FELIKS VOLKHOVSKII

Feliks Volkhovskii

A Revolutionary Life

Michael Hughes

OpenBook
Publishers

https://www.openbookpublishers.com

©2024 Michael Hughes

All external links were active at the time of publication unless otherwise stated and have been archived via the Internet Archive Wayback Machine at https://archive.org/web

Updated digital material and resources associated with this volume are available at https://www.openbookpublishers.com/product/0385#resources

ISBN Paperback: 978-1-80511-194-8
ISBN Hardback: 978-1-80511-195-5
ISBN Digital (PDF): 978-1-80511-196-2
ISBN Digital eBook (EPUB): 978-1-80511-197-9
ISBN HTML: 978-1-80511-199-3

DOI: 10.11647/OBP.0385

Cover image: Portrait originally published in an obituary of Volkhovskii by Nikolai Chaikovskii in *Golos minuvshago*, 10 (2014), 231–35.

Cover design: Jeevanjot Kaur Nagpal

Contents

Everything passes away—suffering, pain, blood, hunger and pestilence. The sword will pass away too, but the stars will still remain when the shadows of our presence and our deeds have vanished from the earth. There is no man who does not know that. Why, then, will we not turn our eyes to the stars? Why?[1]

Mikhail Bulgakov, The White Guard

Everything is what it is: liberty is liberty, not equality or fairness or justice or culture, or human happiness or a quiet conscience.

Isaiah Berlin, Two Concepts of Liberty[2]

> Man is a torch, then ashes soon,
> May and June, then dead December,
> Dead December, then again June.
> Who shall end my dream's confusion?
> Life is a loom, weaving illusion...

Vachel Lindsay, 'The Chinese Nightingale'[3]

---

1   Mikhail Bulgakov, *The White Guard*, trans. Michael Glenny (London: Fontana, 1979), 270.

2   Isaiah Berlin, *Two Concepts of Liberty. An Inaugural Lecture Delivered before the University of Oxford on 31 October 1958* (Oxford: Clarendon Press, 1958).

3   Vachel Lindsay, *The Chinese Nightingale and Other Poems* (New York: The Macmillan Company, 1922).

Preface

The name of Feliks Volkhovskii is not well-known, except perhaps to a small group of scholars interested in the development of the Russian revolutionary movement in the years before 1917, and even among that small band of aficionados his name pales into insignificance besides far better-known figures like Vladimir Lenin and Leon Trotskii. This is partly because Volkhovskii belonged in his final years to the Socialist Revolutionary Party, whose members have often been eclipsed from both scholarly and popular memory, victims of the harsh truth that history remembers the victors better than the losers. The Bolsheviks have by contrast dominated historical attention as the party that took power in October 1917, subsequently transforming Russia from a backward agrarian country into a modern industrial economy, albeit at an almost unimaginable cost in human lives. Even among historians who do study the Socialist Revolutionaries, Volkhovskii remains a surprisingly unknown figure, regularly described as one of the Party's leaders in the years before his death in 1914, and yet remaining elusive when compared with better-known figures such as Viktor Chernov and Ekaterina Breshko-Breshkovskaia. And, when Volkhovskii has received attention, it has typically been for his role in the London emigration in the 1890s when, along with Sergei Stepniak-Kravchinskii and Nikolai Chaikovskii, he played an important role in the campaign to win sympathy in Britain for the Russian revolutionary movement's struggle against the autocratic tsarist state. While some younger historians have started to extend discussion of Volkhovskii to other parts of his revolutionary career, he remains a surprisingly neglected figure, seldom warranting more than a footnote or two in scholarly books and articles focused on other aspects of the Russian revolutionary genealogy.

This lacuna in the scholarly literature is regrettable. As the following chapters will show, Volkhovskii lived through some of the pivotal developments in the history of the Russian revolutionary movement, ranging from the rise of the 'new people' of the 1860s and the growth of populism in the 1870s to the creation of the Socialist Revolutionary Party in the early 1900s. He was imprisoned for his activities three times before he turned thirty, and spent ten years in Siberian exile, before fleeing abroad like many of his fellow revolutionaries to join the fight against tsarist autocracy from the comparative safety of Western Europe. He was a well-known figure in the revolutionary milieu for nearly fifty years, and while it would be a mistake to overestimate his influence on events, a study of his life can help to illuminate the collective story of all those who fought to destroy the tsarist regime.

There is much about Volkhovskii's life that remains obscure. Although there is a vast amount of material in libraries and archives around the world that helps to construct his biography, important gaps remain, in part because few correspondents retained copies of Volkhovskii's letters. This even sometimes extends to the spelling of his name (in later life, Volkhovskii sometimes styled himself Volkhovskoi for reasons that are still not entirely clear). Volkhovskii assiduously maintained files of everything ranging from correspondence through to press clippings, which can be used to cast light on his activities and ideas, but he was inevitably circumspect when writing about certain subjects to avoid the scrutiny of the Russian (and on occasion British) police. Volkhovskii's biography—personal, intellectual, revolutionary—must therefore be built up from countless fragments into some kind of whole, or at least what José Ortega y Gasset called 'a system in which the contradictions of a human life are unified'.

I am perhaps an unlikely biographer of a revolutionary like Volkhovskii. Much of my work over the past few decades has focused on individuals who were firmly ensconced in the social and political establishment of their assorted homelands. I have also spent a good deal of time exploring the lives of conservative-minded figures who sought refuge from the chaos of modernity in an imagined world of social harmony and order. And, as attentive readers of this book will probably realise, my intellectual habitus was firmly shaped during the closing decades of the Cold War. Many Russian specialists educated in those years were instinctively inclined to see the failings of the Soviet regime less as a contingent response to complex domestic and international pressures and more as the logical outcome of a utopian project to remake the world out of Immanuel Kant's 'crooked timber of humanity'. In reality, of course, the Russian revolutionary movement was, like all social and political movements, made up of countless individuals each with their own beliefs and instincts. That is not to deny that utopian aspirations can prove fatal when they leave the world of books and become a primer for human behaviour. The history of the twentieth century has shown all too graphically that they can. Yet many Russian revolutionaries were inspired less by teleological dreams and more by a hatred of the abuses they saw around them. Feliks Volkhovskii was one of them. If the vast scholarly literature on the Russian revolutionary movement that has been published over the past thirty years or so has taught us anything, it is that tidy narrative arcs and precise ideological labels obscure as much as they illuminate, and that the lives of individual revolutionaries were typically shaped by a mixture of ideological and emotional commitment filtered through a web of personal experiences and aspirations.

I have pursued Volkhovskii for many years in archives and libraries across Europe and North America, and although I could not obtain all the documents from the archives that I would like to have seen, I am confident that the material I was unable to consult following Russia's invasion of Ukraine in 2022 would not change the picture that emerges in the following pages. It will hopefully, in future, be possible once again for foreign scholars to work in Russia but, given the uncertainties prevailing at the time of writing, it seemed sensible to complete the book now rather than delay its publication still further. It has indeed already been far too long in the making (although that has had the benefit of allowing me to read much excellent recent work by scholars both in Russia and the West). Many years of involvement in university management slowed the pace of research. So too did the demands of other projects. The coronavirus pandemic and the invasion of Ukraine greatly complicated the collection of material in Moscow and Kyiv. A series of family bereavements diverted attention away from what is, when all is said and done, the less important business of academic writing. The notes and bibliography will hopefully give some sense of the scale of my debt to the research of fellow scholars from around the world. Writing a biography requires engagement with a vast historical landscape and weighty scholarly debates, and for much of the time the biographer must rely on the labours of others, who have often devoted their careers to studying developments that represent just a fleeting moment in the life of the individual under review. I have tried to keep the text as readable as possible by dealing lightly with discussions about such perennial questions as the character of Russian populism and the effectiveness of revolutionary parties in undermining the tsarist regime during its final decades. Scholars with a particular interest in these and other topics will hopefully be able to use the notes to understand how Volkhovskii can be situated within these debates. I have also tried where possible to make use of Soviet and post-Soviet literature that has not always received sufficient acknowledgement by historians in Western Europe and North America. Scholarship is always of necessity a transnational project, even if it can never altogether break free from pressures that undermine efforts to build closer academic ties across political borders.

It is perhaps worth noting here in the light of recent events that Volkhovskii was in many ways a Ukrainian: born in Poltava; brought up in a multilingual milieu; convinced that 'Little Russia' was a place with its own identity and character. His 'Ukrainophilism' was closely bound up with a sense that national sentiment could be used as an agent for revolutionary change, although he was equally sceptical of 'nationalism', recognising how it could be used to cement existing hierarchies and corrupt new ones. There have been some efforts in recent years to claim Volkhovskii as a Ukrainian, which are not without merit, but Volkhovskii was, above all, a man committed to the struggle for freedom of all those living under the rule of the tsarist autocratic state. I have in the text typically used Russian names for individuals and places but have, where it seems more appropriate, included the Ukrainian spelling.

In writing this book I have incurred help from individuals too numerous to name in full. Professor Dominic Lieven has continued to provide wise counsel and support in the thirty-five years since he served as my PhD supervisor. Professor Simon Dixon and Professor David McDonald provided invaluable support in obtaining the grants and fellowships that made the research possible. Professor N. V. Zhiliakova, Dr Aleksandr Mazurov and Andrei Nesterov provided me with material that I could not obtain in the United Kingdom. I was fortunate enough to examine the PhD of Dr Lara Green, whose work has been invaluable in completing the book (Dr Green also kindly made available to me her notes on some archival collections that I had not myself seen for some years). Dr Robert Henderson provided me with helpful advice about archival material in Moscow. Professor Rebecca Beasley sent me proofs of her book on Anglo-Russian cultural relations at a time when the coronavirus pandemic made travel to libraries impossible (I should note that while the first draft of this book was complete before I read Professor Beasley's book, it has been invaluable in helping to contextualise Volkhovskii's literary activities). Dr Helen Grant was kind enough to answer some of my queries about the Garnett family. I have down the years benefitted greatly from conversations about Volkhovskii with many people including, among others, Professor Charlotte Alston, Dr Ben Phillips, and Dr Anat Vernitskii. I also need to thank the reviewers of the manuscript for their suggestions. Maryam Golubeva provided help with translations of some hard-to-decipher handwritten material. Dr Alessandra Tosi and her colleagues at Open Book Publishers, Adèle Kreager, Maria Eydmans, and Rosalyn Sword have been exemplary in their helpfulness and efficiency, and I am delighted to once again be associated with such an innovative organisation. I owe a debt of thanks to audiences at seminars where I have spoken about Volkhovskii in the UK and the United States. I must also extend huge thanks to colleagues from both Russia and Ukraine who have offered practical help, particularly during the final stages of this project, when a new and tragic *smutnoe vremia* (time of troubles) made further visits to both countries impossible. I hope one day to be able to return and thank you all in person.

I owe, too, an enormous debt to staff at archives and libraries around the world, above all at the two institutions which house the biggest collections of Volkhovskii's papers, namely the Hoover Institution Library and Archives (Stanford University) and the Houghton Library (Harvard University). I also owe thanks to staff at other archives and libraries including the Bakhmeteff Archive of Russian and East European Culture (Columbia University); the British Library of Political and Economic Science (LSE) Archives and Special Collections; Gosudarstvennyi arkhiv Rossiskoi Federatsii (Moscow); the International Institute of Social History (Amsterdam); the Leeds Russian Archive (Brotherton Library,

University of Leeds); the Library of Congress Manuscript Division; the McCormick Library of Special Collections (Northwestern University); McGill University Library Rare Books and Special Collections; the National Archives (London); Newcastle University (Philip Robinson Library) Special Collections; Newnham College Cambridge Library; the New York Public Library (Special Collections); the Parliamentary Archives (UK); Rossiiskii gosudarstvennyi arkhiv literatury i iskusstva (Moscow); and the Slavonic Library (National Library of Finland). The research for this project was made possible by generous financial support from the Hoover Institution at Stanford University, the British Academy (award SG2122\210709), and my home institution Lancaster University. Lancaster University also provided funding to support the open access publication of this book.

I owe as ever a great debt to my family, in particular Katie, for their support during the last few difficult years. This book is dedicated to my mother, Anne Hughes, and to the memory of my father, John Pryce Hughes, who sadly died before it was published.

1. Introduction

The Russian political exile Feliks Volkhovskii died in London at the start of August 1914, at the age of sixty-eight, as Europe slid into the maelstrom of war. The outbreak of hostilities represented a defeat for a liberal peace movement that held military conflict to be morally unconscionable and economically destructive.[1] It also revealed the impotence of a socialist internationalism that believed war was the consequence of imperial rivalry for markets in which the workers had no stake.[2] There is no record of how Volkhovskii reacted to the chaos of the July Crisis. His health was poor, and he probably knew little of events taking place beyond the cloistered world of his flat in West London, but if he had known then he would surely have been distraught. Volkhovskii had for many years been one of the most prominent voices in the Russian Socialist Revolutionary Party warning about the threat posed by 'militarism' both to European peace and the cause of revolution in the Russian Empire.

Volkhovskii first arrived in London in 1890, following a dramatic flight from Siberia, where he spent more than a decade in administrative exile for involvement in a society that planned 'at a more or less remote time in the future, to overthrow the existing form of government'.[3] Over

---

1   Among the large literature on the peace movement both in Britain and abroad before the First World War see, for example, Sandi E. Cooper, *Patriotic Pacifism. Waging War on War in Europe, 1815–1914* (New York: Oxford University Press, 1991); Paul Laity, *The British Peace Movement, 1870–1914* (Oxford: Oxford University Press, 2002).

2   For a useful overview of the genealogy of socialist internationalism before 1914, see Patrizia Dogliani, 'The Fate of Socialist Internationalism', in Glenda Sluga and Patricia Clavin (eds), *Internationalisms: A Twentieth Century History* (Cambridge: Cambridge University Press, 2016), 38–60. James Joll, *The Second International, 1889–1914* (London: Routledge and Kegan Paul, 1955) remains a lively if dated account of the Second International.

3   George Kennan, *Siberia and the Exile System*, 2 vols (New York: Century Company, 1891), I, 333.

          https://doi.org/10.11647/OBP.0385.01

the next few years, he became a public figure in Britain, writing and lecturing at length about the harsh treatment meted out to those in Russia who opposed the tsarist government. Along with several other Russian émigrés in London, including Sergei Stepniak-Kravchinskii and Nikolai Chaikovskii, he worked closely with members of the Society of Friends of Russian Freedom producing the newspaper *Free Russia*. Volkhovskii also established friendships with several Britons who played an important role in fostering interest in Russian literature among their compatriots, most notably Edward Garnett and his wife Constance, whose translations of novelists including Leo Tolstoi and Fedor Dostoievskii helped to fuel the Russia craze in Britain during the decades before the First World War.[4]

Volkhovskii made a powerful impression on many of those he met in Britain during the 1890s. Although he never became such a well-known figure as Sergei Stepniak or Petr Kropotkin, he contributed regularly to British newspapers and journals, while his colourful lectures about his time in Russia attracted large audiences up and down the country. His name had already become familiar to many of those interested in Russian affairs when he was still in Siberian exile, thanks to the work of the American writer George Kennan, who first met Volkhovskii when he travelled through the region in the mid-1880s collecting material for a series of articles in *The Century Illustrated Monthly Magazine*. Kennan told his readers in 1888 that

> To me perhaps the most attractive and sympathetic of the Tomsk exiles was the Russian author Felix Volkhofski ... He was about thirty-eight years of age at the time I made his acquaintance, and was a man of cultivated mind, warm heart, and high aspirations ... His health had been shattered by long imprisonment in the fortress of Petropavlovsk; his hair was prematurely gray, and when his face was in repose there seemed to be an expression of profound melancholy in his dark brown eyes.[5]

---

4   For an excellent account that examines how networks of Russian émigrés and British writers helped to fuel the Russia 'craze', see Rebecca Beasley, *Russomania: Russian Culture and the Creation of British Modernism, 1881–1922* (Oxford: Oxford University Press, 2020). Beasley's monograph only appeared when the first draft of this book was completed but has proved invaluable in helping to contextualise Volkhovskii's literary activities.

5   George Kennan, 'Political Exiles and Common Criminals at Tomsk', *The Century Illustrated Monthly Magazine* (henceforth *Century Magazine*), 37, 1 (November 1888), 32–33.

Following his flight from Siberia to London, via North America, Volkhovskii worked closely with Kennan in the campaign to promote Western sympathy for the opposition movement in Russia, and while the two men often disagreed on questions of tactics, the American never lost his affection for his old friend. A few months after Volkhovskii's death, Kennan wrote that he had throughout his life shown 'a fortitude in suffering and indomitable courage in adversity [that] put to shame the weakness of the faint-hearted ... and compel even the cynic and the pessimist to admit that man, at his best, is bigger perhaps than anything that can happen to him'.[6]

Kennan's hagiographic description was echoed by many others who knew Volkhovskii during his years in emigration. The journalist and writer G. H. Perris, who worked closely with Volkhovskii in London, described him as 'the poet and the statesman of revolutionary propaganda' whose 'fiery spirit' never flagged despite years of imprisonment and exile.[7] Sympathetic obituaries in the British press following his death told readers how Volkhovskii had lived 'a life truly great' that illustrated 'the grandeur of fraternity among the toilers of the earth'.[8] J. F. Green, who for a time co-edited *Free Russia* with Volkhovskii, recalled his old friend as 'a charming companion' of 'wide culture'.[9] The Executive Committee of the Society of Friends of Russian Freedom praised the 'sacrifices' he had made for his country.[10]

Kennan's original articles in *Century Magazine* used an almost martyrological language to represent Volkhovskii as a heroic figure who embodied the suffering of critics who dared to oppose the Russian autocratic government. Many of those who subsequently wrote about Volkhovskii echoed this trope by making much of the personal tragedies he had faced while still living in Russia. His first wife died in Italy when he was in prison in St Petersburg awaiting trial. His second wife killed herself after struggling with the hardships of Siberian exile. He lost two children in infancy. Volkhovskii himself seldom referred to these personal tragedies after his flight from Russia, but he was adept during

---

6   George Kennan, *A Russian Comedy of Errors with Other Stories and Sketches of Russian Life* (New York: The Century Company, 1915), 139.

7   G. H. Perris, *Russia in Revolution* (London: Chapman and Hall, 1905), 226.

8   *Daily Herald* (6 August 1914).

9   *Justice* (13 August 1914).

10 *Manchester Guardian* (14 August 1914).

his first ten years in Britain at fashioning a *persona* that dramatised and embodied the anguish endured by many critics of the tsarist regime. He sometimes imitated Kennan by lecturing to audiences dressed in the clothes and chains of a Russian convict (Volkhovskii himself had in fact worn neither while in Siberia). He was also skilled at behaving in ways that dovetailed with the expectations of the social and literary circles in which he moved, presenting himself as an exotic representative of an intriguingly alien country, yet one who could easily accommodate himself within the orbit of Western culture and values. And, in his articles and lectures, he discussed Russian affairs in general—and the Russian revolutionary movement in particular—in ways that were designed to reassure his audience that the values espoused by Russian revolutionaries like himself were consonant with those held by respectable liberals and moderate socialists in countries such as Britain.

There was nevertheless something paradoxical about the efforts made by Volkhovskii and some other political émigrés in Britain to defend a Russian revolutionary movement whose members were often committed to tactics and values profoundly at odds with the political and cultural *mores* of late Victorian and Edwardian Britain. Volkhovskii himself was for the most part ready to endorse the use of terrorism in Russia, both as a natural response to the brutality of the tsarist state and as an ethical means of bringing about political change. He was also a socialist who believed that, in Russia at least, the main value of such liberal appurtenances as universal suffrage and freedom of speech lay in their role in facilitating the struggle for a new social and economic order. Many Britons who sympathised with the struggle against tsarism by contrast viewed the Russian revolutionary movement through a prism shaped by a fusion of the Nonconformist Conscience and hazy memories of a previous generation of European revolutionaries like Lajos Kossuth and Giuseppe Mazzini. It was at best a partial understanding of a complex reality.

There is in fact a real danger of reducing Volkhovskii's career to his role as an intermediary between the Russian revolutionary movement and its British supporters in the years after 1890 (a theme that dominates the way he is discussed in much of the existing literature). The leader of the Socialist Revolutionaries, Viktor Chernov, wrote in his memoirs that 'the life of Feliks Volkhovskii is a history of the Russian revolutionary movement, of which he remained a true and faithful servant his *whole* life' [italics added].[11] Vera Figner, who played a leading role in the Narodnaia volia (People's Will) organisation that assassinated Tsar Aleksandr II in 1881, agreed that 'the whole of his [Volkhovskii's] ... life was devoted to the revolutionary cause'.[12] The focus on Volkhovskii's long and varied revolutionary career was echoed in the obituaries that appeared in Russia following his death. Nikolai Chaikovskii recalled that when he first met Volkhovskii in the early 1870s, his new acquaintance was already a veteran of the revolutionary movement, who had endured two terms of imprisonment.[13] An obituary published a few months later in *Mysl'* focused by contrast on Volkhovskii's work in the final decade of his life, when he played an important role in the Socialist Revolutionary Party, editing many of its publications, and serving on the Foreign Committee that provided material support to revolutionaries organising uprisings across Russia.[14] Both obituaries said much less than the British press about Volkhovskii's role editing *Free Russia* and his work with members of the Society of Friends of Russian Freedom.[15]

One of the main aims of this book is indeed to gently 'shrink' the Volkhovskii familiar to many of his British friends and allies, and instead give more attention to placing him within the development of the Russian revolutionary movement. A good deal of valuable work has been published in recent years discussing Russian revolutionary communities abroad and the integration of Russian revolutionaries within broader transnational revolutionary networks.[16] The limited scholarly attention given to Volkhovskii has similarly focused on his role in shaping American and European attitudes towards Russia in the 1890s and early 1900s, although he has too often been seen primarily as a sidekick to Stepniak, lacking the glamour and brilliance

---

11 V. M. Chernov, *Pered burei* (Moscow: Direct Media, 2016), 203.

12 V. I. Figner, *Posle Shlissel'burga* (Moscow: Direct Media, 2016), 345.

13 N. V. Chaikovskii, Obituary of Volkhovskii, *Golos minuvshago*, 10 (1914), 231–35.

14 Ritina [I. I. Rakitnikova], Obituary of Volkhovskii, *Mysl'*, 40 (January 1915).

15 The same was true of the obituary by N. E. Kudrin that appeared in *Russkoe bogatstvo*, 9 (1914), 364–65, which focused overwhelmingly on Volkhovskii's life before 1890 when he fled Russia.

16 The most important recent work taking this approach is without doubt Faith Hillis's magisterial *Utopia's Discontents: Russian Émigrés and the Quest for Freedom, 1830s–1930s* (New York: Oxford University Press, 2021), which examines how Russian colonies abroad formed part of the broader Russian revolutionary movement, while also shaping and being shaped by their host communities.

of his better-known friend.[17] Much less has been written—particularly in English—about the other parts of his life.[18] Volkhovskii was, as Figner and Chernov recognised, a living embodiment of the development of the Russian revolutionary movement. He came of age in the 1860s under the influence of the revolutionary scientism of 'nihilists' like Nikolai Chernyshevskii and Dmitrii Pisarev. He was imprisoned in 1869 on suspicion of being involved in the network of groups that surrounded Sergei Nechaev, the self-fantasising *enfant terrible* of the Russian revolutionary movement, whose murder of one of his followers was immortalised by Dostoievskii in his novel *Besy* (The *Devils*). Volkhovskii subsequently became a prominent figure in the Chaikovskii milieu that coalesced in the early 1870s, paving the way for the 'Going to the People' movement of 1874, when thousands of young Russians fanned out into the Russian countryside in an effort to draw closer to the people, although he was himself always sceptical of those populists (*narodniki*) who believed that some elusive quasi-mystical wisdom was to be found among the ordinary Russian peasants. Following his exile to Siberia, Volkhovskii largely reinvented himself, playing a significant role in the cultural life of Tomsk, writing numerous short stories and poems, as well as becoming the most prolific contributor to the newly established paper *Sibirskaia gazeta* (*Siberian Gazette*).

---

17   Among the few publications in English devoted to Volkhovskii, see Donald Senese, 'Felix Volkhovsky in London, 1890-1914', in John Slatter (ed.), *From the Other Shore: Russian Political Emigrants in Britain, 1870–1917* (London: Frank Cass, 1984), 67–78; Donald Senese, 'Felix Volkhovskii in Ontario: Rallying Canada to the Revolution', *Canadian-American Slavic Studies*, 24, 3 (1990), 295–310. A good deal of material can also be found in Donald Senese, *S. M. Stepniak-Kravchinskii: The London Years* (Newtonville, MA: Oriental Research Partners, 1987). Volkhovskii's name has also started to occur more frequently in some recent work in English on the Russian revolutionary movement, not least because his papers often include valuable material about other better-known figures. See, for example, Lara Green, 'Russian Revolutionary Terrorism, British Liberals, and the Problem of Empire (1884–1914)', *History of European Ideas*, 46, 5 (2020), 633–48; Lynne Hartnett, 'Relief and Revolution: Russian Émigrés' Political Remittances and the Building of Political Transnationalism', *Journal of Ethnic and Migration Studies*, 46, 6 (2020), 1040–56. Other literature touching on Volkhovskii's time in emigration is discussed in later chapters.

18   For two recent exceptions, see the relevant sections of Ben Phillips, *Siberian Exile and the Invention of Revolutionary Russia, 1825–1917: Exiles, Émigrés and the International Reception of Russian Radicalism* (Abingdon: Routledge, 2022); Lara Green, 'Russian Revolutionary Terrorism in Transnational Perspective: Representations and Networks, 1881–1926' (PhD thesis, Northumbria University, 2019).

Following his flight from Siberia and arrival in London in the summer of 1890, where he became a central figure in the international campaign against tsarist Russia, Volkhovskii continued to play a significant role supporting the development of the Russian revolutionary movement. He was a key figure in the Russian Free Press Fund, which printed radical literature for distribution in Russia, and joined his old friend Stepniak in efforts to overcome the divisions that characterised the Russian revolutionary movement. The two men also sought to build closer links with Russian liberals, a tactic viewed with scepticism by revolutionary luminaries like Petr Lavrov and Georgii Plekhanov, who feared that such cooperation would weaken rather than strengthen the opposition to tsarism. In the chaotic aftermath of the 1905 Revolution, Volkhovskii returned for a time to Russia, where he played a role producing propaganda designed to encourage mutiny in the Russian army and navy, before fleeing the country once again to avoid arrest. In the final years of his life, he served as a regular delegate for the Socialist Revolutionaries at conferences of the Second International. He was, to put it flippantly, something of a revolutionary 'Forrest Gump' whose life can provide a segue into the development of the Russian revolutionary movement.[19]

Vera Figner once suggested that there was 'almost no material' on Volkhovskii in the literature describing the history of the Russian revolutionary movement.[20] Volkhovskii's name in fact appears quite regularly in the memoirs published in such journals as *Byloe* (*The Past*) and *Katorga i sylka* (*Penal Servitude and Exile*), for he was a familiar figure to several generations of revolutionaries, ranging from the 'new people' of the 1860s through to the neo-*narodniki* of the early twentieth century. He was himself a prolific writer of poetry, short stories, literary criticism and polemical journalism. Yet the archival trail is surprisingly thin on material casting light on his ideas and activities. Volkhovskii was a keen correspondent, but while he kept many of the letters he received, only a small number of those he wrote have been preserved. His diaries are episodic and contain little of substance. The records

---

19   The reference is of course to the 1994 film directed by Robert Zemeckis, whose eponymous hero lives a life that intersects with some of the most dramatic events of the history of the United States in the second half of the twentieth century.

20   Figner, *Posle Shlissel'burga*, 346.

of the *Okhrana* and its predecessors contain some material relating to surveillance and interrogation, but they seldom reveal much substance about Volkhovskii's networks and activities.[21] Some useful documents can be found in the archives of the Socialist Revolutionary Party, but even there he remains an elusive figure. Volkhovskii wrote several autobiographical pieces towards the end of his life, both for Russian and Western audiences, but while such accounts are valuable, they need to be read with caution given his penchant for turning his experiences into propaganda. His biography must instead be assembled from sources scattered around the world in archives and long-forgotten publications.

The problem in reconstructing the 'life and times' of Volkhovskii is not, though, simply one of source material. It is also the challenge of locating him within a fast-moving and complex landscape, in which he was sometimes a significant figure, but seldom a pivotal one. Volkhovskii was a highly intelligent man, who had little interest in dogma, and was throughout his life impatient with the ideological squabbles that so often characterised the revolutionary movement. His own outlook was characterised above all by his loathing of the tsarist social and political order and his commitment to ending the exploitation of the Russian *narod*, the 'ordinary' Russian people, idealised and mythologised by generations of educated Russians in ways that were often fantastic and naïve.[22] These two instincts—and they were instincts rather than highly articulated principles—underpinned his ideas and actions for half a century. Yet it was precisely Volkhovskii's impatience with ideology that makes it difficult to delineate his long career in terms of the vocabulary typically used to explore patterns of opposition to tsarism: nihilist, radical, revolutionary, populist, liberal and the like.

This should not come as any surprise. The literature on the Russian revolutionary movement that has appeared over the past twenty-five

---

21 The *Okhrana*, or Department for the Preservation of Public Safety and Order, is often referred to as the tsarist secret police and regularly seen as the predecessor of the better-known secret agencies of the Soviet period. For a useful general history of the *Okhrana*, see Charles A. Ruud and Sergei A. Stepanov, *Fontanka 16: The Tsar's Secret Police* (Montreal: McGill-Queens's University Press, 1999).

22 The word *narod* was used by many members of the Russian intelligentsia to describe the 'ordinary' Russian people, typically the peasantry, although from the 1870s onwards it was increasingly used to describe urban workers as well. The character of the Russian *narod*—whether conservative or revolutionary—was at the heart of much social and political debate throughout the nineteenth century.

years or so has taken seriously the lived experience of its participants. The opening up of archives has combined with new ways of thinking about history to allow a richer exploration than one that focuses simply on ideas and organisations. Biography has once again become recognised as a valuable way of understanding the past, not so much for restoring agency to the individual, but because it shows the uncertain and contradictory motives that influence the actions of both the celebrated and the obscure.[23] Detailed discussion about the ideology espoused by members of the Socialist Revolutionary Party, for example, seems less compelling when research into the situation on the ground shows patterns of complexity and diversity that do not fit easily into neat categories.[24] Even such seminal developments as the split between Bolsheviks and Mensheviks now appear more fluid and uncertain than they once did. The history of opposition to tsarism was characterised by an ever-changing kaleidoscope of individuals and organisations with more-or-less clearly held objectives and ideologies. Too close a focus on ideas and plans runs the risk of assuming that members of the radical opposition thought and acted in line with well-defined ideological principles and a clear sense of tactics. Yet ignoring such things altogether runs the risk of missing how the language and practice of opponents of the tsarist regime were saturated by a conviction that any successful effort to bring about change had to be rooted in a coherent analysis of the possibilities and limitations imposed by Russia's historical situation.

It is in the light of such things, to return to a previous point, that the value of a biography of Feliks Volkhovskii partly rests. It is not only that it can provide a fuller picture of his role within the revolutionary milieu, although that is certainly one of the benefits, given that he has been largely overlooked by historians. Nor is it simply that his career can serve as a prism through which to view wider patterns in the development

---

23   For a useful discussion of the scholarly nature of this development, see Hans Renders, Binne de Haan and Jonne Harmsma (eds), *The Biographical Turn. Lives in History* (Abingdon: Routledge, 2017). Many of the biographies cited in the chapters that follow have perhaps (and quite laudably) been inspired less by strong theoretical views and more by a recognition that studying the lives of individuals can help to understand the times they lived in.

24   The best general discussion in English of the Socialist Revolutionary Party before 1914, which captures its complexity and changing character, remains Manfred Hildermeier, *The Russian Socialist Revolutionary Party Before the First World War* (New York: St Martin's Press, 2000).

of opposition to tsarism. A study of Volkhovskii's biography can also illuminate the many ways that the Russian revolutionary movement can be explored: socially, culturally, intellectually and organisationally. As the following chapters will show, Volkhovskii was in many ways a 'typical' representative of the Russian *intelligentsia*, who came to maturity in the 1860s, and dedicated the rest of his life to undermining the tsarist state and the social and economic order it symbolised and protected. At the same time, though, his life—like all lives—was governed by unpredictable contingencies and the need to respond to the countless changes that took place in Russia during the fifty years before the First World War.

It is this that makes Volkhovskii's career so difficult to describe in terms of a vocabulary that is itself often inadequate or confused. It is hardly a concession to the wilder epistemological shores of postmodernism to recognise that social and political labels have uncertain and shifting meanings. The only practical response is to engage in the kind of linguistic pragmatism that is the staple of most historians (even if they are sometimes reluctant to admit it). The situation can perhaps be best illustrated by looking at a few examples. While the literature on the Russian *intelligentsia* is immense, and perhaps still pervaded by a sense that the holy grail of a precise meaning remains elusive, there is something close to a consensus that it constituted a distinctive social-cultural-psychological milieu, characterised both by its alienation from the dominant *mores* of tsarist Russia and by a moral commitment to promoting the well-being of the victims of the social and political *status quo*.[25] The most astute work on the subject has often focused less on the challenge of defining the *intelligentsia* in terms of its supposedly enduring abstract features and more on exploring the factors that shaped its evolution in a specific historical situation, often through the

---

25 Among the massive and often contradictory literature on the Russian intelligentsia in English see, for example, Isaiah Berlin, *Russian Thinkers* (London: Penguin, 1994); Martin Malia, 'What Is the Intelligentsia?', *Daedalus*, 89, 3 (1960), 441–58; Laurie Manchester, *Holy Fathers, Secular Sons: Clergy, Intelligentsia and the Modern Self in Revolutionary Russia* (DeKalb, IL: Northern Illinois University Press, 2008); Vladimir C. Nahirny, *The Russian Intelligentsia: From Torment to Silence* (New Brunswick, NJ: Transaction Books, 1983); Philip Pomper, *The Russian Revolutionary Intelligentsia* (Wheeling, IL: H. Davidson, 1993); Marc Raeff, *Origins of the Russian Intelligentsia. The Eighteenth-Century Nobility* (New York: Harcourt Brace and World, 1966); Nicholas Riasanovsky, *A Parting of Ways: Government and the Educated Public in Russia, 1801–1855* (Oxford: Clarendon Press, 1976).

prism of particular individuals. The character of the *intelligentsia* was not fixed over the course of half a century. Nor was its development uniform. By examining individual lives, it becomes easier to understand the Russian *intelligentsia* in all its heterogeneity, recognising that any attempt to reduce it to a specific set of features is doomed to fail. Volkhovskii himself was, by any understanding of the term, an *intelligent* whose efforts to bring about revolution shifted over time in response to changing circumstances.

A similar point can be made when addressing the question of whether Volkhovskii was a *narodnik* (or 'populist' to use the English word most often used as a translation). The term itself has long proved elusive, generating extensive academic discussion among scholars about its meaning and relationship to broader European understandings of populism.[26] While Volkhovskii had little interest in ideological questions, he was not really a *narodnik* in the sense suggested by Richard Pipes, who argued in a celebrated article that the term should be limited to a small number of radicals who believed that they should seek to learn from the *narod* rather than lead them 'in the name of abstract, bookish, imported ideas'.[27] Nor was he much interested in the extensive debates that took place about how the tsarist regime needed to be overthrown to forestall the disintegration of the peasant commune in the face of the development of capitalism (fears that have for some historians come to define *narodnichestvo*, at least before the 1880s, as a form of anti-capitalist radicalism).[28] And, more than twenty years later, Volkhovskii contributed little to the earnest discussions within the Socialist Revolutionary Party about questions of post-revolutionary land tenure that so preoccupied Viktor Chernov and many other Party leaders.

Volkhovskii, indeed, wrote almost nothing about the peasant commune and surprisingly little about the Russian peasantry. And yet, in his personal foundation myth, he described how it was the

---

26 See, for example, the important collection edited by Ghita Ionescu and Ernest Gellner, *Populism: Its Meaning and National Characteristics* (London: Weidenfeld and Nicolson, 1969). The character of Russian populism and its treatment in the scholarly literature is discussed in more detail in Chapter 2.

27 Richard Pipes, '*Narodnichestvo*: A Semantic Inquiry', *Slavic Review*, 23, 3 (1964), 441–58 (445).

28 For an interpretation of Russian populism along these lines, see Andrzej Walicki, *The Controversy over Capitalism: Studies in the Social Philosophy of the Russian Populists* (Oxford: Clarendon Press, 1969).

harsh treatment of Russian serfs which he witnessed as a child that
led him to question the legitimacy of the existing order. His first major
'revolutionary' activity was planning the clandestine circulation of
literature in the Russian countryside, as a means of fostering popular
enlightenment through building closer links between the peasantry and
sympathetic members of the *intelligentsia*. In many of his writings about
literature and theatre in the 1880s, Volkhovskii called for the publication
of books and plays crafted to illuminate the culture of the Russian *narod*,
while many of the short stories he wrote throughout his life echoed
motifs from traditional Russian folktales (more often than not with a
distinct radical twist). There is, in short, no neat answer as to whether
Volkhovskii was or was not a *narodnik* given that it is a yardstick that
lacks precise meaning or definition. What remains important is that his
attitude towards social and political questions was shaped by the sense,
so characteristic of the Russian *intelligentsia* of the second half of the
nineteenth century, that there was a moral imperative on all those who
recognised the wretched condition of the Russian *narod* to do everything
in their power to ameliorate it. His ideas and instincts—not to mention
his actions—clearly place him within the network of individuals
and groups that are conventionally assumed to fall within the broad
framework of *narodnichestvo*. And, equally clearly, they distance him
from the tradition of Marxism–Leninism that triumphed in October
1917, three years after Volkhovskii's death.

A rather different issue is whether Volkhovskii was a revolutionary
as opposed to a radical or even a liberal. Much of the ambiguity about
Volkhovskii's status as a revolutionary stemmed from his ideological
flexibility and readiness to work with all those seeking to bring about
change in Russia. It was noted earlier that some leading figures in the
Russian revolutionary movement, like Lavrov, thought that he was
too focused on building bridges with Russian and Western liberals,
yet the tsarist authorities always recognised Volkhovskii as someone
who could pose a serious threat both before he left Russia and later in
emigration. Nor did he himself shrink from the label revolutionary, even
if when writing for a Western audience he typically emphasised how
revolution represented a natural choice in the face of repression, rather
than a commitment to radical social and economic change. Volkhovskii
never had much interest in Russian liberalism as a distinct intellectual

tradition, but he was throughout his career willing to work with those who sat more easily within the confines of (semi-)permitted dissent, whether in Odessa (Ukr. Odesa) in the 1870s or London in the 1890s. While some of his critics saw such a position as evidence of a lack of ideological rigour and revolutionary zeal, it was in large part a reflection of Volkhovskii's pragmatism, and his determination to find the most effective way of undermining the tsarist regime.

All this, in a sense, simply underscores a truth familiar to any biographer: that it is possible in most lives to discern distinct patterns that nevertheless ebb and flow in response to changes and circumstances that disrupt even the most definite narrative arc. Karl Marx was prescient when he observed that 'Men make their own history, but they do not make it as they please'. So, too, is there much truth in the quotation, often attributed to Churchill, that 'when the facts change, I change my mind. What do you do?' The development of the Russian revolutionary movement was for fifty years or more characterised by a struggle between what some nineteenth-century thinkers called necessity and freedom. Or, to put it rather differently, the challenge facing many of its leading representatives lay in reconciling a view of the world influenced by clear ideological preconceptions with the need to respond to ever-changing but nevertheless still constraining circumstances.

Even the most determined of revolutionaries could not avoid altogether the need to adopt new tactics and ideas in response to events. Vladimir Lenin was once seen by many scholars as an ideologue who bent the course of Russian history by his titanic will. Yet, more recent biographies have rightly recognised how he often responded to events in a pragmatic way to advance his long-term objectives.[29] The most interesting questions focus on the extent to which his short-term manoeuvrings became the substance of his revolutionary work. In other words, was Lenin's use of Marxist language simply a cloak for his all-consuming emphasis on making revolution, or was it rather the framework that shaped his activities, while leaving sufficient room to use his agency to respond to circumstances? Common sense suggests there was an element of both. And common sense suggests, too, that

---

29 For a lively biography of Lenin that firmly eschews a teleological approach in favour of one that captures his uncertainties and contradictions, see Robert Service, *Lenin: A Biography* (London: Pan Macmillan, 2010).

the same was true of many other revolutionaries who had to reconcile their intellectual convictions with the stubborn material of history. Volkhovskii's commitment to revolution was the product, above all, of a visceral loathing of the tsarist state and a determination to promote the welfare of the Russian people. His focus was less on doctrine and more on action—weakening the tsarist state at specific moments in time—in order to expand the potential for developing practical ways of improving the material and cultural position of the *narod*.

It is this insight that frames the argument in the pages that follow. Chapter 2 and Chapter 3 examine Volkhovskii's life in Russia before his flight to the west, tracing the genesis of his radical views, and setting them against the wider revolutionary drama, with its progression from the 'nihilism' of the 1860s, through the populism of the 1870s, and on to the bleak years of repression that followed the murder of Aleksandr II in 1881. Chapter 4 and Chapter 5 then explore Volkhovskii's time in Britain in the 1890s, arguing that while he played an important role in mobilising international support for the victims of tsarist oppression, he also remained a significant figure in the broader revolutionary emigration through his role in the production and distribution of propaganda. Chapter 6 and Chapter 7 discuss the last fifteen years of Volkhovskii's life, when he once again firmly established himself within the ambit of the Russian revolutionary movement, as opposed to being a political exile whose career was characterised primarily by his relations with foreign liberals and radicals. There is a sense in which Volkhovskii became increasingly 'revolutionary' during his last years, expressing more openly than before his support for the use of force to destroy the autocratic regime, and questioning the value of working with moderate opposition groups to bring about change. Whether this represented a definite change in his position, or rather the more forceful articulation of views long held, is perhaps a moot point.

Many of the themes that emerge in these chapters are touched on above: Volkhovskii's general lack of interest in the details of ideological discussion; his focus on the *narod*, not as a repository of communal virtue, but rather as the victim of a harsh social and political order; his sometimes ambiguous attitude towards terrorism and political violence; his growing concern over the threat posed to peace by the forces of 'militarism'; and, perhaps above all, his readiness to respond to circumstances in ways that could make him seem inconsistent but were often simply a reaction to the situation in which he found himself. Any biography of Volkhovskii also needs to capture other aspects of his life, not least his work as a poet and short story writer, along with his activities as a critic and translator. Nor were these simply ephemeral interests. Literary activity was central to the nineteenth-century Russian *intelligentsia*, in part because it provided a vehicle for expressing views and sentiments likely to face censorship if articulated in more purely political terms, and partly because culture itself was often seen as a kind of handmaiden to the revolutionary cause. Many of Volkhovskii's short stories and poems were propagandistic in character, but he undoubtedly had real literary ability, as well as very significant talent as a critic. His work was the hallmark of a man who was for all his revolutionary passion something more than a revolutionary. And, as will be seen in the chapters that follow, while some of those who met Volkhovskii could find him domineering and impatient, many others considered him to be, in the words of 'the grandmother of the revolution', Ekaterina Breshko-Breshkovskaia, one of the 'noblest hearts' of the Russian revolutionary movement.[30] What follows is above all a biography of Volkhovskii's public life, but it tries too to capture at least a little of the elusive timbre of a man whose personality impressed so many of those he met as a model of integrity, and who faced the harsh vicissitudes of life with enormous courage and strength.

---

30   Alice Stone Blackwell (ed.), *The Little Grandmother of the Revolution. Reminiscences and Letters of Catherine Breshkovsky* (London: T. Fisher Unwin, 1918), 282.

2. The Making of a Revolutionary

Feliks Vadimovich Volkhovskii was born in July 1846 in Poltava, then a city of some 25,000 people, situated around five hundred miles south of Moscow in modern-day Ukraine.[1] His father Vadim Petrovich Volkhovskii had served as an artillery officer before subsequently taking up a post in the Civil Service as a Collegiate Assessor. The rank was a comparatively modest one. A Collegiate Assessor was only marginally superior to a Titular Councillor, the rank held by Akakii Akakievich Bashmachkin, the downtrodden 'hero' of Nikolai Gogol's short story 'Shinel''('The Overcoat'), who spends his evenings copying official documents by candlelight in a shabby attic room.[2] Vadim Petrovich's situation was somewhat less parlous. He was the eldest of eight children born to Petr Grigorovich Volkhovskii, a major in the Corps of Gendarmes, whose work required him to travel regularly across the empire. Vadim and his seven younger siblings spent most of their time on their mother's small estate of Chepurkivka in the north-west of Poltava province. The family was far from wealthy, and although Vadim Petrovich's childhood passed in modest comfort, he knew from a young age that he would have to earn his own living.

Vadim's father Petr Grigorovich himself retired from the Corps of Gendarmes in 1839, living for a while at Chepurkivka, before seeking a new position to improve his family's finances. He found work managing

---

1   Volkhovskii occasionally wrote that he was born in 1845, a date which appears in some records of his death. See, for example, Newnham College (Cambridge) Library Special Collections, Wallas family papers, PP/Wallas/2/7/6 (Brief biographical note by Volkhovskii). Most other sources are, though, clear that he was born in the following year.

2   'The Overcoat', in Nikolai Gogol, *Diary of a Madman and Other Stories*, trans. Ronald Wilks (London: Penguin, 1972), 71–108. It should be noted that the post of Collegiate Assessor—unlike that of Titular Councillor—did provide hereditary noble status.

          https://doi.org/10.11647/OBP.0385.02

factories in Perm province, but his new career was cut short when he fell
from a horse, suffering a concussion that caused long-term damage to
his memory. In the years that followed, he lived with his brother Stepan
Grigorovich, who later served as Governor of Samara Province, before
the fortuitous death of a relative meant that Petr inherited the estate of
Moisevka (Ukr. Moisivka) in Poltava Province (his brothers renounced
their share of the estate leaving him in sole possession). The Moisevka
estate was a substantial one consisting of 300 male peasants and more
than 2,000 hectares of land.[3] It had acquired some fame in the early 1800s
for the lavish balls hosted there by one Petr Stepanovich Volkhovskii and
his wife Tatiana (it was Tatiana who left the estate to Petr Grigorovich
and his brothers since she had no children of her own). The main house
was built in an elaborate French style, surrounded by acres of parkland,
complete with gazebos and fountains. Some visitors spoke of it in rather
exaggerated terms as a veritable 'Versailles'. A church was added in
1808 (which stands to this day).

The parties held by Petr and Tatiana Volkhovskii attracted the
attention of the authorities on occasion—not least in the revolutionary
year of 1848—when a number of guests belonging to the facetiously-
named Obshchestvo mochemordiia (Society of Boozers) attended
a party at the house where they gave a toast to the French Republic.[4]
Moisevka was also for a time a notable centre of culture, attracting
writers and artists including the poet Taras Shevchenko, whose work
shaped the growth of a Ukrainian national consciousness during the
1840s and 1850s (a portrait of Petr Stepanovich and his wife painted by
Shevchenko hung for many years on the walls of the manor house).[5] By
the time Petr Grigorovich inherited the estate in the early 1850s, though,
the house was very run down.[6] His grandson Feliks later recalled that

3   For details of the estate, see *Prilozheniia k trudam redaktsionnykh kommissii dlia
    sostavleniia polozhenii o krest'ianakh*, 6 vols (St Petersburg: V tip-ii V. Bezobrazova i
    komp., 1860), VI.
4   On the Society, see Danylo Husar Struk (ed.), *Encyclopedia of Ukraine*, 5 vols
    (Toronto: University of Toronto Press, 1993), III, 430. The drunken toast led to a
    number of arrests on suspicion of sedition but all those detained were released.
5   On Shevchenko, see Pavlo Zaitsev, *Taras Shevchenko. A Life*, trans. George N. Luckyj
    (Toronto: University of Toronto Press, 1988).
6   For a brief discussion of the idea of Moisevka as the Ukrainian Versailles,
    along with some photographs of the estate later in the nineteenth century,
    see Volodymyr Panchenko, 'Moisivka, "ukrainskii Versal'"', *Dyen* (16

most of the rooms were shut up and unheated. The mirrors hanging on the walls were cracked and the portraits of half-forgotten ancestors covered with dust. The garden and park were unkempt and returning to wilderness. Volkhovskii had few happy memories of the time he spent at Moisevka as a young boy.

Volkhovskii wrote little about his early life, although on more than one occasion he described how he came to be christened with the distinctively un-Russian name of Feliks. He was throughout his life close to his mother, Ekaterina Matveeva (née Samotsvit), the daughter of a Polish mother and a Ukrainian-Russian father, who lived in the town of Novograd-Volynskii (Ukr. Zviahel) 150 miles west of Kyiv. When he was older, some of those who met Volkhovskii assumed from his name that he was a Polish Catholic, but he was baptised into the Russian Orthodox Church. His mother, who had previously lost two boys and a girl in infancy, vowed that her next child would be christened after the saint whose name-day was celebrated on the day the baby was born. According to her son, writing many years later, a priest in Poltava helpfully pointed out that the full Church calendar for the date of his birth included a reference to Feliks (one of the early popes). Father Ivan told the baby's parents that they should have no qualms about naming a child after a pope who held office before the great schism between the Orthodox and Catholic churches. He also suggested that since Feliks was derived from the Latin *felicitas*—happiness—it was particularly suitable as the given name for the first child of his parents to survive beyond a few days.[7]

Although Feliks was born in the town of Poltava, he moved as a very young child to the family home of his mother in Novograd-Volynskii. Vadim does not seem to have joined his wife and child there, possibly because he was still in the army, although there are hints in Volkhovskii's

January 2014) https://m.day.kyiv.ua/article/marshrut-no1-podorozhi/moysivka-ukrayinskyy-versal.

7   Volkhovskii Papers, Hoover Institution Library and Archives, Stanford University, henceforth Volkhovskii Papers (HIA), Box 11, Folder 5 (Notes headed 'Autobiography'); F. Volkhovskoi (*sic*), 'Otryvki odnoi chelovecheskoi zhizni', Part 1, *Sovremennik* (April 1911), 254–67 (255). During its four-year life (1911-15), *Sovremmenik*, not to be confused with its better-known counterpart of the mid-nineteenth century, published pieces by authors from both the Marxist and *narodnik* wings of the revolutionary movement, and (like the elderly Volkhovskii) determinedly sought to avoid revolutionary sectarianism.

scattered reminiscences that his parents' marriage was not a particularly happy one. Feliks was certainly closer to his mother, who in later years provided what support she could to her son during his time in prison, and later accompanied him to exile in Siberia where she died as a result of the harsh living conditions.[8] Ekaterina Matveeva had married Vadim Petrovich when she was only sixteen or seventeen, following a somewhat perfunctory education, although she subsequently immersed herself in the books of a medical student who lived for a time with the family (which among other things had the unfortunate side effect of turning her into a hypochondriac). She was in her son's later estimation 'naturally timid but extraordinarily kind-hearted'. Feliks also noted that his mother was by instinct 'impulsive' but disciplined enough to learn French and become a good housekeeper.[9]

Feliks had warm memories of his early years spent living with his mother's family in Novograd-Volynskii where he stayed until he was seven or eight. In an article published more than fifty years later, in the journal *Sovremennik* (*The Contemporary*), he lovingly recalled his grandparents' white one-storied house, complete with large windows that gave the building an open and welcoming appearance. Volkhovskii's positive memories were doubtless coloured by his much bleaker experiences a few years later when living with his paternal grandfather at Moisevka, but there was genuine warmth in his recollection of the 'bright and friendly' life that characterised the Samotsvit household. He remembered the household as a 'nest' (*gnezdo*), a word he doubtless chose for its echo of Ivan Turgenev's novel *Dvorianskoe gnezdo* (lit. *Noble Nest*), which had first appeared just a few years after Feliks left Novgorod-Volynskii for Moisevka.[10]

The Samotsvit household was headed by Feliks' maternal grandfather, Matvei Mikhailovich, who had as a young soldier fought against the Napoleonic armies advancing on Moscow. Matvei was

---

8   Volkhovskii subsequently wrote a poem *Mat'*—'Mother'—describing the grief felt by mothers of young Russian political prisoners who suffered 'the torment of waiting' for news about their loved ones. See A. Bichter (ed.), *Poety revoliutsionnogo narodnichestva* (Leningrad: Izd-vo Khudozhestvennaia literatura, 1967), 69.

9   Volkhovskii Papers (HIA), Box 17, Folder 3 (Brief autobiographical notes by Volkhovskii).

10 The account in this and the following paragraphs draws heavily on Volkhovskoi, 'Otryvki', Part 1.

seriously wounded in the leg, an injury from which he never fully recovered, although Feliks remembered him many years later as a vigorous man 'who did not give the impression of being an invalid'.[11] His role as head of the household was nevertheless largely eclipsed by his wife Viktoriia Ivanovna, who also directed life on the family's small country estate, which supplied the Samotsvits with eggs, meat and vegetables. The relationship of the elderly couple was a close one ('two boots made from a single block' in the words of their grandson). They surrounded themselves with numerous relatives who formed part of a large extended family. Several unmarried women—sisters and daughters of the old couple—lived in the house and contributed to the various tasks of household management. An unmarried son occupied a nearby flat and often called in for dinner. The picture of life at Novograd-Volynskii painted by Volkhovskii was one of a self-contained world that seemed impervious to the tribulations of life beyond the white-washed walls of the family 'nest'.

Such tight-knit families were a familiar presence in nineteenth-century Russian literature in stories like Gogol's 'Starosvetskie pomeshchiki' ('Old World Landowners').[12] The texture of life among the provincial Russian gentry during the middle decades of the nineteenth century in fact exhibited enormous variety (which was hardly surprising given its economic and cultural diversity). Although some families focused obsessively on matters of status and money, others placed more emphasis on the importance of emotional intimacy between family members, cutting across the generations and the sexes. Collections of family correspondence from the period often reveal close relations between husbands and wives and parents and children.[13] Feliks Volkhovskii's portrait of his maternal grandparents' household might well have been prompted by nostalgia, as he looked back more than half a century later, but it probably captured something of its spirit as well.

---

11   Volkhovskoi, 'Otryvki', Part 1, 258.
12   Nikolai Gogol, 'Old World Landowners', in *Evenings on a Farm near Dikanka and Mirgorod*, trans. Christopher English (Oxford: Oxford University Press, 1994), 219–40.
13   For a lucid discussion of this theme, see Mary W. Cavender, *Nests of the Gentry. Family, Estate and Local Loyalties in Provincial Russia* (Newark, DE: University of Delaware Press, 2007), 26–58. For a somewhat different view, see Jessica Tovrov, 'Action and Affect in the Russian Noble Family' (PhD thesis, University of Chicago, 1980).

Volkhovskii's warm description of his grandparents' household even extended to the treatment of the house serfs. It was common for historical journals to publish nostalgic accounts about serfdom in the decades after its abolition in 1861, describing the close bonds that had supposedly existed between serfs and serf-owners.[14] In reality, of course, the idea that serfdom was rooted in a benign patriarchal order was largely an illusion.[15] During the years before the emancipation of the serfs, the myth formed a central plank in an ideology designed to underpin the *status quo*, while in the years after 1861 it was fuelled by an underlying sense of unease about the changing pattern of social relationships. Volkhovskii naturally made no effort to defend serfdom when writing his piece for *Sovremennik*, which would have run counter to his whole life's work, but he did recall how the house serfs in the Samotsvit residence lived in comparative comfort in a small annexe attached to the main building. Life in the one-storey white house was characterised by harmony, its peace disturbed only by minor perturbations, and free from the harsh economic exploitation and social control that were before long to trouble Volkhovskii so deeply.

A large part of Volkhovskii's account of his early childhood in Novograd-Volynskii was devoted to the complex ethnic composition of the Samotsvit household ('our nest was mixed').[16] His grandmother had been brought up in a Polish-speaking Catholic family. His grandfather was Russian-speaking and Orthodox. Such differences were for the most part subsumed in a culture of benign tolerance (his mother had as a child been taken to both Orthodox and Catholic services). Russian and Polish were spoken in the house and sometimes mixed up together. 'Ukrainian' was, though, never spoken in the main house. Matvei Mikhailovich spoke only Russian and indignantly challenged the idea

---

14   For three examples of such accounts, see O. I. Kornilova, *Byl' iz vremen krepostnichestva: vospominaniia o moei materi i eia okruzhaiushchem* (St Petersburg: Obshchestvennaia pol'za, 1894); A. Peterson, 'Cherty starinnago dvorianskago byta', *Russkii arkhiv*, 8 (1877), 479–82; I. A. Raevskii, 'Iz vospominanii', *Istoricheskii vestnik*, 101 (1905), 391–409.

15   For two superb (if very different) histories that cast light on both the economics and culture of serfdom, see Stephen Hoch, *Serfdom and Social Control in Russia: Petrovskoe, a Village in Tambov* (Chicago, IL: Chicago University Press, 1986); Tracy Dennison, *The Institutional Framework of Russian Serfdom* (Cambridge: Cambridge University Press, 2011).

16   Volkhovskoi, 'Otryvki', Part 1, 259.

that there was such a thing as Ukrainian nationality (*narodnost'*). He believed that the language spoken by the family's servants was simply a crude form of Russian—a kind of rural patois—rather than a fully-fledged language. Yet Volkhovskii's time at Novograd-Volynskii, and his close relations with some of the household serfs, gave him a facility in the Ukrainian language that he made extensive use of in his later career as a revolutionary publicist. His Ukrainian heritage also played a part in fuelling his hatred of the autocratic Russian state.

Volkhovskii's recollection of his early childhood in Novograd-Volynskii, which appeared half a century after the events he described, was subject to the usual mixture of nostalgia and amnesia that invariably shapes such accounts. Nor was it simply an exercise in autobiography. In the years before the 1917 Revolution, radical journals like *Byloe* and *Sovremennik* published numerous reminiscences by men and women who had been active in the revolutionary movement over the previous few decades.[17] Many of these accounts were rather formulaic, often tracing the author's turn towards revolution as a response to youthful experiences, ranging from resentment about authoritarian family *mores* through to horror at some egregious act of casual brutality. The second part of Volkhovskii's memoir in *Sovremennik*, which appeared in 1912, largely followed this format, counter-posing his time living with his mother's family at Novograd-Volynskii with the very different experiences he had at his paternal grandfather's estate at Moisevka.[18]

Volkhovskii and his mother left Novograd-Volynskii for Moisevka shortly after his grandfather inherited the estate, probably in 1853,

---

17 For a brief discussion of what might be called 'the revolutionary memoir wars', see Ben Eklof and Tatiana Saburova, *A Generation of Revolutionaries. Nikolai Charushin and Russian Populism from the Great Reforms to Perestroika* (Bloomington, IN: Indiana University Press, 2017), 5–6. For a longer discussion by the same authors, see Ben Eklof and Tatiana Saburova, ''Rembrances of a Distant Past': Generational Memory in the Collective Auto/Biography of Russian Populists in the Revolutionary Era', *Slavonic and East European Review*, 96, 1 (2018), 67-93. Also see Stephen Rindlisbacher, 'Living for a "Cause". Radical Autobiographical Writing at the Beginning of the 20th Century', *Avtobiografiя*, 6 (2017), 59–77.

18 Volkhovskoi, 'Otryvki odnoi chelovecheskoi zhizni', Part 2, *Sovremennik* (March 1912), 91–102. The account that follows draws both on this account as well as an unpublished version of Volkhovskii's memoirs written in English contained in Volkhovskii Papers (HIA), Box 11, Folder 3 (Unpublished autobiography). This version of Volkhovskii's autobiography is the fullest available in English of the various autobiographical writings found in his papers.

where they lived for the next three years. The move from one noble
'nest' to another was deeply traumatic for the young Feliks. The brain
injury suffered by Petr Grigorovich a few years before he inherited the
estate had a profound impact on his personality. Although Moisevka
and the neighbouring village of Stepanovka yielded a good income,[19]
their owner was content to live in just two rooms of the thirty-six-
roomed mansion, using one as a study and the second as a bedroom.
He disbanded the well-known serf orchestra that had made Moisevka a
celebrated centre of music and culture in the years before he inherited
the estate (the instruments were given to the musicians but they were
offered no opportunity to play together again).[20] Feliks' mother took
responsibility for managing the household, but she found it difficult to
get any money out of her father-in-law, and the family relied heavily on
produce from the garden. Petr Grigorovich shuffled around the house,
an incongruous figure in wig and slippers, inspiring fear in family and
servants alike through his capriciousness and cruelty. He kept large
black cats which he tortured by burning them with hot tobacco from
his pipe. He also paid a local 'idiot-boy' to chase birds from the lawn
in front of his study, apparently as much for his own amusement as
for its horticultural benefits, a fact that impressed itself indelibly on his
grandson's mind. The house was invariably very silent, in sharp contrast
to the bustling Samotsvit household, and the young Feliks found it hard
to adjust to a place that was so much more emotionally austere than the
one he had previously known. Yet the most lasting consequence of the
three years Feliks spent living with his grandfather was its influence on
his attitude towards serfdom.

Volkhovskii regularly described in later life an incident that took
place during his time at Moisevka which he saw, at least in retrospect, as
a turning point in his outlook:

---

19 Later owners of the estate went bankrupt, and the house itself was taken over by
    the local *zemstvo* in the early twentieth century, but Petr Grigorovich's miserliness
    in the late 1850s seems to have been as much a personal trait as a response to real
    financial problems.
20 Volkhovskii Papers (HIA), Box 17, Folder 3 (Autobiographical notes by
    Volkhovskii). For useful material on serf orchestras, see Richard Stites, *Serfdom,
    Society and the Arts in Imperial Russian Culture: The Pleasure and the Power* (New
    Haven, CT: Yale University Press, 2005), 53-87.

I was only a little seven year old boy when I lived on my grandfather's estate in the south of European Russia. One afternoon, about 5 o'clock, I came to the house of my grandfather's steward to see my playmate, the steward's son. As I passed the stables, a piteous cry reached my ear: a man was crying and entreating on some account. I stopped and listened.

'No lie down' said a coarse voice in which I recognised the voice of the steward.

'O sir, have mercy, pardon me this time, I will do it all' ... entreated the first voice.

At this moment I saw the steward's son was beside me.

'What is the matter?' I asked, overwhelmed with pity & distress.

'Big John is being punished' he answered in a whisper.

'What for?'

'He has not finished his work'.

I stood there feeling myself very unhappy and very ashamed. I could not explain why I was ashamed, but still my cheeks flushed. As the laments and sobs increased intermingled with some tumult then with the whistle of a brandished whip, I peeped into the stables through a hole in the wall and saw 'Big John' lying on the floor with his back bare and his face to the ground. Two strong men held him down—the one by the neck & hands, and the steward was flogging him. Every stroke left a horrible deep-red stripe on John's back.

Volkhovskii went on to describe how he ran to the house where he saw his 'cold unsmiling' grandfather.

I cannot explain how I contrived, child as I was, to understand the connection between that figure which moved before me and the shameful deed which I had just wittnessed [sic]. I know only that at this moment I hated that figure in which I vaguely discerned a landlord, forgetting that it was also my father's father. I felt myself overwhelmed with the consciousness of some great injustice which that man was guilty of and which must be avenged. So I ran after him & struck him childishly with my hands. This was the first revolutionary deed of my life.[21]

* * * * *

---

21   Volkhovskii Papers (HIA), Box 11, Folder 3 (Unpublished autobiography), 1–3.

The account from which these extracts are taken was probably written in the 1890s, when Volkhovskii was living in London, as part of a planned 'volume of reminiscences' for the publisher Unwins (which never appeared). Thomas Unwin had a particular interest in Russia, although he combined it with a shrewd commercial judgement, and suggested to Volkhovskii that his memoirs should focus on 'the more dramatic periods and situations and those which would be likely to interest an English audience'.[22] It is possible to dismiss such stylised narratives as a kind of *post hoc* explanation for Volkhovskii's revolutionary career, an attempt to reduce a complex chain of circumstances into a single pivotal moment, imbued with the kind of drama that Unwin hoped would sell the mooted 'book of reminiscences'.[23] Yet Volkhovskii was consistent in the different accounts he produced, repeatedly claiming in his articles and lectures that the incident had played a pivotal role in prompting his sympathy for the Russian peasantry.

> As I grew older and the questions of moral responsibility began to agitate me, I felt as if all my education and even my existence were stained with the sweat and blood of men who, being my countrymen and my brothers, were insulted and abused while working for my sake. I felt myself indebted to the Russian peasant and I felt that I must by some means pay my debt.[24]

* * * * *

During his time at Moisevka, Volkhovskii missed the easy intimacy between family members that was such a feature of his maternal grandparents' home. Nor did the polyglot atmosphere of the house in Novograd-Volynskii—where the residents spoke a mixture of Russian, Ukrainian and Polish—find much echo in day-to-day life at Moisevka. And yet it was ironically on his father's side of the family that the issue of Ukrainian national identity had once loomed large. Volkhovskii was, on his paternal grandmother's side, a great-grandson of the historian

---

22   Volkhovskii Papers, Houghton Library, Harvard University, henceforth Volkhovskii Papers (Houghton Library), MS Russ 51, Folder 359 (Unwin to Volkhovskii, 1 March 1895, 2 May 1895).

23   A short account of the flogging of Big John later appeared after Volkhovskii's death in George Kennan, *A Russian Comedy of Errors with Other Stories and Sketches of Russian Life* (New York: The Century Company, 1915), 141.

24   Volkhovskii Papers (HIA), Box 11, Folder 3 (Unpublished autobiography), 3–4.

and folklorist Andrei (Andriian) Chepa, who played a significant role in fostering Ukrainian national consciousness during the late eighteenth and early nineteenth centuries.[25] Chepa collected numerous manuscripts about the historical development of the provinces of south-west Russia, freely sharing his work with others, and was involved in initiatives to defend the rights of the heterogeneous Ukrainian nobility at a time when its status within the Russian empire was still uncertain. He also set up a school on his wife's family's estate of Chepurkivka, to provide local peasant children with an education in their own language.[26] Although no supporter of any form of separatism, Chepa's efforts to study the history of the Ukraine marked him out as one of the earliest figures in the Ukrainian cultural renaissance, which took on more political overtones in the decades following his death in 1822. Feliks Volkhovskii may not have known much about his great-grandfather's activities when he was a child, but he certainly knew about them in later life, regularly using the pseudonym Chepa in his writings.

Volkhovskii must also have known, at least when older, that Moisevka had once been a centre for writers who were instrumental in efforts to promote a Ukrainian national identity. It was noted earlier that Taras Shevchenko visited the estate on several occasions during the 1840s (a plinth commemorating the poet stands nearby to this day). His patron, the writer and poet Evgenii Grebenka (Ukr. Yevhen Hrebinka), who wrote some of the earliest 'literary' works in the Ukrainian language, was also a regular visitor (Grebenka was the godson of Petr Stepanovich Volkhovskii whose wife left the estate to Feliks' grandfather). In the summer of 1843, the two men visited the estate on a day when Tatiana Volkhovskaia was hosting a large ball to mark the anniversary of her husband's death, at which Shevchenko recited his poems and addressed

---

25 For useful background on Chepa's life and activities, see S. V. Abrosymova and L. H. Hurai, "A Chepa i nevidomi marhinalii z yoho biblioteky"(Dnipropetrovsk: NGU, 2006), 134–52, http://ir.nmu.org.ua/handle/123456789/1145. See, too, Dmytro Doroshenko, 'First Efforts to Collect and Publish Ukrainian Historical Material', in the special issue of *The Annals of the Ukrainian Academy of Arts and Sciences in the US, Inc*, 5–6 (1957), 92–103 (an English translation from the author's 1923 work).

26 On Chepa and Chepurkivka, including material on the Volkhovskii family, see 'Khutir Chepurkivka', https://www.grebenka.com/index/serbinivka_chepurkivka_serbinivska_silska_rada_grebinkivskij-rajon/0-480.

the audience in Ukrainian.[27] The Moisevka estate may not have provided the youthful Feliks with the unmediated experience of ethnic diversity that he received in Novograd-Volynskii. Yet its history, too, served as a testimony to the complex identity of the Russian Empire's south-western borderlands.

The atmosphere during Volkhovskii's time at Moisevka was made worse by family quarrels that were destined to have significant consequences on the financial fortunes of his family. Petr Grigorovich's wife and Feliks' grandmother, Valentina Andreovna, never joined her husband at Moisevka after he inherited the estate in the early 1850s. Nor, as noted earlier, did Feliks' own father Vadim live with his family there. There were also tensions between Petr Grigorovich's children. In 1857, Vadim's younger brother Esper retired from the army and moved to Moisevka with his wife and children, and shortly afterwards Petr Grigorovich decided to give him the whole estate. Feliks and his mother had already left Moisevka by the time his uncle arrived, suggesting that there were already tensions within the family, almost certainly focused on ownership of the property (a court case between Esper and his brothers dragged on for many years). The second part of Feliks' childhood was lived in an atmosphere of considerable financial insecurity and uncertainty.

In the years following their departure from Moisevka, Volkhovskii and his mother resided for a time at his paternal grandmother's Chepurkivka estate (where some of Vadim's younger siblings still lived). He was educated at home, before moving to the capital to attend the second St Petersburg Gymnasium, founded in 1805 by a decree issued by Tsar Aleksandr I. One of the pupils who studied there at the time was Petr Tkachev, among the most prominent figures in the revolutionary movement of the 1870s, who subsequently condemned the 'crude despotism, ignorance [and] slow-witted teachers' he encountered in his time at school.[28] Tkachev's dismissal of the education he received was too harsh. Although the Gymnasium lacked the social cachet of the better-known Imperial *Lycée*, it enjoyed significant royal patronage, and had a reputation for offering a high-quality education which included

---

27   Zaitsev, *Shevchenko*, 81–82.
28   Deborah Hardy, *Petr Tkachev. The Critic as Jacobin* (Seattle, WA: University of Washington Press, 1977), 19.

numerous lectures from professors at St Petersburg University.[29] Volkhovskii received an equally good education when he was taken by his mother to finish his school education in the gymnasium classes of the prestigious *Richelieu Lycée* in Odessa. He used his time there to develop his knowledge of foreign languages (he had a good command of French, German and English by the time he was eighteen).

Volkhovskii studied in St Petersburg and Odessa at a time when the emancipation of the serfs was creating a ferment in Russian society.[30] The relaxation of censorship in the years following Aleksandr II's accession to the throne, in 1855, allowed debate about a wider range of social, economic and literary questions than had been possible during the reign of Nicholas I.[31] Journals like the original *Sovremennik* and *Otechestvennye zapiski* (*Notes of the Fatherland*) published articles that would not previously have passed the censor. A new generation of radical writers, including Nikolai Chernyshevskii and Dmitrii Pisarev, contributed essays popularising a crude scientific materialism that questioned the aesthetic value of art for art's sake in favour of a realism designed to unmask the ugliness and exploitation of the contemporary world. In Chernyshevskii's words, 'the first purpose of art is to reproduce nature and life, and this applies to all works of art without exception'.[32]

---

29 On the second St Petersburg Gymnasium, including a detailed review of the curriculum, see A. V. Kurganovich, *Istoricheskaia zapiska 75-letiia S.-Peterburgskoi vtoroi gimnazii*, 3 vols (St Petersburg: various publishers, 1880–1905), II, esp. 28–46.

30 Among the large literature in English on emancipation and the other great reforms of the 1860s, see Ben Eklof, Josh Bushnell and Larissa Zakharova (eds), *Russia's Great Reforms, 1855–1881* (Bloomington, IN: Indiana University Press, 1994); Terence Emmons, *Emancipation of the Russian Serfs* (New York: Holt, Rinehart and Winston, 1970); W. Bruce Lincoln, *The Great Reforms. Autocracy, Bureaucracy, and the Politics of Change in Imperial Russia* (Dekalb, IL: Northern Illinois University Press, 1990).

31 For a useful discussion of *glasnost'* in the late 1850s, see W. Bruce Lincoln, 'The Problem of Glasnost' in Mid-Nineteenth Century Russian Politics', *European Studies Review*, 11, 2 (1981), 171–88.

32 Nikolai Chernyshevsky, 'The Aesthetic Relations of Art to Reality', in N. G. Chernyshevsky, *Selected Philosophical Essays* (Moscow: Foreign Languages Publishing House, 1953), 281-381 (364). For a valuable study of Chernyshevskii's aesthetic views, see Irina Paperno, *Chernyshevsky and the Age of Realism: A Study in the Semiotics of Behaviour* (Stanford, CA: Stanford University Press, 1988). For a useful if somewhat polemical essay examining the materialism of Chernyshevskii and others, see Jacob B. Talmon, *Myth of the Nation and Vision of Revolution: The Origins of Ideological Polarization in the Twentieth Century* (Abingdon: Routledge, 2017), 267–84. For a biography of Chernyshevskii, see William F. Woehrlin, *Chernyshevskii: The Man and the Journalist* (Cambridge, MA: Harvard University

Pisarev pithily expressed this new spirit of 'nihilism' with his celebrated aphorism that 'What can be smashed must be smashed. Whatever withstands the blow is fit to survive; what flies into pieces is rubbish'.[33] Although contributors to journals like *Sovremennik* were still forced to use a veiled language to express their views, the liberalisation of the censorship in the late 1850s and early 1860s facilitated the development of a distinctive Russian *intelligentsia*, characterised by its fascination with radical ideas and committed to social and political change.[34]

The term 'nihilism' was first popularised by Turgenev in his 1862 novel *Otsy i dety* (*Fathers and Children*), which provided a vivid picture of the clash between this new generation committed to the values of materialism and aesthetic utilitarianism, and an older generation of liberal-minded gentry who espoused the importance of progress and high art.[35] The most important response to the book came from the pen of Chernyshevskii. If Turgenev's novel provided a wistful insight into the

---

Press, 1971). On Pisarev, see Peter C. Pozefsky, *The Nihilist Imagination: Dmitrii Pisarev and the Cultural Origins of Russian Radicalism (1860–1868)* (New York: Peter Lang, 2003).

33   Quoted in James M. Edie, James Scanlan and Mary-Barbara Zeldin (eds), *Russian Philosophy*, 3 vols (Chicago, IL: Quadrangle Books, 1965), II, 65.

34   Among the large English-language literature on the origins and elusive character of the Russian *intelligentsia*, see Isaiah Berlin, *Russian Thinkers* (London: Penguin, 1994); Martin Malia, 'What Is the Intelligentsia?', *Daedalus*, 89, 3 (1960), 441–58; Laurie Manchester, *Holy Fathers, Secular Sons: Clergy, Intelligentsia and the Modern Self in Revolutionary Russia* (DeKalb, IL: Northern Illinois University Press, 2008); Vladimir C. Nahirny, *The Russian Intelligentsia: From Torment to Silence* (New Brunswick, NJ: Transaction Books, 1983); Philip Pomper, *The Russian Revolutionary Intelligentsia* (Wheeling, IL: H. Davidson, 1993); Marc Raeff, *Origins of the Russian Intelligentsia. The Eighteenth-Century Nobility* (New York: Harcourt Brace and World, 1966); Nicholas Riasanovsky, *A Parting of Ways: Government and the Educated Public in Russia, 1801-1855* (Oxford: Clarendon Press, 1976).

35   Among the voluminous literature exploring the importance of Turgenev's novel, including his popularising of the term nihilism, see Isaiah Berlin's 1970 Romanes Lecture 'Fathers and Children. Turgenev and the Liberal Predicament', in Ivan Turgenev, *Fathers and Sons*, trans. Rosemary Edmonds (London: Penguin, 1979), 7–71; William C. Brumfield, 'Bazarov and Rjazanov: The Romantic Archetype in Russian Nihilism', *Slavic and East European Journal*, 21, 4 (1977), 495–505; Olga Vishnyakova, 'Russian Nihilism: The Cultural Legacy of the Conflict between Fathers and Sons', *Comparative and Continental Philosophy*, 3, 1 (2011), 99–111; Irina N. Sizemskaya, 'Russian Nihilism in Ivan S. Turgenev's Literary and Philosophical Investigations', *Russian Studies in Philosophy*, 56, 5 (2018), 394–404. For Turgenev's views on his novel, written some years after its appearance, see Ivan Turgenev, 'Apropos of Fathers and Sons', in David Magarshack (ed.), *Turgenev's Literary Reminiscences* (London: Faber, 1984), 168–77.

clash of values between two generations, fretting over the destruction of cherished liberal nostrums and ideals, Chernyshevskii's 1863 novel *Chto delat'?* (*What Is to Be Done?*) offered an unambiguous paean of praise for a new generation committed to questioning everything.[36] Thousands of students at Russian universities and gymnasia were enthralled by characters like Rakhmetov, who spent his nights sleeping on a bed of nails, in an unlikely attempt to steel himself for the struggle to bring about revolution. *What Is to Be Done?* helped to forge a new self-consciousness among thousands of educated young Russians, providing them with a model of ways to live that ostentatiously rejected the values of a previous generation.

Volkhovskii was influenced by the new *zeitgeist* even before enrolling in the Law Faculty at Moscow University in 1863. Students at the St Petersburg gymnasium he attended regularly discussed articles appearing in journals like *Sovremennik*. The same was true in Odessa (Lazar Goldenberg, who subsequently worked with Volkhovskii in London in the 1890s, recalled in his memoirs that he first read *What Is to Be Done?* and *Sovremennik* while at school in the city).[37] Volkhovskii himself was familiar with the writings of Chernyshevskii before he enrolled at the University, and regularly read *Sovremennik* and *Kolokol* (*The Bell*), the journal published abroad by Aleksandr Herzen which circulated widely in Russia.[38] And, during his first year as a student in Moscow, Volkhovskii was among the crowd that witnessed the civic execution of Chernyshevskii in St Petersburg's Mytninskaia Square in 1864 (a symbolic 'ceremony' in which the victim was led to the scaffold before being forced to kneel as a sword was broken over their head). The spectacle had a profound effect on the young Volkhovskii, who

---

36 For a collection of essays by Soviet historians that remains useful today, if bearing the ideological preconceptions of the time, see M. V. Nechkina, *Vstrecha dvukh pokolenii. Iz istorii russkogo revoliutsionnogo dvizheniia kontsa 50-kh – nachala 60-kh godov XIX veka. Sbornik statei* (Moscow: Nauka, 1980).

37 Tuckton House Archive, University of Leeds Brotherton Library Special Collections, henceforth Tuckton House Archive (Leeds Brotherton Library), MS 1381/18 (typescript of L. Goldenberg, 'Reminiscences'), 10. Goldenberg appears for a time to have been at the gymnasium with Volkhovskii, although his interest in radical literature developed after he transferred to the Commercial School in Odessa in 1863, where his interest in political questions was roused by news of the suppression of unrest in Poland.

38 Volkhovskii Papers (HIA), Box 17, Folder 3 (Brief autobiographical notes by Volkhovskii).

described how the 'remarkable' and 'talented' author of *What Is to Be Done?* had been condemned to exile for nothing more than publishing ideas about reform that were anathema to 'the narrow class interests of the aristocracy'.[39]

The term 'nihilism' was in practice never more than a convenient label for a diffuse set of ideas and behaviours, while any effort to understand historical change in terms of generations inevitably runs the risk of reducing the complex experiences of countless individuals to a single descriptor.[40] The rise of the 'new people' of the 1860s was nevertheless something more than a literary construct. Nihilism was as much about lifestyle as ideas: a distinctive fashion designed to assert a semiotics of protest (long shabby coats and long hair for men, plain dresses and short hair for women); a new balance of relationships between the sexes; and so forth.[41] Yet ideas still mattered greatly to the young radicals. Was Russia bound to go through the West European experience of political and economic development? Or would it be possible, as Chernyshevskii and others argued, to build a distinctively Russian socialism based on the egalitarian and collective instincts of the Russian people? And how should young members of the *intelligentsia* seek to relate to the Russian *narod*—the ordinary Russian people (overwhelmingly peasants)—who lived in ways that were largely mysterious to those who spent their lives in the city? As the 1860s progressed, the principal differences within the radical-revolutionary movement revolved around such questions, and above all the vexed issue of whether social and political change was best brought about by the violent destruction of the tsarist state, or a more

---

39 For Volkhovskii's account, see F. Volkhovskii, 'Na Mytninskoi ploshchadi', in Iu. G. Oksman (ed.), *N.G. Chernyshevskii v vospominaniiakh sovremennikov*, 2 vols (Saratov: Saratovskoe knizhnoe izdatel'stvo, 1958), I, 31–36.

40 For a valuable discussion of this subject, see Stephen Lovell, 'From Genealogy to Generation. The Birth of Cohort Thinking in Russia', *Kritika*, 9, 3 (2008), 567–94. For a useful application of the concept of generation to Volkhovskii's own radical milieu, see Eklof and Saburova, *A Generation of Revolutionaries*, passim. For a dated if still useful wider discussion of the subject, see Lewis S. Feuer, *The Conflict of Generations. The Character and Significance of Student Movements* (New York: Basic Books, 1969).

41 For a valuable discussion of the 'self-fashioning' of the radical *intelligentsia*, see Christopher Ely, *Underground Petersburg. Radical Populism, Urban Space and the Tactics of Subversion in Reform-Era Russia* (Dekalb, IL: Northern Illinois University Press, 2016). For a useful discussion of the sartorial dimension, see Victoria Thorstensson, 'Nihilist Fashion in 1860s–1870s Russia: The Aesthetic Relations of Blue Spectacles to Reality', *Clothing Cultures*, 3, 3 (2016), 265–81.

gradualist programme that fostered closer relations between the radical *intelligentsia* and the Russian *narod*. It was to become one of the defining tensions in the development of the Russian revolutionary movement in the 1870s.

All these dilemmas lay, though, ahead when Volkhovskii enrolled as a law student at Moscow University in 1863. He spent very little time on his formal studies over the next few years. The quality of lectures at the University varied considerably in the 1860s,[42] and many students preferred to meet informally to discuss the work of writers like Chernyshevskii, a phenomenon that helped to shape the development of a distinct radical subculture.[43] Volkhovskii lived with his mother in a house just off the Arbat near the city centre, but their financial position was precarious, and Feliks spent much of his time earning money through the book trade. A police report written some years later noted that his activities prevented him from attending class regularly. Volkhovskii's work did however give him an insight into the complex web of rules and regulations that defined what could (and could not) be legally published. It also gave him easy access to numerous illegal publications that were in more or less open circulation at the time.

Volkhovskii does not appear to have developed close links with such revolutionary organisations as the first Zemlia i volia (Land and Liberty), although it will be seen later that he was loosely acquainted with some of those involved in the melodramatically named Ad (Hell), whose members were committed to carrying out a programme of assassinations and robbery.[44] He was, rather, one of the thousands of

---

42 For a ponderous but still helpful Soviet history of Moscow University, see Mikhail Tikhomirov et al. (eds), *Istoriia Moskovskogo universiteta*, 2 vols (Moscow: Izd-vo Moskovskogo universiteta, 1955). For useful memoirs of Moscow University in the late 1850s and 1860s, by one of the best-known professors there, see B. N. Chicherin, *Vospominaniia*, 2 vols, I, *Moskovskii universitet. Zemstvo i Moskovskaia duma* (Moscow: Izd-vo. im. Sabashnikovykh, 2010), 5–126.

43 On this subject, see Daniel R. Brower, *Training the Nihilists. Education and Radicalism in Tsarist Russia* (Ithaca, NY: Cornell University Press, 1975), 190–230.

44 On the first Zemlia i volia see Franco Venturi, *Roots of Revolution. A History of the Populist and Socialist Movements in Nineteenth-Century Russia* (Chicago, IL: University of Chicago Press, 1983), 253–84; Nechkina, *Vstrecha dvukh pokolenii*, 287–336. On 'Hell' see, for example, Adam Ulam, *Prophets and Conspirators in Pre-Revolutionary Russia* (New Brunswick, NJ: Transaction Publishers, 1998), 148–68; Venturi, *Roots of Revolution*, 331-53. For a discussion of 'Hell' from a very different standpoint, see Claudia Verhoeven, *The Odd Man Karakazov. Imperial Russia,*

young men and women whose 'nihilism' was shaped by the materialist philosophy pithily expressed in Aleksandr Kropotkin's dictum that 'There is nothing except matter. Away with idealism'.[45] Yet the nihilist creed—if strictly interpreted—was more effective at challenging the *status quo* than it was in identifying alternatives. Many of the young people enthralled by the new thinking were by contrast natural enthusiasts inspired by a desire to find positive ways of improving the welfare of the *narod*. Lazar Goldenberg, who was trained as a chemist, subsequently articulated the sentiments of many 'new people' when he recalled how he had by the late 1860s become increasingly sceptical about the potential of a 'purely scientific method' to foster social and political change.[46] Volkhovskii himself was subsequently to play a significant role in the search for ways in which the *intelligentsia* could further their understanding of the Russian peasant and find ways of bringing enlightenment to the village.

Volkhovskii devoted a good deal of time as a student to his role as secretary of a Little Russian mutual aid society (*kassa*), established by students at Moscow University who came from the south-western provinces of the Empire. The growth of 'Ukrainophilism' was a source of concern for the tsarist authorities throughout the 1860s. The establishment of the Brotherhood of Saints Cyril and Methodius in the turbulent years of 1847–48 had shown that Ukrainian national sentiment could take on a political form.[47] Most of its members supported the creation of a federation of free Slavic states, organised on liberal principles, a position that was hardly compatible with the ideology of

---

    Modernity and the Birth of Terrorism (Ithaca, NY: Cornell University Press, 2009), passim.

45   Brower, *Training the Nihilists*, 159.

46   Tuckton House Archive (Leeds Brotherton Library), MS 1381/18 (typescript of L. Goldenberg, 'Reminiscences'), 11.

47   On the development of Ukrainian national consciousness in this period, especially in relation to Russia, see Serhy Yekelchyk, *Ukraine: Birth of a Modern Nation* (New York: Oxford University Press, 2007), 33–52; Aleksei Miller, *The Ukrainian Question: The Russian Empire and Nationalism in the Nineteenth Century* (Budapest: Central European Press, 2003), 49–60; Johannes Remy, *Brothers or Enemies? The Ukrainian National Movement and Russia from the 1840s to the 1870s* (Toronto: Toronto University Press, 2016). For an imaginative and wide-ranging review of the impact of Romantic Nationalism in the region, see Serhiy Bilenky *Romantic Nationalism in Eastern Europe: Russian, Polish, and Ukrainian Political Imaginations* (Stanford, CA: Stanford University Press, 2012).

Official Nationality, with its emphasis on Orthodoxy, Autocracy and Nationality, designed to help secure the social and political *status quo*.[48] While the Brotherhood was quickly suppressed, interest in Ukrainian identity and culture never faded away, and the appearance of the legal journal *Osnova* (lit. *The Basis*) in 1861 provided a new setting for debate on questions relating to Ukrainian culture and language.[49] The Polish Rebellion of 1863 made the question more sensitive than ever.[50] By the time Volkhovskii matriculated at the University, any interest in the question of Little Russian identity was bound to attract official suspicion.

The Little Russian *kassa* was at least ostensibly designed to provide financial help to any of its members who fell on hard times. Its rules emphasised the need for members to pool their resources and treat each other with a respect that recognised no distinctions or hierarchies.[51] One Soviet historian suggested that the communal values demanded of members were very similar to those of the Chaikovskii-Natanson radical circle that emerged in the early 1870s (to which Volkhovskii belonged).[52] The sixty members met regularly to discuss requests for financial help (some 2,500 rubles was disbursed between 1863 and 1866). The society also maintained a library that provided a meeting place for its members. While the University authorities were aware of the *kassa's* activities it still attracted suspicion. The Third Section, the 'secret police' agency responsible for monitoring subversive activities,

---

18   On Official Nationality, see Nicholas Riasanovsky, *Nicholas I and Official Nationality in Russia, 1825–1855* (Berkeley, CA: University of California Press, 1959). For a brief but useful article on Count Sergei Uvarov, widely and not altogether accurately seen as the main architect of the policy, see Cynthia Whittaker, 'The Ideology of Sergei Uvarov: An Interpretive Essay', *Russian Review*, 37, 2 (1978), 158–76.

49   On the creation and demise of *Osnova*, see Miller, *Ukrainian Question*, 75–96; Remy, *Brothers or Enemies?* 90–108.

50   Miller, *Ukrainian Question*, 97–126. See, too, David Saunders, 'Russia and Ukraine under Alexander II: The Valuev Edict of 1863', *International History Review*, 17, 1 (1995), 23–50. For a general discussion of the Polish factor in developments in 'Right Bank' Ukraine, see Kimitaka Matsuzato, 'Pol'skii faktor v pravoberezhnoi Ukraine s XIX po nachalo XX veka', *Ab Imperio*, 1 (2000), 123–44.

51   The elaborate rules of the Little Russian Society can be found in the State Archive of the Russian Federation (henceforth GARF), f. 95, op. 2, del. 419 (Various records relating to the Malorussian student society).

52   P. S. Tkachenko, *Uchashchaiasia molodezh' v revoliutsionnom dvizhenii 60-70-kh gg. XIX v.* (Moscow: Mysl', 1978), 91.

placed an informer among the members of the organisation.[53] A report later described the organisation as secretive—*neglasno*—but suggested that it had no criminal objectives (*prestupnye tseli*). When its library was seized by police in 1868, eighteen months after Volkhovskii had left the University without graduating, most of its books and papers were found to be 'unobjectionable'.[54]

While Volkhovskii's role as secretary of the Little Russian *kassa* focused on providing practical help to fellow students, his interest in all things Ukrainian was much broader, touching precisely on the sorts of questions that concerned the authorities. Nor was he alone. Several members of the *kassa* subsequently faced arrest and imprisonment for their Ukrainophile sentiments. Volkhovskii himself had been under police surveillance for nearly two years at the time of his first arrest, in February 1868, when a search of his flat discovered numerous pictures of Taras Shevchenko and the eighteenth-century Cossack leader Pavlo Polubotok. It also uncovered numerous books with photographs of individuals dressed in Ukrainian national costume.[55] Such artefacts were bound to appear suspect to the authorities, anxious in the wake of the Polish Revolution of 1863 about the growth of nationalist sentiment in the Empire's western borderlands.

A few months before his arrest, Volkhovskii had sought permission to publish a series of articles sketching out a programme of field work to collect material designed to foster greater understanding of the Ukrainian peasantry, telling the Moscow Censorship Committee that he hoped in due course to publish the articles in book form for easy circulation. The Committee was suspicious of the whole enterprise, suspecting that the author 'in all probability has some other goal that he had not

---

53   On the Third Section in this period, see Sidney Monas, *The Third Section: Police and Society in Russia under Nicholas I* (Cambridge, MA: Harvard University Press, 1961); P. S. Squire, *The Third Department: The Establishment and Practices of the Political Police in the Russia of Nicholas I* (Cambridge: Cambridge University Press, 1968). For the classic pre-revolutionary account of the Third Section and its impact on cultural life in the reign of Nicholas I, see M. K. Lemke, *Nikolaevskie zhandarmy i literatura, 1826–55 gg.* (St Petersburg: Tip-ia A. V. Orlova, 1909). For a recent account, see Igor' Simbirtsev, *Tret'e otdelnie. Pervyi opyt sozdaniia professional'noi spetssluzhbi v Rossiiskoi imperii, 1826–1880* (Moscow: Tsentrpoligraf, 2006).

54   N. F. Bel'chikov, 'Rublevoe obshchestvo. Epizod iz istorii revoliutsionnogo dvizheniia 60-kh godov', *Izvestiia Akademii Nauk SSSR. Seriia vii. Otdelenie obshchestvennykh nauk*, 10 (1935), 941-1001 (942).

55   Bel'chikov, 'Rublevoe obshchestvo', 992.

explained to the Committee', and referred the issue to St Petersburg. A senior official in the capital wrote a detailed report noting warily that the programme to collect information about peasant lifestyles would require the dispatch of enumerators to the countryside. He agreed with the Moscow Committee that the author probably had 'another goal' in mind than a purely scientific one, adding that Volkhovskii had a 'Polish name', and that the area to be surveyed formed part of Poland until the country's final partition in 1795. Permission to publish was refused.[56]

When Volkhovskii was arrested early in 1868, though, it was neither a direct result of his involvement in the Little Russian *kassa* nor a consequence of his plans for publishing material about the Ukrainian *narod*. He was instead taken into custody for his part in establishing the so-called Ruble Society, along with his friend German Lopatin, who had graduated from the Mathematics Faculty of St Petersburg University in 1866. Lopatin had been on the periphery of the revolutionary group that coalesced in the mid-1860s around Ivan Khudiakov in Petersburg and Nikolai Ishutin in Moscow (out of which emerged 'Hell'). Ishutin had for a time audited classes at Moscow University, where he met Volkhovskii through the Little Russian *kassa*, although it is not clear how well the two men knew one another.[57] He was also first cousin of Dmitrii Karakazov, who made an unsuccessful attempt on the life of Tsar Aleksandr II in 1866, for which he was subsequently hanged.[58] Ties between members of the Ishutin and Khudiakov groups had grown closer during 1865, and both men were instrumental in encouraging Karakazov's actions, although most of the young student radicals grouped around them had no knowledge of the plot. Lopatin was arrested and imprisoned for two months following the assassination attempt before being released without charge. He almost certainly knew nothing about Karakazov's plans. The same was true of Volkhovskii despite his slight acquaintanceship with Ishutin.[59]

---

56 Bel'chikov, 'Rublevoe obshchestvo', 986 ff.

57 Philip Pomper, *Sergei Nechaev* (New Brunswick, NJ: Rutgers University Press, 1979), 48–49.

58 For an interesting discussion of Karakazov, which sees his act of violence as something more complex and significant than the act of a deranged misfit, see Verhoeven, *The Odd Man Karakazov*.

59 N. A. Troitskii, *Pervye iz blestiashchei pleiady. Bol'shoe obshchestvo propagandy 1871–1874 gody* (Saratov: Izd-vo Saratovskogo universiteta, 1991), 37.

Lopatin was no Jacobin regicide, instead believing that any attempt
to bring about radical social and political change in Russia should be
founded on a deep understanding of the 'real position and needs' of
the peasantry, which meant that it was necessary 'to draw closer to that
enigmatic sphinx called the *narod'*. Volkhovskii took a similar view.
Indeed, when he first sought permission to publish his programme
for collecting material about the Ukrainian peasantry, Volkhovskii and
Lopatin had already begun to sketch out a plan to create a peripatetic
cadre of 'teachers' who would travel to rural areas and acquaint
themselves with the life and needs of the peasantry.[60] The 'teachers'
would also discuss historical and political questions with members of
the peasant commune, and distribute specially published books, written
in an accessible language on issues ranging from history to economics.
Subscribers would support the whole operation by paying one ruble per
month. In the event, the only book to be published was one by Khudiakov,
Drevnaia Rus' (*Ancient Russia*), which rejected state-centred accounts of
Russia's history in favour of one that condemned the modern system of
autocratic government as a break with the supposedly more egalitarian
traditions of Russia's past.[61]

Lopatin and Volkhovskii exchanged a series of letters discussing
their plans. In January 1868, Lopatin told his friend that fifteen people
who attended a meeting in St Petersburg agreed to support the scheme.[62]
Neither man knew that the mutual friend they asked to carry their letters
between Moscow and St Petersburg was in the pay of the Third Section.
The authorities were concerned enough to arrest the two men in order to
obtain more information about their activities. Volkhovskii described in
one of his unpublished autobiographical accounts how, after his mother
answered a knock at the door late at night,

> The room was filled with people: there was a colonel of gendarmes, a
> police-officer, some gendarmes-soldiers and policemen, and two private
> persons from the neighbourhood who, according to law, are witnesses
> as to the legality of the manner in which the search is conducted ... the

60   A. A. Shilov (ed.), *German Aleksandrovich Lopatin, 1845-1918. Avtobiografiя.*
      Pokazaniia i pis'ma. Stat'i i stikhotvoreniia. Bibliografiia (Petrograd: Gosudarstvennoe
      izdatel'stvo, 1922), 28.

61   Venturi, *Roots of Revolution*, 341.

62   Shilov (ed.), *German Aleksandrovich Lopatin*, 31.

colonel went to my bedroom and, rousing me from my bed, asked where were my papers.

I led him to my desk. The colonel took up a position on my left hand, the police officer on my right, and we began to take out, one by one, the papers which were examined by the officials. Those which were evidently without any significance, were put aside, all the rest were kept by the gendarmes. On a sudden [sic] I perceived in the drawer the important paper which I had forgotten to conceal: it was a list of persons contributing money monthly. My blood ran cold & my breath stopped. If the list were seized, the lodgings of all these persons would be searched at night like mine, something compromising might be discovered and the people would be ruined – all that through my carelessness! The thought of it was almost unbearable to me. Generally in such cases a Russian revolutionist tries to seize the compromising paper and to swallow it. But I could not do it. The sheet was pretty large and they were at my side—two vigorous men. No doubt the paper would be taken out by force even from my mouth ... Luckily my list was written on the opposite side of some advertisements and were lying with the printed side up. I summoned all my self-possession and taking the paper quietly, I showed it to the colonel, keeping it in my hands of course without turning it over.

'Do you want it' I asked smiling.

'Certainly not' answered the colonel, and with an exulting heart but an unaltered face I laid the list aside.[63]

After the search was over, Volkhovskii was driven away by sleigh to a local police station, where he was held for a few hours before being put on a train to St Petersburg under the guard of two gendarmes. Lopatin's home in St Petersburg was also searched, although he had somehow got wind of what was happening, and nothing compromising was found. He was nevertheless arrested and taken to prison where, like Volkhovskii, he was detained for several months.

Volkhovskii was just twenty-one at the time of his arrest, and the next few months introduced him to the challenges of 'solitude and forced idleness' that were to become all too familiar in the years that followed.

---

63 Volkhovskii Papers (HIA), Box 11, Folder 3 (Unpublished autobiography), 8–9. A somewhat different account by Volkhovskii—in another autobiographical manuscript—can be found in George Kennan Papers, 1840–1937, Manuscript Division, Library of Congress, Washington DC, henceforth Kennan Papers (Library of Congress), Box 136.

Much of his captivity was spent in the Peter and Paul Fortress on the banks of the Neva opposite the Winter Palace, although he was regularly taken from the prison in a closed carriage for interrogation by a commission of inquiry made up of eight generals, who cross-questioned the prisoner at length, reacting with anger 'when my answers seemed ... not to be frank enough'. Volkhovskii was according to his own account well-treated, although his interrogators still made him feel like a 'desperate culprit ... they knew all about my doings & that my only chance of a mitigated punishment lay in a frank confession'. In true Kafkaesque fashion, when Volkhovskii asked with what he was charged, he was told by his interrogators that 'I knew as well as [they] did'. The questions put to him repeatedly focused on his relationship with Lopatin and other acquaintances, many of whom had been put under surveillance, and when he failed to give satisfactory answers, he was sent back to his cell for days on end. During questioning he found that 'it took an almost superhuman effort to stay clear of the reefs that lay in my way without dropping a name or a sentence which might produce a fatal result'.[64]

In both published and unpublished versions of his memoirs describing this time of his life, Volkhovskii told how a kindly prison guard acted as a go-between with Lopatin, providing the two men with an opportunity to coordinate their answers when questioned by the examining commission.[65] The authorities were nevertheless convinced that they were both being evasive—'not without cause' as Volkhovskii later observed—and played cat and mouse with the prisoners in an effort to catch them out.[66] Although Lopatin and Volkhovskii denied

---

64 Volkhovskii Papers (HIA), Box 11, Folder 3 (Unpublished autobiography), 12 ff. Volkhovskii subsequently published an account describing his experiences for an English audience in Felix Volkhovsii, 'My Life in Russian Prisons', *Fortnightly Review*, 48 (November 1890), 782-94. He also published an account of his arrest and imprisonment for a Russian audience in 1906, which was broadly consistent with the English version, despite the very different audiences. See F. Volkhovskii, *Druz'ia sredi vragov. Iz vospominanii starago revoliutsionera* (St Petersburg: Knigoizdatel'stvo 'Narodnaia volia', 1906).

65 Volkhovskii's account of his various terms of imprisonment in *Druz'ia sredi vragov* was carefully written to suggest that many guards and even some officers felt sympathy for their prisoners, an approach that was designed to emphasise his views in the wake of the 1905 Revolution that it was possible to build close relations between soldiers (including officers) and revolutionaries.

66 The extensive records of the Third Section's investigation into Lopatin and Volkhovskii can be found in GARF, f. 109, op. 153, del. 172.1–172.3.

anyone else had been involved in the Ruble Society, officials in the Third Section knew that the claim was false, not least because a second raid on Volkhovskii's house had uncovered a list of members (presumably the document he had successfully concealed during the first search). The raid also discovered his account of Chernyshevskii's civic execution which praised the victim as a martyr whose fate should inspire 'deeds' rather than 'helpless whimpering'.[67] It was only after investigators confronted Lopatin with the evidence that he changed his story, telling his inquisitors that he and Volkhovskii had hoped 'to spread enlightenment among the people' by providing them with books that would give them a greater understanding of history and literature. He also claimed unconvincingly that they had not sought approval for their activities because they lacked the right contacts among the bureaucracy.[68]

Although Volkhovskii and Lopatin were evasive in the answers they gave when questioned about the Ruble Society, they were not as the authorities feared planning an armed uprising along the lines set out in some of the revolutionary manifestoes that had circulated in Russia earlier in the 1860s.[69] Volkhovskii still maintained forty years later that the Ruble Society had never been anything more than a loose association of like-minded individuals inspired by a sense of their 'moral debt to the Russian *narod*'.[70] Its programme was indeed in many ways the antithesis of the Jacobinism favoured by the Ishutin-Khudiakov group. Yet both Lopatin and Volkhovskii knew that it was impossible to separate questions of 'enlightenment' and 'propaganda' from questions of organisation. The distinction was also unclear to those charged with maintaining public order.

Lopatin and Volkhovskii were eventually released from prison without charge in the autumn of 1868, in part because of lack of evidence that the Ruble Society was a genuinely revolutionary organisation.

---

67 Volkhovskii, 'Na Mytninskoi ploshchadi', 35.

68 For Lopatin's testimony, see Shilov (ed.), *German Aleksandrovich Lopatin*, 33–43.

69 One of the documents seized in the raid on Volkhovskii's flat was headed 'To the Younger Generation', and the authorities may have been concerned that it was written in a conscious echo of a similarly-named 1862 pamphlet by Nikolai Shelgunov and Mikhail Mikhaikov, which while less sanguinary in tone than some of the more blood-curdling manifestoes of the time still contained demands for an elected Head of State and the transfer of all noble owned land to the peasantry. On Shelgunov and Mikhailov's pamphlet, see Venturi, *Roots of Revolution*, 241–50.

70 Volkhovskii, *Druz'ia sredi vragov*, 4.

Although the Third Section had seized a copy of Volkhovskii's diary, which provided an account of his friendships and activities, they found no detailed evidence that he was involved in a conspiracy to foment revolution.[71] The behaviour of both men was deemed to be the product of youthful exuberance that would fade with time. The Commission of Inquiry also concluded, not altogether accurately, that Lopatin had been the more important figure in establishing the Ruble Society. Volkhovskii and his mother had to sign a formal document promising that Feliks would not engage in any illegal activities. Lopatin was sent from St Petersburg to join his family near Stavropol.[72]

Following his release, Volkhovskii returned to the book trade to earn money, working in the Moscow branch of the bookshop owned by the St Petersburg lawyer Aleksandr Cherkesov, which provided an important meeting place for young radicals in the city. He established friendly relations with Vsevolod Lopatin, the brother of German, and the two men quickly became central figures in a discussion group that included Petr Uspenskii and his sister Nadezhda, along with Uspenskii's future wife Aleksandra Zasulich.[73] Zasulich recalled later that 'We were all very inexperienced: we read the articles of Chernyshevskii in *Sovremennik* and the works of Lavrov, and we welcomed enthusiastically the small number of back copies of *Kolokol* which Uspenskii had been able to obtain'.[74] They also read numerous foreign works in translation.[75] Most participants in the group seem initially to have held views consistent with the ones that inspired German Lopatin and Volkhovskii when founding the Ruble Society, including agreement about the need to develop a closer relationship between the intelligentsia and the *narod*. They were also still heavily influenced by the positivism that was so

---

71 Volkhovskii's episodic diary and other jottings for 1866–67 can be found in GARF, f. 95, op. 2, del. 311. Other material in the same *delo* shows how Volkhovskii had even as a very young man developed the habit of cutting out and keeping cuttings from the Russian press that was to continue till the end of his life.

72 Kennan Papers (Library of Congress), Box 136 (Autobiographical notes by Volkhovskii), 17.

73 Aleksandra was the sister of Vera Zasulich who subsequently became famous for her assassination attempt on the Governor-General of St Petersburg in 1878.

74 Aleksandra Zasulich, 'Vospominaniia shestidesiatnitsy', *Byloe*, 18 (1922), 19–45 (esp. 26–35).

75 For Volkhovskii's views of the circle given at his trial, see *Pravitel'stvennyi vestnik*, 159 (1871).

influential in radical circles in Russia during the 1860s. The group first assembled at Uspenskii's home, but when he was placed in charge at Cherkesov's bookstore he asked for the meetings to be moved to his sister's flat, on the grounds that although they were 'completely innocent' they might provoke suspicion and make his job harder.[76] Nadezhda Uspenskaia shared a flat with Aleksandra Zasulich and another young radical, Mariia Antonova, who noted in her subsequent testimony to the Third Section that some fifteen people usually attended meetings, a number that included several who had been on the fringes of the group involved in Karakazov's attempt on the life of Aleksandr II. She also testified that the group was not interested in politics, something that Volkhovskii claimed too, following his second arrest in April 1869.[77] Such protestations were decidedly disingenuous. The discussions may not have focused on the need for political change, in the narrow sense of the term, but the emphasis on developing a closer understanding between the *intelligentsia* and the *narod* was bound to appear subversive in the eyes of the authorities.

The outbreak of student demonstrations in cities across Russia in the final months of 1868 increased official concern about the threat posed by young radicals. Most of the demands related to immediate grievances, including the right to free speech and free assembly on university premises, but the tough response by the University authorities provoked further anger among the students. The ferment prompted discussion in revolutionary circles about the nature and significance of the unrest. The newspaper *Narodnoe delo* (*The People's Cause*), which was published by Mikhail Bakunin in Geneva, called for the protests to become the basis for a more general *bunt* (rebellion).[78] Many students considered giving up their studies to make a more immediate contribution to the welfare of the peasantry. In the words of Solomon Chudnovskii, who later worked closely with Volkhovskii in south Russia in the early 1870s,

76 *Pravitel'stvennyi vestnik*, 159 (1871).
77 B. P. Koz'min, 'S. G. Nechaev i ego protivniki v 1868–69 gg.', in B. I. Gorev and B. P. Koz'min (eds), *Revoliutsionnoe dvizhenie 1860-kh godov* (Moscow: Izd-vo Vsesoiuznogo obshchestva politkatorzhan i ssyl'no-poslentsev, 1932), 168–226 (192).
78 On Bakunin's views during this period, see Aileen Kelly, *Mikhail Bakunin: A Study in the Psychology and Politics of Utopia* (Oxford: Clarendon Press, 1982), 257–88.

The problem was raised in a ruthlessly categorical and extremely partial form: learning or work? i.e. was it necessary to devote ourselves, even if only temporarily, to our studies, so as to obtain diplomas and then live the life of the privileged professions of the intelligentsia; or should we remember our duty to the people, recall that all our learning had been acquired only by means provided by the people, who work like condemned men and are always hungry? Should we not rather, we students, give up our privileged position, give up scholarship and devote ourselves to learning a craft, so as to take part as simple artisans or labourers in the life of the people, and merge with it.[79]

* * * * *

The student unrest provided the background for the appearance of one of the most unsavoury figures in the history of the nineteenth-century Russian revolutionary movement: Sergei Nechaev. Nechaev was born into a poor background in the town of Ivanovo, 150 miles north of Moscow, but subsequently acquired sufficient education to become a teacher. In 1868 he attended lectures at St Petersburg University. Over the next couple of years, Nechaev became adept at constructing a fantasy world in which he played the starring role, convincing both impressionable young students and experienced revolutionaries like Bakunin that he had at his beck and call a large and well-organised revolutionary organisation.[80] He was active in the student disorders of 1868–69, before fleeing Russia in typically melodramatic manner, circulating a note falsely claiming that he had been arrested by the Third Section. Once in Switzerland, Nechaev co-authored with Bakunin the 'Catechism of a Revolutionary',[81] which opened with the sombre words that 'the revolutionary is a doomed man. He has no private interests, no

---

79 Quoted in Venturi, *Roots of Revolution*, 359.
80 On Bakunin's relations with Nechaev, see Paul Avrich, *Bakunin and Nechaev* (London: Freedom Press, 1987); Michel Confino, *Violence dans le violence: Le débat Bakounine-Nečaev* (Paris: F. Maspero, 1973); Arthur Lehning (ed.), *Michel Bakounine et ses relations avec Sergej Nechaev, 1870–1872* (Leiden: Brill, 1971); Woodford McClellan, *Revolutionary Exiles. The Russians in the First International and the Paris Commune* (London: Frank Cass, 1979), 36-40. For useful general discussions of Nechaev's career, see Pomper, *Sergei Nechaev*; Ulam, *Prophets and Conspirators*, 169–200.
81 Full text available in translation at https://www.marxists.org/subject/anarchism/nechayev/catechism.htm.

affairs, sentiments, ties, property nor even a name of his own'.[82] He also wrote 'The People's Justice' which called for the assassination of leading ministers and journalists. Nechaev returned to Moscow in September 1869, where he assembled a small group of young and impressionable followers, who were enthralled by their leader's fantastic rhetoric. Yet there was something only too real about the murder that Nechaev orchestrated two months later of one of his followers, Ivan Ivanov, ostensibly because he was a police spy (although more probably because Ivanov had the temerity to question Nechaev's leadership). Ivanov was strangled, shot through the head, and his body dumped under the ice of a frozen lake. Nechaev subsequently fled abroad again following the killing. It was the brutality of the murder that provided the inspiration for Dostoievskii's *The Devils*, in which the sordid details of personal rivalry and ideological extremism were elevated into a religious-metaphysical drama.

Volkhovskii briefly met Nechaev early in 1869 at Cherkesov's bookshop, through Vladimir Orlov, who had previously been a teacher in Nechaev's hometown of Ivanovo. Nechaev was using an assumed name and Volkhovskii does not seem to have been aware of his real identity.[83] Volkhovskii also met several times with Petr Tkachev, like him a graduate of the second St Petersburg Gymnasium, who collaborated with Nechaev in trying to build student protests into a more substantial revolutionary movement.[84] The Third Section had continued to monitor Volkhovskii following his release from prison a few months earlier, and in April 1869 arrested him on suspicion of involvement in efforts to provoke student unrest, apparently after intercepting some incriminating material.[85] He was held in prison for more than two years before eventually being acquitted at trial in the summer of 1871.

---

82 The question of Bakunin's contribution to the Catechism has for many years raised considerable debate. For a discussion, see Philip Pomper, 'Bakunin, Nechaev, and the "Catechism of a Revolutionary": The Case for Joint Authorship', *Canadian-American Slavic Studies*, 10, 4 (1976), 535–51.

83 Lehning, *Michel Bakounine*, 290.

84 On Tkachev's role in the Nechaev affair, see Hardy, *Tkachev*, 125–55; B. Koz'min, *P. N. Tkachev i revoliutsionnoe dvizhenie 1860-kh godov* (Moscow: Novyi Mir, 1922), 134–208.

85 For an unpublished and untitled article detailing Volkhovskii's analysis of the significance of the student unrest of 1868–69, which shows the importance he ascribed to such a development, see GARF, f. 109, op. 214, del. 334 (the article

The evidence Volkhovskii gave at his trial was designed to distance himself from the more extreme elements involved in the Nechaev affair. The fact that he was in prison following Nechaev's return to Moscow in autumn 1869 certainly means that he took no part in the events leading up to the murder of Ivanov. Some of those close to Volkhovskii *were* however implicated in the killing, most notably Petr Uspenskii, a key figure in the discussion circle that Volkhovskii joined following his release from his first spell of imprisonment in August 1868 (Uspenskii was subsequently sentenced to fifteen years' hard labour). Volkhovskii was before his arrest also in close contact with Vladimir Orlov who— along with Nechaev and Tkachev—was active in efforts to fan the flames of student unrest into a more far-reaching revolutionary movement. The Soviet historian Boris Koz'min suggested that Volkhovskii was a fierce critic of Nechaev,[86] but his findings are not entirely convincing, not least because Nechaev's sadism and penchant for fantasy meant that he was a difficult figure for Soviet scholars to discuss, except in a way that treated him as a complete aberration in the Russian revolutionary lineage. It seems on balance likely that Volkhovskii was on the periphery of the web of conspiracies woven by Nechaev, particularly during the student unrest of winter 1868–69, but was never a central figure in any of them.[87]

While Volkhovskii was temperamentally opposed to the kind of melodramatic Jacobinism that characterised Nechaev's whole *modus operandi*, he seems for a time to have become more positive about the potential for a 'political' revolution, in which a small group of agitators forcefully seized power to use the state apparatus to foster a social revolution. The best evidence comes from material in his papers found by the police in January 1870 some months after his arrest. One of these manuscripts was a copy of 'A Programme of Revolutionary

---

is not signed but both the style and the handwriting seem to confirm proof of authorship). Volkhovskii's article suggests that he was already convinced that a true revolutionary consciousness could only be fostered in the *narod* by a more politically aware external group.

86 Koz'min, 'S. G. Nechaev i ego protivniki', 190–98.
87 Pomper, *Sergei Nechaev*, 49. The following pages draw heavily on Pomper's discussion of developments in the winter of 1868–69, in particular his questioning of Koz'min's argument that Volkhovskii was in all respects a sharp critic of Nechaev's Jacobinism. It should however be noted that Koz'min's views are supported by some material in the memoir literature. See, for example, Zamfir Ralli-Arborre, 'Sergei Gennadievich Nechaev', *Byloe*, 7 (1906), 136–46 (139).

Action', which roundly condemned any social and economic system based on 'the mastery of the strong over the weak [and] the parasitism of the capitalist on the exhausted worker', suggesting that real change could only come about through 'the annihilation of the nesting places (*istreblenie gnezda*) of the existing power'. It followed that 'social revolution—is our ultimate goal and political [revolution]—is the sole way of achieving this goal'.[88] Such a formulation in effect set down the need for a two-stage revolution in which political change could serve as a conduit for social and economic transformation.

The authorship of the Programme remains uncertain. Although the language is reminiscent of some of Nechaev's publications, including 'Catechism of a Revolutionary', the 'nihilist scientism' is not.[89] Petr Tkachev probably contributed to the Programme: it certainly echoes the views he expressed both at the time and when in exile abroad in the 1870s. Vladimir Orlov may have written part of it as well. The Programme was specific in calling for an uprising in the spring of 1870, with a particular focus on the Ukraine, which raises the prospect that one of the authors may have been Vsevelod Lopatin or Volkhovskii himself (since both men had a good knowledge of the region). Whether or not Volkhovskii contributed to the actual Programme, the Third Section did find a second manuscript written in his hand, which Nechaev's American biographer suggests was a commentary on 'A Programme of Revolutionary Action'.[90] Volkhovskii claimed at his trial that he had copied the words from a letter by an unknown author, to which he planned to draft a reply, an explanation which officials at the Ministry of Justice dismissed as 'extremely unsatisfactory'.[91] It seems reasonable to assume that the notes seized by the Third Section were composed by Volkhovskii and provide some insight into his views during this period.

Volkhovskii's notes show that he was still influenced by the 'scientific' discourse associated with Chernyshevskii and other prominent

88 B. I. Gorev et al. (eds), *Istoriko-revoliutsionnaia khrestomatiia*, 3 vols (Moscow: Novaia Moskva, 1923), I, 81–85. The handwritten version of the Programme was copied by Nadezhda Uspenskaia who belonged to the Volkhovskii circle that met at Cherkesov's bookshop.
89 Pomper, *Sergei Nechaev*, 59.
90 Pomper, *Sergei Nechaev*, 54, 60–62.
91 B. P. Koz'min (ed.), *Nechaev i Nechaevtsy. Sbornik materialov* (Moscow: Gos. sotsialno-ekonomicheskoe izdatel'stvo, 1931), 16; Lehning, *Michel Bakounine*, 291.

journalists and writers of the late 1850s and early 1860s. He wrote with approval how the British historian Henry Buckle used the language of 'force' and 'action' to understand the past and argued that the language of physics could help to cast light on the study of society. Volkhovskii noted that his own reading of history persuaded him that a revolutionary conspiracy was bound to fail unless 'revolutionary ideas' had already percolated into 'the minds of the masses'. Yet he also observed—again using a rather stilted scientific language—that should the 'court' find itself unable to rely on control of armed force then it would easily fall prey to another scientific law: 'the smaller mass participation is in political life, the easier it is to have a political revolution'. Volkhovskii used a laboured metaphor drawn from chemistry to suggest that the seizure of power by a small group—a 'spark'—could pave the way for a social revolution that would create a bedrock of support needed in what was bound to be a violent struggle to defeat 'the people's enemies'.[92] If the government lost the support of the army it would be unable to suppress the desire of the *narod* for radical change.

While Volkhovskii was questioned at some length at his trial in 1871 about the provenance and content of 'A Programme of Revolutionary Action', along with the accompanying commentary, the prosecution focused more attention on his role in the student unrest of 1868–69. The abstruse theoretical tone of the Programme and the accompanying notes may have masked their political radicalism. More likely, though, the prosecution's questions reflected greater official concern about revolutionary actions rather than revolutionary words. Volkhovskii told the Court that he had actively discouraged students in Moscow from submitting group demands to the University authorities, which was illegal, suggesting that they instead submit individual petitions relating to their grievances:

> I said that [a mass petition] cannot lead to anything except claims that the students were acting illegally, and since the only legal way of acting is to be silent they should sit and remain silent: if they could not sit and be silent because they have nothing to eat, then they must find some other

---

92   *Pravitel'stvennyi vestnik*, 163 (1871).

way of getting out of their situation ... But all my efforts at the Moscow meeting did not lead anywhere.[93]

He went on to add that during a trip to St Petersburg, where the unrest had started, he urged students there to take a cautious approach and 'not think that the Muscovites would support them. The whole point of my speech was the same as the one I made before ... that although students have been deprived of the right to file a collective request, they have not been deprived of the right to file individual requests.' Volkhovskii may have been telling the truth, and other witnesses recalled that he was delighted on hearing that students in cities like Odessa were taking a moderate line, but many of those caught up in the Nechaevskoe delo (Nechaev Affair) were understandably less than open in the evidence they gave in Court.

The 1871 trial of Volkhovskii and others charged with inciting student unrest and involvement in the Nechaevskoe delo was conducted in the spirit of the judicial reforms introduced in 1864. The Soviet historian N. A. Troitskii acknowledged that it took place under conditions of almost complete openness despite the lack of a jury. An article in the journal *Delo* (*The Cause*) noted that 'until now everything has taken place in complete secrecy [but now] everything is discussed openly, in the full light of the factual and moral case'.[94] Crowds of sympathisers flooded the courtroom. The defendants tried to transform proceedings into a carnival of protest. Volkhovskii ostentatiously offered a bouquet of flowers to one of the female defendants despite the protests of the gendarme officer in Court. The procedures were periodically interrupted, as the accused were cheered, and the prosecution counsel catcalled. The Government undoubtedly mismanaged the trials that took place in the summer of 1871, not least by prosecuting individuals charged with Ivanov's murder at the same time as those of men and women charged with involvement in the student unrest of 1868-69, creating confusion in the public mind about the seriousness of the alleged offences. The

---

93 *Pravitel'stvennyi vestnik*, 160 (1871). Volkhovskii repeated his assessment of the student protests in his unpublished autobiography. See Volkhovskii Papers (HIA), Box 11, Folder 3 (Unpublished autobiography), 24, where he described his position as 'a very strange and awkward one'.

94 N. A. Troitskii, *Tsarskie sudy protiv revoliutsionnoi Rossii. Politicheskie protsessy v 1871–1880 gg.* (Saratov: Izd-vo Saratovskogo universiteta, 1976), 122.

Third Section agents who attended the trial described the prosecution as inept and the speeches of the defence lawyers as seditious.[95] The men found guilty of Ivanov's murder faced imprisonment rather than the death penalty. Those who were acquitted, like Volkhovskii, were told that 'justice has spoken: from now onwards your place is not among the accused but among free citizens'.[96] Senior figures in the Moscow police believed that 'a dangerous agitator' had escaped justice.[97]

Volkhovskii was surprisingly terse when recalling his trial in the unpublished biographical notes he wrote many years later: 'In 1871 I was at last brought to trial and acquitted'. He acknowledged that he had been arrested in connection with the activities of Nechaev, 'a very skilful agitator ... though not free from wrong principles [who] undertook to organise a rising of the people for the purpose of overthrowing the government'.[98] Nor did Volkhovskii say much more in the pamphlet he published for Russian readers in 1906 describing his early revolutionary career.[99] Nechaev's reputation for deceit and ruthlessness meant that he was by the closing years of the nineteenth century an embarrassment for all the different strands of the Russian revolutionary movement. And, while Volkhovskii later acknowledged that his 'trial was a fair one', he had little desire to dwell on the subject, given that much of his time in exile abroad after 1890 was devoted to efforts to persuade a Western audience of the arbitrary and harsh treatment faced by all those who dared oppose the tsarist state.

Volkhovskii spent more than two years in prison while awaiting trial, spending most of the time in solitary confinement in the Peter and

---

95   For the reports by agents of the Third Section on the trial, see Koz'min, *Nechaev i Nechaevtsy*, 158–88. Volkhovskii argued that the defence lawyers were inspired by the recent legal reforms to see themselves as 'champions of humanitarianism'. See Volkhovskii Papers (HIA), Box 11, Folder 1 (Untitled memoir notes by Volkhovskii on meeting with Stepniak in 1872).
96   Ulam, *Prophets and Conspirators*, 197.
97   Koz'min, *Nechaev i Nechaevtsy*, 173.
98   Volkhovskii Papers (HIA), Box 11, Folder 3 (Unpublished autobiography), 17. In another memoir note, Volkhovskii wrote that the importance of the trial was showing 'the existence of a new moral and social current of thought'. Volkhovskii Papers (HIA), Box 11, Folder 1 (Untitled memoir notes by Volkhovskii on meeting with Stepniak in 1872).
99   Volkhovskii, *Druz'ia sredy vragov*.

Paul Fortress.[100] The prisoners nevertheless managed to communicate with one another, taking advantage of their short periods of exercise to leave notes hidden in scraps of rye bread, which they dropped near to the edges of the paths or placed in knots in the bark of trees. They also communicated by tapping on the walls of their cells, using an elaborate code by which each letter in the alphabet was represented by two numbers, and developing a special shorthand in which a particular sequence of taps represented a whole phrase.[101] Some prisoners became very skilled in this language, but none of these strategies could overcome their sense of isolation, nor ameliorate the harsh conditions they laboured under. Volkhovskii's time in the Peter and Paul Fortress in the years before his trial greatly damaged his health which

> became worse & worse. My memory began to fail me. My nerves were in a dreadful state. I suffered from palpitations of the heart. I frequently had unbearable headache. I lost all appetite and ate only as a duty. In this way I spent in solitary confinement about two years and a half.

It was also during this period that Volkhovskii began to lose his hearing. Although he was eventually moved to a somewhat less harsh regime, prison life continued to 'suck out the best blood of the prisoner and [fill] his heart with despair'.[102]

One of those who had a particularly hard time in prison was Mariia Antonova, who had been active in the discussion circle centred on Cherkesov's bookshop, and was arrested during a raid on the St Petersburg home of Elizaveta Tomilova (Tomilova provided considerable financial support to a number of revolutionaries in the city). Antonova was from a poor background—the daughter of a seamstress—who had nonetheless managed to graduate from a Moscow High School. Volkhovskii later described how, as a 'non-privileged' person, she was only able to afford 'bread & water' while in prison. Nor could her friends find out where she was held. Antonova was also subjected to harassment

---

100 For a recent excellent account of the history of the Peter and Paul Fortress, see Nicholas Romeo Bujalski, 'Russia's Peter and Paul Fortress: From Heart of Empire to Museum of the Revolution, 1825–1930' (PhD thesis, Cornell University, 2020).
101 For a detailed account of the various methods and codes used by prisoners to communicate, see Volkhovskii Papers (HIA), Box 11, Folder 3 (Unpublished autobiography), 28–30.
102 Volkhovskii Papers (HIA), Box 11, Folder 3 (Unpublished autobiography), 31–32.

from one senior police officer, who made her get out of bed at night, covered only with a sheet 'to protect her from the eyes of the crowd of soldiers invading her cell'. She developed typhus and for many days lay delirious in her cell. After a brief stay in the prison infirmary, the authorities transferred her back to the main building, where she was put in a cell with 'a mad woman'. After some months of this harsh treatment, Antonova was cleared of any crime, and released without being brought to trial. Volkhovskii's indignation about her treatment had deep personal roots. He was close to Antonova before their arrest, and the two of them later married in the summer of 1871, after Volkhovskii's acquittal of involvement in the Nechaev conspiracy. Many Russian radicals of the 1860s and 1870s entered marriages of convenience, often to help young females become independent from their families, but Volkhovskii and Antonova appear to have married for love.[103]

Following his release, Volkhovskii felt overwhelmed by the 'bustle and excitement' of the world beyond the walls of the Peter and Paul Fortress.[104] He stayed for a few months in St Petersburg, drawing close to a group of young radicals that had coalesced around Mark Natanson, Nikolai Chaikovskii and Sof'ia Perovskaia. Several members of the group had previously formed a commune in a house at Kushelevka, then on the outskirts of the city, scandalising local society by refusing to adopt the usual conventions of dress code and gender roles, along with the occasional consumption of dogs and cats when their staple diet of horsemeat was in short supply. The circle, in Chaikovskii's words, brought together 'a fairly large group of people who were more or less of one mind, had similar hopes, and were already bound together by a common cause'.[105]

---

103 Constance Garnett noted many years later that Volkhovskii had never been in love with his first wife, but she was writing at a time when he had greatly irritated her, and there is little evidence to support the claim. See Barry C. Johnson (ed.), *Olive and Stepniak. The Bloomsbury Diary of Olive Garnett, 1893–95* (Birmingham: Bartletts Press, 1993), 20.

104 Volkhovskii Papers (HIA), Box 11, Folder 3 (Unpublished autobiography), 34.

105 V. Chaikovskii, 'Cherez pol stoletiia', *Golos minuvshego na chuzhnoi storone*, 16, 3 (1926), 179-97 (181). See, too, the comments by N. A. Charushin in his *O dalekom proshlom. Kruzhok Chaikovtsev. Iz vospominanii o revolitusionnom dvizhenii 1870–kh gg.* (Moscow: Vsesoiuznoe obshchestvo politicheskikh katorzhan i ssylno-poselentsev, 1926), 83–84. On the Kushelevka commune, see Erich E. Haberer, *Jews and Revolution in Nineteenth-Century Russia* (Cambridge: Cambridge University Press,

The ideological profile of the group was still fluid in 1871, despite its members' commitment to 'a common cause', and it went through various permutations over the next few years as branches developed in cities across the Russian Empire. Many individuals who came to occupy a prominent place in the history of the Russian revolutionary movement, including Petr Kropotkin and Sergei Stepniak, were participants in what has generally been known to history as the Chaikovskii circle (although Mark Natanson was the most influential figure before his arrest at the end of 1871).[106] When Volkhovskii first made contact with the young radicals grouped around the Kushelevka commune he declared, according to one account, his wish 'to organise some dirty tricks against the Government' (*ustroit' kakuiu-libo pakost' pravitel'stvu'*).[107] Although he only stayed in St Petersburg a few months, it was long enough to establish good relations with several members of the group, and when he moved to Odessa the following year, the *kruzhok* (circle) he established in the city formed part

---

1995), 44–45; Vera Broido, *Apostles into Terrorists. Women and the Revolutionary Movement in the Russia of Alexander II* (New York: The Viking Press, 1977), 67 ff.

106 The best Russian-language discussion of the Chaikovskii circle remains N. A. Troitskii, *Bol'shoe obshchestvo propagandy, 1871–1874* (Saratov: Izd-vo Saratovskogo universiteta, 1963) updated as Troitskii, *Pervye iz blestiashchei pleiady*. A useful discussion of the different views within the movement can be found in B. S. Itenberg, *Dvizhenie revoliutsionnogo narodnichestva: Narodnicheskie kruzhkii i "khozdenie v narod" v 70-kh godakh XIX v.* (Moscow: Nauka, 1965), 229–46; Martin A. Miller, 'Ideological Conflicts in Russian Populism: The Revolutionary Manifestoes of the Chaikovskii Circle, 1869–1874', *Slavic Review*, 29, 1 (1970), 1–21. For a recent discussion casting light on the culture of the Chaikovskii circle, see Eric M. Johnson, 'Revolutionary Romance. Love and Marriage for Russian Radicals in the 1870s', *Russian History*, 43, 3–4 (2016), 311–37. See, too, A. V. Knowles, 'The "Dook Affair" of the Chaykovsky Circle', *Slavonic and East European Review*, 51, 125 (1973), 554–66. In addition to the accounts by Chaikovskii and Charushin cited above, other useful memoir material casting light on the activities of the Chaikovtsy includes S. L. Chudnovskii, *Iz davnikh let. Vospominaniia* (Moscow: Izd-vo Vsesoiuznogo obshchestva politkatorzhan i ssyl'no-poselentsev, 1934); Peter Kropotkin, *Memoirs of a Revolutionist* (London: Swann Sonneschein, 1908), 243 ff; L. Shishko, *Sergei Mikhailovich Kravchinskii i kruzhok Chaikovtsev* (St Petersburg: Izdanie Vl. Raspopova, 1906); Sergei Sinegub, *Zapiski chaikovtsa* (Moscow: Molodaia gvardiia, 1929), esp. 13 ff.

107 Troitskii, *Bol'shoe obshchestvo propagandy*, 24. Volkhovskii also took part in discussions about the potential for constitutional development in Russia, arguing that there was no social foundation for such liberalism, instead suggesting that members of the *intelligentsia* should seek to mobilise the *narod* behind a socialist programme. See D. A. Klements, *Iz proshlogo. Vospominaniia* (Leningrad: Kolos, 1925), 26.

of the loose network of groups that made up the Chaikovskii movement in the years before the 'Going to the People' movement of 1874.[108]

Many Chaikovtsy (members of the Chaikovskii circle) were influenced by the ideas of Petr Lavrov, the most influential voice arguing that the *intelligentsia* needed to develop a better understanding of the Russian peasantry before they could hope to work effectively for their liberation. There was nevertheless disappointment among some Chaikovtsy at what they believed was the insufficiently revolutionary tone of Lavrov's émigré journal, *Vpered (Forward)*, when it was first published in London in 1873.[109] Some, like Sergei Sinegub, had already turned their attention to developing a programme of education and agitation among the urban workers of St Petersburg and its environs, believing that popular unrest was more likely to break out in the city than the countryside.[110] Others such as Petr Kropotkin were in favour of a more 'Bakuninist' strategy that sought to provoke an uprising among the *narod*.[111] Volkhovskii himself had by now come to believe that political change would prove fruitless if not combined with a programme of agitation and propaganda designed to mobilise widespread radical sentiment. Early in 1872, he travelled south with Antonova, heading first to Stavropol, before settling in Odessa, a town he knew well from his time at the gymnasium ten years earlier. In the two years that followed, Volkhovskii maintained close links with many other Chaikovtsy, including some who were later in

108 On the Going to the People movement in 1874 see, for example, Itenberg, *Dvizhenie revoliutsionnogo narodnichestva*, 266–360.

109 On Lavrov's activities during this period, see Philip Pomper, *Peter Lavrov and the Russian Revolutionary Movement* (Chicago, IL: Chicago University Press, 1972), 143-200; B. S. Itenberg, *P. L. Lavrov v russkom revoliutsionnom dvizhenii* (Moscow: Nauka, 1988), 129–65.

110 Sinegub, *Zapiski chaikovtsa*, 13–17; Pamela Sears McKinsey, 'From City Workers to Peasantry. The Beginning of the Russian Movement "To the People"', *Slavic Review*, 38, 4 (1979), 629–49; Reginald E. Zelnik, 'Populists and Workers. The First Encounter between Populist Students and Industrial Workers in St. Petersburg, 1871–74', *Soviet Studies*, 24, 2 (1972), 251–69.

111 For a useful discussion of the relationship between populism and anarchism within the Chaikovskii circle, see Graham John Gamblin, 'Russian Populism and its Relations with Anarchism, 1870–1881' (PhD thesis, University of Birmingham, 1999), esp. 88–127. See, too, Itenberg, *Dvizhenie revoliutsionnogo narodnichestva*, 218–29.

exile with him in Siberia or London, among them Chaikovskii, Stepniak, Kropotkin and Leonid Shishko.[112]

Although Volkhovskii's health was poor, visitors to the small flat he shared with Antonova in Odessa were impressed by the strength of his personality, as well as the determination with which he built up a radical *kruzhok* of around one hundred members. Solomon Chudnovskii, who became a key figure among the Odessa Chaikovtsy, praised Volkhovskii for his 'original [and] brilliant mind'.[113] Nikolai Charushin, who had known Volkhovskii back in St Petersburg, recalled in his memoirs that when he first visited Odessa in 1873, the *kruzhok* headed by his old friend had already adopted a clear strategy of building close links with workers in the various *artely* (small workshops) scattered across the city. He also noted that this focus on urban workers—rather than the peasantry— echoed the priorities of the St Petersburg Chaikovtsy.[114] Another leading *narodnik* activist, Sergei Kovalik, agreed that the principal focus of the Odessa group was on the workers rather than the *intelligentsia*.[115] Russian populism was from its earliest days less exclusively agrarian in focus than sometimes imagined.[116]

Odessa provided a promising background for radical activities. The city was by 1870 the third biggest urban centre in the Russian Empire.

112 For a fascinating account which traces the careers of many of the Chaikovtsy who came to Britain, see Rebecca Beasley, *Russomania. Russian Culture and the Creation of British Modernism, 1881–1922* (Oxford: Oxford University Press, 2020).

113 Chudnovskii, *Iz davnikh let*, 52. For a description of Chudnovskii as Volkhovskii's 'right hand', see Charushin, *O dalekom proshlom*, 143.

114 Charushin, *O dalekom proshlom*, 122.

115 S. F. Kovalik, *Revoliutsionnoe dvizhenie semidesiatykh godov i protsess 193-kh* (Moscow: Izd-vo Vsesoiuznogo obshchestva politkatorzhan i ssyl'no-poselentsev, 1928), 83. A rather different view is offered by Troitskii who emphasises the role of students in the Odessa circle. See Troitskii, *Bol'shoe obshchestvo propagandy*, 24-25.

116 Among the large literature on populism, including both its character and ideological content, see Christopher Ely, *Russian Populism* (London: Bloomsbury, 2022); Richard Pipes, 'Narodnichestvo: A Semantic Inquiry', *Slavic Review*, 23, 3 (1964), 441–58; Venturi, *Roots of Revolution*; Andrzej Walicki, *The Controversy over Capitalism: Studies in the Social Philosophy of the Russian Populists* (Oxford: Clarendon Press, 1969); Richard Wortman, *The Crisis of Russian Populism* (Cambridge: Cambridge University Press, 1967). See, too, Ghita Ionescu and Ernest Gellner (eds), *Populism: Its Meaning and National Characteristics* (London: Weidenfeld and Nicolson, 1969). For an important recent collection by Russian scholars, see G. N. Mokshin et al. (eds), *Narodniki v istorii Rossii*, 2 vols (Voronezh: Istoki, and Izdatel'skii dom VGU, 2013–16). Also see G. N. Mokshin (ed.), *Kul'turnoe narodnichestvo 1870–1900-kh gg. Khrestomatiia* (Voronezh: Izdatel'skii dom VGU, 2016).

Tens of thousands worked in the docks and factories.[117] Many more were
employed in the quarries that ringed the city. Odessa had a large Jewish
population, prominent in professional and commercial occupations,
which increased both their visibility and their vulnerability in a city
experiencing the strains and stresses of modernisation (a violent pogrom
had erupted in 1871).[118] By the time Volkhovskii and his wife arrived in
1872, Chudnovskii had already established good ties with radicals in
Odessa and Kherson,[119] and over the next year the two men built up
a circle that contained both workers and members of the *intelligentsia*,
including several who subsequently became active in Narodnaia volia
at the end of the 1870s: Andrei Zheliabov, Andrei Franzholi and Martin
Langans. Franzholi and Lagans were originally active in Kherson, but
moved to Odessa in the early summer of 1873, impressed by what
Volkhovskii had already achieved in the city (both men already knew
Chudnovskii well).[120] The *kruzhok* produced a *samizdat* (self-published)
newspaper *Vpered*—edited by Volkhovskii and Chudnovskii—which
was widely read by students in Odessa and circulated in other major
Russian cities including Kyiv and St Petersburg. The paper was
eclectic in scope. Volkhovskii focused on political and literary topics.
Chudnovskii contributed articles on social and economic questions.[121]
Pavel Aksel'rod, who was living in Kyiv at the time, later recalled that
the ability of the Odessa circle to produce such a publication was of
'great significance in our eyes'.[122]

117 For a fascinating history of Odessa, including material on social and economic
    issues as well as local administration, see Patricia Herlihy, *Odessa. A History,
    1794-1917* (Cambridge, MA: Harvard Ukrainian Research Institute, 1986). For a
    very different approach to the city's history, see Evrydiki Sifneos, *Imperial Odessa:
    Peoples, Spaces, Identities* (Leiden: Brill, 2018).
118 For a useful discussion of the social and economic background of Odessa and
    its impact on the development of Volkhovskii's group, see Haberer, *Jews and
    Revolution*, 57 ff. On the 1871 pogrom, see Steven J. Zipperstein, *The Jews of Odessa.
    A Cultural History, 1794-1881* (Stanford, CA: Stanford University Press, 1985), esp.
    114-128.
119 For his memories of these activities, see Chudnovskii, *Iz davnikh let*, 37-49.
120 The best account of the Volkhovskii group in Odessa can be found in Langans's
    memoirs, reproduced in P. L. Lavrov, *Narodniki-propagandisty 1873-1878 godov* (St
    Petersburg: Tip-ia Andersona i Loitsianskago, 1907), 215ff.
121 Chudnovskii, *Iz davnikh let*, 54-56.
122 For Aksel'rod's memoirs of this period, including a trip to Odessa where he met
    Zheliabov, see P. B. Aksel'rod, *Perezhitoe i peredumannoe* (Cambridge: Oriental
    Research Partners, 1975), 68-93.

Members of Volkhovskii's Odessa group played a significant role importing illegal literature from Western Europe for onward circulation throughout the Empire. Some of the clandestine material was brought into the port by ship. Still more came by land across the Austrian border, a process masterminded by Chudnovskii (jokingly referred to by Volkhovskii as his Minister of Communications). The import of literature from Austria was often disrupted by the authorities, but while in December 1873 alone the police intercepted more than 1,500 items including ninety-two copies of Lavrov's *Vpered*, the Odessa circle continued to send material north to other groups of Chaikovtsy in Moscow and St Petersburg.[123] Volkhovskii's group maintained close ties with such groups both through clandestine written communication and more direct personal links. Nikolai Charushin visited Odessa on several occasions (he was probably instrumental in the merger of the Odessa and Kherson groups). So, too, did Chaikovskii.[124] Aksel'rod visited from Kyiv. Several members of the Odessa group had, like Volkhovskii, lived in St Petersburg when the Chaikovskii-Natanson circle was taking shape there, and these networks helped to build a sense of common identity, even though the movement was never more than a loose federation of groups without any definite ideological or organisational unity.

The Odessa Chaikovtsy were well-organised, carefully targeting much of their propaganda at the seasonal workers in the city's many *artely* in the hope that they would carry their new-found radicalism back to the countryside. In late 1873 they conducted a detailed census of workplaces in the city to help them decide where to focus their activities. Volkhovskii himself developed a reputation for insisting on rigid discipline within his Odessa *kruzhok* (something that Chaikovskii still remembered more than forty years later when writing his old friend's obituary).[125] One early chronicler of the circle remarked that its existence was safe-guarded by an emphasis on 'unusual conspiratorialness'

---

123 B. B. Bazilevskii (ed.), *Gosudarstvennyia prestupleniia v Rossii v XIX veke*, 3 vols, III, *Protsess 193-kh* (St Petersburg: Sklad pri knigoizdatel'stve Donskaia Rech', 1906), 138. Lavrov was well-aware of Volkhovskii's activities in Odessa, See Boris Sapir (ed.), *Lavrov. Gody emigratsii*, 2 vols (Dordrecht: D. Reidel, 1974), I, 95 (Lavrov to German Lopatin, 2 January 1874).

124 On the visits of Charushin and Chaikovskii to Odessa, see Chudnovskii, *Iz davnikh let*, 78-79.

125 N. V. Chaikovskii, Obituary of Volkhovskii, *Golos minuvshago*, 10 (1914), 231–35.

(a view echoed by the leading Soviet historian of the Chaikovtsy).[126] Martin Langans believed it was among the best organised circles of the period.[127] Those who wished to join the circle were left in no doubt about the commitment expected of them. When Zheliabov was deciding whether he wanted to join the group, he asked a senior member of the Volkhovskii circle whether he could justify putting a decision to help the masses above his duty to his family, and was told in no uncertain terms that the cause should come first.[128] Volkhovskii's own influence as leader depended in large part on his intellectual and personal qualities, but he also possessed a steeliness that some of his contemporaries overlooked, along with a determination to act according to his own judgement. Indeed, he effectively abandoned his leadership of the Odessa group in the spring of 1874 in part because of his frustration that its members seemed reluctant to accept the discipline necessary for an underground organisation. There may also have been growing differences over questions of tactics and ideology.

Volkhovskii was sceptical about the possibility of an immediate peasant *bunt*,[129] and the focus of his group was on distributing propaganda and creating new cells in other towns and cities along the Black Sea coast. Although he spent some time at a small farm outside Odessa in 1873, it was a move inspired less by an attempt to draw close to the people, and more by the hope of evading surveillance.[130] It seems that only a minority of his group took part in the 'Going to the People' that took place in the summer of 1874, although Franzholi and several others did go as 'teachers' to the countryside at the end of 1873, returning some months later having achieved little thanks to the watchful eye of the local authorities.[131] In June 1874, Langans went to the country, in the

126 Troitskii, *Bol'shoe obshchestvo propagandy*, 24.
127 Lavrov, *Narodniki-propagandisty*, 215–16.
128 David Footman, *Red Prelude. The Life of the Russian Terrorist Zhelyabov* (Westport, CT: Hyperion Press, 1979), 48. For further details about Zheliabov's time in the circle, including its leading figure's hostility to the anarchism of Bakunin, see N. P. Asheshov (ed.), *Andrei Ivanovich Zheliabov: Materialy dlia biografii i kharakteristiki* (Petrograd: Izdanie Petrogradskogo soveta rabochikh i krasnoarmeiskikh deputatov, 1919), 19–22.
129 R. V. Filippov, *Iz istorii narodnicheskogo dvizheniia na pervom etape "khozdeniia v narod" (1863–1874)* (Petrozavodsk: Karel'skoe knizhnoe izd-vo, 1967), 184–85.
130 *Stenograficheskii otchet po delu o revoliutsionnoi propagande v Imperii* (St Petersburg: n.p., 1878), I, 411.
131 N. A. Morozov, 'Andrei Franzholi', *Byloe* (March 1907), 283–89.

guise of a cooper, planning to spread propaganda among the peasantry in Poltava and Kyiv provinces (he was quickly arrested).[132] Differences over the wisdom of 'Going to the People' may have contributed to the growth of tension between Volkhovskii and other members of the Odessa group. Some like Andrei Franzholi seem for a time to have drifted towards a Bakuninist-inspired anarchism,[133] calling for armed resistance to oppose the wave of arrests spreading across south Russia, a sentiment that was almost certainly not shared by Volkhovskii.[134] Others like Zheliabov simply drifted away to other underground organisations in Odessa.[135] Volkhovskii was himself arrested in the late summer of 1874 as the result of a tip given to the police by an informant.

Volkhovskii showed little interest in ideological questions while living in Odessa and was ready to cooperate with all those who wanted to bring about change. He became friends with N. A. Novosel'skii, 'one of the most prominent and talented civic leaders in Odessa',[136] who gave him temporary work organising his private collection of books and papers. Novosel'skii was also instrumental in obtaining a post for Volkhovskii in the municipal duma at a salary of 1,500 rubles a year.[137] Volkhovskii used his contacts to raise funds from liberal sympathisers in Odessa (his *kruzhok* also benefitted from donations by two of its wealthy members). During the two years he spent in the city, Volkhovskii therefore held a responsible job that brought him into contact with influential figures, while also running Odessa's largest and most effective illegal organisation. Whether his willingness to cooperate with non-revolutionaries in Odessa was shared by other members of his group is unclear, but it was above all evidence of his pragmatism, rather than any moderation or lack of revolutionary fibre. It also prefigured the strategy Volkhovskii pursued twenty years later in London, when along with Stepniak he sought to cultivate the support of liberals in both

---

132 Troitskii, *Pervye iz blestiashchei pleiady*, 240.

133 Lavrov, *Narodniki-propagandisty*, 220.

134 For a brief discussion of some of the divisions in the circle, see Filippov, *Iz istorii narodnicheskogo dvizheniia*, 284.

135 For a general discussion of the Going to the People movement in south Russia, see Itenberg, *Dvizhenie revoliutsionnogo narodnichestva*, 322–38.

136 Chudnovskii, *Iz davnikh let*, 53.

137 Volkhovskii Papers (HIA), Box 11, Folder 3 (Unpublished autobiography), 35.

Britain and Russia, arguing that they had a common interest in the fight
for political reform.

Volkhovskii's time in Odessa also showed his continuing interest
in the question of Ukraine's place in the Russian Empire. Soviet
historians who wrote about the Odessa circle said little about how
its members viewed the question of Ukrainian identity, not least
because the ideological canons that shaped their research typically
downplayed the national question when tracing the history of the
revolutionary movement. There was in fact discussion throughout the
1870s in revolutionary circles about the relationship between Ukrainian
socialists and their counterparts in 'Great' Russia.[138] Both Bakunin and
Lavrov were avowed federalists who were happy to acknowledge the
distinctive nature of Ukrainian identity. Petr Tkachev in exile abroad
was by contrast impatient of such sentiments which he feared would
undermine the revolutionary cause.[139] In 1875, the Ukrainian radical
Serhii Podolinskii told Valerian Smirnov, who worked closely with
Lavrov in the production of *Vpered*, that Volkhovskii was among those
who experienced no contradiction between his Ukrainophilism and
his support for the broader revolutionary movement.[140] Volkhovskii
would probably have agreed. He certainly believed that the growth of
Ukrainian national sentiment could help to foster opposition to tsarism
in the south-western provinces of the Empire.

Volkhovskii wrote at least two pieces during his time in Odessa
that were designed to harness Ukrainian national sentiment to the
revolutionary cause. The first was a translation into Ukrainian of a short
story by Mariia Tsebrikova, 'Dedushka Egor' ('Old Man Egor'), that had
appeared legally in Russian in the journal *Nedelia* (*The Week*) in 1870,
which told how an elderly peasant was exiled to Siberia for protesting
against unjust taxation of the peasantry. It was subsequently reprinted

138 For a useful discussion, see S. V. Kalinchuk, 'Revoliutsionnye narodniki i
     ukrainofily 1870–1880-kh gg.: sotrudnichestvo ili sopernichestvo?', in Mokshin et
     al. (eds), *Narodniki v istorii Rossii*, II, 82–106.
139 For a useful recent discussion of attitudes towards the state within Russian
     populism, see Fei Khaitin, *Federativnye idei v politicheskoi teorii russkogo
     narodnichestva: A. I. Gertsen, M. A. Bakunin, P. A. Lavrov, P. N. Tkachev* (St
     Petersburg: Aleteiia, 2018).
140 Roman Serbyn, 'In Defence of an Independent Ukrainian Socialist Movement.
     Three Letters from Serhii Podolynsky to Valerian Smirnov', *Journal of Ukrainian
     Studies*, 7, 2 (1982), 3–32 (esp. 22).

as a brochure and circulated widely by *narodniki* in the south-western provinces of the Empire. Volkhovskii's translation was apparently never published (presumably because of his arrest in the summer of 1874).[141] A second piece Volkhovskii wrote in Ukrainian, 'A True Word of a Breadwinner', was more overtly 'agitational' in character, attacking large landowners for increasing their wealth at the expense of the peasants.[142] Although aimed at readers within the Tsarist Empire, it was published in Lvov (Ukr. L'viv), where copies were seized by the Austrian authorities (the publisher Ostap Terletskii was subsequently put on trial). Volkhovskii himself seemed to have little interest in the potential impact of the growth of Ukrainian nationalism beyond the borders of the Russian Empire, even though a large part of the population in the Habsburg-ruled province of Galicia was 'Little Russian' in culture and language, perhaps suggesting that his interest in Ukrainian identity was for the most part secondary to his concern with fomenting opposition to tsarism. He was nevertheless later in life on good terms with important figures in the Ukrainian national movement—including Mykhailo Drahomanov and Lesia Ukrainka—while 'A True Word of a Breadwinner' served as a reminder of the threat posed by nationalism to both the main multinational empires of central and eastern Europe.

Volkhovskii was taken to Moscow following his arrest in Odessa, in August 1874, where he was taken to a police station and held in 'the smallest cell I was ever confined in'.[143] He was subsequently moved to the Butyrka prison. Volkhovskii's whereabouts was only discovered when one of his friends visited his original place of detention, disguised as a senior government official, demanding to know where the prisoner had been taken. The ruse was successful and the clerk on duty gave the bogus visitor the information he wanted. Although Volkhovskii was held in solitary confinement, one of the guards helped him to communicate with other prisoners, as well as with family and friends who were still at

---

141 Serbyn, 'In Defense of an Independent Ukrainian Socialist Movement', 14.

142 F. Volkhovskii, 'Pravdyve slovo Khliboroba', in M. Drahomanov (ed.), *Lysty do I. V. Franka i inshykh 1887–1895* (L'viv: Nakladom ukrainsko-ruskoi vydavnychoi spilky, 1908), 358–69. The first published version appeared in 1876. For a discussion of how Drahomanov's Ukrainian nationalism shaped his relations with Russian socialists, which casts light on broader patterns, see V. N. Kudriashev, 'M. P. Dragomanov i russkie sotsialisty: diskussiia o federalisme', *Vestnik Tomskogo gosudarstvennogo universiteta*, 336 (July 2010), 82–85.

143 Volkhovskii Papers (HIA), Box 11, Folder 3 (Unpublished autobiography), 37.

liberty (Antonova had come to Moscow following her husband's arrest, leaving her children in Odessa with their grandmother).[144] Among the messages passed to Volkhovskii was one from Sergei Stepniak, asking if his friend wanted to attempt to escape, but the authorities somehow got wind of the plot and moved him to a more secure section of the prison.[145]

Stepniak worked closely with another former member of the Chaikovskii movement, Nikolai Morozov, in planning to free Volkhovskii, but both men recognised that escape would be impossible unless they could find a pretext for him to leave the prison temporarily (early hopes of using a rope ladder to enable the prisoner to escape over the wall were dashed when he was moved to a new cell).[146] Following further clandestine communication, a new plan was developed in which Volkhovskii would ask the prison authorities to take him to the home of an official investigating his case, a sleigh ride away, saying that he was now ready to provide further information about his activities. His would-be rescuers would then 'spring' him from captivity on the street. Things did not work out as hoped. Stepniak was called to St Petersburg by comrades in the Russian capital who were deeply sceptical about the plans (another Chaikovets, Dmitrii Klements, had already made it clear that he thought the plan was folly).[147] The plot to free Volkhovskii was therefore left in the hands of Vsevelod Lopatin, who had been part of

---

144 News of Volkhovskii's arrest also reached Petr Lavrov in London, who regularly discussed the fate of Volkhovskii and Vesvelod Lopatin with the latter's brother. See Sapir (ed.), *Lavrov. Gody emigratsii*, I, 205–06 (Lavrov to German Lopatin, c. November 1874); I, 229 (Lavrov to German Lopatin, 30 December 1874).

145 For Volkhovskii's account of his first meeting with Stepniak, see Volkhovskii Papers (HIA), Box 11, Folder 1 (Untitled memoir notes by Volkhovskii on meeting with Stepniak in 1872).

146 The description of the escape attempt is taken from the draft of Volkhovskii's own memoirs, along with the published memoirs of Vsevelod Lopatin and Nikolai Morozov (who discussed the plans extensively with Stepniak). There were significant differences between these accounts which were striking enough for Lopatin to publish his account in part to put right what he believed to be the inaccuracies in Morozov's article. See the relevant sections of Nikolai Morozov, 'Vo imia bratstva', *Golos Minuvshago* 11 (1913), 122–61; 12 (1913), 117–67; Vselvod Lopatin, 'Osvobozhdenie F. V. Volkhovskago', *Golos Minuvshago*, 4 (1914), 217–21; Volkhovskii Papers (HIA), Box 11, Folder 3 (Unpublished autobiography), 42. See, too, Sapir (ed.), *Lavrov. Gody emigratsii*, I, 479–80 (Lavrov to German Lopatin, 12 October 1879). Morozov gave a somewhat different account of the escape in his memoirs. See N. A. Morozov, *Povesti moei zhizni*, 3 vols (Moscow: Nauka, 1965), II, 224 ff.

147 Klements, *Iz proshlogo*, 31.

the discussion group whose members were caught up in the *Nechaevskoe delo* in 1869, before subsequently joining a group of Chaikovtsy in Kyiv. Lopatin was sceptical about the likelihood of success, but he was persuaded to go ahead with the plan by Antonova, who was desperate to free her husband. Things at first went smoothly. When Volkhovskii caught sight of the sleigh with his wife on board, he threw snuff in the face of the gendarme escorting him, hoping to temporarily blind the officer and make his escape. The snuff did not have the desired effect. The gendarme chased after Volkhovskii, who had no time to leap into the sleigh, instead desperately jumping on to the runners as he called on the driver to take off. His pursuer caught him by the collar and wrestled him to the ground—the gendarme apparently suffered some injuries— and the prisoner was eventually overpowered. A policeman patrolling nearby arrested Lopatin (Antonova escaped). Volkhovskii was taken back to prison, and shortly afterwards moved from Moscow to the Peter and Paul Fortress in Petrograd, where he spent the next two years.

Volkhovskii probably saw his wife for the last time during the ill-fated rescue attempt in Moscow. Antonova made her way back south to Odessa, devastated by the failure of the attempt to free her husband. Her health was declining rapidly (she was almost certainly suffering from tuberculosis and had some rheumatic condition which made it difficult for her to walk). She moved abroad in the hope of recovering her health, helped by Stepniak, travelling first to Switzerland and then to Italy. She was nevertheless in a 'deplorable' state by the summer of 1875.[148] One of those who met her during this time recalled that she was 'thin, small, her face shrivelled and almost of a greenish hue'.[149] By 1876 she was living in Sicily, where Stepniak again joined her for a time, before heading to Naples in a hopeless quest to cure her illness. She died early in 1877. It was the first of many personal tragedies that were to plague Volkhovskii over the next ten years. The couple's young son died while his father was still in prison (his daughter Sof'ia survived, later joining her father in his Siberian exile, before becoming an actress at the Mariinskii Theatre and wife of the celebrated actor

148 Sapir (ed.), *Lavrov. Gody emigratsii*, I, 301 (Lavrov to German Lopatin, undated letter).

149 Tuckton House Archive (Leeds Brotherton Library), MS 1381/26 (typescript of later parts of L. Goldenberg, 'Reminiscences'), 27.

Nikolai Chaleev-Kostromskoi).[150] Volkhovskii's mother died soon after accompanying her son into exile. His second wife, who he met and married in Siberia, committed suicide. One of the couple's young daughters died just two years later when she was only three years old. All these tragedies still lay ahead in 1874, though, as Volkhovskii was forced to come to terms with the failure of his escape attempt and the prospect of spending many more years in prison.

---

150 For Chaleev-Kostromskoi's memoirs of his theatrical career, see N. F. Chaleev-Kostromskoi, *Vospominaniia* (Kostroma: DiAr, 2006). Some sources suggest that the young Volkhovskii child who died in the 1870s was in fact a girl.

3. Prison, Poetry and Exile

When Volkhovskii was sent to the Peter and Paul Fortress in St Petersburg following his unsuccessful escape attempt in Moscow, he found 'everything altered for the worse' from the time he had first been incarcerated there five years earlier. The only window in his cell looked out on a high wall and he could 'only get light enough to read by putting my solitary chair upon the table, and then sitting on the chair'. The cell was so damp that there were pools of water on the floor. The food was poor and opportunities for exercise infrequent.[1] Still worse than the physical conditions were the psychological strains of solitary confinement.

> All the intense longings of a human soul are kept without any food. No work or occupation to escape the torture of over-active imagination which prevents you from enjoying reading, by showing you images of what you are craving for and never get, or of the possible sufferings of those near and dear to you.[2]

In the draft notes he wrote many years later for his autobiography, Volkhovskii recalled how political prisoners in the Peter and Paul Fortress were dressed in 'linnen [linen], sleepers [slippers] and a long dressing-gown, presenting the strange appearance of a patient in a Russian hospital' (the hospital metaphor was used in the memoirs of many other prisoners, including his old comrade from Odessa Solomon Chudnovskii).[3] The process undermined any sense of individuality.

---

1   Felix Volkovsky, 'My Life in Russian Prisons', *Fortnightly Review*, 48 (November 1890), 782-94 (792).

2   Volkhovskii Papers (HIA), Box 11, Folder 3 (Unpublished autobiography), 52.

3   Volkhovskii Papers (HIA), Box 11, Folder 3 (Unpublished autobiography), 51; S. L. Chudnovskii, *Iz davnikh let. Vospominaniia* (Moscow: Izd-vo Vsesoiuznogo obshchestva politkatorzhan i ssyl'no-poselentsev, 1934), 124. See, too, Leo Deutsch, *Sixteen Years in Siberia. Some Experiences of a Russian Revolutionist*, trans. H. Chisholm (London: John Murray, 1904), 49. For some illuminating comments about the experience of imprisonment, and its psychological impact, see Ben Eklof

    https://doi.org/10.11647/OBP.0385.03

Like many prisoners held in solitary confinement, Volkhovskii dreaded losing his mind in the face of silence and isolation, not least because his deafness meant that he found it hard to communicate through the system of coded pipe-tapping used by prisoners to keep in touch with one another.[4] He kept his sanity by composing 'a long poem of which the subject was taken from Russian history', committing it to memory, since he had no pen or paper to write it down (the final version consisted of 178 verses).[5]

The idea of the Peter and Paul Fortress as a Russian Bastille was a well-established motif in the Russian imagination—it was a theme in many popular ballads—although conditions actually improved there during the third quarter of the nineteenth century. Even Volkhovskii acknowledged that prisoners held in the new block, built in the early 1870s, fared better than those incarcerated elsewhere in the prison (although he still found it a kind of 'monstrous tomb'). Political prisoners were usually allowed to read, while communication with the outside world was surprisingly easy, thanks to guards who smuggled messages in and out for a small fee. Yet the suffering incurred by political prisoners during the 1860s and 1870s was still very real. The fact that generations of prisoners who later wrote about their experiences had a political agenda in embellishing their stories does not invalidate all they had to say.[6] The Peter and Paul Fortress was far from being a 'comfortable hotel'

---

and Tatiana Saburova, *A Generation of Revolutionaries. Nikolai Charushin and Russian Populism from the Great Reforms to Perestroika* (Bloomington, IN: Indiana University Press, 2017), 114 ff. For a valuable discussion of the nature of prison memoirs, see Sarah J. Young, *Writing Resistance. Revolutionary Memoirs of Shlissel'burg Prison, 1884–1906* (London: UCL Press, 2021).

4   For a recent article on the importance of pipe-tapping as a form of communication, see Nicholas Bujalski, '"Tuk, tuk, tuk!" A History of Russia's Prison Knocking Language', *Russian Review*, 81, 3 (2022), 491–510.

5   Volkhovskii Papers (HIA), Box 11, Folder 3 (Unpublished autobiography), 54–55.

6   For a brief but nuanced discussion of the psychological impact of punishment on prisoners, see Eklof and Saburova, *Generation of Revolutionaries*, 111–14. For a helpful discussion of radical autobiographical writing in Russia before 1917, see Ben Eklof and Tatiana Saburova, "Rembrances of a Distant Past': Generational Memory in the Collective Auto/Biography of Russian Populists in the Revolutionary Era', *Slavonic and East European Review*, 96, 1 (2018), 67-93. See, too, Stephen Rindlisbacher, 'Living for a "Cause". Radical Autobiographical Writing at the Beginning of the 20th Century', *Avtobiografiя*, 6 (2017), 59–77; Young, *Writing Resistance*.

as one historian has suggested.[7] The rituals of prison confinement and the challenge of isolation warped many prisoners' experiences of space and time. A significant number were driven to despair and suicide.

Volkhovskii was at the end of 1875 transferred from the Peter and Paul Fortress to the House of Preliminary Detention, in part because one of the officials investigating his case feared that he was about to go insane, although other Chaikovtsy like Sinegub were moved around the same time. The material conditions were no better than in the Peter and Paul Fortress—some memoirs suggest the food was worse—but the discipline was more relaxed. Prisoners could wear their own clothes which helped to restore a sense of self. Although Volkhovskii was in solitary confinement, the gaolers talked to him, and he could hear 'muffled sounds of life around my cell'. He nevertheless still experienced fits of 'nervous irritation, during which I felt I could commit murder.'[8] And, while prisoners found it comparatively easy to obtain news from the outside world, the information they received could make their isolation harder to bear. Volkhovskii was a prisoner in the House of Preliminary Detention when he first heard about the deaths of his wife and child.

Although no copy survives of the long historical poem Volkhovskii composed in prison to help him stay sane, many other verses he wrote in the ten years before his exile to Siberia in 1878 were published. While a few appeared in legal journals in Russia itself, most were smuggled out and printed abroad.[9] The act of writing poetry at first glance hardly seems to reflect the kind of nihilist world view articulated by such fictional characters as Bazarov, the (anti-)hero of Turgenev's *Fathers and Children*, whose thorough-going materialism meant that he had little time for such fripperies as music and art. Yet literature was of great importance to writers like Chernyshevskii and Pisarev.[10] Chernyshevskii's *What Is to Be Done?* had proved so influential precisely because it provided

---

7   Orlando Figes, *A People's Tragedy. The Russian Revolution, 1891–1924* (London: Pimlico, 1996), 123.

8   Volkhovsky, 'My Life in Russian Prisons', 793.

9   Volkhovskii was known by the middle of the 1870s to be collecting revolutionary verses for publication abroad, which duly appeared as the collection *Iz-za reshetki* (Geneva: Rabotnik, 1877). See N. A. Morozov, *Povesti moei zhizni*, 3 vols (Moscow: Nauka, 1965), II, 178.

10   For discussions of both writer's aesthetic views, see Irina Paperno, *Chernyshevsky and the Age of Realism: A Study in the Semiotics of Behaviour* (Stanford, CA: Stanford University Press, 1988); Peter C. Pozefsky, *The Nihilist Imagination: Dmitrii Pisarev*

role models for young radicals who were determined to emancipate
themselves from the conventions of the society around them. Much
of the prose and poetry Volkhovskii wrote in the 1860s and 1870s was
similarly didactic in character. He nevertheless displayed a literary
sensibility that at times sat uneasily with the aesthetic *credo* articulated
by 'nihilists' like Chernyshevskii.

Volkhovskii's first published literary work was his contribution to V.
V. Butuzov's translation of Bayard Taylor's *Hannah Thurston: A Tale from
American Life*, which appeared in *Sovremennik* in 1864 when he was just
eighteen years old (Taylor was an accomplished travel writer and poet,
who served as American Consul in St Petersburg in 1862–63, which
doubtless increased interest in the novel among Russian readers).[11]
Volkhovskii won the commission after he was recommended to the
journal by his father, Vadim Petrovich, who seems to have developed
connections there. During the following ten years or so, he worked on
several further translations, including John Lubbock's *Prehistoric Times
as Illustrated by Ancient Remains* and Herbert Spencer's *Social Statics*
(although the latter was banned soon after publication). Volkhovskii
also translated poetry from English into Russian for various 'thick'
journals including *Vestnik Evropy* (*Herald of Europe*). In 1872, he
published under the pseudonym L. M. N., a translation of Thomas
Hood's 'Gold', which half-jestingly condemned those who pursued
the acquisition of wealth 'To the verge of a church yard mold'.[12] He
also translated Henry Longfellow's *The Arsenal at Springfield*. In 1876,
Volkhovskii contributed an anonymous translation of a Serbian poem
'The Song of a Citizen' to *Novoe vremia* (*New Times*) which appears to
have passed the censor despite its radical tone, probably because of
the widespread sympathy at the time in Russia for Balkan Christians
fighting to throw off Ottoman rule.[13]

and the Cultural Origins of Russian Radicalism (1860–1868) (New York: Peter Lang,
2003).

11   The translation was serialised in *Sovremennik* (1864), Nos 6–10. On Volkhovskii's
contribution, along with a useful bibliography of his writings before his flight
from Russia, see I. G. Iampol'skii, 'K bibliografii F. V. Volkhovskogo', *Uchenye
zapiski Leningradskogo gosudarstvennogo universiteta*, 349, *Seriia filologicheskikh nauk*,
74 (1971), 184–90.

12   *Vestnik Evropy* (February 1872), 695.

13   *Novoe vremia* (5 December 1876).

Much of Volkhovskii's work as a translator was motivated by the need for money (even when in prison he was determined to find ways to support his family). The same may have been true of the numerous articles and poems he published in the slew of pedagogical journals that began to appear in Russia during the 1870s. Volkhovskii nevertheless developed a real interest in education in general and female education in particular. In a series of articles published in *Pedagogicheskii muzei* (*Pedagogical Museum*), he lamented the absence of a clear theoretical foundation in many discussions of pedagogy, including the widespread lack of understanding of its psychological dimension. He also argued that despite recent improvements, the books published for children in Russia were of lower quality than those produced abroad, and suggested that young readers could benefit from being introduced at an early age to the classics of Russian and foreign literature (including translations of Trollope and Dickens).[14] Volkhovskii's reviews of new children's books were often scathing,[15] and it was partly for this reason that he started to compose numerous short poems that were designed to engage the interest and enthusiasm of youthful readers in ways that existing material could not.

The poems published by Volkhovskii in journals like *Sem'ia i shkola* (*Family and School*) and *Vospitanie i obuchenie* (*Education and Upbringing*) were typically aimed at very young children, complete with a powerful beat and rhyming couplets that made them easy to recite. Many included references to animals that talked or magically came to life after being built by children out of paper.[16] Others were loosely based on stories from various Russian chronicles.[17] A number were described as 'songs'. Some of the poems were illustrated, including 'Babushka' ('Grandmother'), which described how a little girl was anxious to come to the aid of her grandmother who was worn out by endless work at

14 F. V-skii, 'Zadachi zhurnala, posviashchennago voprosam zhenskago obrazovaniia', *Pedagogicheskii muzei*, 6 (20 March 1876), 345–51; A. Chepa (Volkhovskii), 'Odin iz istochnikov detskoi literatury', *Pedagogicheskii muzei*, 10 (20 October 1876), 567–75. Volkhovskii published a number of reviews in *Pedagogicheskii muzei* of articles appearing in the journal *Zhenskoe obrazovianie* which began to appear at the start of 1876.

15 See, for example, the unsigned review of M. B. Chistiakov, 'Byloe i vozmozhnoe. Novyia povesti dlia starshago vozrasta', *Delo*, 1 (1877), 64–70.

16 A. Chepa (Volkhovskii), 'Vas'ka'; Petushok', *Sem'ia i shkola*, 4 (1877), 537–38.

17 'Pesnia pro boiarina Artomona Matveeva', *Sem'ia i shkola*, 8 (1877), 7–14.

her sewing machine.[18] A few combined humour with a none-too-subtle attack on self-important authority figures who failed to recognise that honest labour alone deserved true respect.[19] Such radical motifs were however generally muted, although they were subsequently to become more pronounced in the stories that Volkhovskii published when living in Siberian exile in the 1880s, and even more so during his time in Britain in the early 1900s, when he wrote a number of *skazki* (fairy tales) that sought to subvert the established order of tsars and landowners in the vernacular of traditional folk tales.

While the poems Volkhovskii wrote for children during the 1870s were for the most part simple entertainments, the same was not true of the verses he penned for adults in the same period.[20] Many *narodniki* wrote verses during these years with rousing titles like 'The Songs of the Workers of Young Russia' (Sergei Sinegub) and 'Battle Cry' (Nikolai Morozov).[21] Volkhovskii himself started writing poetry seriously in the late 1860s, when in prison awaiting trial over the Nechaevskoe delo. In 1871 he published anonymously in *Vestnik Evropy* a poem 'Terplenie' ('Patience'), which began with a reflection on how, as he sat in his cell, he came to realise that 'the most important thing in life is patience'.[22] Such sentiments were not, though, typical of the verses he composed over the following few years (almost none of which appeared legally in Russia). More characteristic were poems with such titles as 'Nashim ugneteliam' ('To Our Oppressors') and 'Progress'. 'To Our Oppressors' concluded with the ringing words that 'the garland [of freedom] will be plucked from the despot / And returned to the people'. 'Progress' ended with a rousing declaration that despite being in prison, normally a place of despair and suffering, the author was 'On the contrary full of joy / Beyond myself with happiness / Seeing the powerful spirit of progress / Even in a time of imprisonment'.[23]

---

18   A. Chepa (Volkhovskii), 'Babushka', *Sem'ia i shkola*, 2 (1878), 252–53.

19   A. Chepa (Volkhovskii), 'Pro Kozla', *Vospitanie i obuchenie*, 4–5 (1880), 7.

20   A useful discussion of Volkhovskii's poetry can be found in V. A. Domanskii, 'F. V. Volkhovskii—neglasnyi redaktor "Sibirskoi gazety"', in E. A. Kol'chuzhkin et al. (eds), *Russkie pisately v Tomske* (Tomsk: Vodolei, 1996), 147–66.

21   For selections of poems by Sinegub and Morozov see, for example, V. N. Orlov et al. (eds), *Poety-demokraty 1870–1880-kh godov* (Leningrad: Sovetskii Pisatel', 1968).

22   *Vestnik Evropy* (October 1871), 767–68.

23   A. Bichter (ed.), *Poety revoliutsionnogo narodnichestva* (Leningrad: Izd-vo Khudozhestvennaia literatura, 1967), 53, 57. It is difficult to date the composition

Still more striking, perhaps, was the poem 'Tam i zdes'' ('Here and There'), which was written in 1872, when Volkhovskii was at liberty and living in south Russia:

> There in the far-away west
> The proletarian leads the struggle,
> He is becoming stronger in the fight against cruelty,
> Is strengthening, multiplying, growing.
>
> Here, in the gloomy east,
> The proletarian is fast asleep;
> He does not think of the time
> Of deliverance and remains silent.
>
> But then the student awoke
> And rubbed his eyes,
> And looked to the west:
> Would God's thunder soon be heard?
>
> He will wake up the worker,
> Will establish a common interest with him
> And hand in hand will secure
> Bread, freedom and progress.

The language was striking both for its emphasis on 'the proletarian' (rather than the peasant) and the pivotal role of the student in mobilising the workers.[24] The poem was of course written at a time when Volkhovskii was encouraging members of his circle in Odessa to focus on building close relations with local workers rather than agitating among the rural population out on the steppe.

Volkhovskii suggested that some of his poems could be put to music, making use of tunes that were 'already in use among the working class', which his mother smuggled out during visits to her son at the Peter and Paul Fortress. Although he did not know it at the time, he later discovered that several poems had 'found their way among the masses, and one of them, at least, ha[s] even become a favourite!'[25] They also found an

---

of Volkhovskii's poems precisely, despite the best efforts of Soviet scholars, since many were written long before they first appeared in any published form.

24 *Poety revoliutsionnogo narodnichestva*, 60.

25 F. Volkhovsky, 'Peter the Weaver', *Free Russia* (1 May 1900). Volkhovskii was told about the popularity of his 'songs' by Peter Alekseev who was in prison with him in 1876–77. For Volkhovskii's memory of 'the real peasant' Alekseev, see his

audience among a section of the radical *intelligentsia*. The writer Vladimir Korolenko recalled that Volkhovskii's 1872 poem 'Krichi' ('Cry Out')— which called on its readers to 'Cry out about equality, brotherhood and freedom'—was often sung aloud by groups of students heading to the countryside during the Going to the People movement that took place in the summer of 1874.[26]

Some of the poems that Volkhovskii wrote in the 1870s were more personal in tone. In his poem 'U okna' ('Through the Window'), which was headed by a verse in Ukrainian from Taras Shevchenko ('I do not know whether I am alive or dead'), Volkhovskii described the dreary passage of time in prison, where 'the heart and mind fall asleep / there are no desires, no wishes'.[27] Still more intimate was the poem 'M. A.' [Mariia Antonova]. After lamenting how he felt 'poorer than poverty itself' at the prospect of never seeing his wife again, Volkhovskii concluded with a fatalistic cry that 'All this is so; all this will be', despairing at his failure to express the depth of his feelings in words: 'But my God how poor all this is / As a way of expressing my love'.[28] Many of Volkhovskii's poems, including 'Progress' and 'M. A.', were published under a pseudonym in the collection *Iz-za reshetki* (*From Behind Bars*) that appeared in Geneva in 1877.[29] So too was his poem 'Mat'' ('Mother'), which described the anguish suffered by women who were unable to discover the whereabouts of their children who had been arrested and placed in detention by the authorities.[30]

Much of the poetry Volkhovskii composed in the 1870s was re-published many years later by a press closely associated with the Socialist Revolutionary Party,[31] and subsequently anthologised during

---

pamphlet *Russkii tkach. Petr Alekseevich Alekseev* (n.p.: Tip-ia Rabochago Znameni, 1900).

26 *Poety revoliutsionnogo narodnichestva*, 61.
27 *Poety-demokraty 1870–1880-kh godov*, 90.
28 *Poety revoliutsionnogo narodnichestva*, 66. The poem was presumably written when Volkhovskii heard of his wife's death, although the text makes it hard to date with certainty, not least given the final lines: 'I love you immensely / And am ready to die for you'.
29 *Iz-za reshetki*. Volkhovskii was the *de facto* editor of the collection, contributing his own poems under the pseudonym A. Chornyi, but his editorial role was not acknowledged in the printed volume.
30 *Poety revoliutsionnogo narodnichestva*, 69.
31 F. Volkhovskoi (*sic*), *Sluchainyia pesni* (Moscow: Knigoizdatel'stvo L. I. Kolevatova, 1907).

the Soviet period as a product of 'revolutionary populism', but even his warmest admirers would be hard-pressed to consider it as part of the Russian literary canon. Volkhovskii himself would probably have agreed. In one piece he wrote that,

> I know my verse is often bad,
> It is crude, without a golden touch,
> Often in it the heart sighs,
> And it sounds dissonant and tuneless...

He went on, though, to suggest that the mere act of writing such 'trifles' could help to protect against the threat of being 'smothered by tears'.[32] Volkhovskii's verse of the 1870s—much of it composed in prison—was designed both to encourage those who sought to overthrow tsarism as well provide a way for him to maintain his sanity.

Volkhovskii was by the mid-1870s instrumental in collecting poems by his fellow prisoners for publication abroad. Although his own work on educational issues appeared legally, suggesting that the authorities were surprisingly relaxed at the prospect of prisoners continuing to write and publish, the fact that so much agitational verse was smuggled out of prison indicates that the repressive apparatus of the tsarist state was often characterised by the same indolence and corruption as the rest of the bureaucracy. While political prisoners like Volkhovskii were treated better than common criminals, the uncertain freedoms they carved out in their daily routines were less the result of concessions by the authorities, and more minor triumphs that exploited the failings of the punitive system tasked with crushing critics of the tsarist government.

****

Significant changes took place in the web of individuals and organisations that made up the Russian revolutionary movement in the years Volkhovskii spent in prison following his third arrest in 1874. He had been astute in his scepticism about the Going to the People movement that culminated in the chaos of the 'mad summer' of that year. Although the peasantry's response to the wave of urban incomers was not as

---

32   Volkhovskoi, *Sluchainyia pesni*, 24.

hostile as sometimes suggested,[33] many of the new arrivals had little understanding of the harsh realities of rural life, and the subsequent tensions illuminated the gulf between the *narod* and members of educated society. Some newcomers were denounced to the authorities for criticising the tsar, often by the local priest, although in other cases they received a warmer welcome. Many found themselves unable to earn a living despite their best efforts to learn a rural craft. Most soon realised that their romanticised image of the Russian peasantry had little in common with the flesh and blood population they encountered in the villages.[34]

The debacle of the Going to the People prompted many radicals who remained at liberty to reconsider both their focus and their tactics. The demonstration that took place in Kazan Square in St Petersburg, in December 1876, was organised by members of the embryonic second Zemlia i volia group, including the future Menshevik leader Georgii Plekhanov,[35] and was intended to mobilise urban workers to protest in the streets. The previous year, Mark Natanson began work bringing together 'illegals' who remained at liberty—his fellow revolutionary Dmitrii Klements christened them 'troglodytes'—in an effort (in Vera Figner's words) to 'unite them in a common goal'.[36] Petr Tkachev abroad in Switzerland continued to promote the virtues of a Jacobinism that emphasised the need for violent action against the representatives of

---

33 For a superb article examining this theme and challenging many traditional views about the 'mad summer', see Daniel Field, 'Peasants and Propagandists in the Russian Movement to the People of 1874', *Journal of Modern History*, 59, 3 (1987), 415–38. For a more traditional account of events, see Franco Venturi, *Roots of Revolution. A History of the Populist and Socialist Movements in Nineteenth-Century Russia* (Chicago, IL: University of Chicago Press, 1983), 504–06.

34 For a brief review of the way in which educated Russians of different outlooks constructed the peasantry as a blank canvas on which to build their own hopes, see Michael Hughes, 'Misunderstanding the Russian Peasantry: Anti-Capitalist Revolution or Third Rome?', in Helga Schultz and Angela Harre (eds), *Bauerngesellschaften auf dem Weg in die Moderne. Agrarismus in Ost Mitteleuropa 1880 bis 1960* (Wiesbaden: Harrassowitz, 2010), 55–67.

35 Pamela Sears McKinsey, 'The Kazan Square Demonstration and the Conflict between Russian Workers and *Intelligenty*', *Slavic Review*, 44, 1 (1985), 83–103. For a detailed if somewhat dated discussion of the development of Zemlia i volia over the months and years that followed, see Deborah Hardy, *Land and Freedom: The Origins of Russian Terrorism, 1876–1879* (Westport, CT: Greenwood Press, 1987).

36 Quoted in Christopher Ely, *Underground Petersburg. Radical Populism, Urban Space and the Tactics of Subversion in Reform-Era Russia* (Dekalb, IL: Northern Illinois University Press, 2016), 172.

state power.[37] Although there was little real pattern underpinning this revolutionary kaleidoscope, there was a growing recognition of the need to avoid a repetition of the chaos of 1874, as well as a burgeoning sense that a focus on agitation and propaganda among the peasantry was unlikely by itself to unleash the forces needed to create lasting social and political change.

There is little available material to provide an insight into Volkhovskii's views on these developments during the years he spent in prison, before appearing in front of a special session of the Senate in the autumn of 1877, as a defendant in the celebrated Trial of the 193. It was the third mass trial of the year (the defendants at the first trial were accused of involvement in the Kazan Square demonstration, while those involved in the second Trial of 50 were charged with belonging to a secret organisation seeking the 'overthrow of the existing order'). The Government's decision to stage high-profile trials was prompted by an expectation that 'the well-disposed social classes' would rally to support the Government when confronted with a public airing of 'the delirious ravings of a fanatical imagination'.[38] Such hopes were to prove forlorn.

During the months leading up to the trial, most prisoners were, like Volkhovskii, held in solitary confinement in the House of Preliminary Detention. Charushin described the regime there as more relaxed than in the Peter and Paul Fortress, providing more opportunities for communication between prisoners, although he also remembered that after several years of isolation he found it hard to interact at all with other people.[39] Sergei Sinegub recalled that the prisoners created informal clubs, using clandestine forms of communication to swap information and recite poetry to one another.[40] Ekaterina Breshko-Breshkovskaia later described the atmosphere in the House of Preliminary Detention as 'lively and even jolly'.[41] The arrival of a new head of the prison administration in the summer of 1877 increased tension, though, which

37 On Tkachev during this period, see Deborah Hardy, *Petr Tkachev. The Critic as Jacobin* (Seattle, WA: University of Washington Press, 1977), 247–77.

38 Quoted in Venturi, *Roots of Revolution*, 585.

39 N. A. Charushin, *O dalekom proshlom. Kruzhok Chaikhovtsev. Iz vospominanii o revolitusionnom dvizhenii 1870–kh gg.* (Moscow: Vsesoiuznoe obshchestvo politicheskikh katorzhan i ssylno-poselentsev, 1926), 194.

40 Sergei Sinegub, *Zapiski chaikovtsa* (Moscow: Molodaia gvardiia, 1929), 184.

41 Ekaterina Breshko-Breshkovskaia, *Skrytye korny russkoi revoliutsii. Otrechenie velikoi revoliutsionerki, 1873–1920* (Moscow: Tsentrpoligraf, 2007), 136. See, too, N. A.

exploded in dramatic fashion when General F. F. Trepov, Governor of St Petersburg, made a visit to the prison.[42] When one of the prisoners who went by the name of Bogoliubov failed to raise his cap,[43] Trepov reacted with fury, and appeared to onlookers to strike the offending article off the prisoner's head.[44] The Governor also ordered that Bogoliubov be flogged for his insolence. When news of the decision was announced, the prisoners howled abuse and shook the bars of their windows, continuing their protests for many hours. Eventually the prison guards were commanded to restore order by force.

Volkhovskii made a good deal of the incident in his unpublished memoirs, claiming that Trepov had first insisted on inspecting the quarters of the women prisoners, despite complaints from the female warden that such a visit was unseemly. He described how the guards responded to protests by dragging prisoners out of their cells and

> beat them mercilessly ... One of the prisoners was gazing out of the window, when the door flew open. He was caught by his feet and dragged down. As the windows in the cell are high from the floor and beneath an iron wash-basin is fastened to the wall, he fell with his face on it and got a severe wound. A blanket was thrown over another—a refined student and an artist, to prevent him from defending himself, and he was beaten till he fainted.

'[T]wo strong policemen with the faces of excited bulldogs' forced their way into Volkhovskii's cell, submitting him to 'a shower of heavy blows', although he fared better than some other prisoners who were thrown into punishment cells close to a massive oven where they 'got blood-poisoning from the vile atmosphere'.[45] The whole affair was to have long-term consequences. When the flogging became common knowledge, several revolutionaries still at liberty vowed

---

Troitskii, *Tsarskie sudy protiv revoliutsionnoi Rossii. Politicheskie protsessy v 1871–1880 gg.* (Saratov: Izd-vo Saratovskogo universiteta, 1976), 188.

42 Richard Pipes, 'The Trial of Vera Z', *Russian History*, 37, 1 (2010), 1–82 (13 ff.).

43 The real name of the prisoner was A. S. Emelianov who had been arrested the previous year for his participation in the Kazan Square demonstration. On Emelianov's career during this time, see Pipes, 'Trial of Vera Z', 8–11.

44 For accounts of the Bogoliubov incident and the riot that followed see, for example, Sinegub, *Zapiski chaikovtsa*, 181–96.

45 Volkhovskii Papers (HIA), Box 11, Folder 3 (Unpublished autobiography), 60–61; Morozov, *Povesti moei zhizni*, II, 195.

to take revenge, and in January 1878 the twenty-eight-year-old Vera Zasulich shot and wounded Trepov after seeking an audience at his office. She was subsequently tried and found not guilty, an acquittal that provided stark evidence of how significant sections of 'the well-disposed classes' were in fact better disposed to the radicals than they were to the government.[46]

The Trial of the 193, which took place a few months before Zasulich's trial, showed how hard it was for the government to mobilise opinion against its radical critics (the cases were heard before a Committee of the Senate, in part because the government was wary about the unpredictability of juries, making the subsequent decision to try Zasulich in a regular court so surprising).[47] Volkhovskii described the Trial of the 193 as a 'mock trial' in the account he wrote twenty years later for a Western audience. He was less keen to emphasise the chaotic nature of the proceedings, which would not have fitted well with his attempt to promote an image of tsarist Russia as an embryonic police state. Nor did he note that defendants were permitted defence lawyers or that many journalists were allowed to watch proceedings. The accused often treated the Courtroom as a place to meet old friends, after months in solitary confinement, creating an atmosphere that turned the trial into a site of protest. Many defendants initially refused to appear at all. Some like Sergei Sinegub resisted when efforts were made to transport them to 'Court'. And, when the defendants did eventually come before the senators, some took the opportunity to disrupt proceedings and attack the 'judges'. Ippolit Myshkin, who had been arrested in Siberia in 1875, where he had gone on an ill-fated mission to rescue Chernyshevskii from exile, declared in a scathing speech,

---

46   On Zasulich's attempt on Trepov's life and subsequent trial, see Jay Bergman, *Vera Zasulich: A Biography* (Stanford, CA: Stanford University Press, 1983), 19–62; Pipes, 'The Trial of Vera Z'; Anna Siljak, *Angel of Vengeance: The "Girl Assassin", the Governor of St. Petersburg, and Russia's Revolutionary World* (New York: St Martin's Press, 2008), 189–247. For a useful memoir by one of her contemporaries, the liberal jurist A. F. Koni, see his *Vospominaniia o dele Very Zasulich* (Moscow: Direct Media, 2015).

47   The best general account of the Trial of the 193 remains N. A. Troitskii, *Tsarskie sudy*, 157 ff. Among the many memoir accounts of those involved in the trial (and were on good terms with Volkhovskii), see Breshko-Breshkovskaia, *Skrytye korny russkoi revoliutsii*, 144–55; Charushin, *O dalekom proshlom*, 196–206; Chudnovskii, *Iz davnikh let*, 134–59; Sinegub, *Zapiski chaikovtsa*, 196–201.

this is not a tribunal but a useless comedy; or something worse, something
more repulsive, more shameful than a brothel. There a woman sells her
own body out of necessity. Here, senators trade with the lives of others,
with truth and justice; trade in fact with all that is dearest to humanity
out of cowardice, baseness, opportunism, to gain large salaries.[48]

Eight members of the Odessa *kruzhok*—in addition to Volkhovskii—
faced charges at the Trial of the 193, including Chudnovskii, Zheliabov
and Langans. Volkhovskii's first appearance before the Court took
place towards the end of October 1877, just a week after the start of
proceedings, when he began by telling the Court that:

Before I address the matter of my culpability, I must ask permission to
explain ... issues relating to my deafness and my declining health that
have come about as a result of the six years solitary confinement that
I have experienced since 1868. I lost almost all my hearing ... this puts
me in an exceptional position in relation to everything that takes place
in this hall; I can hear almost nothing ... and at every moment risk not
understanding properly everything that is taking place around me.

He was given permission to come closer to the 'judges' so that he could
hear them more clearly. Volkhovskii then continued with a long speech
that defended his own integrity in the face of a process that lacked any
moral legitimacy.

I want all honourable people to understand that ... I consider the current
proceedings to be those of an administrative commission and not a court.
I protest against such a state of affairs. I want all honourable people to
understand that I wash my hands of all this ... I am appearing here only
because compelled to by physical force and I decline both witnesses and
defence lawyers and ask immediately to be taken from this hall.[49]

The guards led a still-protesting Volkhovskii away.

Volkhovskii was brought back to Court the following day when
his speech was at first less provocative (he began by apologising for
his earlier rudeness). He instead focused on procedural issues, once

---

48   Venturi, *Roots of Revolution*, 590.
49   *Stenograficheskii otchet po delu o revoliutsionnoi propagande v Imperii* (St Petersburg:
     n.p., 1878), I, 32–33 (transcript of sitting held 25 October 1877). Further
     material from the trial can be found in B. Bazilevskii (ed.), *Gosudarstvennyia
     prestupleniia v Rossii v XIX veke*, 3 vols, III, *Protsess 193-kh* (St Petersburg: Sklad pri
     knigoizdatel'stve Donskaia Rech', 1906).

again asking permission not to appear in person before the Court. The presiding Senator K. K. Peters noted that he had only refused such permission the previous day because he thought it would help the 'not young' Volkhovskii—he was thirty-one—to get the hearing over as soon as possible. The prisoner for his part expressed 'gratitude in the highest degree' for such courtesy, before going on to use a tortured chess metaphor to describe his position, irritating Peters who interrupted him exclaiming 'Enough, enough, be quiet'. Volkhovskii responded by once more asking permission to leave the Court. The President angrily declared 'Take the defendant away in view of the disrespect (*neuvazhenie*) he has shown the Court'.[50] Some other prisoners who were watching proceedings shouted out that they too wanted permission to leave.

Many witnesses who appeared over the next few weeks were asked about Volkhovskii's activities, including the sister of his late wife Mariia Antonova, as well as others who had known him when he was living in Odessa. His defence lawyer was present throughout and questioned some of the witnesses, including the gendarme attacked by Volkhovskii in his escape attempt three years earlier. Volkhovskii's later description of proceedings as a 'mock trial' was, as already noted, misleading (or at least simplistic). Most defendants were found not guilty of the charges they faced. Among those acquitted were several who were shortly to become involved in terrorism, including Sof'ia Perovskaia and Andrei Zheliabov, both later sentenced to death for their part in the assassination of Aleksandr II in March 1881. The sentences of those found guilty varied. Nikolai Charushin and Sergei Sinegub were condemned to nine years hard labour in Siberia. Volkhovskii and his old friend from Odessa, Solomon Chudnovskii, escaped more lightly. They were sentenced to deprivation of civil rights and exile for life to Siberia but without hard labour.

The defendants who had been found guilty were returned to prison, before being sent eastwards to Siberia to serve their sentences in the spring of 1878. A number signed an open letter, drafted by Volkhovskii, setting out their beliefs and hopes for the future of the revolutionary cause.

---

50 *Stenograficheskii otchet*, I, 41–43.

The trial of the Russian popular revolutionary (social revolutionary) party has officially ended: the so-called verdict has been issued in its final form, and all that remains to the official powers is to send us, the condemned, to hard labour and exile as decreed. Having left the field of activity as a result of captivity, but having honourably paid our dues ... we consider it our right and our duty to turn to you, comrades, with these few words .... We call on our comrades resolutely to pursue with renewed energy and a redoubled courage that holy (*sviatoi*) goal for which we exposed ourselves to persecution and for which we are ready to struggle and suffer to our last breath.[51]

****

The period that followed the Trial of the 193 was indeed an important watershed in the development of the revolutionary movement. Zasulich's attempt on Trepov's life marked the beginning of a new wave of assassinations and attempted assassinations. Sergei Stepniak returned to Russia from Switzerland in the summer of 1878, inspired by Zasulich's actions, and in early August stabbed to death General N. V. Mezentsev (Director of the Third Section). The authorities responded by declaring that violent activities against government officials would be heard in the military courts.[52] The move had little effect. A few months later, Grigorii Goldenberg killed General Dmitrii Kropotkin (the Governor of Kharkov, Ukr. Kharkiv). The revolutionary organisation Zemlia i volia took on a more definite form and became, in the words of one of the leading historians of the period, 'the organizing centre of the entire revolutionary Populist movement'.[53]

The question of terrorism eventually split Zemlia i volia, leading to the creation in 1879 of Narodnaia volia, which was dedicated to using terror to undermine the tsarist government including, if possible, the assassination of the tsar himself.[54] Among its members were some who

51 Bazilevskii, *Gosudarstvennyia prestupleniia v Rossii*, III, 303.
52 Jonathan Daly, *Autocracy under Siege: Security Police and Opposition in Russia, 1866–1905* (DeKalb, IL: Northern Illinois Press, 1998), 23. For a fuller discussion of the events surrounding Mezentsev's death, see Ely, *Underground Petersburg*, 210–15.
53 Venturi, *Roots of Revolution*, 597. On Zemlia i volia, see Hardy, *Land and Freedom*.
54 For a valuable account of *Narodnaia volia* by a Soviet historian, which has stood the passage of time surprisingly well, see S. S. Volk, *Narodnaia volia, 1879–1882* (Moscow: Nauka, 1966). Those who rejected terrorism, including Plekhanov, formed the group Black Repartition on which see E. R. Ol'khovskii, 'K istorii "Chernogo Peredela" (1879–1881 gg.)', in L. M. Ivanov et al. (eds),

had been part of Volkhovskii's circle in Odessa in the early 1870s including
Zheliabov and Langans. Narodnaia volia quickly established itself as an
effective terrorist group—in many ways the first of its kind—developing
a cell-based infrastructure that minimised the danger of penetration by
the Third Section.[55] Its members were far from unified in their ideological
views, not least as to whether the use of terror was designed to pave the
way for a peasant *bunt*, or rather to secure political reforms that could
facilitate the struggle for further social and economic revolution. While
such questions were played out on the pages of Narodnaia volia's main
journal, edited by Lev Tikhomirov, the commitment to terror was the
binding rationale of the group. Volkhovskii had been living in exile in
Siberia for a year at the time when Narodnaia volia came into existence. If
he had remained at liberty, then he (like many other former Chaikovtsy)
would probably have come to accept the use of terror as a necessary
weapon in the struggle against tsarism, not least as a means of exacting
political concessions from the Government. Volkhovskii was often
described in later years by other members of the Russian revolutionary
movement as a *narodnovolets* (a member of Narodnaia volia). He made
little effort to reject the label.

It is perhaps strange that Volkhovskii did not receive such a harsh
sentence at the Trial of the 193 as the one handed out to other former
Chaikovtsy like Charushin. He had long been seen by the Third Section

Obshchestvennoe dvizhenie v poreformennoi Rossii (Moscow: Nauka, 1965), 124–78.
For a collection of memoirs of those involved, see S. S. Volk et al. (eds), *"Narodnaia
volia" i "Chernyi peredel": vospominaniia uchastnikov revoliutsionnogo dvizheniia v
Peterburge v 1879–1882 gg.* (Leningrad: Lenizdat, 1989).

55   For an influential article examining whether Narodnaia volia can be considered
the first modern terrorist group, see Lindsay Clutterbuck, 'The Progenitors of
Terrorism: Russian Revolutionaries or Extreme Irish Republicans?', *Terrorism and
Political Violence*, 16, 1 (2004), 154–81. For a broader comparative analysis of the
origins of modern terrorism, see Carola Dietze, *The Invention of Terrorism in Europe,
Russia, and the United States* (London: Verso, 2021). For an imaginative argument
that Russian terrorism was actively shaped by literary models of terrorists, see
Lynn Ellen Patyk, *Written in Blood. Revolutionary Terrorism and Russian Literary
Culture, 1861–1881* (Madison, WI: University of Wisconsin Press, 2017). For
biographies of key individuals who turned to terrorism in the late 1870s see, for
example, David Footman, *Red Prelude. The Life of the Russian Terrorist Zhelyabov*
(Westport, CT: Hyperion Press, 1979); Lynne Hartnett, *The Defiant Life of Vera
Figner: Surviving the Russian Revolution* (Bloomington, IN: Indiana University
Press, 2014); Evgeniia Taratuta, *S. M. Stepniak-Kravchinskii. Revoliutsioner i pisatel'*
(Moscow: Khudozhestvennaia literatura, 1973).

as a 'dangerous' agitator,[56] while his speech in Court singled him out as one of the ringleaders among prisoners seeking to boycott proceedings. The 'judges' may have spared him hard labour on account of his poor health, but the stenographic record of the trial suggests they had little detailed knowledge of the scale of his activities in Odessa, since witnesses who described his time there were usually very vague. Banishment to Siberia was nevertheless still a severe punishment, even without hard labour, for exiles had to adapt to a harsh climate and isolation from all they had previously known.[57] Those who did not possess independent means also faced the challenge of earning a living. Volkhovskii's journey to Siberia was uneventful, even though the perils and dangers faced by convicts and exiles on the long trip eastwards had become part of revolutionary mythology since 1825, when the government of Nicholas I sent into exile army officers who had taken part in the Decembrist conspiracy. Nor (as a member of a noble family) did he have to wear chains. He was instead transported by train to Nizhnii Novgorod, and then by barge to Perm, from where he was taken by a relay of horses to the small town of Tiukalinsk a hundred miles north of Tomsk. He was to remain there for the next two years.

Volkhovskii later recalled Tiukalinsk as a 'wretched town' of some fifteen hundred people.[58] The inhabitants received little news from the outside world, while the authorities closely monitored the mail of exiles who had been sent there. Volkhovskii was joined by his mother Ekaterina Matveeva, although his daughter Sof'ia seems to have remained for a time in European Russia, only travelling to Siberia when her father moved to Tomsk two years later. Volkhovskii also met

---

56 B. P. Koz'min (ed.), *Nechaev i Nechaevtsy. Sbornik materialov* (Moscow: Gos. sotsialno-ekonomicheskoe izdatel'stvo, 1931), 173.

57 For an excellent general discussion of Siberian exile in the nineteenth century, see Daniel Beer, *The House of the Dead: Siberian Exile under the Tsars* (London: Penguin, 2016). For the earlier period, see Andrew A. Gentes, *Exile to Siberia, 1590–1822* (Basingstoke: Palgrave Macmillan, 2008); Andrew A. Gentes, *Exile, Murder and Madness in Siberia, 1823–1861* (Basingstoke: Palgrave Macmillan, 2010). For two excellent if contrasting general histories of Siberia, see Janet M. Hartley, *Siberia. A History of the People* (New Haven, CT: Yale University Press, 2014); Alan Wood, *Russia's Frozen Frontier: A History of Siberia and the Russian Far East, 1581–1991* (London: Bloomsbury, 2011).

58 For Volkhovskii's memories of this time, see his article 'The Suffering of Russian Exiles', *New Review*, 18, 3 (1890), 414–26. See, too, Volkhovskii Papers (HIA), Box 17, Folder 3 ('Sketches Continued').

and married a fellow exile, Aleksandra Khorzhevskaia, who had been sentenced to exile in Siberia at the Trial of the 50. Khorzhevskaia was like Volkhovskii originally from Ukraine. She had gone to Zurich in 1872 to study in the Medical Faculty of the University, where she met Vera Figner and other members of the Fritsche circle of young female radicals,[59] before returning to Russia to live under an assumed name in Moscow and Odessa. The conditions faced by Volkhovskii and his small family were difficult. They lived together with the exiled writer Grigorii Matchet in a two-roomed wooden hut with bare walls lined with moss to keep out the cold. Volkhovskii worked as a bookbinder and house painter to support their meagre existence (the government provided a stipend of just six rubles per month). It was almost impossible to buy food except at the Saturday market. The intense cold and poor food were severe enough to undermine the health of Volkhovskii's mother (the fact that the local doctor was an alcoholic did nothing to help matters).[60] She died less than a year after arriving in Tiukalinsk.

The harsh living conditions were not the only challenge facing Volkhovskii and his wife. On arrival in Tiukalinsk, Volkhovskii was taken to the police station, where he was told that all his correspondence would be read. He was also instructed not to leave the town even to bathe in a nearby lake.[61] The treatment of exiles by the authorities in Siberia depended a good deal on the personality and caprice of officials. The appearance of a new police chief (*Politseiskii nadziratel'*), just a few months after Volkhovskii's arrival, made life more difficult. The officer appeared on several occasions at Volkhovskii's cabin, often drunk, and flew into a rage when the inhabitants treated him with barely concealed contempt. The situation facing political exiles was generally worse in small towns like Tiukalinsk than in bigger cities. The material conditions were harsher, and there was little cultural life, while the local population was often hostile. When living in London many years later, Volkhovskii recalled that the main challenge he faced in Tiukalinsk was not so much

---

59 Vera Figner, *Memoirs of a Revolutionist*, trans. Richard Stites (DeKalb, IL: Northern Illinois University Press, 1991), 39–40.

60 Chudnovskii, *Iz davnikh let*, 243. Volkhovskii Papers (HIA), Box 17, Folder 3 ('Sketches Continued'), 3. Some fragments of information about his mother's long-term health before moving to Siberia can be found in F. Volkhovskii, 'Pamiati cheloveka i grazhdanina', *Letuchie listki*, 25 (15 October 1895).

61 Volkhovskii Papers (HIA), Box 17, Folder 3 ('Sketches Continued'), 1-2.

the shortage of food, but rather the relentless sense that 'Your time, your home, your peace, your family life do not belong to you'.[62]

Volkhovskii himself moved to Tomsk in the summer of 1881, where his wife had moved a few months earlier, probably on account of her poor health.[63] The following year Khorzhevskaia gave birth to a daughter Vera (the couple were not married at the time which subsequently created numerous bureaucratic problems). Another daughter, Katia, was born three years later. The couple were also joined in Tomsk by Volkhovskii's older child Sof'ia. The move to a large city was undoubtedly welcome to Volkhovskii, both because it offered a more congenial social and intellectual environment, as well as new opportunities to earn a living through writing and journalism. Although Tomsk was home to the notorious Forwarding Prison, soon to be made famous by George Kennan in his articles for *Century Magazine* condemning the 'exile system', the city of some 40,000 people was one of the liveliest centres of cultural life east of the Urals. It had for many years boasted a large wooden theatre, complete with chandelier and red upholstered seating, which was replaced in 1885 by a new stone building.[64] It also boasted one of the biggest bookshops in Siberia, owned by the entrepreneur P. I. Makushin, who in 1881 established the weekly *Sibirskaia gazeta*, the first privately-owned newspaper east of the Urals.[65] It quickly became one of the most widely read papers in Siberia, and Volkhovskii one of its most assiduous

62   Felix Volkhovsky, 'Suffering of Russian Exiles', 418.
63   Some documents suggest that Volkhovskii in fact travelled to Tomsk with Khorzhevskaia. See Gosudarstvennyi arkhiv Tomskoi oblasti (henceforth GATO), f. 3, op. 4, del. 820 (Letter from the Main Administration of Western Siberia to the Tomsk Governor V. I. Mertsalov, 9 September 1881).
64   Iu. I. Rodchenko, 'Istoriia pervogo Tomskogo teatra, 1850–1882 gg. (na materiale "Tomskikh gubernskikh vedomostei" i "Sibirskoi gazety")', *Vestnik Tomskogo gosudarstvennogo universiteta*, 366 (2013), 78–81. For a valuable discussion of the role of Tomsk theatre in cultural life, see O. B. Kafanova, 'Dialog kul'tur v teatral'nom khronotope Tomska na rubezhe XIX–XX vv.', *Knigoizdanie* 3 (2014), 45–64.
65   Among the large literature on *Sibirskaia gazeta*, see L. L. Ermolinskii, *Sibirskie gazety 70–80-kh godov XIX veka* (Irkutsk: Izd-vo. Irkutskogo universiteta, 1985), 37–104; L. S. Liubimov, *Istoriia Sibirskoi pechati* (Irkutsk: Izd-vo. Irkutskogo univesiteta, 1982), 67–77; and especially N. V. Zhiliakova, *Zhurnalistika goroda Tomska (XIX–nachalo XX veka): stanovlenie i razvitie* (Tomsk: Izd-vo Tomskogo universiteta, 2011), esp. 128–61. I am indebted to Professor Zhiliakova both for her extensive published work on journalism in Tomsk and for providing me with material I could not otherwise obtain.

contributors, as well as one of the *de facto* editors.[66] Makushin was also involved in numerous other civic initiatives to improve education and eliminate illiteracy in the town itself.[67] There were also plans to build a new University in Tomsk, a proposal first approved by Tsar Aleksandr II in 1878, although it was only put into effect a decade later.

The growth of civil society in late imperial Russia—the constellation of independent societies and publications operating outside the formal control of the state—was as striking in Siberia as it was in European Russia.[68] George Kennan nevertheless painted a grim picture of the situation endured by the political exiles he met in Tomsk in 1885 in his critical account of the Siberian exile system:

> The number of politicals in Tomsk, at the time of our visit, was about thirty, including six or eight women. Some of them were administrative exiles, who had only just arrived from European Russia; some were *poslentsi*, or forced colonists, who had been banished originally to 'the most remote part' of Siberia, but who had finally been allowed to return in broken health to a 'less remote part'; while a few were survivors of the famous '193', who had languished for years in the casemates of the Petropavlovsk fortress, and had then been sent to the plains of Western Siberia.
>
> I was struck by the composure with which these exiles would sometimes talk of intolerable injustice and frightful sufferings. The men and women who had been sent to the province of Yakutsk for refusing to take the oath of allegiance to Alexander III, and who had suffered in that arctic wilderness all that human beings can suffer from hunger, cold, sickness, and bereavement, did not seem to be conscious that there was anything very extraordinary in their experience ... as a rule, both men and women

---

66 For a discussion of Volkhovskii's role at *Sibirskaia gazeta*, see Domanskii, 'F. V. Volkhovskii'.

67 For a useful description of civil society in Tomsk during these years, see V. P. Zinov'ev et al. (eds), *Obshchestvenno-politicheskaia zhizn' v Tomskoi gubernii v 1880– 1919 gg.: khronika*, 3 vols. (Tomsk: Izd-vo Tomskogo universiteta, 2013), I. Further material about social and economic developments in Tomsk, as seen through the prism of official publications, can be found in V. V. Shevtsov, *Pravitel'stvennaia periodicheskaia pechat' Sibiri (vtoraia polovina XIX–nachalo XX veka)* (Tomsk: Izd-vo Tomskogo universiteta, 2016).

68 In addition to V. P. Zinov'ev et al., *Obshchestvenno-politicheskaia zhizn' v Tomske'*, see the useful encyclopaedia of organisations and individuals edited by M. V. Shilvoskii et al., *Obshchestvenno-politicheskaia zhizn' Sibiri v kontse XIX–nachale XX veka* (Novosibirsk: Parallel, 2019).

referred to injustice and suffering with perfect composure, as if they were nothing more than the ordinary accidents of life.[69]

Kennan's words eliding the situation at Tomsk with the experiences of those who had been sent to towns like Iakutsk, a far more remote place thousands of miles to the east, was something of a rhetorical sleight of hand designed to paint a devastating picture of the exile system for his readers. His private notes show that he knew the situation of political exiles varied enormously from place to place and that in Tomsk 'The treatment of exiles ... is generally quite good'.[70]

While Kennan believed there were around thirty political exiles in Tomsk, the real figure was probably higher, certainly if it includes the many Polish exiles living in the city.[71] During the 1880s, several former Chaikovtsy lived in the town, including Volkhovskii's old comrade from Odessa, Solomon Chudnovskii, who greatly impressed Kennan as 'a bright and talented publicist' who met the challenges of exile with 'energy and courage'.[72] Aleksandr Kropotkin—brother of Petr—was also exiled to Tomsk where he subsequently committed suicide.[73] Other notable members of the exile community in Tomsk included the writer Konstantin Stanukovich, who spent three years in the town, after being sent there as punishment for his contacts with political exiles living in Western Europe. The former Chaikovets Dmitrii Klements lived for a time in Tomsk and contributed regularly to *Sibirskaia gazeta*.[74] The exile colony also included S. P. Mokievskii-Zubok, M. S. Moroz and V. P. Aleksandrov, along with the prominent female radicals Liubov' and

69 *Century Magazine*, 37, 2 (December 1888), 174.
70 Kennan Papers (Library of Congress), Box 20, Diary/Book No. 24 (Miscellaneous notes on exiles), 15, 18.
71 Chudnovskii, *Iz davnikh let*, 248. On the exile of Poles to Siberia in the third quarter of the nineteenth century, see Andrew A. Gentes, *The Mass Deportation of Poles to Siberia, 1863–1880* (Cham: Palgrave Macmillan, 2017).
72 *Century Magazine*, 37, 1 (November 1888), 31.
73 On Aleksandr Kropotkin see T. V. Vagina, 'Kniaz' Aleksandr Kropotkin: Pechal'nyi udel nesostoiavshegosia talenta', *Vestnik arkhivista*, 1 (2017), 226–38.
74 On Klements' contributions to the Siberian press, including *Sibirskaia gazeta*, see S. I. Gol'dfarb, *D. A. Klements. Revoliutsioner, uchenyi, publitsist* (Irkutsk: Izd-vo Irkutskogo universiteta, 1986), 40 ff. See, too, the 2022 article by M. V. Balakhnina, 'Sotsial'no-ekonomicheskie i politichestkie aspekty sostoianiia Sibirskogo kraia v 1880-e gg. v publikatsiiakh D. A. Klementsa v "Sibirskoi gazete"', *Interexpo GEO-Siberia* (2022), 10–14, https://scholar.archive.org/work/bxh6lpr5uva5bfod3som4wl7ci.

Aleksandra Kornilov, who had both been active in the Chaikovskii circle from its earliest days when Mark Natanson was still its leading figure.[75]

The exiles' presence helped to strengthen the cultural life of Tomsk. Many of them were active in societies like The Society for Spreading Popular Education, which attracted enthusiastic support both from the local *intelligentsia* and the exile community. So too did initiatives to establish schools in the town and the wider province. Political exiles were well-represented in the audience at many of the public lectures offered on subjects ranging from literature to the ethnography of Siberia. Chudnovskii contributed regularly to the official Tomsk Yearbook. He also obtained permission to take part in two ethnographic expeditions to eastern Siberia, later recalling that the local authorities generally took a tolerant line towards political exiles living in the town,[76] although he acknowledged that much depended on the personality of the governor and other leading officials. Dmitrii Klements was allowed to carry out extensive ethnographic research on Siberia throughout the 1880s.[77] Exiles living in Tomsk could even on occasion meet with political prisoners passing through the town *en route* to other places of exile in Siberia. There was indeed significant support among the city's residents for the exiles. Lev Deich—who subsequently became a leading figure in the Menshevik Party—later recalled how when he was being transported through the town, 'two young girls, scarcely over school-age, suddenly broke through our escort of soldiers, and rushed upon us ... The girls ran like squirrels through our midst, announced themselves as the two sisters P., gave each of us a hasty kiss, and paid no attention to the calls of the officers and soldiers'.[78]

The most important figure among the liberal *intelligentsia* of Tomsk was Petr Makushin, the founder of *Sibirskaia gazeta*, whose publishing house produced numerous books about Siberian history and culture.[79] The first edition of *Sibirskaia gazeta* that appeared in March 1881, when

---

75 For a series of pen portraits of the exile community in Tomsk, see Chudnovskii, *Iz davnikh let*, 254 ff.
76 Chudnovskii, *Iz davnikh let*, 251.
77 For Klements' extensive ethnographic activities in Siberia, see Gol'dfarb, *Klements*, passim.
78 Deutsch, *Sixteen Years in Siberia*, 153–54.
79 On Makushkin and his educational activities, see for example *Kapital sel'skikh bezplatnykh bibliotek v Sibiri* (Tomsk: Tip-litografiia Sibirskago t-va pechatnago dela, 1907); *Poluvekovoi iubilei P. I. Makushina 1866–1916 gg.* (Tomsk: n.p., 1917); G.

Volkhovskii was still living in Tiukalinsk, set out a manifesto declaring its aim of 'monitoring the development of local life, focusing the attention and interest of local society on its needs [and] giving all its energy to the development of a local independent cultural life ... Public education (*narodnoe prosveshenie*) in Siberia, the situation and needs of the Siberian peasant and the incomer, and the rapid reform of the old pre-reform order ... [these] will be the main tasks that the *Sibirskaia gazeta* will focus on'.[80] Interest in the ethnographic character of Siberia was a defining feature of many of those who contributed to *Sibirskaia gazeta*. Chudnovskii travelled through Yenisei province and later toured the Altai region of Siberia looking at patterns of settlement.[81] Aleksandr Adrianov, a native-born Siberian who served for several years as editor, also explored the Altai and wrote extensively about his experiences there. Grigorii Matchet contributed stories on village life in Siberia. And Volkhovskii, as will be seen later, wrote numerous poems and short stories with a Siberian setting.

Sibirskaia gazeta was following a sensitive path in emphasising the need for a Siberian intelligentsia attuned to local needs.[82] Students from Siberia had gathered in informal discussion circles at Moscow and St Petersburg universities from the late 1850s and 1860s. Among their number were Nikolai Iadrinstsev and Grigorii Potanin, who were both deeply interested in the ethnography of Siberia, and later became critics of the Government for treating the region as a colony rather than a place with a distinctive identity.[83] Iadrintsev believed that the boundary between 'Populism' and 'Siberianism' was necessarily uncertain (he later wrote that 'Populism in its general specific form was dominated

K. Krepkin, *Revnitel'sveta—P. I. Makushin: 50 let prosvetitel'noi deiatel'nosti* (Tomsk: n.p., 1916).

80 *Sibirskaia gazeta*, 1 (1 March 1881).

81 Chudnovskii, *Iz davnikh let*, 253. See, too, S. L. Chudnovskii, *Eniseiskaia guberniia: k trekhsotletnemu iubileiu Sibiri (statistiko-publitsisticheskie etiudy)* (Tomsk: n.p., 1885); S. L. Chudnovskii, *Pereselenicheskoe delo na Altae* (Irkutsk: Vostochnoe obozrenie, 1889).

82 For a useful summary of this theme, see N. G. O. Pereira, 'The Idea of Siberian Regionalism in Late Imperial and Revolutionary Russia', *Russian History*, 20, 1–4 (1993), 163–78.

83 Iadrintsev was closely involved in the planning for George Kennan's Siberian expeditions and provided him with numerous letters of introduction. Kennan Papers (Library of Congress), Box 6, Kennan to Smith (*Century Magazine*), 30 May 1885.

by a current that sprung from the capital. But how is real populism possible without the participation of the intellectual and civil life of the province').[84] By the 1880s, 'Siberianism' had evolved a distinctive character in which populist elements, including a focus on the welfare and education of the peasantry, were combined with a desire to foster a Siberian consciousness that acknowledged how the vast territory east of the Urals was a region with its own character and needs. *Sibirskaia gazeta* articulated a similar set of principles. It was a combination that could easily fall foul of the authorities, anxious that such sentiments might encourage the growth of liberal and revolutionary sympathies.

Volkhovskii's move to Tomsk was prompted in part by his hope of getting regular work at *Sibirskaia gazeta*. His Ukrainophilism had already shown that he recognised how regionalism in all its forms could mobilise opposition to the autocratic system of government, and Siberian motifs came to feature prominently in his writings during the 1880s. Volkhovskii was still under surveillance throughout his time in Tomsk,[85] and he seems to have been wary of developing relations with the more radical elements in the town's underground, preferring to work with liberals like Makushin. Much of his literary work of the 1880s was published in *Sibirskaia gazeta* and fell firmly within the ambit of a 'legal' populism that emphasised the importance of promoting the welfare of the *narod*, while remaining more circumspect about how such a goal could be achieved.[86] The shift echoed a broader change in the character of Russian populism, at a time when the repressive policies pursued by the tsarist government were largely successful in containing the challenge posed by revolutionary groups.[87] Volkhovskii certainly believed that

---

84   Quoted in Dmitri Von Mohrenschildt, *Toward a United States of Russia: Plans and Projects of Federal Reconstruction of Russia in the Nineteenth Century* (London: Assoc. University Press, 1981), 110.

85   See, for example, GARF, f. 102, op. 78, del. 252 (Intercepted correspondence between Volkhovskii and Machtet); GATO, f. 3, op. 4, del. 820 (1882 Report sent by Tomsk Police Chief to the Tomsk Governor about Volkhovskii).

86   For useful discussions of liberal populism, see B. P. Baluev, *Liberal'noe narodnichestvo na rubezhe XIX–XX vekov* (Moscow: Nauka, 1995); G. N. Mokshin, *Evoliutsiia ideologii legal'nogo narodnichestva v poslednei trety XIX–nachale XX vv.* (Voronezh: Nauchnaia Kniga, 2010).

87   On the development of the Russian revolutionary movement in the 1880s and early 1890s, see Norman M. Naimark, *Terrorists and Social Democrats. The Russian Revolutionary Movement under Alexander III* (Cambridge, MA: Harvard University Press, 1983); Derek Offord, *The Russian Revolutionary Movement in the*

his time working for *Sibirskaia gazeta* was productive. Several years after
he fled Russia, he told Chaikovskii that 'I had five years' editorial and
newspaper experience and clearly my work in Siberia bore good fruit'.[88]
He also believed that *Sibirskaia gazeta* had 'without doubt had a good
impact on the growth of Siberian social thought'.[89]

Successive editors saw *Sibirskaia gazeta* not simply as a local
newspaper, but rather one that should provide its readers with a
broad view of the world, and it typically included extensive coverage
of foreign and domestic news as well as reports from correspondents
across Siberia. The paper also published accounts of explorations and
ethnographic investigations along with numerous short stories and
poems. Volkhovskii contributed to *Sibirskaia gazeta* under a series of
assumed names—most frequently Ivan Brut—although some of his
work was uncredited. He played a key role in encouraging the paper's
focus on *belles-lettres* after his move to Tomsk, penning the theatre
reviews himself, and writing many of the paper's distinctive *feuilletons*.
In the months following the closure of *Sibirskaia gazeta*, in 1888, he noted
that he had on average been paid twenty-five rubles a month for his
contributions to the paper and sixty-two rubles at times when he was
required to devote all his time to editorial work.[90]

Volkhovskii's status as a political exile meant that he could not
formally serve as the editor of *Sibirskaia gazeta*, although he performed
the role informally when Adrianov was away from Tomsk.[91] He was

1880s (Cambridge: Cambridge University Press, 1986). For a useful discussion
of the concept of 'cultural populism', see G. N. Mokshin, 'Osnovnye etapy
istorii "Kul'turnogo" narodnichestva', *Vestnik Rossiiskogo universiteta druzhby
narodov. Ser. istoriia Rossii*, 15, 2 (2016), 19–28. For useful brief reviews of the
historiography of populism in the final decades of the nineteenth century, see
V. A. Isakov, 'Sushchnost' rossiiskogo radikalizma vtoroi poloviny XIX veka v
istoriograficheskom protsesse', in G. N. Mokshin et al. (eds), *Narodniki v istorii
Rossii*, 2 vols (Voronezh: Istoki, and Izdatel'skii dom VGU, 2013–16), I, 8–25; M.
D. Karpachev, 'O novykh i starykh podkhodakh k periodizatsii istorii russkogo
narodnichestva', in G. N. Mokshin et al. (eds), *Narodniki v istorii Rossii*, II, 7–19.

88   Gol'dfarb, *Klements*, 42.
89   Gol'dfarb, *Klements*, 57. For some further useful comments about Volkhovskii's
     views of provincial journalism, see N. V. Zhiliakova, 'Obsuzhdenie
     professional'nykh tsennostei zhurnalista v perepiske F. V. Volkhovskogo i V. G.
     Korolenko', *Zhurnalistskii ezhegodnik*, 3 (2014), 38–42.
90   Iampol'skii, 'K bibliografii F. V. Volkhovskogo', 188.
91   For an article emphasising Volkhovskii's *de facto* editorial role, see Domanskii, 'F.
     V. Volkhovskii'. Adrianov seems to have taken a rather different view, complaining

certainly one of the most prolific contributors throughout its seven-year life, as well as an active member of the collective that met to discuss the newspaper's contents, although Makushin and Adrianov took the lead when dealing with the authorities over such questions as censorship. The paper maintained good relations with other newspapers that took a 'Siberianist' editorial line, including *Sibir* (*Siberia*),[92] published in Irkutsk, and Iadrintsev's *Vostochnoe obozrenie* (*Eastern Review*) which was produced in St Petersburg.[93] Iadrintsev himself took a keen interest in *Sibirskaia gazeta* during its early years, and was instrumental in bringing about the departure of the lawyer E. V. Korsh from its editorial board, ostensibly for his lack of concern with Siberian issues, although the conflict also reflected deep clashes of personality.[94] Korsh subsequently became editor of a new Tomsk newspaper, *Sibirskii vestnik* (*Siberian Herald*), which engaged in polemics with *Sibirskaia gazeta* on a range of issues throughout the second half of the 1880s.

Volkhovskii's role in fostering the 'literary turn' of *Sibirskaia gazeta* reflected both his interests as an author—whether as poet, critic or short story writer—as well as his belief that *belles-lettres* could shape the moral and political views of the public. Although recent efforts by Russian scholars to present him as a literary figure of significance in his own right are perhaps too ambitious,[95] he was without doubt an astute critic, while his best creative work displayed real sensitivity and imagination. Volkhovskii wrote dozens of theatre columns for *Sibirskaia gazeta*. Some of these described local theatrical performances, that were typically staged in Tomsk by touring companies, while others offered

---

in a letter to Potanin that he carried out much of the work 'alone'. For Adrianov's correspondence with Potanin, see N. V. Zhiliakova (ed.), *Sibirskaia gazeta v vospominaniiakh sovremennikov* (Tomsk: NTL, 2004), 133–40.

92 On *Sibir*, see Ermolinskii, *Sibirskie gazety 70–80-kh godov*, 37–104.

93 S. I. Gol'dfarb, *Gazeta "Vostochnoe Obozrenie" 1882–1906* (Irkutsk: Izd-vo Irkutskogo universiteta, 1997).

94 For Korsh's account of the dispute, see E. V. Korsh, 'Vosem' let v Sibirii', *Istoricheskii vestnik*, 5 (1910), 424-49 (esp. 436–37). See, too, Zhiliakova, *Zhurnalistika goroda Tomska*, 138–39.

95 See, for example, N. V. Zhiliakova, 'Mezhdu literaturoi i zhurnalistikoi: fel'etony F. V. Volkhovskogo v "Sibirskoi Gazete"', *Amerikanskoe issledovanie v Sibiri*, 9 (2008), 333–45. Also see A. E. Mazurov and N. V. Zhiliakova, '"Kartinka mestnogo nastroeniia": Obstoiatel'stva zapreshcheniia i soderzhanie pervogo fel'etona "Sibirskoi gazety" (1881)', *Vestnik Tomskogo gosudarstvennogo universiteta. Filologiia*, 66 (2020), 308–17.

more general reflections on the social significance of dramatic art. Volkhovskii's criticism was rooted in Chernyshevskii's aesthetic views, telling readers of his column that the theatre should show 'what takes place in life',[96] and 'cultivate positive feelings and aspirations that foster in people a sense of human dignity [and] a selfless commitment to truth'.[97] He also ascribed a pivotal role to the critic, as a representative of the *intelligentsia*, who he believed had a duty to help the public understand the significance of what they saw on stage:

> The reviewer writes for the public. In this regard he must keep in mind two tasks: 1) clarifying the social significance of the relations, characters and circumstances which define the content of the play; 2) the development of taste in society, cultivating in it correct aesthetic views and understandings in relation to literature and dramatic art.[98]

* * * * *

Volkhovskii fulminated in many of his columns against actors who were too mannered, suggesting that such a mode of performance emphasised the artifice of theatrical performance and undermined its impact on the audience. His reviews of productions staged in the Tomsk theatre were nevertheless both livelier and more subtle than his somewhat laboured aesthetic *credo* might have suggested. His analysis of performances of Aleksandr Gribodev's *Gore ot uma* (*Woe from Wit*) and Gogol's *Revizor* (*Inspector-General*), which were both staged soon after he arrived in Tomsk, included detailed critiques of everything from the costumes through to the performances of individual actors. One young actor in *Woe from Wit* was judiciously praised for being 'in general not bad, at times good. One must remember that he is young and establishing himself'.[99] Volkhovskii was more critical of the production of *Inspector-General*, suggesting that its emphasis on the 'external' comedic elements undermined the play's satirical treatment of the banality of provincial society. He was more positive in his review of (the now long-forgotten) *Nishchie dukhom* (*Beggars of the Spirit*) by Nikolai Potekhin—who had

---

96   *Sibirskaia gazeta*, 42 (20 October 1885). Volkhovskii's early columns of theatre criticism were written under the pseudonym F. Poltavchuk (a name inspired by his place of birth).
97   *Sibirskaia gazeta*, 43 (24 October 1882).
98   *Sibirskaia gazeta*, 48 (28 November 1882).
99   *Sibirskaia gazeta*, 48 (28 November 1882).

himself been arrested in the 1860s for revolutionary activity—praising the play for its attacks on provincial bureaucrats and merchants who enriched themselves while impoverishing the lives of those around them.[100]

It is difficult not to see a tension between Volkhovskii's formal commitment to an unimaginative aesthetic realism and his intuitive recognition of culture as a form of dialogue that at its best avoided any overt didactic function. His willingness to marginalise the shibboleths articulated by a previous generation of radical Russian critics was most visible in the numerous feuilletons he wrote for *Sibirskaia gazeta*. It was a form of writing that defies easy characterisation—a mixture of fiction, poetry and essay—but one that was popular in Russian periodicals and newspapers in the second half of the nineteenth century.[101] While such a genre was not necessarily incompatible with the theories advanced by the 'men of the sixties',[102] many of the most popular feuilletons displayed a whimsy that owed little to the aesthetic principles set down by Chernyshevskii since, as Volkhovskii himself came to realise, effective social commentary could take different forms from the realism of *What Is to Be Done?* The *feuilletons* he contributed to *Sibirskaia gazeta* were often fuelled by a search for new ways of using his talent to condemn the corruption of Russian society and the incompetence of its government.

Many of Volkhovskii's *feuilletons* showed the influence of writers like Nikolai Gogol and Mikhail Saltykov-Shchedrin, who regularly satirised the abuses of the world around them by juxtaposing the familiar and bizarre. The most astute scholar of his *feuilletons* rightly notes that he often conflated both space and time, fostering a dreamlike atmosphere in which strange or bizarre happenings took place in the familiar world of Tomsk or some other 'real' Siberian setting.[103] The unfeeling *chinovniki* (civil servants) and merchants who populated many of his sketches were figures in a fictional and sometimes farcical world, as well as 'aesopian' exemplars of a corrupt social and political order. Many of the *feuilletons* formed part of cycles— 'Ordinary Notes on an Extraordinary

100 *Sibirskaia gazeta*, 43 (24 October 1882).
101 For the development of the feuilleton form in Russia, see Katia Dianina, 'The Feuilleton: An Everyday Guide to Public Culture in the Age of the Great Reforms', *Slavic and East European Journal*, 47, 2 (2003), 187–210.
102 Domanskii, 'F. V. Volkhovskii', 154.
103 Zhiliakova, 'Mezhdu literaturoi i zhurnalistikoi', 336–37.

World', 'The Siberian Museum', 'Chronicles of a Peaceful Town'—which allowed figures who sometimes appeared as characters in one story to act as narrators in another. Volkhovskii's work appeared under various pseudonyms: Foma, Achinskii, Prostoi smertny (A Mere Mortal) and above all Ivan Brut. These pseudonyms themselves sometimes became characters in the stories they narrated to readers. Volkhovskii intended his work both to entertain his readers and encourage them to think critically about the world around them.

Volkhovskii's best-known story from this period was probably 'Noch' na novy god' ('New Year's Eve'), which appeared in *Sibirskaia gazeta* in 1884, before being published separately the following year.[104] The story describes the experiences of a 'typical' 'thickset' Siberian merchant— Egor Popov—as he sees in the New Year alone. During a series of strange encounters, which reveal Popov as a grasping speculator who has little interest in the welfare of others, the clock steadfastly refuses to advance to strike in the new year. Although Popov himself is discontented with his life—'he felt vaguely that everything was wrong'—he dismisses out of hand the ideas expressed by a procession of visitors who attack the authorities and condemn the accumulation of capital as theft. While frequent references to the decanter of vodka in front of Popov offer a mundane explanation for the uncanny series of events, the fantastic elements are presented as literal happenings, portraying the main character as the face of a corrupt merchant class standing in the way of progress. The story somewhat surprisingly passed the censor without trouble when it first appeared, but the subversive message subsequently raised official suspicion, and it was deemed to be 'an openly revolutionary homily' (*propovel*').[105]

While 'New Year's Eve' provided a critique of contemporary Russian (and Siberian) society, Volkhovskii's populism and 'Siberianism' was articulated more clearly in another story, 'S novym godom' ('Happy

---

104 Ivan Brut (Volkhovskii), *Noch na novyi god* (Tomsk: Sibirskaia gazeta, 1885). On the practice of various Siberian papers in publishing some of the work that appeared in their columns in book form, see N. V. Zhiliakova, 'Knizhnye proekty redaktsii sibirskikh gazet (na primere Tomskoi "Sibirskoi gazety" 1880-e gg.)', *Knigoizdanie*, 1 (2012), 89–97.

105 Domanskii, 'F. V. Volkhovskii', 162. The interpretation of Volkhovskii's feuilletons in the following paragraphs draws heavily on Domanskii's work, as well as that of Prof. Zhiliakova, who kindly provided me with detailed lists of all the feuilletons written by Volkhovskii.

New Year') published in *Sibirskaia gazeta* the previous year.[106] The story focuses on a writer who—rather in the tradition of Aleksandr Radishchev's *Journey from St Petersburg to Moscow*—seeks to make sense of the country through which he is travelling (in this case Siberia). The ordinary world dissolves into fantasy when 'Siberia' appears before the traveller in the guise of a beautiful woman:

> Her features were severe but her eyes glowed with kindness. The hem of her dress was edged at the front and the sides with the colour of the sea. Rich blue ribbons were wrapped around her and ran down her in stripes like waves. Her head was crowned with a beautiful diadem, that seemed like a profile of the Altai mountains, in the middle of which was a large opal which shimmered with all the colours of the rainbow like a large lake. A necklace made up of all the different rocks of the Urals decorated her neck.

The personification of Siberia as a female form was not in fact an original motif (Iadrintsev had written in a similar vein the previous year in *Vostochnoe obozrenie*).[107] Yet Volkhovskii's female figure also carried a shield covered with words of a distinctively radical character: 'Brothers let us love one another'; 'there are no rights without duties and no duties without rights'; 'knowledge is light and ignorance is darkness'; and (most surprisingly in view of the censorship) 'the instruments of production belong to the working people'. The tale goes on to tell how the wealth and nobility of Siberia is stolen and desecrated by those interested only in selfish material gain.

In another story—'Moi Tost' ('My Toast')—Volkhovskii again juxtaposed the mundane and the fantastic.[108] The unnamed central character makes a toast at a party to Siberia, resulting in general merriment among the listeners, who think of it simply as a freezing country that is home to an ignorant peasantry. The maker of the toast is mortified and withdraws to another room, where out of the smoke of the fire appears the form of a Siberian 'fairy', who engages him in a dialogue that convinces him that he was right to think of his homeland as a place where 'the heart of humanity beats' and where 'burns the flame of life lighting up the earth'. The hero recognises his duty to stay in

---

106 *Sibirskaia gazeta*, 1 (2 January 1883).
107 Zhiliakova, 'Mezhdu literaturoi i zhurnalistikoi', 342.
108 *Sibirskaia gazeta*, 6 (16 February 1883).

his homeland to help Siberia develop its distinctive identity and future. Once again—as in 'Happy New Year'—Volkhovskii portrayed Siberia not simply as an abstract geographical space but rather a place with its own distinctive spirit and potential.

Siberian motifs also loomed large in the poetry Volkhovskii wrote during his time in Tomsk. Some of his verses appeared in *Sibirskaia gazeta*, often over the telling pseudonym of 'a Siberian poet',[109] and in 1889 he published (as Ivan Brut) an edited collection *Otgoloski Sibiri* (*Echoes of Siberia*) which contained work by some twenty contributors including himself.[110] In the lengthy introduction, Volkhovskii argued that although 'Siberia has not up to this point produced a single authentic (*tsel'nyi*) poet', there already existed the 'sparks' of a new Siberian poetry. He was nevertheless concerned that the local population did not yet understand Siberia's real identity. *Echoes* was designed to show that there were already poetic voices expressing a sense of the region's distinctive self-consciousness.

Volkhovskii's own contributions to *Echoes of Siberia* were less obviously political than the verses he had written in the 1870s. He took his family every summer to a *dacha* a few miles from Tomsk—where his *sojourns* in the countryside seem to have had a considerable impact on him—giving him an opportunity to see the natural landscape up close.[111] Siberian themes figured prominently in poems like 'The Songs of a Siberian Poet', which acknowledged that although 'There are no gay Siberian tunes', there was already 'In its poetry ... great sternness / Through its verses you can / Discern its manly thoughts / And the power of its noble dreams'.[112] Other poems like 'Gorelyi les' ('The Burnt Forest') were more intimate in tone, using natural images as a backdrop to reflections on lives that were lived and sometimes lost under difficult circumstances. The same was true of 'Solovei' ('The Nightingale'), written over a period of years, which in its published form appeared to serve as an elegy to his second wife ('Dear little bird ... / You have flown

---

109 See, for example, *Sibirskaia gazeta*, 40 (5 October 1886).

110 Ivan Brut (ed.), *Otgoloski Sibiri. Sbornik stikhotvorenii raznykh avtorov* (Tomsk: Tip-ia Mikhailova i Makushina, 1889).

111 For Volkhovskii's request for permission to leave the city see, for example, GATO, f. 3, op. 4, del. 820 (Letter from Volkhovskii to the acting Governor, 28 May 1883).

112 Brut, *Otgoloski Sibiri*, 3–4. Like many other poems in the collection, 'The Songs of a Siberian Poet' had first appeared in *Sibirskaia gazeta*.

away from here'). A close reading of Volkhovskii's poems of the 1880s can certainly find political motifs, including one which celebrated how the opening of Tomsk University would allow 'the sun to shine with a new strength', yet there was an absence of the kind of rhetoric that characterised his poetry of the 1870s, with its focus on the awakening of the proletariat and the suffering of those imprisoned for daring to support political change. *Echoes of Siberia* was published legally, which doubtless helps to explain the moderate tone of Volkhovskii's poems, but there was also real passion in his commitment to capturing the area's distinctive landscape and character.

Some isolated political motifs can be found in a few of the children's stories that Volkhovskii published during his time in Tomsk. Six of these tales were published in 1888 in a collection that appeared under the familiar pseudonym of Ivan Brut (a number had already appeared in print before).[113] Some were retellings of traditional folktales. Others were pure literary creations. Several of the stories included in *Shest' skazok* (*Six Fairy Tales*) were fables with no apparent political overtones, such as the one describing the woes of an elderly dog rejected by its master, who conspired with a wolf to win back his place by pretending to rescue the child of the house from a lupine aggressor. Another told of the fate of a lump of clay transformed into a china cup that is smashed by a spoilt child, after they burn their lips when drinking tea, before being glued back together by a beggar woman who uses it to feed broth to her sickly granddaughter. Such stories with their familiar motifs of talking animals and sentient objects were intended above all as entertaining fables designed to articulate a wisdom that reflected ironically upon the foibles of the world.

Other stories in *Shest' skazok* had a more obviously radical tone. 'Lesnaia pomeshchitsa' ('A Forest Landowner') begins with a lyrical description of a colony of small birds that live and work in harmony on the banks of a Siberian river. This paradise of avian cooperation disintegrates when a family of crows demand that the trees they roost in should be respected as their own private domain. When fire rips

---

113   Ivan Brut, *Shest' skazok* (Moscow: Tipo-litografiia I. N. Kushnereva, 1888). Several stories in the collection were later translated into English and published under Volkhovskii's own name as *A China Cup and Other Stories for Children* (London: T. Unwin Fisher, 1892).

through the part of the forest where the crows live, all are burnt to death
except for the mother and one of her fledglings, who linger for a while
before they too die lamenting that they have been offered no help. The
other birds revert to their previous life 'rejoicing as before in the whole
of God's creation'. It is hard to read the story of the forest landowner—
the ironic name given to the female crow who nests there—as anything
other than a socialist fable. Nor is it possible to miss the radical moral
of the story 'Kak petushok Krasnyi-Grebeshok za pravdu postoial'
('How Scarlet-Comb the Cock Defended Justice'), which tells how a
Polish landlord who stole a grindstone from one of his serfs gets his
comeuppance at the hands of a young cockerel, who pursues him for
months demanding that he return the stone. The landlord in desperation
eventually shoots the bird, though only manages to wound it, and the
following night it pecks out one of his eyes. Realising that he will only
get peace by restoring the grindstone to its rightful owner, the landlord
orders it to be sent back to the village, to the delight of the young bird
who has fought so hard for justice.

The story of Scarlet-Comb needs to be read against the background
of a widespread Russian folklore tradition in which animals restore
justice to the human world, just as 'The Forest Landlord' can be seen as
a fable emphasising the dangers of selfishness, rather than a polemical
tract about how private property leads to egoism and division. And it
would certainly be unwise to imagine that all the tales in *Shest' skazok*
were crafted primarily as radical propaganda to win over young minds.
Volkhovskii later claimed that he first told the stories to his young
daughter, Vera, and only published them so that they could be enjoyed
by other young children.[114] The experience of writing such pieces
nevertheless helped him develop his aptitude for articulating ideas of
justice and fairness in a simple and accessible way.

Volkhovskii's work for *Sibirskaia gazeta* provided him with congenial
duties and extra income to support his young family, but the situation
in Tomsk was still difficult for all political exiles, both materially and
psychologically. Volkhovskii regularly wrote to the local authorities
asking for financial help to support his family.[115] He also earned money

---

114 Volkhovsky, *China Cup* ('The Tale About How All These Tales Came to Light').
115 See, for example, GATO, f. 3, op. 4, del. 820 (Volkhovskii to the Tomsk Governor,
     August 1882; Volkhovskii to the Tomsk Governor, 4 February 1883).

at various times working in a bank and at a government office (although his earnings there led to a reduction in the small amount of money he received as a political exile).[116] Volkhovskii's situation was made more fraught by continuing police surveillance which, although less onerous than at Tiukalinsk, still created considerable strain and constantly threatened to lead to a new clash with the authorities. The situation was not made any easier by the sloth and incompetence of the local bureaucracy (Volkhovskii regularly faced official obstacles, not least over his passport and residence papers, and it took him several years to obtain a formal statement that his designated place of exile was Tomsk).[117] The suicide of his old friend Aleksandr Kropotkin in 1886 appears to have been a consequence both of the stress of exile and concern about money.[118] The suicide of Volkhovskii's wife the following year reflected her irrational fear that she had become a burden to her husband and children (even though she had, in George Kennan's words, 'worked herself to death' taking up sewing to keep her family afloat).[119]

Khorzhevskaia's death left her husband with three daughters to raise alone: Sof'ia (from his first marriage to Mariia Antonova), Vera, and Katia. Volkhovskii's earnings from *Sibirkskaia gazeta* were barely enough for his family to live on, despite being supplemented by the extra income he made contributing to other newspapers including *Vostochnaia obozrenie*. The crisis came to a head in 1888 when *Sibirskaia gazeta* was closed down permanently by the authorities in Tomsk, ostensibly because of an article about the opening of the new University, although more probably because of concern both about its 'Siberian' orientation and the role played by political exiles in the paper's production.[120]

---

116 GATO, f. 3, op. 4, del. 820 (Report sent by Tomsk Chief of Police to the Tomsk Governor, n.d. but probably 1885 or 1886).

117 GATO, f. 3, op. 4, del. 820 (Volkhovskii to the Tomsk Governor, 19 April 1885).

118 For a report of Kropotkin's death, see *Vostochnoe obozrenie* (21 August 1886).

119 George Kennan Papers, 1856-1987, New York Public Library (Manuscripts and Archives Division), henceforth Kennan Papers (NYPL), Box 6, Folder 3, Kennan to Frost, 12 October 1887.

120 On the closure of *Sibirskaia gazeta*, see Zhiliakova, *Zhurnalistika goroda Tomska*, 157–58. Volkhovskii himself noted that the authorities were determined to reduce the number of political exiles in Tomsk following the opening of the new University there, in 1888, not least to limit their potential influence on the student body. Volkhovskii Papers (HIA), Folder 17, Box 3 ('Sketches continued'), 7. For a useful discussion about how the opening of Tomsk University became embroiled in disagreements over 'Siberianism', see N. V. Zhiliakova, '"V zashchitu

Volkhovskii wrote in desperation to the committee of the Society for the Provision of Aid to Writers and Scholars in Need, asking for financial help to ease the parlous situation of his family:

> My oldest daughter is going into the 6th class of the gymnasium and the middle one will this winter begin study there: but all the expenses mount up and I, in truth, do not know what I will do in August when I must pay for both of them not to mention clothes, books, textbooks, etc.[121]

His request does not seem to have met with any response.

The strain of exile affected even those who had, like Volkhovskii, already endured many years in solitary confinement. The visit of George Kennan to Siberia in 1885–86 was welcomed by many exiles precisely because it seemed to provide a link to the outside world. Kennan established particularly close friendships with Volkhovskii and Chudnovskii during his time in Tomsk, visiting them most days when he was in the city,[122] later writing how on his departure Volkhovskii hugged him, saying that 'in bidding you good-bye, I feel as if something were going out of my life that would never again come into it'.[123] Kennan was given a good deal of material by Volkhovskii and other members of the Tomsk exile community while in Siberia, including detailed lists of prisoners and extracts from *Sibirskaia gazeta*,[124] which he later used when writing his articles for *Century Magazine*. He also continued to correspond fitfully with Volkhovskii after his return to the USA.[125] Kennan was anxious to persuade his readers that the political exiles he encountered in cities like Tomsk were courageous opponents of a brutal system of autocratic rule rather than

> crazy fanatics, or men whose mental processes it is difficult to understand. On the contrary, they are simple, natural, perfectly comprehensible, and often singularly interesting and attractive. One sees at once that they

umstvennogo tsentra": polemika "Sibirskogo vestnika" i "Grazhdanina" po povodu otkrytiia Imperatorskogo Tomskogo Universiteta (1888)', *Vestnik Tomskogo gosudarstvennogo universiteta. Filologiia*, 17, 1 (2012), 129–39.
121 Iampol'skii, 'K bibliografii F. V. Volkhovskogo', 188.
122 Chudnovskii, *Iz davnikh let*, 262–64; George Kennan, *Siberia and the Exile System*, 2 vols (New York: The Century Co., 1891), I, 322 ff.
123 *Century Magazine*, 37, 1 (November 1988), 34.
124 For some of this material see Kennan Papers (NYPL), Box 3, esp. Folder 10.
125 See, for example, Kennan Papers (Library of Congress), Box 1, Volkhovskii to Kennan, 13 July 1887; 9 December 1888. On the problems faced by Kennan in keeping up correspondence with Siberian exiles, in part due to interception of letters, see Kennan Papers (NYPL), Kennan to Frost, Box 6, 11 October 1886.

are educated, reasonable, self-controlled gentlemen, not different in any essential respect from one's self.[126]

Kennan may have been naïve in failing to acknowledge that many of the political exiles he met were committed to a socialism that would have been antithetical to many of his readers in Western Europe and North America (although in lectures to American audiences he acknowledged that he did not always share the 'visionary and over-sanguinary hopes and plans for the future of their country' expressed by some of them).[127] Nor did he deny that many of them supported terrorism,[128] arguing that such a tactic was simply a response to the actions of the tsarist government, while men like Volkhovskii possessed a generosity of spirit that set them apart from the 'wrong-headed fanatics of the anarchistic type with which we in the United States ha[ve] become so familiar' (Kennan doubtless had in mind the Chicago Haymarket bombings of 1886 that were widely attributed at the time to foreign-born anarchists).[129] He told one correspondent how 'I went to Siberia regarding the political exiles as a lot of mentally unbalanced ... bomb-throwers and assassins and ... when I came away from Siberia I kissed these same men good bye with my arms around them and my eyes full of tears'.[130]

The friendship between Kennan and Volkhovskii was without doubt genuine. Although it was difficult for the two men to communicate once Kennan had returned home, Volkhovskii wrote a good deal about the personal challenges he faced in the period following the death of his wife. In February 1889, he told Kennan both about the closure of *Sibirskaia gazeta* and the poor health of his youngest daughter Katia, who was 'still sick and has grown so thin that it is painful to look at her. She

---

126 *Century Magazine*, 37, 1 (November 1888), 34. Kennan noted in his private correspondence that he had been surprised on first meeting with political exiles that 'They are more reasonable, better-educated, less fanatical, and have far more moral character than the Nihilists I had pictured to myself'. Kennan Papers (Library of Congress), Box 6, Kennan to Smith, 16 July 1885.

127 Kennan Papers (NYPL), Box 4, Folder 6 (Notes for a lecture on 'Russian Political Exiles').

128 Stepniak noted in a letter to Kennan that the main difference between them was that Kennan thought the use of terror was 'excusable and comprehensible' whereas he thought it was 'obligatory' and 'as moral as anything can be'. Kennan Papers (Library of Congress), Box 1, Stepniak to Kennan, 23 March 1888.

129 The words are taken from the Preface to Kennan, *Siberia and the Exile System*, I, iv.

130 Kennan Papers (Library of Congress), Box 6, Kennan to Miss Dawes, 15 December 1886.

sleeps badly and often I have to be up all night taking care of her. This, together with constant fear for her life, disorders my nerves terribly, and undermines what health I have left ... It is very hard, sometimes, my dear fellow, to live in this world!' He went on to note that he was finding it impossible to earn any money through journalism ('I have sent four manuscripts to St. Petersburg, but none of them has been published').[131] The situation got worse over the following weeks. Volkhovskii had for some years taken his family to one of the villages near Tomsk each summer, to enjoy life in the Siberian countryside, and he did so once again early in the spring of 1889 in the hope that it would improve Katia's health. Things at first went well, but in early May he wrote to Kennan that

> Fate has dealt me another blow. My youngest Katie died a month or two since of pneumonia ... She was about three years old—and such a dear lovable child! But whose child is not dear and lovable?

> No! I can't write any more about it! This is the second time within a few days that I have tried to write you of her—but I cannot—it hurts me too much! As long as I am busy and can talk or write of other things, it seems as if the wound were healed; but let my thoughts once go to her, and I feel such grief and pain that I don't know what to do with myself.[132]

Volkhovskii's pain was doubtless made worse by the fact that he had already lost two wives and a young son. The tragedies he encountered while still in Russia were later to become part of a mythology—or perhaps a martyrology—built up by some of those who met him following his flight to Britain. Kennan himself contributed to the process by printing extracts from the letters about Katia's death in *Siberia and the Exile System* (the book published in 1891 that was based closely on his *Century Magazine* articles). Volkhovskii's correspondence was in fact as much concerned with the challenge of establishing effective communication between Siberian exiles and their sympathisers abroad as it was with more personal reflections about the hardships he faced, but Kennan was shrewd enough to realise that highlighting the story

---

131 The translation is that of George Kennan and is reproduced in Kennan, *Siberia and the Exile System*, I, 336. The full letter in Russian can be found in Kennan Papers (Library of Congress), Box 1.

132 Kennan, *Siberia and the Exile System*, I, 337. The full letter can again be found in Kennan Papers (Library of Congress), Box 1.

of Katia's death could dramatise the plight of all those exiled by the tsarist government, and help mobilise opposition to the tsarist regime in Western Europe and North America.[133] Yet none of this detracts from the desperate personal and financial position in which Volkhovskii found himself after the closure of *Sibirskaia gazeta*, which not only deprived him of a living, but also denied him the chance to use his talents as a writer.

Volkhovskii moved from Tomsk to Irkutsk in Eastern Siberia in the spring of 1889, a few weeks after his daughter's death. He had been offered a job there in a bank, and although the work was not particularly congenial, it did at least hold out the prospect of a salary. The town was located near Lake Baikal, and Volkhovskii welcomed the chance to see at first hand another part of Siberia (he had occasionally used the pseudonym 'Baikal Poet' when publishing his work). Irkutsk like Tomsk had a vibrant cultural life, despite being a place of exile for many, and the town was home to the newspaper *Sibir*. Volkhovskii had contributed to the paper in the past and doubtless hoped he would be able to gain some new commissions. He was not, though, able to stay in Irkutsk for long. The Governor-General, A. P. Ignat'ev, ordered that he leave the town since his presence was prejudicial to public order.

The loss of Volkhovskii's job meant that his financial future was as uncertain as ever. He decided to head for the city of Troitskosavsk (Kiakhta), on the Russian-Mongolian border, leaving his younger daughter Vera behind in Irkutsk (his older daughter Sof'ia appears to have remained in Tomsk before subsequently returning to European Russia). Volkhovskii may have headed to Troitskosavsk because it was the home of his old friend and fellow Chaikhovets Nikolai Charushin, who had over the previous two years toured Siberia taking numerous photographs illuminating the area's ethnic heritage,[134] but he had almost certainly already decided to flee Russia given that he had lost any hope

---

133 Volkhovskii had been out of Russia for more than a year by the time *Siberia and the Exile System* was published and it seems likely that Kennan consulted him about the publication of their correspondence.

134 Volkhovskii noted in his autobiographical notes that he had received a job offer in Irkutsk, although he struggled to get official permission to make the move, a bureaucratic obstacle that demoralised him still further and added to his eventual decision to flee Russia. See Volkhovskii Papers (HIA), Box 17, Folder 3 ('Sketches continued'), 7–8. On Charushin's photographic tours, see Eklof and Saburova, *A Generation of Revolutionaries*, 169–83.

of earning a living or expressing his views legally. In September 1889, Volkhovskii made his way to the Amur River, hoping to catch a steamer that would take him to the Pacific Ocean and a passage to North America and freedom.

Volkhovskii's flight from Siberia was an escape from oppression and poverty and grief. He had during the previous twenty years spent six years in prison and a further ten in exile. Some former members of the Chaikhovskii movement followed his example in escaping abroad, including Leonid Shishko, who fled Siberia for Europe in 1890, where he worked closely with Volkhovskii in producing revolutionary literature. Other old friends like Charushin and Chudnovskii remained in Siberia, returning to European Russia a few years later, after an imperial decree provided an amnesty to many political exiles. There is no way of knowing whether Volkhovskii would have followed their example if he had been given permission to return home at a time when he was still living in Siberia. His decision to flee abroad was certainly a brave one given that he had never left Russia before. It is not clear if he had any definite plans, although his friendship with Kennan had opened his eyes to the possibility of mobilising international opinion against the tsarist regime, and he was hopeful of using his skill as a writer and propagandist abroad in ways that would be impossible in Russia. He certainly planned to meet up with his old friend once he reached America. Volkhovskii's journey was, though, to prove anything but straightforward.

4. Selling Revolution

The only sources of information about Volkhovskii's flight from Siberia to North America come from Volkhovskii himself. The *Times* published an interview with him soon after he arrived in Britain, describing how the strain of exile had 'broken' his health and left 'his forehead deeply lined by terrible hardship and deprivations'.[1] Volkhovskii also gave details of his escape to George Kennan, who subsequently published an account in his book *Siberia and the Exile System*, which was closely based on his earlier articles in *Century Magazine*.[2] Volkhovskii and Kennan both knew that a dramatic narrative could highlight the plight of those who challenged the tsarist regime, while the *Times* interview was conducted by William Le Queux, already making a name for himself as the author of melodramatic novels describing how the government in St Petersburg imprisoned its critics in dank dungeons or condemned them to forced labour in Siberia.[3] There is however no reason to doubt the basic outlines

---

1   *Times*, 11 October 1890. Volkhovskii gave several interviews over the following years providing more details about his escape including his use of a false passport. See, for example, the highly-coloured account in *Chums*, 3, 118 (12 December 1894).

2   George Kennan, *Siberia and the Exile System*, 2 vols (New York: The Century Co., 1891), I, 339–43. Kennan gave a somewhat more detailed and possibly less accurate account shortly after Volkhovskii's death in George Kennan, *A Russian Comedy of Errors with Other Stories and Sketches of Russian Life* (New York: The Century Company, 1915), 162–69. For a valuable biography of Kennan with a particular focus on his role in assisting the revolutionary cause, see Frederick F. Travis, *George Kennan and the American-Russian Relationship, 1865–1924* (Athens, OH: Ohio University Press, 1990). Volkhovskii also gave details of his escape to his friend George Perris which informed the account that appeared in G. H. Perris, *Russia in Revolution* (London: Chapman and Hall, 1905), 226–35.

3   Chris Patrick and Stephen Baister, *William Le Queux. Master of Mystery* (Purley: C. Patrick and S. Baister, 2007), 23–28. On Le Queux's changing views on Russia, see Michael Hughes, 'William Le Queux and Russia', *Critical Survey*, 32, 1–2 (2020), 119–38. Among Le Queux's novels set in Russia see, for example, *Guilty Bonds* (London: Geo. Routledge and Sons, 1891).

     https://doi.org/10.11647/OBP.0385.04

of the story Volkhovskii told to Kennan and Le Queux. His escape from
Siberia was arduous and dangerous even if it also subsequently had the
potential to serve as good propaganda.

In August 1889, Volkhovskii left Troitskosavsk on the Mongolian
border and headed to Stretinsk, described a few years earlier by one
British traveller as a 'good-sized' town and the chief port on the upper
reaches of the Amur River.[4] From here he took a steamer down to the
town of Khabarovsk. He then travelled up the Ussuri River and across
Lake Khanka before moving on to Vladivostok, where he persuaded the
captain of a British coal steamer bound for Japan to take him on board.
The journey from Troitskosavsk was filled with drama. Volkhovskii at
one stage had to dress as an army officer to escape the attention of the
authorities. He arrived at Lake Khanka just in time to catch one of the last
ferries to make the crossing before the winter ice made passage by boat
impossible. Nor were his problems over when he arrived in Nagasaki
from Vladivostok. The Japanese government routinely returned escaped
Russians to the tsarist authorities, and Volkhovskii was unlucky enough
to register at a hotel that was run by a Russian, who viewed the new
arrival with suspicion. He was fortunate in winning the sympathy of the
local American consul, who helped Volkhovskii to pass himself off as a
US citizen, and a few days later he was able to move on to Yokohama.
From here he took passage on the British steamer *Batavia* headed for
Vancouver. Kennan noted in his account that Volkhovskii so impressed
the officers and his fellow passengers with his courtesy and courage that
they raised the money he needed to continue his journey from Vancouver
on to the East Coast.[5] A few days after landing he reached Toronto,
where he was welcomed by Lazar Goldenberg, who had travelled from
his home in New York to greet the new arrival.

Kennan first heard that Volkhovskii had arrived in Canada in
November 1889, when he received a letter from his old friend telling him

---

4   Henry Lansdell, *Through Siberia* (London: Samson Low, 1882), 438.
5   For further details on Volkhovskii's flight, see Kennan Papers (NYPL), Box 6,
     Folder 3, Kennan to Frost, 28 December 1889. Volkhovskii's memories of the
     kindness he received from his fellow passengers can be found in his introduction
     to G. Kennan, *Sibir i ssylka v dvukh chastiakh* (St Petersburg: Izdanie Vl. Raspopova,
     1906), 24–26.

that 'I am at last free'.[6] The two men met in early December in Albany in upstate New York (Kennan later wrote that he thought Volkhovksii 'was in better health than I expected' but had 'a peculiar hunted expression in his eyes').[7] They talked for twelve hours, after which Kennan went south to continue his latest lecture tour, while Volkhovskii crossed back into Canada and headed for the city of Berlin in Ontario.[8] Berlin was the home of Allan Huber, who had been a passenger on the *Batavia*, and over the next few months he provided Volkhovskii with a home and financial support.[9] Throughout the time he spent in Canada, Volkhovskii lived under the pseudonym Felix Brant, since his young daughter Vera was still in Irkutsk, and her father feared that it would be impossible to smuggle her out of the country if the Russian authorities knew he had fled abroad.[10]

During the eight months he spent in Canada, Volkhovskii was extraordinarily energetic in campaigning to raise sympathy for the victims of tsarist oppression (the 'cause' as he regularly described it in letters to Kennan). Within a few weeks of arriving in Ontario, he was giving lectures about his experiences, despite his poor command of spoken English (one newspaper noted that he spoke for three hours 'though his inability at speaking in the English tongue proved somewhat of a disadvantage to him').[11] Kennan's recent articles in *Century Magazine* had made the plight of exiles in Siberia a topical issue, and Volkhovskii attracted many collaborators, including a young Mackenzie

6   Kennan Papers (Library of Congress), Box 1, Volkhovskii to Kennan (no date though late November 1889).

7   Kennan, *Siberia and the Exile System*, I, 339.

8   Kennan noted in a letter that he was happy to pay all Volkhovskii's expenses until he could 'establish himself', but was unable to offer him hospitality in person, since he was moving so frequently on his lecture tour. Kennan Papers (NYPL), Box 6, Folder 3, Kennan to Frost, 28 December 1889.

9   The following two paragraphs draw on the letters from Volkhovskii to George Kennan, held in Box 1 of his papers at the Library of Congress, as well as Donald Senese, 'Felix Volkhovskii in Ontario: Rallying Canada to the Revolution', *Canadian-American Slavic Studies*, 24, 3 (1990), 295–310.

10   Kennan Papers (NYPL), Box 6, Folder 3, Kennan to Frost, 28 December 1889. Kennan told Frost, who had accompanied him on his trip to Siberia four years earlier, that Volkhovskii was afraid his children would be held 'hostage'.

11   *Manitoba Free Press* (12 January 1890). Volkhovskii was inspired by seeing how effective Kennan's lectures were, and for some years to come he consciously modelled himself on his friend, giving lectures wearing chains to dramatise the plight of Siberian exiles.

King (later Prime Minister of Canada).[12] Numerous local newspapers published interviews with him about his experiences in Russia. Despite his recent flight from Siberia, Volkhovskii was still receiving news from Russia, although he was cautious to say nothing in public that might compromise any of his sources there.[13] He also regularly discussed with Kennan ways of encouraging greater interest in Russian developments among Canadians and Americans.

Volkhovskii not only used his lectures and articles to condemn the tsarist government's harsh treatment of political exiles. He also worked hard to challenge popular misapprehensions about the 'nihilists'. In a piece for *The Globe* (the leading Toronto paper) he sketched out a taxonomy of the revolutionary movement that distinguished between 'oppositionists', 'revolutionists' and 'terrorists'.[14] Volkhovskii was wary of talking in public about 'socialism', instead emphasising that the immediate task of the opposition in Russia was to achieve more political rights, a course of action urged on him by George Kennan, who recognised that such a language was more likely to attract popular support. Kennan introduced his friend at several of his lectures, perpetuating the ruse that the speaker was really 'Felix Brant', ending his prefatory remarks with stories about how 'Volkhovskii' was supposedly still suffering in exile in far-off Siberia.

While Volkhovskii's lectures focused primarily on the harsh treatment of prisoners by the Russian government, along with the need for constitutional rather than economic reform, Kennan was still anxious that the 'cause' might become too strongly associated in the mind of the North American public with socialism and anarchism. He was also cautious about a proposal put forward by Volkhovskii to set up a North American society to mobilise international criticism of the Russian government. Kennan's hesitations may have been prompted in part by a desire to protect his own lucrative lecture tours, but they also reflected his understanding that the image of the Russian revolutionary

---

12 For further details, see Donald Senese, 'Willie and Felix: Ill-Matched Acquaintances', *Ontario History* 84, 2 (1992), 141–48.

13 Kennan Papers (Library of Congress), Box 1, Volkhovskii to Mrs Kennan, 27 April 1890.

14 [*Toronto*] *Globe* (15 February 1890). Donald Senese has rightly pointed out that such a *schema* was concerned more with matters of tactics than fundamental questions about the nature of the society that should be built in Russia.

movement needed to be carefully crafted, at a time when there was growing public concern in America about the development of violent challenges to the established economic and political order.[15]

Kennan's caution was probably a factor in encouraging Volkhovskii to move to Britain in the summer of 1890, to work with Stepniak, although in a letter written to Kennan while still in Canada, Volkhovskii noted that geography alone meant that cities like London and Paris were bound to be the centre of efforts to influence developments in Russia.[16] He also wanted to be in London to greet his daughter Vera—plans had already been put in motion to smuggle her out of Russia—while in private correspondence with Stepniak he suggested that Kennan was despite his best efforts largely 'alone' in the struggle in North America to expose the corruption and brutality of the tsarist government.[17] Volkhovskii's departure from Canada did not signal anything like a break with Kennan. The two men often worked closely together in the years that followed. There was nevertheless a marked difference in their views. Kennan was an American liberal whose support for the 'cause' was rooted in a half-articulated sense of the universal value of the rule of law and constitutional government. Volkhovskii saw political reform in more instrumental terms as one element in the struggle for fundamental social and economic change.

Despite these ambivalences, Volkhovskii's time in Canada was extraordinary both for its energy and ambition. He had arrived in the country in late November as a penniless immigrant who spoke poor English.[18] In just a few months he had shown that he could rouse significant public support for change in Russia. And, guided by Kennan, he was shrewd enough to present Western audiences with an image of

---

15 Travis notes that Kennan was always well aware of the financial benefits that could flow from writing and lecturing on Russia, even if such pecuniary considerations were not his major concern, and certainly cannot explain why he came to take such a positive view of the Russian revolutionary movement following his trip to Siberia in 1885–86. Travis, *George Kennan*, 95, 225.

16 Kennan Papers (Library of Congress), Box 1, Volkhovskii to Kennan, 13 April 1890.

17 Russian State Archive of Literature and Art (henceforth RGALI), f. 1158, op. 1, ed. khr. 232, Volkhovskii to Stepniak, 12 February 1890.

18 For Volkhovskii's comments on improving his English while in Canada, see Kennan Papers (Library of Congress), Box 1, Volkhovskii to Mrs Kennan, 27 April 1890.

Russian revolutionaries as moderates rather than wild-eyed socialists committed to using dynamite and assassination to smash the existing order. There was of course nothing particularly original in this objective. Kennan had been trying to do something similar with his articles in *Century Magazine*, while Stepniak's *Underground Russia*, which first appeared in English in 1883, had painted a picture of Russian nihilists as morally responsible men and women who had only turned to terrorism in the face of brutal repression.[19] The most striking feature of Volkhovskii's time in Canada was the speed with which he grasped the potential for building opposition to tsarism abroad, even though he had never previously travelled overseas, nor possessed many substantial contacts outside Russia with anyone other than Kennan.

****

When Volkhovskii arrived in London from Canada, in the early summer of 1890, he was following in the footsteps of many of his compatriots.[20] The city had for years provided a refuge for political exiles fleeing tsarist Russia. Aleksandr Herzen lived in London in the 1850s and 1860s. Petr Lavrov spent time there during the 1870s. Many other Russian revolutionaries, including Mikhail Bakunin and Sergei Nechaev, also passed through the city. Few of these visitors made any great effort to immerse themselves in British society,[21] instead treating London as a place where they could live free from the threat of arrest and extradition, while continuing to work with other Russian exiles across Europe in building opposition to the tsarist government.[22] This

---

19 Sergei Stepniak, *Underground Russia* (London: Smith Elder, 1883). For an interesting piece examining Stepniak's complex attitude towards terrorism through the prism of his writings, see Lynn Ellen Patyk, 'Remembering "The Terrorism": Sergei Stepniak-Kravchinskii's *Underground Russia*', *Slavic Review*, 68, 4 (2009), 758–81. Also see Peter Scotto, 'The Terrorist as Novelist: Sergei Stepniak-Kravchinksii', in Anthony Anemone (ed.), *Just Assassins: The Culture of Terrorism in Russia* (Evanston, IL: Northwestern University Press, 2010), 97–126.

20 For a discussion of Russian revolutionaries abroad during the mid nineteenth century, see Martin A. Miller, *The Russian Revolutionary Emigres, 1825–1870* (Baltimore, MD: Johns Hopkins University Press, 1986).

21 For an argument that Herzen did in fact actively seek to influence British attitudes, see Monica Partridge, 'Alexander Herzen and the English Press', *Slavonic and East European Review*, 36, 87 (1958), 453–70.

22 For useful discussions of Russian revolutionary publishing in London in the second half of the nineteenth century, see Charlotte Alston, 'News of the Struggle:

pattern began to change in the 1880s, when several former Chaikovtsy moved to London, and began to make a determined effort to shape British attitudes towards the Russian government and its revolutionary opponents. Sergei Stepniak and Petr Kropotkin contributed numerous articles to the British press, including some that tried to explain to British readers why the Russian revolutionary movement had turned to the use of terror in the 1870s.[23] Perhaps more important than their words, though, was the way in which both men came to embody the 'cause' in a manner that seemed congenial to the *mores* of late Victorian society. Reports in the British press routinely described Kropotkin as 'gentle' and 'kind-hearted'.[24] Much was made of his 'noble blood' and his 'noble antecedents'.[25] Oscar Wilde described him as a Christ-like figure. Stepniak was widely portrayed as a man of 'mystery',[26] whose powerful stature was reminiscent of 'the gentleness of great powerful beasts',[27] with an 'expression [of] ferociousness' that could not mask an underlying 'shadow of sadness'.[28] Such images of moral commitment and self-sacrifice bore little resemblance to the picture of the Russian revolutionary movement that had previously characterised reports in British newspapers and journals.

Stepniak's efforts to shape British perceptions of Russia were not limited to journalism and fiction. He also devoted considerable effort

---

the Russian Political Press in London, 1853–1921', in Constance Bantman and Ana Claudia Suriani da Silva (eds), *The Foreign Political Press in Nineteenth-Century London* (London: Bloomsbury, 2017), 155–74; Martin A. Miller, 'The Transformation of the Russian Revolutionary Émigré Press at the End of the Nineteenth Century', *Russian History*, 16, 2 1 (1989), 197–207; Kate Sealey Rahman, 'Russian Revolutionaries in London, 1853–70. A. I. Herzen and the Free Press Fund', in Barry Taylor (ed.), *Foreign Language Publishing in London, 1500–1907* (London: British Library, 2002), 227–40; Helen Williams, 'Vesti i slukhi: The Russian Émigré Press to 1905', *Revolutionary Russia*, 13, 2 (2000), 45–61.

23   Among the numerous examples, see, for example, Sergius Stepniak, 'Terrorism in Russia and Terrorism in Europe', *Contemporary Review*, 45 (January 1884), 325–41; Prince Kropotkin, 'The Russian Revolutionary Party', *Fortnightly Review*, 37 (May 1882), 654–71. For a general discussion of this issue, including a discussion of some of Stepniak's 'terrorist' novels, see Michael Hughes, 'British Opinion and Russian Terrorism in the 1880s', *European History Quarterly*, 41, 2 (2011), 255–77.

24   *Faringdon Advertiser and Vale of the White Horse Gazette* (13 April 1889); *Freeman's Journal* (27 October 1887).

25   *Norwich Mercury* (11 May 1887).

26   *Glasgow Evening Post* (30 November 1889).

27   *Lakes Herald* (6 August 1886).

28   *Freeman's Journal* (26 December 1887).

in the late 1880s to establishing a society designed to mobilise 'the working of public opinion of the civilised countries in favour of our cause'.[29] Following a number of tentative discussions with socialists including Annie Besant and George Bernard Shaw, his efforts finally bore fruit in 1890 with the creation of The Society of Friends of Russian Freedom (SFRF), which he hoped would shape the attitudes of a section of the British establishment towards Russia.[30] The process was given added momentum by growing public anger in Britain at reports about the killing of a group of exiles at Iakutsk in Siberia.[31] In setting up the SFRF, Stepniak worked closely with the Newcastle solicitor Robert Spence Watson, the long-serving President of the National Liberal Association,[32] and (in Stepniak's words) 'perhaps the most influential man out of Parliament and also one of the best and cleverest men I ever met'.[33] While Stepniak had at first been inclined to sound out socialists like Shaw and Besant, within a few years he came to realise that the planned society was likely to be more influential if it drew support from leading figures in the British social and political establishment.

---

29   Kennan Papers (Library of Congress), Box 1, Stepniak to Kennan, 26 March 1889.

30   On the origins of the SFRF, see Barry Hollingsworth, 'The Society of Friends of Russian Freedom: English Liberals and Russian Socialists, 1890–1917', *Oxford Slavonic Papers*, New Series, 3 (1970), 45–64. See, too, John Slatter, 'Stepniak and the Friends of Russia', *Immigrants and Minorities*, 2, 1 (1983), 33–49. Useful material can also be found in Donald Senese, *S. M. Stepniak-Kravchinskii: The London Years* (Newtonville, MA: Oriental Research Partners, 1987), 46–71; D. M. Nechiporuk, *Vo imia nigilizma. Amerikanskoe obshchestvo druzei russkoi svobody i russkaia revoliutsionnaia emigratsiia, 1890–1930 gg.* (St Petersburg: Nestor-Istoriia, 2018), 40–61.

31   Robert Henderson, 'The Hyde Park Rally of 9 March 1890: A British response to Russian atrocities', *European Review of History / Revue européenne d'histoire*, 21, 4 (2014), 451–66.

32   David Saunders, 'Stepniak and the London Emigration: Letters to Robert Spence Watson, 1887–1890', *Oxford Slavonic Papers*, New Series, 13 (1980), 80–93. Stepniak told Petr Lavrov in Paris that Spence Watson was 'very strongly with us'. See S. M. Stepniak-Kravchinskii, *V Londonskoi emigratsii*, ed. M. E. Ermasheva (Moscow: Nauka, 1968), 270 (Stepniak to Lavrov, 6 February 1890).

33   Kennan Papers (Library of Congress), Box 1, Stepniak to Kennan, 26 March 1889. Stepniak was first introduced to Spence Watson by his close friend and correspondent, Edward Pease, who was a central figure in the founding of the Fabian Society in 1884. The two men first met Spence Watson in 1888, and by February of the following year the Englishman had become a firm advocate of the 'cause', providing both moral and financial support. See Spence Watson / Weiss Papers, Newcastle University Special Collections, henceforth Spence Watson / Weiss Papers (Newcastle University), SW 1/17/83, Stepniak to Spence Watson, 23 March 1889.

Along with Spence Watson, he organised a public appeal, suggesting that sympathy for the cause of the 'Russian Liberals' (*sic*) should be natural in a country like Britain, where 'Mazzini, Garibaldi, Kossuth, and many another patriot of foreign name, are familiar as household words, and beloved as more than national heroes'.[34] The appeal led to the formation of a Managing Committee to oversee the new Society that included among its members eight Members of Parliament (MPs) and several prominent academics and journalists. A smaller Sub-Committee chaired by Spence Watson managed the day-to-day affairs of the new organisation (other members included the publisher Thomas Unwin, and the prominent member of the Fabian Society, Edward Pease).[35] The Society's monthly newspaper—*Free Russia*—first appeared in June 1890 edited by Stepniak himself.[36]

Many members of the Society were, like Spence Watson, not only Liberals, but also life-long Quakers, and natural proponents of a 'Nonconformist Conscience' that sought to articulate dissenting values in public life.[37] The amalgam of instincts and values associated with the Nonconformist Conscience also helped to shape responses to developments abroad, whether fostering humanitarian intervention

---

34   Spence Watson took the lead in publicising the appeal apparently to provide it with a suitable imprimatur of respectability. See, for example, *Pall Mall Gazette* (10 February 1890). See, too, Stepniak-Kravchinskii, *V Londonskoi emigratsii*, 266 (Spence Watson to Stepniak, 12 December 1889); 267 (Spence Watson to Stepniak, 22 December 1899); 268 (Spence Watson to Stepniak, 22 January 1890). Stepniak for his part was clear that the appeal was very much the work of English supporters, declining to have his name appended to it, although he kept a close eye on efforts to create a new Society devoted to the cause of Russian Freedom. See Spence Watson / Weiss Papers (Newcastle University), SW 1/17/84, Stepniak to Spence Watson, 15 November 1889; SW 1/17/85, Stepniak to Mrs Spence Watson, 15 December 1889; SW 1/17/86, Stepniak to Spence Watson, 19 December 1889.

35   Stepniak expressed himself well-pleased that the high profile of many committee members was likely to make it easier to raise money. See Spence Watson / Weiss Papers (Newcastle University), SW 1/17/91, Stepniak to Spence Watson, 14 April 1890.

36   For the decision to name the paper *Free Russia*, see Stepniak-Kravchinskii, *V Londonskoi emigratsii*, 279 (Spence-Watson to Stepniak, 25 February 1890). On Spence Watson's favourable view of the first number, see Stepniak-Kravchinskii, *V Londonskoi emigratsii*, 285 (Spence Watson to Stepniak, 28 May 1890).

37   The only biography of Spence Watson remains Percy Corder, *The Life of Robert Spence Watson* (London: Headley Bros., London, 1914). On the elusive concept of the Nonconformist Conscience, see D. W. Bebbington, *The Nonconformist Conscience: Chapel and Politics, 1870–1914* (London: George Allen and Unwin, 1982).

to relieve human suffering, or garnering support for opponents of governments who mistreated and abused their people.[38] Yet the nature of such support could create significant division. Spence Watson had, as a young man, praised the national liberation movements in southern and south-eastern Europe, arguing that leaders like Kossuth and Mazzini were justified in using force to free their compatriots from oppression. He was in later life ready to accept, albeit reluctantly, that bringing about political change in Russia might similarly involve violence (even though he served for a time as President of the Peace Society).[39] Many other supporters of the SFRF were by contrast convinced that the use of force could never be justified whatever the value of the ends it was designed to achieve. It was a disagreement that regularly caused tension within the Society during the first ten or fifteen years of its existence.[40]

The SFRF also attracted many Fabians (the Fabian Society had been set up in 1884, and while its early supporters articulated a variety of creeds, its best-known members espoused a somewhat ill-defined 'reformist' socialism). Edward Pease, Graham Wallas and Adolphe Smith all took part in running the Society. Other supporters from the Fabian movement include Edith Nesbit and her husband Hugo Bland (the two had woven a Russian theme into their jointly authored novel *The Prophet's Mantle*, in the person of a Russian aristocrat and revolutionary named Michael Litvinoff, who was almost certainly modelled on Kropotkin).[41] The

---

38   Luke Kelly, *British Humanitarian Activity in Russia, 1890–1923* (Cham: Palgrave Macmillan, 2017), 32 ff.

39   For Spence Watson's views on civil disobedience, see his *The Proper Limits of Obedience to the Law* (Gateshead: Howe Brothers, 1887).

40   Spence Watson himself was clearly still nervous in the first few months of 1890 about Stepniak's radicalism, asking the publisher Thomas Unwin to sound out Kennan's views of him. Kennan for his part noted that while 'Stepniak belongs to the extreme wing of the Russian revolutionary party' his writings were 'so far as I have had an opportunity of testing them ... substantially true'. Spence Watson / Weiss Papers (Newcastle University), SW 1/17/92, Unwin to Spence Watson, 7 March 1890.

41   Nesbit and Bland published the book under the name Fabian Bland, *The Prophet's Mantle* (London: Drane, 1889). For a useful discussion of the book, see Matthew Ingleby, 'Double Standards: Reading the Revolutionary Doppelgänger in *The Prophet's Mantle*', in Darrah Downes and Trish Ferguson (eds), *Victorian Fiction beyond the Canon* (Basingstoke: Palgrave Macmillan, 2016), 181–199; Julia Briggs, *A Woman of Passion. The Life of E. Nesbit, 1858–1924* (London: Hutchinson, 1987), 71–76. See, too, Haia Shpayer-Makov, 'The Reception of Peter Kropotkin in Britain, 1886–1917', *Albion*, 19, 3 (1987), 373–90.

division between 'Liberals' and 'Fabians' was never a precise one. J. F. Green, who served for many years as Treasurer of the SFRF, left the Liberal Party to join the Fabians and later served as a Labour MP. The journalist G. H. Perris, who for many years contributed extensively to *Free Russia*, resigned from the Liberals in 1907 to join the Labour Party in protest at the signing of the Anglo-Russian Convention.[42] More radical figures were also involved in the Society from time to time, although Stepniak was anxious that their presence should not weaken efforts to change perceptions of Russian revolutionaries in Britain, nor undermine the 'respectable' character of the SFRF. William Morris attended many meetings of the Society in the early 1890s,[43] a few years after he had broken with the Social Democratic Foundation to create the anarchist-inspired Socialist League, while the Marxist Theodore Rothstein was for a period an active contributor to *Free Russia*.[44] And, as will be seen in later chapters, in the years after 1900 the Society increasingly drew its support from more left-wing figures active in the trade unions and the Independent Labour Party (ILP).

The SFRF was only a few months old when Volkhovskii arrived in London at the start of July 1890, where many members of the Russian exile community already knew him from their time in Russia, including former Chaikovtsy like Stepniak, Kropotkin and Nikolai Chaikovskii himself.[45] He was also a familiar figure to British readers of Kennan's *Century Magazine* articles. Stepniak was delighted to have the chance to work with a man he had known for many years, not least because he

42 On Perris, see Robert Gomme, *George Herbert Perris 1866–1920: The Life and Times of a Radical* (Oxford: Peter Lang, 2003).

43 On the origins of Morris's interest in Russia, see Evgeniia Taratuta, *S. M. Stepniak Kravchinskii—Revoliutsioner i pisatel'* (Moscow: Khudozhestvennaia literatura, 1973), 332–34; E. P. Thompson, *William Morris. Romantic to Revolutionary* (London: Merlin Press, 1996), 306–07.

44 On Rothstein see David Burke, 'Theodore Rothstein, Russian Émigré and British Socialist', in John Slatter (ed.), *From the Other Shore. Russian Political Emigrants in Britain, 1880–1917* (London: Frank Cass, 1984), 81–99. A longer discussion of Rothstein and a more general discussion of radical Russian émigrés in London can be found in David Burke, *Russia and the British Left. From the 1848 Revolution to the General Strike* (London: I. B. Tauris, 2018). For a sense of Rothstein's Marxist views in the 1890s, see his piece 'The Russian Revolutionary Movement' in *Justice* (1 May 1897).

45 For a valuable first-hand account of the London emigration in the 1890s, see Dioneo [I. V. Shklovskii], 'Staraia londonskaia emigratsiia', *Golos minuvshego na chuzhoi storone*, 4 (1926), 41-62.

already found the demands of editing *Free Russia* very onerous, even before the first issue appeared, telling Spence Watson that producing the paper was 'a serious business' that 'weighs heavily upon me'. He also admired the 'tremendous' speed with which Volkhovskii had launched his career as a lecturer on Russian affairs in Canada.[46] Volkhovskii himself was at first disappointed by the situation in London, believing that public interest in Russian affairs was more muted in Britain than in North America, in contrast to what he had expected to find. He was also deeply frustrated that everything seemed to be done at a slow pace. Volkhovskii was, though, pleased to find that the Committee of the SFRF was made up of 'powerful and influential' people who provided the 'cause' with the establishment *imprimatur* it still lacked on the other side of the Atlantic.[47] In the weeks following his arrival in London, he set to work with his usual energy, quickly establishing himself among the Russian political exile community and emerging as a central figure in producing *Free Russia*. He brought to the job the skills in newspaper production that he had developed while in Siberia. Volkhovskii was well-aware of Stepniak's shortcomings in this regard, telling Lazar Goldenberg in America that his friend was not 'a practical man', and would never be able to provide answers to detailed questions about such mundane things as production runs and printing costs.[48]

The first editorial that appeared in *Free Russia* may have surprised readers whose interest in Russia had been fostered by Kennan's *Century Magazine* articles on the suffering of Russian exiles.[49] The author—presumably Stepniak himself—argued that 'as Russians, we cannot regard the ill-treatment of political offenders by the Russian government as our greatest grievance'. More important still were 'the wrongs inflicted on millions of peasantry, the stifling of the spiritual life of our whole gifted race [and] the corruption of public morals'. The editorial noted that while foreigners could not 'join those who fight the autocracy upon Russian soil', they were able to foster 'a moral ostracism

---

46   Spence Watson / Weiss Papers (Newcastle University), SW 1/17/91, Stepniak to
     Spence Watson, 14 April 1890.
47   Kennan Papers (Library of Congress), Box 1, Volkhovskii to Kennan, n.d. but
     probably August 1890.
48   Tuckton House Archive (Leeds Brotherton Library), MS 1381/351, Volkhovskii to
     Goldenberg, dated 20 November (probably 1892).
49   'Our Plan of Action', *Free Russia* (1 June 1890).

of the Russian autocracy' that would make 'its position ... untenable'. It was a strategy that Stepniak had outlined in a letter to Kennan the previous year.[50]

The second issue of *Free Russia* included a long piece about Volkhovskii's arrival in London,[51] using the language of innocent suffering that was to become such a familiar trope in the British press,[52] reassuring readers that he had never been involved in 'terrorism or the like'. The article also noted that Volkhovskii had now dropped the pseudonym of Felix Brant, since his young daughter Vera had arrived in Britain, removing any danger that she might be 'laid hold of by the Russian government, as had happened with the children of several political offenders'. Her flight had been dramatic. George Kennan later wrote that he played an important role in planning the escape, using his contacts at the American Embassy in St Petersburg,[53] although friends of Volkhovskii were instrumental in transporting her from Irkutsk to European Russia. She was smuggled out of the country by Mikhail Hambourg, a former Professor at the Moscow Conservatoire, who had briefly returned to Russia after moving to Britain the previous year. One of Hambourg's sons later recalled that 'our family consisted at that time of four boys (including myself), and a girl, and our passport had five children's names on it, though I was already in England. So my father conceived the idea of taking Volkowsky's child along with his own children, and dressing her up as a boy, to pass her off as myself'.[54] The attempt was successful. Vera subsequently remembered how the party had

> arrived in London late at night, and next morning my father came for me. I remember his arrival very clearly, but not until he came forward

---

50   Kennan Papers (Library of Congress), Box 1, Stepniak to Kennan, 26 March 1889.
51   'Felix Volkhovsky', *Free Russia* (1 September 1890). Such measures were of course commonly used during the Soviet period, to discourage defections, although it is difficult to identify many cases where the tsarist government made use of such a tactic.
52   See, for example, *Glasgow Herald* (14 October 1890), which spoke of Volkhovskii's 'martyrdom'; see, too, *Westmorland Gazette* (18 October 1890).
53   Kennan, *Siberia and the Exile System*, I, 343. It seems from other accounts that Kennan may have exaggerated his role in facilitating Vera's escape. See, for example, Kennan Papers (Library of Congress), Box 1, Volkhovskii to Kennan, 1 November 1890.
54   Mark Hambourg, *From Piano to Forte: A Thousand and One Notes* (London: Cassell, 1931), 28..

and lifted me off the ground as he used to do, did I realise that, at last, I was really with him, and although I felt very happy, I began to cry. When we arrived at the house where my father was then staying I gave him my doll, as I had been told to do. Inside its head had been placed some letters, which were dangerous to send by post. Then the head had been sewn on, and, of course, no one suspected that a little girl of eight and a sawdust doll were carrying forbidden letters across the frontier. This was the end of my adventure, which was really no adventure at all.[55]

Volkhovskii and Stepniak had known each other since the early 1870s, even maintaining a fitful correspondence when the former was still in Siberian exile. Stepniak told Kennan in 1889 that 'Felix is one of my dearest friends and a man whom nobody can ever forget after knowing him'.[56] It was this long history of personal trust that encouraged him to give Volkhovskii a central role in *Free Russia* and the SFRF. He also provided his friend with introductions to some of the most prominent editors in London. Volkhovskii wrote two long articles shortly after his arrival, one for the *Fortnightly Review* ('My Life in Russian Prisons'), and a second for the *New Review* ('Sufferings of Russian Exiles'). The narrative Volkhovskii set out in 'My Life in Russian Prisons' was designed to emphasise his moderate political views, noting that there was in the propaganda he distributed in Russia 'never any thought of attacking the Czar personally. It was the system we attacked and not the individuals who maintained it'.[57] Such words (which were decidedly disingenuous) were designed to distance him in the minds of readers from the killers of Aleksandr II. While Stepniak had previously defended terrorism in his books and articles as a legitimate tool in the struggle against autocracy, telling Kennan in 1889 that he supported 'the use of dynamite and bombs in Russia',[58] he too was, by the early 1890s, increasingly cautious about expressing sympathy for the strategy pursued by Narodnaia volia ten years before. Both men recognised that the association of the Russian revolutionary movement with terrorism would make it harder to win sympathy in Britain.

---

55 Vera Volkhovsky, 'How I Came from Siberia', *Free Russia* (1 February 1900).
56 Kennan Papers (Library of Congress), Box 1, Stepniak to Kennan, 1 February 1889.
57 F. Volkhovsky, 'My Life in Russian Prisons', *Fortnightly Review*, 48 (November 1890), 782-94 (790).
58 Kennan Papers (Library of Congress), Box 1, Stepniak to Kennan, 26 March 1889.

Volkhovskii used his own experiences to highlight in 'Sufferings of Russian Exiles' the shortcomings of the petty-minded officials who used their power to intimidate those condemned to exile in Siberia:

> What is it that makes a Russian 'political' miserable even if he do not suffer from physical privations? To this I will answer unhesitatingly: It is the feeling of one's complete dependence upon the whims of every official to whom one is subjected; it is the consciousness that one is a bond slave of every brute wearing a State uniform, and that one must put up with all his caprices, submit to his arrogance, and endure insults inflicted by him sometimes out of sheer wantonness.[59]

He went on to echo a theme that was a staple of many accounts of the iniquities of tsarism: the abuse of female prisoners and exiles by the regime ('Women and girls placed at the mercy of these brutes are subjected to risks so horrible that it is painful even to think of it'). Such abuses did of course happen. Yet Volkhovskii's own time in Siberia in the 1880s showed how the experience of exile was often complex and contradictory. While his family suffered from enormous material deprivation, which contributed to his wife's mental instability and suicide, Volkhovskii's pivotal role at *Sibirskaia gazeta* demonstrated how a significant degree of freedom could exist alongside poverty and fear. Such nuances were not easy to convey to a foreign audience, and were in any case pushed to the margins, since they could easily compromise efforts to mobilise support for the 'cause' among foreign publics.

Volkhovskii began lecturing on behalf of the SFRF within a few months of arriving in Britain. In the middle of December 1890, he spoke 'about his life' before 'a large audience' at the Portman Rooms in London, calling on his audience to do everything they could to help victims of tsarist persecution still in Russia.[60] Over the following weeks he lectured in towns and cities across Britain. In January he spoke in Leicester ('in excellent English' according to one newspaper report).[61] The following month he gave a series of talks in the north-east of England on the

---

59 F. Volkhovsky, 'The Suffering of Russian Exiles', *New Review*, 18, 3 (1890), 414–26 (415).

60 *Birmingham Daily Post* (19 December 1890). According to one of those present, Volkhovskii 'kept up the interest of the audience' despite speaking in 'not very distinct' English. See, too, Kennan Papers (Library of Congress), Box 1, Unwin to Kennan, 19 December 1890.

61 *Leicester Chronicle* (17 January 1891).

'horrors of autocracy'.[62] By March he was lecturing in Scotland.[63] His talks were generally well-received, while extensive reporting in the local press helped to amplify their impact, although a few accounts sounded a rather quizzical note about what practical steps Volkhovskii expected his audience to take to promote the cause of Russian freedom.

Volkhovskii gave at least one hundred talks during his first three years in Britain, many attended by large numbers of people, and he was by the end of 1892 regularly billed as a 'Famous Russian Exile'. His lectures typically focused on using his own experiences as a living testimony to the brutality of the Russian autocracy. Many press accounts in turn presented him as the embodiment of suffering. One local paper in north-east England told readers that the 'iron of Russian oppression' had 'entered into [Volkhovskii's] body and soul'.[64] An Inverness paper noted that 'in manner and appearance, M. Volkhovsky himself bore out the burden of his narrative. His face and frame were thin and wearied looking'.[65] A newspaper in Lancashire described how Volkhovskii's experiences had made him 'prematurely old'.[66] Other reports described him as 'an enlightened and cultured man',[67] who had suffered persecution just for seeking the kind of 'constitutional government ... such as we enjoy'.[68] Volkhovskii carefully crafted his lectures to focus on subjects that were most likely to attract the sympathy of his audience, avoiding discussion of controversial topics like terrorism or socialism, in favour of graphic descriptions of the sufferings of Russian exiles and prisoners. He also showed himself adept at developing a *persona* that reassured his audience he shared their values despite his foreign accent and bearing.[69]

Volkhovskii also quickly immersed himself in the day-to-day production of *Free Russia*. He edited the paper for several months after

---

62 *Sunderland Daily Echo and Shipping Gazette* (24 February 1891).
63 *Perthshire Advertiser* (13 March 1891).
64 *Shields Daily Gazette* (24 February 1891).
65 *Inverness Courier* (16 December 1892).
66 *Blackburn Standard* (10 December 1892).
67 *Western Mail* (9 December 1891).
68 *Sunderland Daily Echo and Shipping Gazette* (27 February 1891).
69 For a helpful discussion of ideological congruences between Russians associated with the SFRF and their English hosts, revolving around the values of a benign and socially-conscious imperialism, see Lara Green, 'Russian Revolutionary Terrorism, British Liberals, and the Problem of Empire (1884–1914)', *History of European Ideas*, 46, 5 (2020), 633–48.

Stepniak left Britain in December 1890 for a long lecture tour in the US, just a few weeks after first arriving in London from Canada, a reflection of the trust that existed between the two men. Stepniak's wife Fanni went so far as to refer to it as Volkhovskii's paper in this period.[70] He also began to contribute articles to the paper under his own name. In December 1890, *Free Russia* carried a detailed account of Volkhovskii's interview with the Irish Republican Michael Davitt, who had served a lengthy prison sentence in the 1870s for arms smuggling,[71] and retained radical views on questions of land reform even though he had moved away from advocating violence to end British rule in Ireland. Volkhovskii's interview largely avoided controversial questions. Davitt for his part told his interviewer that he was sympathetic to the cause of Russian freedom ('a suffering Russian is as near to me as an Irishman') and noted that he was aware that much 'nonsense' was talked in Britain about the 'so-called Russian nihilists'. Volkhovskii told the Irishman that he was, like many Russian exiles, well-aware of the shortcomings of the British political system. He nevertheless stressed that he still believed that constitutional reform in Russia could 'give to the Russian people better conditions for development than a bureaucratic autocracy'. He added that it was impossible to 'have

---

70   *Indianapolis News* (1 June 1891). For the reasons why Stepniak was so determined to go on a lecture tour of the USA, see Stepniak-Kravchinskii, *V Londonskoi emigratsii*, 286–87 (Stepniak to Pease, 14 August 1890). Also see Michael J. Lyons, 'An Army Like that of Gideon. Communities of Transnational Reform on the Pages of Free Russia', *American Journalism*, 32, 1 (2015), 2–22; Nechiporuk, *Vo imia nigilizma*, 88 ff; Travis, *George Kennan*, 199–206. On the international dimension of anti-tsarist radicalism see, for example, Ron Grant, 'The Society of Friends of Russian Freedom (1890–1917): A Case-Study in Internationalism', *Scottish Labour History Society*, 3 (1970), 3–24; Green, 'Russian Revolutionary Terrorism'; Lutz Häfner, 'An Entangled World at the Beginning of the Twentieth Century: Socialist Revolutionary Terrorism, Transatlantic Public Sphere and American Capital', in Franz Jacobs and Mario Keßler (eds), *Transnational Radicalism. Socialist and Anarchist Exchanges in the 19th and 20th Centuries* (Liverpool: Liverpool University Press, 2021), 23–56; Faith Hillis, *Utopia's Discontents: Russian Émigrés and the Quest for Freedom, 1830s–1930s* (New York: Oxford University Press, 2021).

71   F. Volkhovsky, 'My Interview with Michael Davitt', *Free Russia* (1 December 1890). The two men continued to write to one another in the years that followed. See, for example, Tuckton House Archive (Leeds Brotherton Library), MS 1381/358, Davitt to Volkhovskii, 3 July 1896. Davitt himself visited Russia several times in the early 1900s, to see at first-hand anti-Jewish violence, writing a book *Within the Pale. The True Story of Anti-Semitic Persecutions in Russia* (New York: A. S. Barnes and Co., 1903).

everything at once'. His words were telling. Volkhovskii saw political freedom—at least in Russia—as a pathway to more radical social and economic change.

Volkhovskii's correspondence shows that he continued to play a pivotal role in editing *Free Russia* even after Stepniak returned from America in the summer of 1891.[72] The paper polemicised furiously with writers who sought to whitewash the tsarist regime, including the former editor of the *Pall Mall Gazette* William Stead, along with 'the MP for Russia' Olga Novikova.[73] Novikova was a well-connected Russian *grande dame*, and friend of William Gladstone, who spent much of her time in London trying to influence British foreign policy in a Russophile direction (George Kennan described her as 'a dangerous antagonist' who was 'personally adroit' and 'skilful in newspaper controversy').[74] Even more reviled was Harry de Windt, who used his account of a journey through Russia, *Siberia as It Is* (1892), to challenge George Kennan's description of the harsh character of the Russian penal system.[75] De Windt had little knowledge of Russia, and his trip to Siberia almost certainly received indirect financial support from the Russian government through Novikov, who had excellent links with senior officials including the influential Konstantin Pobedonostsev, Procurator of the Holy Synod, and sometime tutor of the future Tsar Nicholas II.[76] In April 1892, an unsigned piece in *Free Russia*—the sarcastic tone is characteristic of Volkhovskii—attacked foreign travellers who wrote books about Russia that were no more than 'floating impressions of

72 For Volkhovskii's correspondence with Stepniak in the early 1890s, see RGALI, f. 1158, op. 1, ed. khr. 232.

73 The name was applied flippantly by Disraeli, but was happily appropriated by Novikov, and used by Stead in the collection of her letters he edited. See W. T. Stead, *The M.P. for Russia. Reminiscences and Correspondence of Madame Olga Novikoff*, 2 vols (London: Melrose, 1909). Among Novikov's numerous pieces in the British press (or translations into English of pieces in the Russian press) see Olga Novikoff, 'A Cask of Honey with a Spoonful of Tears', *Contemporary Review*, 55 (February 1889), 207–15; 'Russia and the Re-Discovery of Europe', *Fortnightly Review*, 61 (April 1897), 479–91.

74 Tuckton House Archive (Leeds Brotherton Library), MS 1381/225, Kennan to Goldenberg, 27 March 1893.

75 Harry de Windt, *Siberia as It Is* (London: Chapman and Hall, 1892).

76 On Pobedonostsev see Robert Byrnes, *Pobedonostsev: His Life and Thought* (Bloomington, IN: Indiana University Press, 1968); A. Iu. Polunov, *K. P. Pobedonostsev v obshchestvenno-politicheskoi i dukhovnoi zhizni Rossii* (Moscow: Rosspen, 2010).

tourists who do not speak a word of Russian'. The author argued that such 'superficial' works showed 'malice' in failing to provide the kind of honest account that would help 'in the formation of a truly enlightened public opinion'.[77] He suggested that readers should give more credence to books by well-informed foreigners like Kennan and his fellow American Edmund Noble.[78]

Free Russia devoted a good deal of attention during its first few years to religious freedom in Russia, a sensitive issue for many of its readers, particularly those from a nonconformist background. It printed many pieces describing the harsh treatment of non-Orthodox Christian groups, including the Stundists, evangelical protestants whose doctrine and practice was closely related to the German Mennonites.[79] The paper also subsequently covered the plight of the Doukhabors after it was dramatically raised by Tolstoi.[80] Numerous articles condemned the harsh treatment of the country's Jewish population, including a long piece by Stepniak in the second number, deploring 'the disgraceful' antisemitism of the tsarist government.[81] *Free Russia* also devoted significant attention to the parlous situation of the Russian peasantry, particularly during the famine that swept through the countryside in 1891-92, which led to hundreds of thousands of deaths. The tsarist government's response was widely condemned as inadequate, both in Russia and beyond, and the SFRF sent two 'commissioners' to investigate the situation. It also set up a fund to aid relief efforts.[82] The editorial policy of *Free Russia* was, in short, carefully designed to appeal to the nonconformist-humanitarian instincts that characterised so many of its readers. Stepniak and

---

77 Opening editorial, *Free Russia* (1 April 1892).

78 See, for example, Edmund Noble, *The Russian Revolt: Its Causes, Condition and Prospects* (Boston: Houghton Mifflin, 1885).

79 See, for example, G. Lazarev, 'The History of Elisey Sukach, the Stundist', *Free Russia* (1 May 1893). For a very helpful discussion of how concern about religious freedom related to broader humanitarian issues, see Kelly, *British Humanitarian Activity in Russia*, 85–111.

80 For a brief overview of Tolstoi's intervention, see, for example, Nina and James Kolesnikoff, 'Leo Tolstoy and the Doukhobors', *Canadian Slavonic Papers*, 20, suppl. 1 (1978), 37–44.

81 Stepniak, 'The Jews in Russia', *Free Russia* (1 September 1890).

82 For an excellent discussion of responses in Britain to the famine, see Kelly, *British Humanitarian Activity*, 53–84. See, too, Richard Robbins, *Famine in Russia, 1891-1892: The Russian Government Responds to a Crisis* (New York: Columbia University Press, 1975).

Volkhovskii were both astute enough to craft the 'pitch' of the paper in ways that would encourage its readers to see the situation in Russia through a sympathetic lens.

The articles in *Free Russia* were regularly mentioned in the mainstream press, both national and local, which helped to increase the paper's influence. The creation of the SFRF in 1890 had also been widely reported, usually with approval, and in the years that followed many newspapers routinely carried accounts of meetings held by the Society both in London and the provinces.[83] Supporters used articles and letters in the press to reassure readers that the Society was run by such respectable figures as Spence Watson, who would never sanction the use of its funds 'to support offences against morality, law and order'.[84] Despite such positive coverage, though, membership of the SFRF never rose above a few hundred. Sales of *Free Russia* were generally disappointing (and declined further as time went by). Volkhovskii told Kennan at the end of 1890 that five thousand copies of *Free Russia* were printed, but it is not clear how many were sold rather than distributed *gratis*, while the print run was sharply reduced soon afterwards.[85] Financial woes were to preoccupy supporters of the 'cause' right down to the outbreak of the First World War in 1914.

Stepniak's lengthy visit to America, in the first half of 1891, was prompted by his long-standing conviction that successfully mobilising international opinion against the tsarist government depended on increasing support there (not least as source of funds). He had suggested to Kennan two years earlier that funds should be raised in the USA to establish a new journal to provide 'active and direct assistance to those who are fighting at such awful disadvantages for the cause of Russian emancipation'.[86] Stepniak's 1891 trip was largely designed to build on this earlier proposal. He told Kennan during his visit that 'English soil' was 'violently not favourable' to promoting the 'cause', and suggested that *Free Russia* should be transferred to New York and

---

83 See, for example, the account of a 'packed' meeting in *Daily News* (3 December 1891).

84 *Worcestershire Chronicle* (12 December 1891), letter to the editor by Albert Webb.

85 Kennan Papers (Library of Congress), Box 1, Volkhovskii to Kennan, 1 November 1890.

86 Kennan Papers (Library of Congress), Box 1, Stepniak to Kennan, 26 March 1889.

Volkhovsky should come over with it as the acting editor and ... you should become what the French call *Redacteur Politique*. You will certainly have no difficulty in agreeing with Volk[hovsky] ... you will not be compelled to devote to the paper more time than you can afford. With your name at the head of it, the paper will immediately appeal to a broad public and is sure to be a viable business. Now it seems to me that only if it becomes self-supporting is the paper worth publishing. Otherwise it is simply a waste of time and energy.[87]

Kennan was sceptical, pointing out that while he himself believed in the need for such a paper in America, the times were not propitious for raising the necessary capital.[88] It also seems unlikely that Volkhovskii would have been ready to return to north America, not least because Vera was settling in Britain, although he did recognise the importance of efforts to build support there.[89] He told Kennan in April 1891 that while the movement in Britain was 'going on all right ... we simply creep along from month to month. Please, make the Americans understand, that [*Free Russia*] cannot improve either in size or content without having direct pecuniary support from America'.[90]

Such hopes were not to be realised. Stepniak at first had some modest success in building up support for the American version of the SFRF.[91] The American Society drew much of its membership from a small number of families who had been active in the abolitionist movement and subsequently played a role in various reform campaigns. Yet, although it won some support in Boston and New York, attracting several

---

87   Kennan Papers (Library of Congress), Box 2, Stepniak to Kennan, 29 March 1891.
88   For evidence that Kennan despite his reservations was still keen to ensure the success of *Free Russia* in America, see Kennan Papers (Library of Congress), Box 1, Volkhovskii to Kennan, 1 November 1890. See, too, Luckton House Archive (Leeds Brotherton Library), MS 1381/77, Goldenberg to Garrison, 24 October 1891.
89   By May 1891, Stepniak too seems to have recognised that Volkhovskii might be reluctant to edit a North American edition of *Free Russia*, noting that 'I for my part would not press upon him to go: everything that has to succeed must be done willingly and with a cheerful heart'. See Kennan Papers (Library of Congress), Box 2, Stepniak to Kennan, 9 May 1891.
90   Kennan Papers (Library of Congress), Box 2, Volkhovskii to Kennan, 2 April 1891.
91   On the American SFRF see Nechiporuk, *Vo imia nigilizma*, passim; Travis, *Kennan and the American-Russian Relationship*, 195–248. For a more general discussion of American attitudes towards Russia in this period, see David S. Foglesong, *The American Mission and the "Evil Empire". The Crusade for a "Free Russia" since 1881* (Cambridge: Cambridge University Press, 2007), 7–33.

high-profile figures like Mark Twain,[92] the Society struggled to acquire real momentum. Membership seldom rose to more than two hundred or so. Stepniak corresponded regularly with influential figures in the American Society—including Francis Garrison, Edmund Noble and Lillie Chace—but even his energy could not build widespread popular support for the 'cause'. The Society published an American edition of *Free Russia*, although it mainly reprinted articles from the English version, along with extra pieces judged to be of particular interest to American readers. George Kennan himself appears to have been decidedly ambivalent about the American edition of *Free Russia*. Although he was supportive in the early days, giving advice about questions of pricing and distribution to Lazar Goldenberg,[93] who oversaw the production of the paper in New York, he privately doubted whether members of the American SFRF possessed the expertise to build on his work raising interest in Russian affairs. He also believed that the paper should be produced in Russian as well as English, to increase its circulation both inside the Tsarist Empire and among émigré communities abroad, and by 1893 he was actively raising money for a new publication.[94] Although he discussed the project with Stepniak and Volkhovskii on a trip to Europe, Kennan seems to have been oblivious to the problems that his plans would pose to *Free Russia* on both sides of the Atlantic, not least by increasing their financial challenges still further.

While the US Senate's ratification of a new version of the extradition treaty with Russia early in 1893 provoked significant protest across the country, and for a time held out the prospect of providing new life to the 'cause',[95] the Society's energetic campaign against the treaty ultimately had little impact. Edmund Noble noted at the end of the year that the

---

92   Mark Twain told Stepniak that he had read *Underground Russia* with 'a deep and burning interest'. See Stepniak-Kravchinskii, *V Londonskoi emigratsii*, 298 (Samuel Clements to Stepniak, 23 April 1891). For a longer discussion of Twain's relationship with the American SFRF, see John Andreas Fuchs, 'Ein Yankee am Hofe des Zaren: Mark Twain und die *Friends of Russian Freedom*', *Forum für osteuropäische Ideen und Zeitgeschichte*, 15, 2 (2013), 69–86.
93   Tuckton House Archive (Leeds Brotherton Library), MS 1381/163, Kennan to Goldenberg, 30 July 1890; MS 1381/174, Kennan to Goldenberg, 22 October 1890.
94   Tuckton House Archive (Leeds Brotherton Library), MS 1381/233, Kennan to Goldenberg, 9 May 1893.
95   For examples of mass protest meetings and lectures, see *Buffalo Commercial* (20 March 1893); *Boston Globe* (15 June 1893). For a report of Volkhovskii's attack on the treaty in a lecture in Britain, see *Chicago Tribune* (2 March 1893).

interest provoked by the publication of Kennan's articles in *Century Magazine* a few years earlier was 'dying out'.[96] The US edition of *Free Russia* never sold many copies and finally folded in 1894.[97] The reasons for the failure of the American movement were many, but Kennan was not alone in thinking that the Russian revolutionary movement was too bound up in the public mind with political extremism and violence. Mark Twain's celebrated outburst of 'Thank God for dynamite', which he made after attending one of Kennan's lectures, was not shared by most of his compatriots.[98] The association of 'immigrants' and 'violence' was damaging at a time when nativist sentiment was becoming a pronounced feature of American life. It was also a challenge faced by Stepniak and Volkhovskii back in London as they tried to make the 'cause' respectable in the eyes of the British public.

Volkhovskii wrote many of the unsigned articles that appeared in *Free Russia* in the first half of the 1890s highlighting the fate of those arrested or exiled by the tsarist regime. His reports focused on the treatment of prisoners and exiles, rather than their actions and beliefs, typically arguing that the victims were opposed to violence and condemned simply for demanding reforms that would be unexceptional in a country like Britain. In May 1892, Volkhovskii described a recent meeting in St Petersburg, where a group of 'workmen ... assembled to celebrate the First of May as the holiday of the working people ... and to proclaim the rights of labour in Russia and her solidarity in political and social aspirations with the rest of the civilised world'.[99] He went on to describe how the speakers—whose 'plain common sense' shone through their sometimes 'clumsy phraseology'—traced their genealogy back to 'the educated Russians of the sixties and seventies who were called in Russia "revolutionists", and abroad "nihilists", and who created a whole political movement in their country'. Volkhovskii

---

96 Tuckton House Archive (Leeds Brotherton Library), MS 1381/301, Noble to Goldenberg, 6 December 1893.

97 On the difficult financial position of the American edition of *Free Russia*, see Tuckton House Archive (Leeds Brotherton Library), MS 1381/89, Garrison to Goldenberg, 20 April 1892; MS 1381/92, Goldenberg to Garrison, 23 April 1892; MS 1381/125, Garrison to Goldenberg, 11 December 1893.

98 'The Movement in America', *Free Russia* (1 September 1890). Further useful information can be found in Louise J. Budd, 'Twain, Howells, and the Boston Nihilists', *New England Quarterly*, 32, 3 (1959), 351–71.

99 F. Volkhovsky, 'May-Day Celebrations in Russia', *Free Russia* (1 May 1892).

praised the speakers for favouring 'evolutionist methods' to bring about change: 'by the ballot, the press, public agitation, organization'. The article was calculated to re-enforce in the minds of readers of *Free Russia* that the Russian opposition movement was shaped above all by a desire for political freedom.

In reality, of course, the revolutionary movement of the 1860s and 1870s included numerous figures who were convinced that change could only come to Russia through violence. And even participants in more 'moderate' groups, like the Chaikovtsy, openly or tacitly recognised that a popular uprising could never be entirely bloodless. Such subtleties were doubtless lost on readers of *Free Russia*, who were encouraged to see the Russian revolutionary movement through a kind of 'Whig' prism, as one that sought the rights and liberties taken for granted in countries like Britain. It was a language that Volkhovskii sometimes even used in private correspondence. When he wrote to Kennan in the spring of 1891, acknowledging a cheque for £25 to help 'comrades lingering in penal servitude in Siberia', he asked him to pass on thanks to 'those generous Americans who, enjoying personal freedom and welfare, thought it their moral duty to assist their brethren in mankind who, in another country, suffer because of having honestly served the cause of truth and honesty'.[100]

The difficulty of reassuring cautious supporters of the 'cause' was made more challenging by developments in continental Europe. While 'Fenian fire' had provoked most concern in Britain during the 1870s and 1880s,[101] by the start of the 1890s 'anarchism' was becoming the new *bête noire*, seeming to threaten social and political order across Europe and America. London became home to significant numbers of anarchist exiles during the 1880s and 1890s, particularly from France and Italy,[102]

---

100 Kennan Papers (Library of Congress), Box 2, Volkhovskii to Kennan, 2 April 1891.
101 Christy Campbell, *Fenian Fire. The British Government Plot to Assassinate Queen Victoria* (London: Harper Collins, 2002) argues that the best-known plot was in fact orchestrated from within the British state. For a broader discussion, see Niall Whelehan, *The Dynamiters: Irish Nationalism and Political Violence in the Wider World, 1867–1900* (Cambridge: Cambridge University Press, 2012).
102 See Constance Bantman, *The French Anarchists in London, 1890–1914: Exile and Transformation in the First Globalisation* (Liverpool: Liverpool University Press, 2013); Pietro Di Paola, *The Knights Errant of Anarchy. London and the Italian Anarchist Diaspora (1880–1917)* (Liverpool: Liverpool University Press, 2013). A lively if somewhat idiosyncratic discussion of the European revolutionary movement

and although political extremism was less globalised than sometimes imagined, much of the British press treated anarchist violence as an alien phenomenon that found little resonance in British political culture.[103] Such a language also tended to lump together foreign radicals in an undifferentiated way that associated Russian 'revolutionaries' with the kind of bombings and assassinations seen in cities across Europe throughout the final decade of the nineteenth century.

Free Russia was forced to address the question as early as its second issue, when it reported on the trial in Paris of a number of 'so-called Russian dynamiters', who were caught building explosives supposedly for use either in Russia or in an attack on the Tsar should he visit the French capital.[104] An article in the paper bitterly attacked the French government for using the affair to 'ingratiate themselves with the Russian government' by taking action against 'revolutionaries' working to destroy tsarism. It also suggested that the Russian police had been 'able to have their own way in Paris, as if it were a Russian provincial town', and noted that a 'provocating agent' paid by the Russian government had played 'a conspicuous part' in events.[105] It was a shrewd analysis. Petr Rachkovskii, head of the Foreign Agency of the *Okhrana* in Paris, had employed an *agent provocateur* named Abraham Hekkelman (*pseud.* Landezen) to persuade the conspirators to manufacture explosive devices, in the hope that the French authorities would on discovering the plot take a harder line towards enemies of the Tsar in the French capital.[106] While the author of the *Free Russia* article on 'The Paris

---

during this period can be found in Alex Butterworth, *The World that Never Was: A True Story of Dreamers, Schemers, Anarchists and Secret Agents* (London: Bodley Head, 2010).

103 For a useful discussion of how press coverage of anarchism in Britain shaped opinion, see Haia Shpayer-Makov, 'Anarchism in British Public Opinion, 1880–1914', *Victorian Studies*, 31, 4 (1988), 487–516. As noted earlier in this chapter, though, Petr Kropotkin attracted remarkably positive press coverage in Britain despite his professed anarchism, perhaps reflecting a pervasive sense that an anarchist drawn from the ranks of the nobility, who was comfortable in 'polite society', was less threatening than the anonymous 'others' who inhabited the run-down clubs and meeting rooms of Soho and the East End.

104 For a discussion of the Paris 'plot', see Butterworth, *The World That Never Was*, 264–71.

105 'The Paris Trial', *Free Russia* (1 September 1890).

106 For details of Rachkovskii's time in Paris, see Fredrick Zuckerman, 'Policing the Russian Emigration in Paris, 1880–1914: The Twentieth Century as the Century of Political Police', *French History and Civilisation*, 2 (2009), 218–27. For a broader

Trial' could not be familiar with all the details of the affair, they were astute enough to recognise that it signalled the Russian government's determination to make it harder for its opponents to find refuge abroad. The article was probably written by Volkhovskii shortly after his arrival in London. He certainly recognised that such incidents could do great harm to the 'cause', telling Kennan in November 1890 that it was still widely believed in Britain that *Free Russia* and the SFRF were animated by principles 'analogous with the Russian dynamiters'.[107]

The arrest of the Walsall anarchists in 1892 raised more immediate challenges for members of the London emigration, given that the affair took place in Britain itself. The circumstances behind the plot remain somewhat murky, although once again it was prompted by the use of an *agent provocateur*, a French anarchist Auguste Coulon, who was employed by Inspector William Melville of the Special Branch (Melville was to become something of a nemesis for Russian revolutionaries in Britain over the next few years).[108] The group, which included several Britons, planned to manufacture bombs reportedly destined for use in Russia. The trial of the participants inevitably attracted a good deal of press attention, given the sensational nature of the charges,[109] and *Free Russia* once again worked hard to persuade its readers that the whole affair should not diminish the integrity of the Russian opposition movement. It published a short article noting that one of the accused, Fred Charles,

---

discussion of the Russian secret police abroad, see the same author's *The Tsarist Secret Police Abroad: Policing Europe in a Modernising World* (Basingstoke: Palgrave Macmillan, 2003). See, too, V. S. Brachev, *Zagranichnaia agentura departmenta politsii (1883–1917)* (St Petersburg: Stomma, 2001). For a fascinating if not entirely accurate summary of Rachkovskii's career, including his involvement in revolutionary activities, see SR Party Archive, International Institute of Social History, Amsterdam, henceforth SR Party Archive (Amsterdam), 1048 ('Karera Rachkovskago'). For a still valuable discussion of the foreign activities of the Okhrana, including the work of Rachkovskii, see Ben B. Fisher (ed.), *Okhrana. The Paris Operations of the Russian Secret Police* (Washington, D.C.: Central Intelligence Agency, 1997), which contains a series of declassified articles first written in the 1960s. See too the account based on the findings of a Commission established in 1917 by the Provisional Government to examine the activities of the Okhrana abroad, V. K. Agafonov, *Zagranichnaia okhranka* (Petersburg: Kniga, 1918).

107 Kennan Papers (Library of Congress), Box 1, Volkhovskii to Kennan, 1 November 1890.

108 On the case of the Walsall anarchists, see Andrew Cook, *M. MI5's First Spymaster* (London: Tempus, 2004), 87–93; Butterworth, *The World That Never Was*, 297–300.

109 See, for example, the summary of the trial in the *Daily Telegraph* (5 April 1892).

had said that he was happy to be involved in the manufacture of explosives since he thought they were destined for use in Russia rather than Britain. The author of the unsigned article—again almost certainly Volkhovskii—noted sarcastically that:

> We are very much obliged to Citizen Charles for his touching solicitude for Russia (though we would have entreated him to leave her well alone), and we fully endorse his implicit condemnation of the use of violence in this country ... As a warning to others, whatever be your opinion of the use of bombs in Russia, the moment you hear of their being manufactured *in England* you may say with certainty that Russia's spies and *agents provocateurs* are at the bottom of it. Some fools may become their prey.[110]

The wording was designed to reassure readers that the struggle for Russian freedom would not spill over onto the streets of Britain. Yet the phrase 'whatever be your opinion of the use of bombs in Russia' hinted at the argument long advanced by Stepniak, and tacitly accepted by Volkhovskii, that terrorism could be ethical if it was directed to resisting oppression and promoting liberty (as they believed had been the case with Narodnaia volia). It was a balancing act designed not to offend the religious and political sensitivities of readers, while acknowledging that bringing about change in Russia could demand actions that would seem morally reprehensible to many in a country like Britain. *Free Russia* throughout the 1890s effectively presented terrorism as an 'oriental' response to an 'oriental' despotism—but one in which 'the terrorists' were fighting for political reforms that were occidental in character.

Free Russia was on more comfortable ground when discussing Russian literature rather than terrorism. Volkhovskii was instrumental in strengthening the paper's literary 'turn', although the process itself had a distinctly political colour, since he hoped that introducing readers to the richness of Russian culture would show how autocratic rule had not suppressed the creative instincts of the Russian people. The burgeoning interest in Russian literature also provided Volkhovskii himself with an entrée to literary society in his new homeland. A year after arriving

---

110 'The Walsall Bombs', *Free Russia* (1 May 1892). Stepniak had told Kennan some years earlier that foreigners should avoid becoming directly involved in the struggle against tsarism. See Kennan Papers (Library of Congress), Box 1, Stepniak to Kennan, 26 March 1889.

in Britain, he met the literary critic Edward Garnett, who worked as a reader for various publishers including T. H. Unwin. Garnett had along with his wife Constance already developed a considerable interest in Russian writers including Turgenev and Tolstoi (which they read in French translations).[111] Constance Garnett later recalled how:

> One day in 1891 Edward on coming back from London told me 'I have met a man after your heart—a Russian exile—and I have asked him down for a weekend'. This was Felix Volkhovsky, who had recently escaped from Siberia and he soon became a great friend. He had no home and ... it was arranged that he should make our cottage his headquarters. He insisted on paying for his board (unlike most Russians) and brought his little girl, Vera, a charming child rather pathetic—about eight years old. He was a curious mixture—on one side a fanatical almost Puritanical revolutionary, pedantic and strict, ready to go to the stake rather than disown or disguise opinions really of no practical importance ... on the other hand, pleasure-loving, vain, rather intriguing, a tremendous 'ladies man', a first-rate actor, fond of dancing. One day he was a pathetic broken-down old man —very sorry for himself —the next day he would look 20 years younger, put a rose in his button-hole, and lay himself out—very successfully—to please and entertain. His terrible deafness— the result of seven years imprisonment in the Peter Paul fortress—made him a tiring companion. But he did me two great services—for which I shall always feel grateful. He made me go out for rather long walks every day ... to the great benefit of my health... and he suggested my learning Russian and gave me a grammar and a dictionary ... Also it was through him I came to know Stepniak.[112]

Volkhovskii gave Constance various stories by Ivan Goncharov to translate,[113] and was so impressed by the results that he handed them to Stepniak, who agreed that she had a rare ability to capture the spirit of Russian literature in English prose.[114] Over the next twenty-five years,

---

111 On the Garnetts, see Helen Smith, *The Uncommon Reader: A Life of Edward Garnett* (London: Jonathan Cape, 2017); Richard Garnett, *Constance Garnett: A Heroic Life* (London: Sinclair-Stevenson, 1991).

112 Garnett Family Papers, Charles Deering McCormick Library of Special Collections, Northwestern University, henceforth Garnett Papers (Northwestern University), Box 14, Folder 5 (Constance Garnett memoir notes), 58–59.

113 Garnett Papers (Northwestern University), Box 14, Folder 5 (Constance Garnett memoir notes), 78.

114 Garnett, *Constance Garnett*, 81. For a discussion of how Constance's background helped shape her interest in Russia, see the paper by Colin Higgins, 'The Guttural Sorrow of the Refugees—Constance Garnett and Felix Volkhovskii in the British

Constance became a prolific translator of Russian literature. Her work played a pivotal role in facilitating the Russia craze by making available in English works of writers including Dostoievskii, Tolstoi and Chekhov.[115]

For Edward's sister Olive, who regularly met Volkhovskii at her brother's cottage in Surrey, he served as a kind of emblematic figure whose *persona* shaped her view of all things Russian:

> It seems that it is a Russian characteristic to live in a world of theories and talk of them with great ease as one would ask for a piece of bread and butter. Volkhovskiy indeed breathes theories. I think this must be good for the national character, and it certainly trains the mind and makes life much more interesting ... When Volkhovskii is here we live in quite a little Russian world. It is so curious to wake from Siberia to a Surrey lane.[116]

Although Olive and Constance both found the Russian a tiring guest, given his deafness, they were grateful for the part he played in opening their eyes to his country's culture. The Garnett family in turn gave Volkhovskii contacts with literary London. Edward Garnett introduced him to Thomas Unwin, who encouraged Volhovskii to write his

Museum', *Materialy X Mezhdunarodnogo seminara perevodchikov*, https://www.repository.cam.ac.uk/items/ee5b06e9-4ba2-43e4-a40f-4c1b4ed29f96.

115 For an important book examining the impact of Russian culture on British culture, including extensive discussion of the role of members of the London émigré community, see Rebecca Beasley, *Russomania. Russian Culture and the Creation of British Modernism, 1881–1922* (Oxford: Oxford University Press, 2020). Another lucid discussion of the relationship between the literary and political activities of Russian emigres in London in the late 19th century can be found in Carol L. Peeker, 'Reading Revolution. Russian Émigrés and the Reception of Russian Literature in Britain c. 1890–1905' (DPhil thesis, University of Oxford, 2006). Further useful material on Anglo-Russian literary relations can be found in W. Gareth Jones (ed.), *Tolstoi and Britain* (Oxford: Berg, 1995); W. J. Leatherbarrow (ed.), *Dostoievskii and Britain* (Oxford: Berg, 1995); Patrick Waddington (ed.), *Ivan Turgenev and Britain* (Oxford: Berg, 1995).

116 Garnett Papers (Northwestern University), Box 21, Olive Garnett to Richard Garnett, 17 November 1891. Olive made numerous references to Volkhovskii in her diary. See Barry C. Johnson, *Tea and Anarchy! The Bloomsbury Diary of Olive Garnett, 1890–1893* (London: Bartlett's Press, 1989). A valuable discussion of Olive's sympathies with Russian radicals in Britain can be found in Anat Vernitski, 'Russian Revolutionaries and English Sympathizers in 1890s London. The Case of Olive Garnett and Sergei Stepniak', *Journal of European Studies*, 35, 3 (2005), 299–314. A useful discussion of Olive Garnett, including material relating to her views of Volkhovskii, can be found in Frances Reading, 'Olive Garnett and Anglo-Russian Cultural Relations from the Crimean War to the Russian Revolutions, 1855–1917' (PhD thesis, University of Kent, 2022).

autobiography, although the project was never completed.[117] Unwin also commissioned him to translate some of Vladimir Korolenko's short stories,[118] several of which were serialised in *Free Russia*, along with one of Volkhovskii's own pieces 'The "New Life": A Siberian Story' (a translation of his 1884 story 'New Year's Eve'). Volkhovskii also provided an introduction to the English translation of Hermann von Samson-Himmelstern's *Russia under Alexander III*.[119] In 1892, Volkhovskii published a translation of some of the children's tales he had written many years earlier, hoping both to earn money and pique the interest of a younger readership in Russia.[120] He noted sadly in the epilogue to the book that he had originally told the stories to his daughter since her mother was too weary to think up any of her own. The throwaway line would have meant little to Volkhovskii's readers, who knew nothing of his second wife's breakdown and suicide, but his words inevitably cast a little retrospective light on the human cost of exile.

Volkhovskii's friendship with the Garnett family introduced him to a milieu characterised by a distinctive mix of literary ambition and political radicalism. It was through the Garnetts that he first met Ford Maddox Ford and members of the Rossetti family.[121] Ford knew the Garnetts and the Rossettis from childhood in Bloomsbury—the Rossettis were cousins—and was fascinated by Russian literature from his youth. His sister Juliet was later to marry the Russian émigré David Soskice, who played an important role in the SFRF, editing *Free Russia* when Volkhovskii was living abroad in 1904–06. Three of the Rossetti children—Olivia, Arthur and Helen—founded an anarchist journal *The Torch* in 1891, at the precocious ages of, respectively, sixteen, fourteen

117 Volkhovskii Papers (Houghton Library), MS Russ 51, Folder 359, Unwin to Volkhovskii, 1 March 1895; 2 May 1895.

118 F. V. Volkhovsky and V. G. Korolenko, *Russian Stories Vol. I. Makar's Dream and Other Stories* (London: T. Fisher Unwin, 1892).

119 Hermann von Samson-Himmelstern, *Russia under Alexander III. And in the Preceding Period* (London: T. Fisher Unwin, 1893).

120 Felix Volkhovsky, *A China Cup and Other Stories for Children* (London: T. Unwin Fisher, 1892).

121 Some insights into the family life of the young Ford Maddox Ford (at that time Ford Maddox Heuffer), can be gleaned at second hand from the book by his sister Juliet M. Soskice, *Chapters from Childhood: Reminiscences from an Artist's Granddaughter* (New York: Harcourt Brace and Co., 1922). There are scattered references to the Garnett family in Ford Maddox Ford's own reminiscences *Return to Yesterday* (London: Victor Gollanz, 1931).

and eleven.[122] Over the next few years, the journal attracted prominent anarchist contributors, including Louise Michel and Enrico Malatesta, and was circulated widely at radical political meetings across the capital. Many years later, Helen and Olivia wrote a fictionalised memoir of this time, *A Girl among the Anarchists*, in which one of the characters was loosely modelled on Volkhovskii.[123] During his first few years in London, then, Volkhovskii found himself in a milieu that must have seemed eerily reminiscent of the *kruzhki* he had known back in Russia, in which intense literary and political interests were animated by a critical spirit that sought to transform the world.

While Volkhovskii was a central figure in promoting the 'cause' during the years following his arrival in London, he was—like Stepniak—determined to contribute more directly to the struggle for change, focusing much of his attention on bringing greater unity to the notoriously fissiparous Russian opposition movement. Even before leaving Canada for Britain, Volkhovskii told George Kennan that he believed 'the whole Russian emigration and all the dissatisfied elements of Russia feel the need to unite as quickly as possible for an amicable general course of action and in particular the founding of a free Russian organ in emigration'. He acknowledged that the different factions 'do not know how to come to an agreement', but went on to note, with a certain lack of humility, that:

> I stand outside parties and I have many friends in Russia, therefore the eyes of the emigration have inevitably turned to me and I am sure that my presence alone will greatly help the success of the coming together. My position is completely unique and it would be a sin against the cause of Russian freedom to scorn it; moreover even the personal lines of my character are such that, speaking without boastfulness, wherever fate has thrown me—Moscow, Odessa, Stavropol, Tyukalinsk, Tomsk— everywhere I either created a circle or in another form served as a unifying cement between people.[124]

122 For a still valuable account of British anarchism in this period, see John Quail, *The Slow Burning Fuse. The Lost History of the British Anarchists* (London: Paladin, 1978).
123 Isabel Meredith (pseud.), *A Girl among the Anarchists* (London: Duckworth, 1903).
124 Quoted in Donald Senese, 'Felix Volkhovsky in London, 1890–1914', in John Slatter (ed.), *From the Other Shore: Russian Political Emigrants in Britain, 1870–1917* (London: Frank Cass, 1984), 67–78 (74).

Volkhovskii emphasised the importance of fostering greater unity among opposition parties in a letter to Stepniak, written eighteen months later, when staying with the Garnetts at their cottage in Surrey. He took issue with Stepniak's use of the term 'our party' in a manuscript that his old friend had asked him to comment on.[125] Volkhovskii noted that while many Russian socialists used the term, it was not always clear what was meant by it: 'socialist', 'militant (*voinstvuiushchaia*) revolutionary', 'old Narodnaia Volia', '*narodniki* [of] 72–74?'. He argued there was no socialist party in Russia, just socialists, and while there were many different groups, each with their own programmes, he and Stepniak did not belong to any of them. Volkhovskii agreed with Stepniak's argument that in the sphere of politics 'our programme is the programme of the Russian liberals', although he questioned his friend's acceptance of the need for a constitutional monarchy, emphasising that the focus should instead be on the principles of 'popular representation, local self-government, and freedom of conscience and a free press'. Above all, though, Volkhovskii believed that opponents of the tsarist autocracy needed to focus on what united them in order to be effective in extracting concessions from the regime.[126] It echoed the approach he had adopted at a local level twenty years earlier in Odessa, when he had built close relations with liberals in the local Duma, while building an illegal *kruzhok* dedicated to spreading propaganda among workers in the city.

Volkhovskii's letter to Stepniak suggests that he was a more influential actor in the project to create a 'National Front' against autocracy than has sometimes been recognised.[127] There was indeed something very ambitious, and perhaps even grandiloquent, about articulating such a strategy at a time when the revolutionary movement was becoming increasingly divided between its Marxist and *narodnik* wings.[128] The development of 'legal' Populism and 'legal' Marxism added to these

---

125 The manuscript Volkhovskii commented on was almost certainly Stepniak's pamphlet 'Chego nam nuzhno' discussed further below.

126 RGALI, f. 1158, op. 1, ed. khr. 232, Volkhovskii to Stepniak, 26 August 1891.

127 For a discussion of the strategy, see Donald Senese, 'S. M. Kravchinskii and the National Front Against Autocracy', *Slavic Review*, 34, 3 (1975), 506–22.

128 For a lucid discussion of the division, see Andrzej Walicki, *The Controversy over Capitalism: Studies in the Social Philosophy of the Russian Populists* (Oxford: Clarendon Press, 1969).

complexities.[129] And, to make things more difficult still, the Russian liberals were in the early 1890s too weak and divided to consider developing close relations with revolutionary groups, even if they shared a common objective of working for constitutional reforms.[130] Any successful attempt to build a united progressive opposition was bound to raise complex ideological and tactical questions, as well as encountering the personal tensions that invariably added to the bitter divisions within the Russian revolutionary movement, both at home and in emigration. Volkhovskii's confidence in such a project was at least in part a reflection of his own lack of interest in the kind of ideological debate that was so important to many members of the Russian revolutionary *intelligentsia*. His impatience was perhaps understandable, but it sometimes blinded him to the scale of the divisions within the Russian opposition movement, and the likely challenges that would need to be faced in overcoming them.

Petr Lavrov in Paris was sceptical both about plans to mobilise international opinion against the tsarist government as well as prospects for achieving any real unity among members of the opposition. While he had in his *Istoricheskie pis'ma* (*Historical Letters*) emphasised the moral duty of the *intelligentsia* to promote the interests and welfare of the *narod*, twenty years of exile had shown him that abstract ethical doctrine

---

129 On this topic, see Arthur P. Mendel, *Dilemmas of Progress. Legal Marxism and Legal Populism* (Cambridge, MA: Harvard University Press, 1961); G. N. Mokshin, *Evoliutsiia ideologii legal'nogo narodnichestva v poslednei trety XIX–nachale XX vv.* (Voronezh: Nauchnaia Kniga, 2010).

130 Among the voluminous literature on Russian Liberalism in the nineteenth century see, for example, Anton A. Fedyashin, *Liberals under Autocracy. Modernization and Civil Society in Russia, 1866–1904* (Madison, WI: University of Wisconsin Press, 2012); Derek Offord, *Portraits of Early Russian Liberals. A Study of the Thought of T. N. Granovsky, V. P. Botkin, P. V. Annenkov, A. V. Druzhinin, and K. D. Kavelin* (Cambridge: Cambridge University Press, 1985); Randall Poole, 'Nineteenth-Century Russian Liberalism: Ideals and Realities', *Kritika: Explorations in Russian and Eurasian History* 16, 1 (2015), 157–81; Susanna Rabow-Edling, *Liberalism in Pre-Revolutionary Russia. State, Nation, Empire* (Abingdon: Routledge, 2019); Vanessa Rampton, *Liberal Ideas in Tsarist Russia. From Catherine the Great to the Russian Revolution* (Cambridge: Cambridge University Press, 2020); Paul Robinson, *Russian Liberalism* (Ithaca, NY: Northern Illinois University Press, 2023); Konstantin I. Shneider, *Mezhdu svobodoi i samoderzhaviem: istoriia rannego russkogo liberalizma* (Perm: Permskii gos. natsional'nyi issledovatel'skii universitet, 2012); Andrzej Walicki, *Legal Philosophies of Russian Liberalism* (Oxford: Clarendon Press, 1987). A useful collection of essays by Russian scholars translated into English can be found in the special edition of *Russian Studies in Philosophy* 60, 2 (2022).

was often a poor guide to action.[131] His critical idealism had in any case been increasingly supplanted by a materialism that emphasised the importance of economic factors in social development. Although he responded positively to Stepniak's initial plans to publish a newspaper intended to win the sympathy of a Western audience for the Russian opposition movement,[132] Lavrov was by the spring of 1891 anxious that *Free Russia* was focusing too much on the need for constitutional change in Russia, rather than more forcefully supporting the struggle for social and economic revolution.[133] It was a view that had been put to him by several prominent exiles, including the veteran London-based *narodovolets* (member of Narodnaia volia) E. A. Serebriakov, who were sceptical about the value of winning support from Western and Russian liberals. Volkhovskii was editing *Free Russia* at the time, as Stepniak was in America, and he urged his old friend to come back to help repair relations with Lavrov.[134] Stepniak's return eased the tension, for a while, but relations between Lavrov and members of the London emigration remained cool throughout the following decade.

Another important centre in the Russian revolutionary emigration was found in Geneva, where Georgii Plekhanov, Vera Zasulich and Pavel Aksel'rod formed the nucleus of Gruppa 'Osvobozhdenie truda' (Emancipation of Labour Group), which played a pivotal role in the development of Russian Marxism. Plekhanov unlike Zasulich had opposed the use of terror in the 1870s, 'sharing the contempt for political action',[135] and his subsequent adoption of Marxism represented a

131 Peter Lavrov, *Historical Letters*, trans. James P. Scanlan (Berkeley, CA: University of California Press, 1967). Lavrov's views in exile are best understood through the prism of his correspondence, much of which can be found in Boris Sapir (ed.), *Lavrov. Gody emigratsii*, 2 vols (Dordrecht: D. Reidel, 1974). The evolution of Lavrov's views is also discussed in B. S. Itenberg, *P. L. Lavrov v russkom revoliutsionnom dvizhenii* (Moscow: Nauka, 1988); Philip Pomper, *Peter Lavrov and the Russian Revolutionary Movement* (Chicago, IL: Chicago University Press, 1972).

132 Stepniak-Kravchinskii, *V Londonskoi emigratsii*, 270–73 (Stepniak to Lavrov, 6 February 1890); 273–74 (Lavrov to Stepniak, 15 February 1890).

133 Stepniak-Kravchinskii, *V Londonskoi emigratsii*, 291–96 (Lavrov to E. E. Lineva, 2 April 1891). A copy of the original letter, in French, can be found in Volkhovskii Papers (HIA), Box 18, Folder 5.

134 Stepniak expressed his views about 'our Paris friends' in a letter to Edward Pease. See Stepniak-Kravchinskii, *V Londonskoi emigratsii*, 301–02 (Stepniak to Pease, late April or early May 1891).

135 Leszek Kolakowski, *Main Currents of Marxism*, 3 vols (Oxford: Oxford University Press, 1978), II, 330.

continuing rejection of the kind of voluntarism that had found expression in the rise of Narodnaia volia.[136] Zasulich had also come to reject terror, a change that was informed not so much by ethical considerations, but rather because she believed that it could not serve as an effective means of creating lasting social and economic change.[137] Both Plekhanov and Zasulich respected Stepniak, and had in the early 1880s suggested that he become a member of the Emancipation of Labour Group,[138] even though he was at the time one of the most prominent defenders of using terror to combat repression. While Stepniak was alive, the members of Group were usually ready to avoid harsh polemics with the London emigration, although relations soured markedly at the end of 1892 when an article appeared in the German edition of *Free Russia* (*Frei Russland*) criticising Marxist Social Democrats for dividing the revolutionary movement.[139] The gulf between Plekhanov's doctrinal Marxism and the emphasis of Stepniak and Volkhovskii on prioritising unity among opponents of the tsar hindered close relations between the two groups (perhaps ironically given that an alliance between revolutionaries and bourgeoisie could easily be presented as a logical Marxist strategy in a quasi-feudal country like Russia). It was a tension that later exploded after Stepniak's death in 1895.

The commitment of Stepniak and Volkhovskii to building greater unity within the Russian opposition movement was central to the creation of the Russian Free Press Fund (RFPF). Although Stepniak took the lead in setting up the RFPF, Volkhovskii played a more important role over the following years, working with other émigrés including several who were active Chaikovtsy in the early 1870s (Stepniak himself was seldom closely involved in the day-to-day running of the Fund). Chaikovskii

---

136 On Plekhanov see Samuel H. Baron, *Plekhanov. The Father of Russian Marxism* (London: Routledge and Kegan Paul, 1963); S. V. Tiutiukin, *G. V. Plekhanov. Sud'ba russkogo marksista* (Moscow: Rosspen, 1997).

137 On Zasulich's move towards Marxism, see Jay Bergman, *Vera Zasulich: A Biography* (Stanford, CA: Stanford University Press, 1983), 63–101.

138 Baron, *Plekhanov*, 128. The invitation was apparently made as early as 1883.

139 For details of this incident, see V. Ia. Laverychev, 'Otnoshenie chlenov gruppy "Osvobozhdenie Truda" k burzhuaznomu liberalizma', in V. Ia. Laverychev (ed.), *Gruppa "Osvobozhdenie Truda" i obshchevstvenno-politicheskaia bor'ba v Rossii* (Moscow: Nauka, 1984), 167-95 (esp. 187–88).

was on the committee that ran the RFPF. So too was Leonid Shishko,[140] who had long been close to Stepniak and Chaikovskii, although he spent most of his time in Paris where he ran the Fund's bookshop, among other activities. Other émigrés active in the RFPF included Egor Lazarev, first arrested for participation in the Going to the People movement of 1874, and Lazar Goldenberg, a central figure in the student riots of 1869.[141] Both Lazarev and Goldenberg had been closely involved in running the American edition of *Free Russia* before moving to Europe.[142]

Also active in the RFPF was Wilfrid Voinich, a somewhat mercurial Pole, who had fled from exile in Siberia to Britain, where he married Ethel Boole, daughter of the mathematician George Boole (Ethel subsequently played a significant role in helping to run *Free Russia* and translated some of the material published there).[143] Voinich acted for a time as business manager for the Fund, which ran a bookshop from its offices in Hammersmith, although he was seldom on easy terms with any of his colleagues (his relationship with Volkhovskii became particularly tense).[144] Voinich subsequently opened his own bookshop in central London, and though he continued for a time to help distribute the Fund's literature, his association with the 'fundists' began to fade by

---

140 On Shishko, see F. Volkhovskii (ed.), *Pamiati Leonida Emmanuilovicha Shishko* (n.p.: Partiia Sotsialistov-Revoliutsionerov, 1910).

141 For Goldenberg's memories of this time, including his rejection of Nechaev's attempt to use student unrest to foster a wider *bunt*, see Tuckton House Library (Leeds Brotherton Library), MS 1381/18 (typescript of L. Goldenberg, 'Reminiscences'), 14-18.

142 For a discussion of the two men's activities in America, see Nechiporuk, *Vo imia nigilizma*, passim.

143 For discussion of Ethel's activities during the 1890s see, for example, Taratuta, *Stepniak*, passim. A more detailed account of Ethel's life can be found in Evgeniia Taratuta, *Nash drug Etel' Lilian Voinich* (Moscow: Pravda, 1957). The article appeared as a supplement to the literary journal *Ogonek*. On Voinich's arrival in London, and Volkhovskii's initial (and positive) views about him, see Kennan Papers (Library of Congress), Volkhovskii to Kennan, 1 November 1890. Although Voinich drifted away from members of the Fund in the second half of the 1890s, at least one agent of the *Okhrana* still believed as late as 1906 that he was involved in funding arms shipments to further revolution in Russia. See Okhrana Archive, Hoover Institution Library and Archives, Stanford University, henceforth Okhrana Archive (HIA), Index VIk, Folder 23, Farce to Rachkovskii, 3 February 1906 (microfilm 108).

144 A great deal about Voinich's career in the 1890s remains mysterious. See for example the cryptic letters, including one written on SFRF headed paper, held by the Grolier Club of New York available at https://www.colinmackinnon.com/attachments/Russian_Letters.pdf.

the middle of the 1890s. He was followed as manager by Lazarev, before he moved on to Switzerland in 1896 after eighteen months in post,[145] to be replaced in turn by Goldenberg, who condemned his predecessor for being too lax in carrying out his duties. The charge may not have been a fair one. Goldenberg took pride in his practical skills—among other things he spent many years earning a living through installing electric generators—and he had a low opinion of the practical capacities of many of those he worked with.[146] Lazarev had in fact corresponded regularly with Russian revolutionary émigrés across Western Europe and North America, soliciting and editing contributions for various publications, as well as participating in discussions about how the Fund could best support the revolutionary movement in Russia.[147] The RFPF's annual reports suggest that it was reasonably well-managed throughout the 1890s.[148] Its publications certainly proved more lucrative than *Free Russia*, the revenue coming from the sale of books and pamphlets to Russian communities across Europe, although some material was also smuggled into Russia where it found a wide readership. Finances nevertheless remained tight. Volkhovskii had to make efforts throughout the 1890s to borrow money for the Fund from sympathetic Britons.[149]

The Fund sold 'classic' radical literature by authors ranging from Herzen to Drahomanov, including some in Polish, as well as publishing many new works (nearly thirty by 1900). The range of these new publications—both in terms of ideology and subject—was

---

145 For useful material on Lazarev's earlier career, when still in Russia, see E. E. Lazarev, *Moia zhizn'. Vospominaniia, stati, pis'ma, materialy* (Prague: Tip-ia Legiografiia, 1935). Useful material on his life after moving to Switzerland can be found in N. A. Ekhina, 'Emigranty, revoliutsionery i koronovannye osoby: "russkaia volost'" E. E. i Iu. A. Lazarevykh v Bozhi nad Klaranom', *Ezhegodnik Doma russkogo zarubezh'ia im. Aleksandra Solzhenitsyna* (2014–15), 20–30.

146 Tuckton House Archive (Leeds Brotherton Archive), MS 1381/26 (typescript of later parts of L. Goldenberg, 'Reminiscences'), 54–55. Goldenberg noted in his memoirs that the Committee of the Free Press Fund had sent him a telegram asking him to 'come and save us', adding that when he arrived in London, he found the Fund's premises in Hammersmith in a terrible state of disorder.

147 Some sense of the scale of the Fund's activities, including the material submitted for publication and the role of the individuals associated with it, can be found in Volkhovskii Papers (HIA), Box 8 (various folders); Box 10 (various folders).

148 See, for example, SR Party Archive (Amsterdam), 111 (1893 Report and Accounts for the RFPF).

149 See, for example, Volkhovskii Papers (HIA), Box 8, Folder 3, Lionel Hobhouse to Volkhovskii, 20 May (no year).

strikingly eclectic. During its ten-year life, the Fund published Vladimir Burtsev's *Za sto let* (*Over a Hundred Years*), which contained a valuable documentary record of the Russian revolutionary movement, as well as books and pamphlets on such subjects as religious persecution and the censorship of Tolstoi's works. S. L. Dickstein contributed a Marxist exposition of the labour theory of value complete with an afterword by Plekhanov. Also published by the Fund was a Russian translation of Eduard Bernstein's revisionist *Die Voraussetzungen des Sozialismus* (*The Prerequisites for Socialism*). The choice of publications reflected the ideological tolerance that the fundists believed was necessary to create a broad opposition movement.

Among the earliest of the Fund's publications were pamphlets by Stepniak and Volkhovskii calling for closer relations between revolutionaries and liberals. Stepniak's 1892 *Chego nam nuzhno?* (*What Do We Need?*) provided a programmatic statement of its author's commitment to building a broad opposition that bridged the (uncertain) gap between revolutionaries and liberals, while remaining firmly committed to the principle that 'socialism is the strongest moral force in modern society'.[150] He urged all revolutionary factions to accept the principle that political change should precede radical social and economic reform ('regarding the introduction of socialism into life we are evolutionists ... We believe that political liberty gives all that is needed for the solution of the social question'). Stepniak also argued that political change could best be secured by members of the *intelligentsia* committed to decisive action,[151] rather than peasants or workers, and urged liberals to recognise that violence was often a necessary means of securing political concessions. The pamphlet, despite its comparatively moderate tone, defended the principle that 'bombs and dynamite' could be vital in bringing about political change.

---

150 S. Stepniak, *Chego nam nuzhno? i Nachalo kontsa* (London: Izdanie Fonda Russkoi Vol'noi Pressy, 1892).

151 For a brief but useful discussion of Stepniak's changing views, including his scepticism about the revolutionary potential of the *narod* throughout the last twenty years of his life, see A. I. Kondratenko, 'Ot khozhdeniia v narod—k sozdaniiu fonda vol'noi russkoi pressy. S. M. Stepniak-Kravchinksii, ego politicheskie vzgliady i propagandistskaia deiatel'nost' v kontekste obshchestvennogo dvizheniia v Rossii 1870–1890-kh godov', *Istoriia: Fakty i Simboly*, 3, 12 (2017), 62–72.

It was almost certainly the manuscript of *Chego nam nuzhno?* that Volkhovskii was commenting on a few months earlier when he suggested that Stepniak should make it clear that he did not belong to any specific party or faction. The pamphlet was nevertheless an expression of both men's views as well as the fundists more generally. The same was true of Volkhovskii's 1894 pamphlet *Chemu uchit 'Konstitutsiia gr. Loris-Melikova'?* (*What Are the Lessons of the Loris-Melikov Constitution?*), a reference to the political reforms put forward by the Minister of Interior in 1881, which were abandoned after the assassination of Aleksandr II.[152] Volkhovskii argued that the refusal of Aleksandr III to take forward the reforms showed how liberal opinion had been mistaken in refusing to support Narodnaia volia. He echoed Stepniak in calling for a political revolution, arguing that the government would only make concessions if it was scared by the 'bogeyman' (*buk*) of revolution.[153] In acknowledging that violence might be needed to force the tsarist government into making concessions, both Stepniak and Volkhovskii showed themselves ready to write in terms that they would probably have avoided—or at least softened—when addressing a British or American audience.

The Russian Free Press Fund also produced a fly-sheet—*Letuchie listki*—that appeared regularly from the end of 1893. It was edited by Volkhovskii, who often included long editorial articles on subjects ranging from international politics to observations about the rule of Nicholas II,[154] although Nikolai Chaikovskii became increasingly involved in its production during the second half of the 1890s. The first number noted that 'in our hands we have accumulated many fragments of information, obtained from both Russian correspondents and the foreign press, which we are not able to publish in the form of pamphlets'.[155] The *listki* were designed to collate this material, presenting readers with news about developments in Russia in general, and the opposition movement in particular. The factual tone was intended to preserve its independence in the fractious debates that raged within the Russian

---

152 F. Volkhovskii, *Chemu uchit 'Konstitutsiia gr. Loris-Melikova'?* (London: Russian Free Press Fund, 1894).

153 For a somewhat different interpretation, that focuses more on Volkhovskii's positive views of liberal reforms, see Senese, *Stepniak-Kravchinskii*, 76–77.

154 F. Volkhovskii, 'Gladston i imperatorskaia diplomatiia', *Letuchie listki*, 31 (23 April 1896); 'Koronatsiia', *Letuchie listki*, 32 (20 May 1896).

155 *Letuchie listki*, 1 (25 December 1893).

opposition movement both in Russia and abroad. The *listki* typically had a print run of a few thousand, although on occasion the number rose to 10,000, probably more than any other émigré publication. Volkhovskii sent copies to senior officials in Petersburg in the hope of appealing to the more liberal *chinovniki*.[156] The *listki* circulated widely both in Russia and abroad, providing an important source of information about revolutionary developments inside the Tsarist Empire, although its silence on tactical and ideological questions did little to moderate the sceptical view among some émigrés about the 'National Front' strategy pursued by Stepniak and Volkhovskii.[157]

The growing number of pages in each edition of the *listki* suggests that its editors had no problem obtaining information (a good deal was translated and included in more digestible form in *Free Russia*).[158] Some material was sent from Russia through the regular mail. Volkhovskii used a series of aliases—'Ivan', Jenkins, Miss Privik—to deceive the tsarist authorities so that they would not open letters and packages addressed to him.[159] The same was true of other members of the Fund. Many Britons who were sympathetic to the 'cause' also received and forwarded correspondence.[160] A good deal of material was sent via third countries such as Sweden.[161] Some was sent in code.[162] The records of the *Okhrana* show that such ruses were not always successful. The Russian secret police were adept in the art of perlustration, intercepting letters before forwarding them seemingly unopened, in order to fool the recipient into assuming they had a secure means of communication

---

156 *Letuchie listki*, 15 (9 February 1895).

157 The best account of this strategy remains Senese, 'S. M. Kravchinskii and the National Front against Autocracy'.

158 Senese by contrast suggests that members of the London emigration sometimes struggled to fill the pages of the *listki* although without much evidence to support the claim. See Senese, *Stepniak-Kravchinskii*, 83.

159 Volkhovskii Papers (HIA), Box 17, Folder 9 (Archivist's note).

160 See, for example, Volkhovskii Papers (Houghton Library), MS Russ 51, 345, Cecily Sidgwick to Volkhovskii (n.d.).

161 Michael Futrell, *Northern Underground. Episodes of Russian Revolutionary Transport and Communications through Scandinavia and Finland, 1863–1917* (London: Faber, 1963), 37.

162 For an example of the code sheet used to decrypt information, along with other useful material about the transportation of illegal material, see Volkhovskii Papers (HIA), Box 10, Folder 6.

which the authorities could then 'tap' into in the future.[163] The *Okhrana* also had more code-breaking expertise than any other police force in the world. The vulnerability of the mail meant that a good deal of material was carried out of Russia by tourists and students travelling to Western Europe. Exile communities across Europe also sometimes forwarded information to London. The sheer quantity of information published in the *listki* shows that information continued to flow out of Russia despite the best efforts of the tsarist authorities to maintain a 'fence around the empire'.

It was still more challenging to smuggle printed material *into* Russia. Some copies of *Free Russia* and *Letuchie listki* were printed on thin paper that made them easier to conceal in luggage.[164] Volkhovskii had in the 1870s played an important role, along with Chudnovskii, in the clandestine import of illegal books and journals into Russia, either shipped through Odessa or smuggled across the frontier with the Habsburg Empire. Twenty years later, the RFPF revived the Odessa corridor. Both Wilfrid and Ethel Voinich had links with Ukrainians living in the Austro-Hungarian Empire which they used to smuggle literature across the Russian border. Ethel visited Lvov (Ukr. L'viv) on several occasions, where she met Ukrainian nationalists including Mykhailo Pavlik and Mykhailo Drahomanov, who introduced her to individuals ready to take material into Russia.[165] Volkhovskii also established cordial relations with radicals in Sweden and Finland—the latter was at the time part of the Tsarist Empire—who helped to smuggle printed material into Russia with the help of trade unionists in north-east England.[166] Both the Northern Underground and the Odessa corridor were subsequently used in the early twentieth century to smuggle guns and explosives into Russia, an enterprise in which several members of the London emigration were involved, but in the 1890s the contraband

---

163 For a detailed account of the development of these techniques in Russia over many centuries, see V. S. Izmozik, *"Chernye kabinety". Istoriia rossiiskoi perliustratsii. XVIII-nachalo XX veka* (Moscow: Novoe literaturnoe obozrenie, 2015).

164 Volkhovskii Papers (HIA), Box 17, Folder 6, Volkhovskii to Aström, 10 February 1895.

165 Taratuta, *Nash drug Etel' Lilian Voinich*, 20 ff.

166 For the role of trade unionists in Britain in assisting the dispatch of illegal material to Russia, see Volkhovskii Papers (HIA), Box 10, Folder 5, Tom Chambers to Volkhovskii, 29 September 1897; J. H. Bell to Volkhovskii, 11 October 1897; Volkhovskii to Bell (n.d.).

seems to have been limited to printed works. The cost of such operations was prohibitive, particularly given that it was virtually impossible for the Fund to receive payment from Russia, but Volkhovskii was confident that material produced in London by the Fund played an important role in helping to build effective revolutionary networks.

The dispatch of money to Russia raised—if anything—still more difficult challenges. The SFRF from its inception launched appeals for funds to help alleviate the victims of famine in Russia. Other appeals were made for money to support the families of political prisoners. Many British supporters of the 'cause' were anxious that their donations should not be used to support terrorism or other forms of violence.[167] The surviving records of the Society do not give any insight into how the money was distributed, but such concerns were almost certainly not ill-founded. When Constance Garnett first visited Russia in 1894, she took with her both letters and cash that Stepniak asked her to distribute, although it is not clear who received the money (her son later wrote that while the money was ostensibly designed for humanitarian relief, there was some doubt whether it would 'get into the right hands').[168] Other visitors also acted as financial couriers. There was no way of knowing how such money would be used. The SFRF noted in its appeals to the British public that donors could specify how they wanted their gifts to be spent, but even if the money was not used to finance any form of violent action, the boundary between 'humanitarian' and 'political' activities was at best uncertain. The accounting distinctions in the Society's records were in any case almost meaningless. Funds that found their way to Russia were not managed in ways familiar to donors accustomed to the more transparent finances of a club or society in late Victorian Britain.

The plans put in motion by Stepniak and Volkhovskii to develop a 'National Front' against autocracy were naïve in underestimating the personal and ideological divisions within the Russian opposition movement. While it was in principle reasonable to hope that a focus on constitutional reform could alleviate the concerns of moderates, most Russian liberals were well aware that many of their putative revolutionary

---

167 See, for example, Volkhovskii Papers (Houghton Library), MS Russ 51, Folder 345, Cecily Sidgwick to Volkhovskii (n.d.).

168 David Garnett, *The Golden Echo* (New York: Harcourt, Brace and Co., 1954), 11.

allies saw such a development as a step on the road to more fundamental social and economic revolution. And, in any case, many revolutionary *narodniki* shared Petr Lavrov's sense that a real revolution could never be brought about by political means. Yet although the challenges facing efforts to build a common front against autocracy were formidable, the mere prospect of such a development caused considerable anxiety back in St Petersburg. The authorities in Russia were not always adept at following the twists and turns of the émigré imbroglio, but they were intensely sensitive to developments beyond the Empire's borders, not least because critics of tsarism used exile abroad to continue the struggle for change. The London emigration was, for much of the 1890s, viewed as a powerful threat to the security of the tsarist regime. The following chapter examines how ministers and *chinovniki* in St Petersburg, along with Russian diplomats and police officials in Western Europe, sought to contain the threat supposedly posed by the small number of exiles grouped around *Free Russia* and the Russian Free Press Fund.

5. Spies and Trials

The emphasis placed by Stepniak and Volkhovskii on building a broad coalition of opposition to the tsarist regime, bringing together liberals and revolutionaries both in Russia and abroad, echoed changes that were taking place in Russia itself. The former leader of the Chaikovskii circle, Marc Natanson, was instrumental in the 1893 formation of a new Partiia narodnogo prava (Party of Popular Rights), designed to serve as a kernel for a broad-based liberation movement.[1] While the membership was small, it attracted support from scholars and writers including the *narodnik* theorist Nikolai Mikhailovskii and the writer Vladimir Korolenko,[2] who urged critics of the tsarist autocracy to unite whatever their other ideological differences. The Party's manifesto published in February 1894 included such characteristically 'liberal' demands as universal suffrage, freedom of religious belief and judicial

---

1   On the Party of Popular Rights, see the dated but still excellent V. V. Shirokova, *Partiia "Narodnogo prava". Iz istorii osvoboditelnogo dvizeniia 90-kh gg. XIX veka* (Saratov: Izd-vo Saratovskogo universiteta, 1972). A shorter account in English can be found in Shmuel Galai, *The Liberation Movement in Russia, 1900–1905* (Cambridge: Cambridge University Press, 1973), 59–65. Of great value both here and elsewhere in this chapter is G. Michael Hamburg, 'The London Emigration and the Russian Liberation Movement: The Problem of Unity, 1889–1897', *Jahrbücher für Geschichte Osteuropas*, 25, 3 (1977), 321–39.

2   On Mikhailovskii's role, see James H. Billington, *Mikhailovsky and Russian Populism* (New York: Oxford University Press, 1958), 157–60. Some details of Korolenko's activities, including his trip to Britain and America in 1893, can be found in Evgeniia Taratuta, *S. M. Stepniak-Kravchinskii. Revoliutsioner i pisatel'* (Moscow: Khudozhestvennaia literatura, 1973), 481–85. See, too, Charles A. Moser, 'Korolenko and America', *Russian Review*, 28, 3 (1969), 303–14. Also see Richard Garnett, *Constance Garnett: A Heroic Life* (London: Sinclair-Stevenson, 1991), 102–04. For a useful discussion of 'liberal populism', a label that can perhaps be applied to Korolenko and others grouped around the journal *Russkoe bogatstvo*, see B. P. Baluev, *Liberal'noe narodnichestvo na rubezhe XIX–XX vekov* (Moscow: Nauka, 1995); G. N. Mokshin, *Evoliutsiia ideologii legal'nogo narodnichestva v poslednei trety XIX–nachale XX vv.* (Voronezh: Nauchnaia Kniga, 2010).

    https://doi.org/10.11647/OBP.0385.05

independence. Although it was broken up shortly afterwards, members of the Natanson circle had during the previous year started to develop links with like-minded Russian émigrés abroad. Korolenko visited Britain and America in 1893, as a kind of unofficial ambassador of the circle, meeting Stepniak and Volkhovskii in London. He also met with Egor Lazarev in Chicago (Lazarev himself soon departed for Paris, with the intention of founding a new journal there, although he was forced to move to London after coming under pressure from the French authorities).[3] Although these meetings yielded little of real substance, they symbolised a willingness among at least some members of the opposition movement to work together, despite their differences, as well as the potential for building closer ties between critics of the tsarist regime both at home and abroad.

The *Okhrana* devoted considerable energy to keeping abreast of these developments. Petr Rachkovskii, as head of the Paris *agentura* (agency), recognised that a more united opposition movement could pose a powerful challenge to the Russian government. He was also intensely aware that close ties between political exiles abroad and critics of the tsarist government in Russia itself could make the threat still more menacing. Rachkovskii had been concerned about the activities of the Society of Friends of Russian Freedom and the Russian Free Press Fund from the moment they were established. He first visited London in 1891 to get a better sense of the situation there,[4] and was concerned enough by what he saw to devote a good deal of time and effort over the following years to undermining the activities of Stepniak, Volkhovskii and others. Volkhovskii wrote in 1897 in an unpublished history of the SFRF that

> throughout the [first] seven years of its existence the Society of Friends of Russian Freedom as well as the whole pro-Russian movement never ceased to be the objects of the fiercest and most unscrupulous attacks ... the most determined of these was the campaign of 1894 when articles aimed at undermining the influence of the Society and the progress of the movement were almost simultaneously smuggled into the English, French, German & Russian press ... it was just that time when several bombs which exploded in public places of Spain, France, and even England have worked up the fears of the public at large to a pitch at

---

3   Hamburg, 'London Emigration', 328–29.
4   Robert Henderson, *Vladimir Burtsev and the Struggle for a Free Russia* (London: Bloomsbury, 2017), 37.

which the commands of cool reason and the securities of liberty become indangered (*sic*) ... the faithful servants of the Tsar's irresponsible rule poured out the vilest calumnies against Stepniak, Dr Spence Watson, F. Volkhovsky and others ...[5]

The 1894 campaign mentioned by Volkhovskii was the culmination of a sustained effort by the *Okhrana* to counter the threat posed by Russian revolutionaries in London. Rachkovskii had for some years been confident that he could rely on the French authorities, and particularly the Paris Sûreté, to help contain the threat posed by Russian political exiles in France.[6] The situation was more difficult in Britain, where public suspicion of Russia was greater. Rachkovskii requested funds from St Petersburg as early as 1890 to increase the capacity of the Paris *agentura* to monitor developments in London, since it was becoming an increasingly important centre of opposition, a suspicion confirmed by the arrival of Volkhovskii, Voinich and (early in 1891) Vladimir Burtsev. Over the next few years, he orchestrated extensive efforts to infiltrate the networks around the SFRF and the RFPF, while encouraging senior officials in St Petersburg to put pressure on the British government to follow its French counterpart in taking action to prevent Russian exiles from organising effectively.

Stepniak was for Rachkovskii the *bête noire* of the London émigrés, both for his rhetorical defence of terrorism and his assassination of General Mezentsev in St Petersburg in 1878. It was perhaps curious that the head of the Paris *agentura* did not make more of the killing when organising 'smear campaigns' against the London emigration in the early 1890s. While Stepniak's role as an assassin was well-known in revolutionary circles, many Britons and Americans who met him seemed oblivious to the idea that his rhetorical defence of terrorism reflected (in the most brutal sense of the term) 'hands-on' experience. The *New York Tribune* noted as early as February 1890 that Stepniak had killed Mezentsev,[7] but such suggestions seem to have been widely

---

5   Volkhovskii Papers (HIA), Box 6, Folder 16 (Unpublished and untitled article by Volkhovskii on the history of the SFRF).

6   For a useful discussion of Rachkovskii's time in Paris, see Fredrick Zuckerman, 'Policing the Russian Emigration in Paris, 1880–1914: The Twentieth Century as the Century of Political Police', *French History and Civilisation*, 2 (2009), 218–27.

7   *New York Tribune* (2 February 1890). For attempts by George Kennan to counter the claims, which he feared could damage support for the 'cause' in North America, see RGALI, f. 1158, op. 1, ed. khr. 232, Volkhovskii to Stepniak, 12 February 1890.

discounted, or indeed simply added to Stepniak's mystique. Rachkovskii was presumably anxious, at least for a time, not to add to this aura of revolutionary glamour by making more of the murder.

The other figure in the London emigration who attracted particular attention from Rachkovskii was Vladimir Burtsev,[8] who had previously been a member of Narodnaia volia, for which he was condemned to exile in Siberia before escaping abroad in 1888. Burtsev lived for a time in Switzerland, where he edited a short-lived journal *Svobodnaia Rossiia* (*Free Russia*), before fleeing to Constantinople. Here he boarded a British ship, under the protection of a captain who refused to surrender him to Turkish and Russian officials, on the grounds that the ship was English territory, and he—the captain—was a gentleman (Volkhovskii later organised a fund-raising campaign to buy him a silver cup).[9] Burtsev arrived in Britain in January 1891, and was quickly spirited away from the docks by Volkhovskii, in order to shield him from the attention of tsarist informers (the two men remained on good terms in the years that followed).[10] Rachkovskii was nevertheless still able to keep the Minister of the Interior P. N. Durnovo informed about Burtsev's movements (reports that were sometimes forwarded to Tsar Aleksandr III for comment).[11] Burtsev played an important role over the next two decades both in chronicling the history of the revolutionary movement and in unmasking tsarist *agents provocateurs* and infiltrators.[12] Why he attracted such attention from the tsarist authorities during his first few years in London is nevertheless something of a mystery. Although he subsequently published a journal in 1897 that included a piece calling for the assassination of the Tsar—an incident discussed later in this

---

8   On Burtsev's revolutionary career before arriving in London in early 1891, see Henderson, *Vladimir Burtsev*, 9–69. Dr Henderson's book (and the associated PhD thesis) have been invaluable in preparing this chapter.

9   *Times* (19 January 1891).

10 Volkhovskii had been receiving information about Burtsev's movements for some time before his arrival in London. See, for example, Spence Watson / Weiss Papers (Newcastle University), SW 1/19/1, Volkhovskii to Spence Watson, 2 January (1891). For an example of later correspondence between Volkhovskii and Burtsev see, for example, Volkhovskii Papers (HIA), Box 1, Folder 12, Burtsev to Volkhovskii, 10 December 1894.

11 Hamburg, 'London Emigration', passim.

12 On Burtsev's place in the emigration, see David Saunders, 'Vladimir Burtsev and the Russian Revolutionary Emigration (1888–1905)', *European History Quarterly*, 13, 1 (1983), 39–62.

chapter—he was during the first half of the 1890s generally in favour of building a broad opposition movement rather than reviving the terrorist strategy of Narodnaia volia. It may be that it was precisely this prospect that concerned Rachkovskii.

Rachkovskii did not at first consider Volkhovskii to pose such a threat as Stepniak or Burtsev. Volkhovskii was himself in exile when Narodnaia volia assassinated Aleksandr II in 1881, and took no part in the conspiracy, although it was noted in a previous chapter that he would probably have become an active supporter if he had remained at liberty. There is certainly no evidence to suggest that he disagreed with Stepniak's view that the terrorists who killed Aleksandr II had been inspired by anything other than the highest ethical motives. And, in pamphlets such as *Chemu uchit 'Konstitutsiia gr. Loris-Melikova?'*, Volkhovskii strongly implied that violence was likely to be needed to extract political concessions from the tsarist government. Rachkovskii, at least for a time, underestimated Volkhovskii's role in the London emigration.

The novelist Ford Maddox Ford, who had good links with the Russian colony in London in the two decades before the First World War, wrote in his memoirs how during this time:

> The fact England was the international refuge for all exiles was not agreeable to the Russian police who filled the country with an incredible number of spies. There must have been at least one for every political exile and the annoyance they caused in the country was extreme. I remember between 1893 and 1894 going home for longish periods almost every night from London University to a western suburb with Stepniak, Volkhofsky or Prince Kropotkin who were then the most prominent members of the Russian extreme left and who were lecturing at the University on political economy, Russian literature and, I think, biology respectively. And behind us always lurked or dodged the Russian spies allotted to each of these distinguished lecturers. Them Stepniak or Volkhofsky dismissed at Hammersmith Station, as often as not with the price of a pint, for the poor devils were miserably paid, and also because, the spies and their purpose being perfectly well known in the district where the Russians lived they were apt to receive very rough handling from the residents who resented their presence as an insult to the country. One or two quite considerable riots were thus caused in the neighbourhoods of Hammersmith proper and Ealing.[13]

---

13 Ford Maddox Ford, *Return to Yesterday* (London: Victor Gollanz, 1931), 133–34.

Ford's recollections may have owed as much to imagination as to reality. The idea that London was full of Russian spies was a common perception at the time.[14] In reality, though, the number of 'spies'—whether *Okhrana* informants or retired British police officers paid to keep Russia émigrés under surveillance—was never very large in the years before 1914.[15] But nor were Ford's recollections altogether false. Rachkovskii was anxious to monitor the Russian émigré colony in London, employing agents to report on the activities of those involved in running *Free Russia* and the Russian Free Press Fund, with the result that by the end of the nineteenth century the cost of operations in Britain was consuming a very significant part of the budget of the *Okhrana*'s Foreign Agency.[16]

Rachkovskii's principal agent in London was a Frenchman, Edgar Farce, who had previously worked for the Paris *agentura* before moving to the British capital in the late 1880s.[17] Although the detail in his reports was quite limited, consisting of little more than descriptions of the comings and goings of members of the Russian community, leavened with French translations of articles in *Free Russia*, his letters to Rachkovskii still provided useful information. They also give an interesting insight into the importance Farce attached to the various members of the émigré community, given that he only had the resources to organise surveillance of a small number of them at any one time (Farce carried out some surveillance in person although he also paid a small number of informants). Volkhovskii figures as much as any other Russian in the reports Farce sent to Paris in the first half of the 1890s (his name

---

14   See, for example, the report by the Vienna correspondent in the *Times* (3 January 1891).

15   On the operations of the Paris *agentura* and its various branches across Europe see, V. K. Agafonov, *Zagranichnaia okhranka* (Petrograd: Kniga, 1918); V. S. Brachev, *Zagranichnaia agentura departmenta politsii (1883–1917)* (St Petersburg: Stomma, 2001); Richard J. Johnson, 'Zagranichnaia Agentura: The Tsarist Political Police in Europe', *Journal of Contemporary History*, 7, 1 (1972), 221–42; Charles A. Ruud and Sergei A. Stepanov, *Fontanka 16: The Tsar's Secret Police* (Montreal: McGill-Queens's University Press, 1999), 79–100; Frederick Zuckerman, *The Tsarist Police Abroad* (New York: Palgrave Macmillan, 2003). Some sense of the number of agents employed in Western Europe can be found in S. V. Deviatov et al. (eds), *Terrorizm v Rossii v nachale XX v.*, *Istoricheskii vestnik*, 149 (Moscow: Runivers, 2012), 179–88. The list is very incomplete.

16   For useful discussions of expenditure by the *Okhrana* abroad, see Agafonov, *Zagranichnaia okhranka*, 28–54 (in particular the summary chart on 53–54).

17   On Farce, see Robert Henderson, *The Spark That Lit the Revolution. Lenin in London and the Politics That Changed the World* (London: I. B. Tauris, 2020), 118–20.

occurs with about the same frequency as Voinich and Burtsev and more regularly than Stepniak's). The fact that Rachkovskii does not seem to have queried Farce's *modus operandi* suggests that both men recognised that Stepniak was, for all his charisma and popularity, seldom the central figure in the work of *Free Russia* and the Free Press Fund.

Farce occasionally got access to letters dispatched by members of the émigré community, apparently through subterfuge rather than perlustration,[18] although he does not seem to have made much sustained attempt to develop personal relations with Russian exiles in London. Many of his reports contained accounts of Volkhovskii's movements, in particular his meetings with Voinich and other fundists, as well as descriptions of his research at the British Museum Library.[19] Farce also followed members of the fund transporting boxes of publications to the East End, presumably destined for Russia, although the Frenchman was not certain.[20] He heard early on about the growing tension between Voinich and the other fundists (his reports rightly suggested that the break may not have been as definite as sometimes assumed).[21] Farce tried valiantly to keep up with the movements of the most prominent fundists, regularly providing detailed lists of names and addresses, and periodically reported on rumours of bomb plots, but without providing any evidence that his 'marks' were involved in such activities.

Farce did not always understand the significance of what was taking place in front of him, not least because Rachkovskii regularly failed to provide him with relevant information. When Farce noted towards the end of 1894 that a certain Lev Beitner had arrived in London, where he spent much of his time with his 'great friend' Burtsev,[22] Rachkovskii apparently neglected to tell him that Beitner was an *Okhrana* informant

---

18   See, for example, Okhrana archive (HIA), Index IIb, Folder 2, Farce to Rachkovskii, 25 October 1895 (microfilm 13).

19   Okhrana Archive (HIA), Index IIb, Folder 2, Farce to Rachkovskii, 18 June 1894 (microfilm 13). See, too, Colin Higgins, 'The Guttural Sorrow of the Refugees—Constance Garnett and Felix Volkhovsky in the British Museum', *Materialy X Mezhdunarodnogo seminara perevodchikov* (2016), www.repository.cam.ac.uk/handle/1810/252929bb.

20   Okhrana Archive (HIA), Index IIb, Folder 2, Farce to Rachkovskii, 18 June 1895 (microfilm 13).

21   Okhrana Archive (HIA), Index IIb, Folder 2, Farce to Rachkovskii, 29 January 1895 (microfilm 13).

22   Okhrana Archive (HIA), Index IIb, Folder 2, Farce to Rachkovskii, 8 November 1894 (microfilm 13).

paid to report on Burtsev. Yet Farce's reports show that he did have some insight into the networks that shaped the activities of the Russian Free Press Fund. He knew that Volkhovskii and Voinich were the key figures involved in the practical business of producing and distributing the Fund's publications (at least before Voinich stood down from his role). Farce also recognised the important part played by Lazarev during his time in London, in 1894–96, although he does not seem to have obtained copies of the voluminous correspondence Lazarev maintained with Russian exiles across Europe, which provided much of the material that appeared in *Letuchie listki*. Stepniak and Chaikovskii were more detached from day-to-day operations (although Chaikovskii became increasingly active after Lazarev's departure for Switzerland). Farce's reports also show how Russian émigrés who came and went across the channel provided a critical link between the London emigration and its counterparts in Western Europe. The transnational character of the Russian revolutionary emigration was also well-known to Special Branch, including Inspector Melville, who had himself spent much of his early career in France monitoring the movement of political radicals to and from Britain.[23]

Rachkovskii claimed as early as 1891 that he had 'complete control' of the situation in London, in part through the recruitment of an informer with access to the inner workings of the SFRF.[24] It seems unlikely this was true. Efforts were made in 1892 to use an eccentric Pole named Boleslaw Maliankewicz to infiltrate the Society, but he proved desperately unreliable, sending back implausible reports that the mild-mannered William Morris had made a series of blood-curdling suggestions at one of its meetings.[25] Lev Beitner was subsequently more successful, establishing friendly relations with Volkhovskii and other émigrés active in the SFRF and the RFPF,[26] but his reports too seem to

23   Andrew Cook, *M. MI5's First Spymaster* (London: Tempus, 2004), 47–57. For a discussion of the development of Special Branch including the monitoring of subversives both foreign and domestic, see Bernard Porter, *The Origins of the Vigilant State: The London Metropolitan Police Special Branch before the First World War* (London: Weidenfeld and Nicolson, 1987). See, too, Ray Wilson, *Special Branch: A History* (London: Biteback Publishing, 2015), Chapter 2.
24   Henderson, *Vladimir Burtsev*, 37.
25   Henderson, *Vladimir Burtsev*, 57.
26   Some insight into the seemingly cordial relationship between the two men can be gleaned from the material in Volkhovskii Papers (Houghton Library), MS Russ 51,

have contained little of real value. Nor was the Russian government at first any more successful when trying to use formal diplomatic channels to persuade its British counterpart to take a robust line towards Russian exiles in London. Early in 1892, the Russian ambassador in London, Baron E. E. Staal, complained to the British Foreign Office that:

> The number of Russian revolutionaries and nihilists based in England, which was already considerable, has acquired, during these past years, a number of recruits expelled from Switzerland, France and elsewhere. The activities of this emigration, under the aegis of the 'right of asylum' have grown in intensity and are currently conducted by such coryphees of terrorist revolution as Prince Kropotkin, Chaikovskii, Kravchinskii (the assassin of General Mezentsev, known under the name of Stepniak), Felix Volkhovskii, Vladimir Burtsev, Michel Voinich (Kelchevskii), Michel-Moise Harmidor (Baranov), Hesper Serebriakov, Stanislaw Mendelssohn and his wife Marie, Aleksandr Lavrenius and many others besides.[27]

The Memorandum went on to complain about the publication of 'the grossest calumnies' against the Russian government in *Free Russia*, as well as Stepniak's pamphlet *Chego nam nuzhno?*, which defended 'military plots ... bombs, dynamite'. The British Prime Foreign Secretary (and Prime Minister) Lord Salisbury was not unsympathetic, although he knew it would be almost impossible to secure a conviction without evidence of definite wrongdoing, a bland response that predictably caused frustration in the Russian capital, cementing a view that English judges under the guise of defending the 'ancient traditions of asylum' were really nit-picking and pedantic.[28] Rachkovskii in Paris fumed with frustration.

The campaign orchestrated against the London emigration referred to by Volkhovskii in his history of the SFRF, which erupted at the start

Folder 190, Beitner to Volkhovskii (various dates).

27 I am indebted to the research of Dr Robert Henderson who located the original version of the Memorandum, a copy of which can be found in The National Archives Kew (henceforth TNA), FO 65/1429. The translation given here is that of Dr Henderson in his 'Vladimir Burtsev and the Russian Revolutionary Emigration: Surveillance of Foreign Political Refugees in London, 1991–1905' (PhD thesis, Queen Mary College University of London, 2008), 98.

28 See, too, the untitled document in the Okhrana Archive (HIA), Index Vc, Folder 1 (microfilm 69), which appears to cover much the same ground as Staal's memorandum, although the language is not identical.

of 1894, marked a new phase in the efforts of the Russian authorities
to control what they saw as a significant threat. In January 1894, the
New Review published an article on 'Anarchists: Their Methods and
Organisation' (the timing was probably a response to the start of George
Kennan's high-profile lecture tour of England in early January).[29] The
first part of the article, by 'Z', attacked foreign anarchists who had
flocked to Britain over the previous few years as 'unscrupulous agents
of the new terror', and 'expert swindlers' of 'the worst character', who
espoused political ends to mask their own criminality. The second part,
by 'Ivanoff', focused more closely on the Russian 'nihilists' in London,
using a language that echoed the Memorandum handed to the Foreign
Office two years earlier. It challenged the idea that the 'nihilists' were
people of honour and integrity, in the tradition of Kossuth and Mazzini,
instead conflating them with the anarchists so roundly condemned by
Z. Ivanoff argued that no self-respecting Briton should associate with
men and women whose sole object was to use violence ('dynamite') to
overthrow 'human civilization'.[30]

Although Ivanoff did not refer to Stepniak by name, he made
no effort to conceal the principal object of his attack. He condemned
'Stepniak' for his 'grandiloquent but empty verbosity' and 'shallow
theories of free love', but above all for his brutal murder of Mezentsev
('the murderer, sneaking on tip-toe, assaulted the General, plunging
the kitchen-knife into his abdomen' before repeatedly twisting round
the knife in 'the open wound'). Volkhovskii as deputy editor of *Free
Russia* was second only to Stepniak as a target. Ivanoff described how
Volkhovskii toured the country giving 'highly-coloured' accounts of
his time in Russian prisons to attract financial contributions from the
citizens of cities like Leicester and London. He also deplored the way
in which politicians 'sing his praises' and presented his experiences
as evidence of the brutality of the Russian government. The unsubtle
theme of Ivanoff's polemic was that British supporters of the 'nihilists'
had been unwittingly duped by Russian exiles in London, who were
working to promote violent revolution, while hiding their true intentions
behind a veneer of moderation. The dramatic explosion of a bomb in

29   For a report of Kennan's first lecture, see *Times* (9 January 1894).
30   Z and Ivanoff, 'Anarchists: Their Methods and Organisation', *The New Review*, 10,
     56 (January 1894), 1–16.

Greenwich Park, a few weeks after the article appeared, can only have helped to bolster Ivanoff's case, even though the only fatality was the French anarchist carrying the device.[31]

Ivanoff was almost certainly a pseudonym for Rachkovskii (who had down the years acquired great experience writing such pieces for the French press). The article may have been drafted some time before, perhaps in 1892, but could not at that stage find a publisher. The identity of Z is unclear, but may have been Inspector Melville, who worked closely with Rachkovskii over the following years in harassing Russian revolutionaries in London. Melville later recalled that Rachkovskii was 'a very hospitable man and a genial character' who 'always called upon me at New Scotland Yard'. He noted the Russian employed several agents in London, 'ostensibly to look after the Nihilists', and was accompanied by many more whenever he visited the British capital in person. Melville was nevertheless 'somewhat suspicious of [Rachkovskii]' although 'without exactly knowing why'.[32] Even so, the two men cooperated closely throughout the 1890s, and although Rachkovskii never obtained the same influence with the British police that he had in Paris, he was undoubtedly successful both in countering the influence of *Free Russia* and the SFRF as well as disrupting the activities of the Free Press Fund.

Ivanoff's article predictably attracted a vigorous response from members of the London emigration and their supporters (*Letuchie listki* published a translation of a detailed rebuttal by Spence Watson).[33] Stepniak penned a long piece in the following month's *New Review* in the form of a piece titled 'Nihilism as It Is', noting that Ivanoff's article had almost certainly been 'fathered by the Russian police' in order to damage the reputation of the émigrés grouped around *Free Russia* and the SFRF. He argued that anarchism had almost no presence as an ideology in the Russian revolutionary movement, which was largely though not entirely true, and added that the principal focus of 'the Russian people' was on

---

31   For reports about the Greenwich Park bomb and growing concern about foreign anarchists in London see, for example, *Daily Telegraph* (17 February 1894; 27 February 1894); *Times* (17 February 1894); *Freeman's Journal* (17 February 1894); *Globe* (16 February 1894). It was of course the Greenwich Park bomb incident that provided the inspiration for Joseph Conrad's 1907 novel *The Secret Agent*.

32   TNA, KV 1/8 (Memoir by William Melville), 15.

33   Robert Spence Watson, 'Grianul', grom, da ne iz tuchi', *Letuchie listki*, 3 (23 March 1894). The piece was presumably translated by Volkhovskii.

the struggle 'to obtain a Constitutional government'. He dismissed as 'moonshine' the idea that Russians involved in the SFRF and the Free Press Fund were involved in dynamite plots. He also seemed to dismiss, though in rather guarded terms, the charge that he had been involved in the Mezentsev murder, suggesting that if 'unimpeachable evidences' existed then the Russian government should arrange for him to be arraigned before an English court. He ended by noting that Ivanoff's accusations would 'never injure my reputation in the eyes of sensible people'.[34]

Despite this robust response, there was a certain amount of substance in the attacks by Z and Ivanoff, while Stepniak's claim that the Russian revolutionary movement was focused above all on constitutional reform was at best misleading. The furore certainly had an impact on the way that the SFRF and Russian exiles were viewed in Britain over the following year.[35] A number of papers reproduced extracts from Stepniak's 'Nihilism as It Is', noting his rebuttal of Ivanoff's charges, but typically without much comment.[36] Even papers that were generally supportive of the 'cause', like the *Daily News*, were conspicuously quiet in their response. A Liberal government headed by Gladstone had been returned in the General Election that took place in the summer of 1892, which may explain why Rachkovskii for a time refrained from launching such a public diatribe against the London emigration, hoping that the Russian government could use diplomatic pressure to encourage its British counterpart to take a tougher line against Stepniak, Volkhovskii and others. The publication of 'Anarchists: Their Methods and Organisation' certainly raised concern within the government. Several Liberal MPs withdrew from the General Committee of the SFRF, possibly under pressure from Gladstone himself, so as to distance themselves from the controversy. The articles by Z and Ivanoff inevitably raised concern about whether support for the 'cause' was appropriate for members of the political establishment.

---

34   S. Stepniak, 'Nihilism as It Is (A Reply)', *The New Review*, 10, 57 (February 1894), 215–22.
35   See, for example, *Beverley and East Riding Recorder* (3 February 1894); *Glasgow Herald* (6 December 1894); *Wells Journal* (4 January 1894).
36   See, for example, *Globe* (2 February 1894).

Ivanoff's article also helped to illuminate the ambiguous attitude of many British supporters of the 'cause' towards the use of force to bring about change in Russia. Stepniak and Volkhovskii had for some years engaged in a kind of semi-conscious self-fashioning, which allowed them to 'fit in' with the *mores* of late Victorian society, even as they simultaneously embodied an alien culture that intrigued so many Britons caught up in the Russian craze.[37] Ivanoff's article undoubtedly came as a shock to those, such as Olive Garnett, who had lionised Stepniak (she described the article in her diary as 'a clever mixture of truth unfavourably represented & falsehood in the guise of truth').[38] Like many others, Olive struggled to reconcile 'her' Stepniak with the murderer who twisted the knife round and round in Mezentsev's stomach (although both she and her sister-in-law Constance Garnett agreed that, while they condemned Stepniak's act, they retained 'implicit confidence' in him).[39] Nor was she alone in being more comfortable with abstract justifications of terrorism than the grisly reality of murder and violence. Many members of the SFRF—particularly those from a nonconformist background—had always been concerned about the issue. There is no firm evidence that publication of 'Anarchists: Their Methods and Organisation' led to a drop in membership of the SFRF or a decline in subscriptions to *Free Russia*. It did nevertheless raise questions that Stepniak and Volkhovskii had for some years carefully tried to keep unasked. Constance Garnett noted in the middle of 1894 that her publisher had refused to include a Preface by Stepniak to her translation of Turgenev's *Rudin* given the recent revelations about his earlier life.[40] A few months earlier, when Volkhovskii was due to speak

---

37　For the classic discussion of 'self-fashioning' and the malleability of self in the context of Renaissance England, see Stephen Greenblatt, *Renaissance Self-Fashioning: From More to Shakespeare* (Chicago, IL: Chicago University Press, 1984).

38　Barry C. Johnson (ed.), *Olive and Stepniak. The Bloomsbury Diary of Olive Garnett, 1893–95* (Birmingham: Bartletts Press, 1993), 19. The entry is headed 29 December 1893—the edition of *The New Review* containing the article by Ivanoff was published just before the New Year. Volkhovskii first heard about the appearance of the article from Olive.

39　Richard Garnett, *Constance Garnett*, 114.

40　Garnett Papers (Northwestern University), Box 11, Folder 2, Constance Garnett to Richard Garnett, 18 June 1894.

at Oxford at the height of the Ivanoff controversy, a friend warned him that even among supporters 'the Anarchist scare is on their minds'.[41]

Although Stepniak did not 'go to ground' in the last two years of his life, he appeared far less than before in public, and contributed fewer articles to the press. While the reasons are not altogether clear, Ivanoff's diatribe certainly compromised his effectiveness as the public face of the 'cause', even if some newspapers believed that he had enjoyed the 'best of the argument' in the polemical struggle with the authors of 'Anarchists: Their Methods and Organisation'.[42] Volkhovskii increasingly took the lead throughout 1894 in the public campaign against the Russian government. Two weeks after the *New Review* article first appeared, he addressed a large audience in Piccadilly, at which he dismissed talk of 'the daggers and bombs of the Nihilist' as 'an old song'. He also repeated the familiar argument that there was no moral equivalence between the architects of 'a Barcelona outrage'—a reference to the bombs thrown by anarchists in the city's opera house a few weeks earlier—and the use of violence by 'a Russian *intelligent* to who[m] all other expressions of dissent were denied'.[43]

Volkhovskii also shaped the response of *Free Russia* to the new landscape created by Ivanoff. In February 1894, he contributed a lengthy piece arguing that attacks on the SFRF in Russian newspapers, including *Moskovskie vedomosti* (*Moscow News*), were evidence that the Russian government was feeling threatened. He also poured scorn on the idea that members of the Society were closet anarchists hoping to overthrow society.[44] The following month, he wrote a piece attacking an article in *Novoe vremia* (*New Times*) that called for greater international action against anarchists, and rejected the charge that members of the London emigration could spend money raised by the SFRF as they wished (an accusation that carried the clear implication that funds were used to support violent activity).[45] And then, in May 1894, Volkhovskii published the first part of a long article on *The Claims of the Russian Liberals*, which was designed to persuade its British and American

---

41 Volkhovskii Papers (HIA), Box 18, Folder 6, Charlotte Sidgwick to Volkhovskii, 22 February 1894.
42 *Liverpool Mercury* (30 January 1894).
43 *Pall Mall Gazette* (29 January 1894).
44 F. Volkhovsky, 'A Beneficial Attack', *Free Russia* (1 February 1894).
45 F. Volkhovsky, 'Belligerent Impotence', *Free Russia* (1 March 1894).

readers that the autocratic government in St Petersburg would never willingly make political concessions.[46]

Volkhovskii argued in *Claims* that liberal members of the various *zemstva* (provincial assemblies) in Russia had given up hopes of bringing about political change, since their appeals were always ignored by the government, with the result that those who hold 'the landed property of the Empire' and 'to a large extent the different branches of manufacture and trade look with great dissatisfaction upon the present arbitrary Russian rule'. He went on to suggest that 'The peaceful elements of society, after having kept for years loyal to the fantastic idea of replacing the present arbitrary mode of government by a representative one while at the same time remaining loyal to the autocracy, came finally to the conclusion that the present autocratic Russian Government would never give up its unnatural prerogatives' unless forced to do so. Volkhovskii was in some ways echoing the line he had taken in his earlier pamphlet on the planned Loris-Melikov reforms, although he was more cautious about suggesting to his English-language readers that the tsarist government would only offer reform in response to the threat of revolution, instead writing more vaguely about 'the pressure of popular wishes'. *Claims of the Russian Liberals* was designed to persuade its readers in Western Europe and North America—*contra* Ivanoff—that opposition to the tsarist government was not confined to 'a small number of troublesome people full of perverted ideas'. Volkhovskii instead wanted his readers to understand that the sharp binary between anarchist and loyal subject, implicit in the pieces by both Z and Ivanoff, did not exist in Russia, and that a broad opposition was emerging there in response to the government's consistent refusal to offer any kind of reform. He concluded with an optimistic suggestion that the recent appearance of the Popular Rights Party showed how public opinion 'is no longer a myth. History cannot be stopped, and it is not impossible that even our generation will see yet great political changes in Russia'.

---

46 The first part of the article by Volkhovskii, 'The Political Claims of the Russian Liberals', appeared in *Free Russia*, 1 May 1894, and continued in the following two numbers. He subsequently reprinted his articles with slight changes in a pamphlet that appeared in *Nihilism as It Is. Being Stepniak's Pamphlets Translated by E. E. Voynich, and Felix Volkhovsky's 'Claims of the Russian Liberals' with an Introduction by Dr R. Spence Watson* (London: T. Fisher Unwin, 1894). The quotations in the following paragraph are taken from the pamphlet.

Claims of the Russian Liberals was published in book form in the autumn of 1894 along with other material, including Stepniak's *Nihilism as It Is*, and a translation of the letter sent by Narodnaia volia to Aleksandr III after the assassination of his father offering to end violence in return for political concessions. The collection was designed, in the words of Spence Watson, who wrote the Introduction, to introduce the 'reader ... to the inner life of the so-called, and mis-called, Nihilists'. He went on to suggest, both inaccurately and naively, that the various pieces taken together showed how:

> the fundamental objects of all Russian Revolutionists (however they may call themselves or be called by others) are the same; that their struggle is for freedom, national and personal; and they forcibly urge the necessity of laying aside all matters which are not absolutely essential, and of working closely and unitedly together for those fundamental objects which all alike hold dear.[47]

The response in the British press was less than overwhelming. While many newspapers and journals noted that they had received a copy of *Nihilism as It Is*, few went on to print reviews, evidence perhaps that the recent attacks by Z and Ivanoff had hit home. One of the reviews that did appear, in the *Pall Mall Gazette*, questioned how Stepniak could 'with an easy conscience, recommend the sort of bomb-throwing, palace-hoisting, train-wrecking which may kill or maim dozens of innocent persons, as well as the one whose death is intended'.[48] It was a telling statement at a time when fears about anarchist violence were on the rise in Britain. Newspapers and journals were becoming more cautious about eulogising Russian revolutionaries as the innocent victims of tsarist oppression.

Volkhovskii continued to use *Free Russia* to try to convince readers that support for political reform was growing in Russia. At the end of 1894, he wrote a piece telling readers about a proposal for a new constitution that had recently been received in London, based on the principle of limited hereditary monarchy and the development of new local and national assemblies with the power to approve legislation.[49]

---

47 *Nihilism as It Is*, ix.
48 *Pall Mall Gazette* (8 February 1895).
49 F. Volkhovsky, 'A Constitution for Russia', *Free Russia* (1 November 1894). The full document can be found in *Letuchie listki*, 11 (Prilozhenie) (31 October 1894).

The document was drafted by a prominent Russian jurist and distributed covertly in Moscow and St Petersburg. While Volkhovskii had some doubts about elements of the proposed constitution—not least because he was a convinced Republican—he believed that its appearance was 'an event of great political importance' (the Free Press Fund printed 3,000 copies for distribution back to Russia). Rachkovskii in Paris agreed, from a very different perspective, warning his superiors in Petersburg that the proposal was evidence of a growing movement to seek political reform through 'broad-based social activism'.[50]

At the time Volkhovskii wrote his piece for *Free Russia*, he could not know that the unexpected death of Aleksandr III a few weeks later at the age of forty-nine, from kidney disease, would raise the whole question of the role of representative bodies in the life of the Empire. He spent the last few weeks of 1894 lecturing up and down Britain, hoping to counter the lingering damage caused by Ivanoff,[51] but was perturbed to find that many in the audience believed that the new Tsar Nicholas II would soon address the kind of abuses routinely highlighted by *Free Russia*. Similar sentiments were expressed by several newspapers. In January 1895, Volkhovskii warned that the British press was attributing to the new Tsar intentions that 'were really only their own wishes'.[52] He repeated the caution in a short speech introducing Egor Lazarev at a meeting in Oxford. It was therefore no surprise to Volkhovskii when Nicholas II, at a meeting with representatives from the *zemstva*, dismissed any thoughts of convening some form of National Assembly as 'senseless dreams'. The incident seemed to confirm his argument in *Claims of the Russian Liberals* that the tsarist government would not make even the most modest of political concessions unless forced to do so. The following month, *Free Russia* printed an article by Stepniak roundly declaring that 'the whole nation cannot take the path leading to mental suicide; the gauntlet thrown down by the Tzar will be taken up. He wants war; there will be war. But by whom, and how will it be

---

50 Hamburg, 'London Emigration', 330.
51 See, for example, the reports of meetings in Derby and Clitheroe in *Derby Daily Telegraph* (16 November 1894); *Preston Herald* (15 December 1894).
52 F. Volkhovsky, 'The Dangers of the Present Attitude of the Press', *Free Russia* (1 January 1895).

carried on? The Tzar has challenged—not the revolutionists alone—but the whole of Russian society'.[53]

Volkhovskii used the pages of *Letuchie listki* to support calls for a national assembly, printing a copy of an Open Letter to Nicholas II that was circulating in Russia, which argued that such a proposal was not designed to destroy the government but rather prevent it from 'digging its own grave'.[54] Other documents reproduced in the *listki* included a call for an end to censorship. In an editorial 'The Next Step', which appeared in May 1895, Volkhovskii called for a the creation of a new publication that would bring together the whole Russian opposition 'from the most moderate to the most extreme' ('ot samoi umerennoi do samoi krainei').[55] The proposal attracted support from some liberals and liberal-minded *narodniki* back in Russia, and by the summer the idea had been floated that the *listki* could itself become such an organ, although the prospect caused some tensions within the London emigration (developments that were followed with care by Rachkovskii in Paris).[56] A number of Russian moderates, including the writer Petr Boborykin, visited London in the second half of 1895 to discuss plans. The substance of the discussions is not altogether clear, but it seems that an agreement was reached by the start of December to produce a new journal that would replace *Letuchie listki* and articulate a definite constitutional-liberal position, although probably with some *narodnik* overtones. Liberals in Russia would provide the necessary funds. Some of the fundists, particularly Chaikovskii, were anxious that associating themselves with a new publication focused on political reform could limit their ability to pursue more radical objectives. It was therefore agreed that the Fund should retain the freedom to decide what else it published and that the alliance with Russian liberals and liberal populists would come to an end once constitutional reform had been achieved.

---

53 S. Stepniak, 'The Tzar's Speech', *Free Russia* (1 March 1895).
54 Details of the address by the Tver *zemstvo* appeared in *Letuchie listki*, 15 (9 February 1895). The 'Otkrytoe pis'mo Nikolaiu II' was printed in *Letuchie listki*, 16 (20 February 1895). A copy can be found in Volkhovskii Papers (Houghton Library), MS Russ 51, Folder 110. For further details about the Open Letter, which was drafted by Petr Struve, see Galai, *Liberation Movement*, 27.
55 F. Volkhovskii, 'Sleduiushchii shag', *Letuchie listki*, 20 (20 May 1895).
56 For some brief comments on the plan for a new journal, see V. L. Burtsev, *Bor'ba za svobodnuiu Rossiiu. Moi vospominaniia* (Moscow: Direct Media, 2014), 95–96. See, too, Hamburg, 'London Emigration', esp. 332–33.

Stepniak was not for the most part a central figure in these developments.[57] Lazarev had by contrast taken an increasingly prominent role in shaping the Fund's strategy since his arrival in London from the USA in 1894 (a move that the government in Petersburg believed was itself part of a strategy to unify the Russian revolutionary movement in Western Europe).[58] Chaikovskii was also involved in the discussions. Volkhovskii's role was pivotal both in terms of initiating the idea for a new journal and discussing it with visitors from Russia. He was also intended to act as *de facto* editor, although Stepniak would have the formal role, replicating the situation at *Free Russia*.[59] The new journal was to be called *Zemskii sobor* (*Assembly of the Land*), the name of the assembly that met in the sixteenth and seventeenth centuries, which had by the nineteenth century become a symbol in some quarters of the principle that Russian society should be consulted by the government on all important matters.[60] The readiness of the London emigration to accept such a title at first glance seemed to represent a concession to 'liberalism', or indeed Slavophilism, but the notion of the Land as the authentic voice of the people also had clear affinities to the radical *narodnik* tradition. The term *Zemskii sobor* was fluid enough to appeal to revolutionaries and liberals alike as the title of a publication designed to bring together different strands of opinion behind a programme of political reform.

The new journal never appeared. On 23 December 1895, Stepniak was on his way to Volkhovskii's home in west London to discuss final plans for launching *Zemskii sobor*, when he was run down by a train

---

57 Taratuta, *Stepniak-Kravchinskii*, rather evades the issue of Stepniak's changing views and his position in the London emigration in the year before his death, and says surprisingly little about many of the issues surrounding the possible publication of a new journal.

58 For a remarkably perceptive if not entirely accurate analysis of developments by a senior official in a memorandum for Aleksandr III, see P. N. Durnovo, 'Aleksandr III i russkie emigranty', *Byloe*, 7 (1918), 198–203. For a different view of Lazarev's role, see Donald Senese, *S. M. Stepniak-Kravchinskii: The London Years* (Newtonville, MA: Oriental Research Partners, 1987), 81–82.

59 Hamburg, 'London Emigration', 333.

60 For a useful discussion, see Ivan Sablin and Kuzma Kukushkin, 'The Assembly of the Land (Zemskii Sobor). Historiographies and Mythologies of a Russian "Parliament"', in Ivan Sablin and Egor Moniz Bandeira (eds), *Planting Parliaments in Eurasia, 1850-1950: Concepts, Practices and Mythologies* (London: Taylor and Francis, 2021), 103-49.

and died instantly. The official verdict was one of accidental death. York Powell, Regius Professor of Modern History at Oxford, told the Coroner's Court that Stepniak had been in good spirits when he met him a couple of days earlier. Chaikovskii said there had been other 'near misses' at the same crossing before. Much was made of the fact that the deceased had his head buried in a book as he walked across the track.[61] Private correspondence suggests that some of those who knew Stepniak thought that it might have been a case of suicide.[62] Stepniak had found the previous two years difficult, not least because of the poor state of his marriage, while the attack by Ivanoff had undermined his reputation among many in Britain. Yet his death was not without serious consequences for the London emigration. It removed from the scene a man whose reputation and charisma had for some years glued together individuals with a range of temperaments and ideologies while raising the profile of the fundists in the wider revolutionary movement.

Hundreds of people followed Stepniak's funeral cortege to Waterloo Station from where his body was taken thirty miles south-west to Woking Crematorium. Volkhovskii organised the funeral arrangements. The speakers at the funeral who spoke about Stepniak's life reflected both his Europe-wide reputation and the increasingly transnational nature of the European revolutionary movement: Kropotkin, Malatesta, Edward Bernstein, Eleanor Marx, Keir Hardie, William Morris.[63] The *Times* noted two days later that the funeral had provided a strange meeting place for 'Socialists, Nihilists, Anarchists, and outlaws of every country'.[64] Stepniak's death also caused enormous dismay among his English admirers. *Free Russia* carried many eulogies. Spence Watson praised Stepniak as 'strong, true, single-minded, earnest for the truth wherever it may lead'. Volkhovskii echoed these sentiments and boldly addressed the question of terrorism, repeating the familiar trope that while the use of terror might seem shocking to British people, it had

---

61 *Times* (27 December 1895).
62 See, for example, Volkhovskii Papers (Houghton Library), MS Russ 51, Folder 362, Spence-Watson to Volkhovskii, 14 January 1896.
63 A detailed description of the circumstances surrounding the death and funeral of Stepniak can be found in Egor Lazarev, 'Smert' S.M. Kravchinskago Stepniaka', *Letuchie listki*, 28 (18 January 1896). Some sense of the response to Stepniak's death can also be found in the letters and telegrams sent to Volkhovskii when the news first broke, which can be found in Volkhovskii Papers (HIA), Box 3, Folders 15–16.
64 *Times* (30 December 1895).

been justified under Russian conditions of the late 1870s and early 1880s. He referred provocatively to the murder of Aleksandr II in 1881 as 'an enormous moral service', even though it had not achieved its immediate objectives, a failure which he argued had led Stepniak to turn his attention away from terrorism towards building 'a broad and strong popular movement'. Volkhovskii's eulogy was a shrewd programmatic statement designed to distance the SFRF from any suspicion of active support for terrorism while preserving a revolutionary martyrology that looked to the dead as inspiration for the living: 'Let us not offend, then, his memory by even one moment of despair. On the contrary, let us rally closer together, Friends of Russian Freedom, let us double our efforts in our righteous cause, and victory will be ours'.[65]

Volkhovskii formally replaced Stepniak as editor of *Free Russia* at the start of 1896, although he had effectively been performing the role for some time, and over the next few years he contributed many signed articles as well as editorials and other pieces that were published anonymously. The main English contributors remained J. F. Green, formally listed for a time as joint editor, G. H. Perris, and Herbert Thompson (author of *Russian Politics* and founder of one of the most active provincial branches of the SFRF in Cardiff).[66] Both the tone and style of *Free Russia* changed somewhat in the years after 1895. Volkhovskii himself began to give freer rein to the sarcasm that flowed easily from his pen. He was sharply critical of moves by some Anglican clergy to develop closer links between the Russian Church and the Church of England.[67] When the Bishop of Peterborough made some complimentary remarks about his Russian hosts, in a lecture given a few months after returning from the Coronation of Nicholas II, Volkhovskii published a piece by one 'L. Varinski' suggesting that his lordship 'would do well to strengthen his sight by putting on his spectacles' (the article was almost certainly penned by Volkhovskii himself).[68] The following year, he suggested that the only reason some Russian clergy were interested in developing

---

65   F. Volkhovsky, 'The Russian Bayard', *Free Russia* (1 February 1896).

66   Herbert M. Thompson, *Russian Politics* (London: T. Fisher Unwin, 1895).

67   On efforts to develop closer relations between the Church of England and the Russian Church during this period, see Michael Hughes, 'The English Slavophile: W. J. Birkbeck and Russia', *Slavonic and East European Review*, 82, 3 (2004), 680–706.

68   L. Varinski, 'The Bishop of Peterborough on Russia', *Free Russia* (1 December 1896).

closer relations with their Anglican counterparts was to 'beguile naïve people'.[69] Volkhovskii's tone was sharp enough to prompt suggestions in some quarters that *Free Russia* was hostile to religion, a view firmly countered by Spence Watson, who noted that such suggestions were nonsense since political and religious freedom could never be separated.[70]

Volkhovskii also started to give more attention to social and economic questions on the pages of *Free Russia*, a focus shaped by the rapid changes that were taking place in Russia itself. The appointment of Sergei Witte as Finance Minister,[71] in 1892, had marked the start of a new economic programme centred on borrowing money abroad to finance a programme of rapid industrialisation at home. The policy dramatically increased economic growth, resulting in a sharp rise in the population of cities like Moscow and St Petersburg, and a concomitant increase in labour radicalism among an impoverished and demoralised workforce. The growth of industry also fostered the growing popularity of Marxist ideology in Russia,[72] at least in some quarters, given that the social and

69 'The Russian Clergy', *Free Russia* (1 October 1897). The article was anonymous, but both the content and tone give little doubt about its author.

70 R. Spence Watson, 'The "Anglo-Russian" and Religious Persecution in Russia', *Free Russia* (1 August 1897). The suggestion had been made, rather curiously, in Jacob Prelooker's paper the *Anglo-Russian*, which seems to have aimed to win over some of the more moderate readers of *Free Russia*. On Prelooker and the *Anglo-Russian*, see John Slatter, 'Jaakoff Prelooker and the Anglo-Russian', in John Slatter (ed.), *From the Other Shore: Russian Political Emigrants in Britain, 1870-1917* (London: Frank Cass, 1984), 49–66.

71 For an excellent biography of Witte, see Sidney Harcave, *Count Sergei Witte and the Twilight of Imperial Russia. A Biography* (Abingdon: Routledge, 2015). For a book focusing more on Witte's economic policy, see Theodore Von Laue, *Sergei Witte and the Industrialization of Russia* (New York: Columbia University Press, 1963).

72 For useful discussions of the rise of Marxism in Russia see, for example, John Keep, *The Rise of Social Democracy in Russia* (Oxford: Clarendon Press, 1963); Richard Kindersley, *The First Russian Revisionists. A Study of 'Legal Marxism' in Russia* (Oxford: Clarendon Press, 1962). Much useful material on the complex relationship between the development of Marxist ideas and revolutionary parties in Russia can be found in the relevant sections of biographies of key figures including Abraham Ascher, *Pavel Axelrod and the Development of Menshevism* (Cambridge, MA: Harvard University Press, 1972); Samuel H. Baron, *Plekhanov. The Father of Russian Marxism* (London: Routledge and Kegan Paul, 1963); Stephen F. Cohen, *Bukharin and the Bolshevik Revolution. A Political Biography, 1888–1938* (London: Wildwood House, 1974); Israel Getzler, *Martov: A Political Biography of a Russian Social Democrat* (Cambridge: Cambridge University Press, 1967); Robert Service, *Lenin: A Political Life. Vol. 1, The Strengths of Contradictions* (Basingstoke: Macmillan, 1985); S. V. Tiutiukin, *G. V. Plekhanov. Sud'ba russkogo marksista* (Moscow: Rosspen, 1997).

economic changes taking place seemed to provide a foundation for the kind of class conflict that Marx believed was the *leitmotif* of historical development. Many surviving *narodniki* of the 1870s, including Volkhovskii, were also acutely aware that the development of an urban working class was changing the character of Russian society and creating the foundation for new and potentially more effective opposition to tsarism.

Free Russia reported extensively on the strikes that broke out in major cities in Russia, including one that erupted among textile workers in St Petersburg in the spring of 1896 (the paper established a special fund to support the strikers). Volkhovskii contributed articles on such questions as 'The Maximum Working Day', reflecting his growing conviction that labour unrest could force government concessions.[73] There are hints that some members of the SFRF were perturbed by the new tone in *Free Russia*. The coalition between 'Liberals', 'Fabians' and 'Socialists'—which had always formed the foundation of the movement in Britain to support change in Russia—was by its nature vulnerable to such fissures. The extent of the change in the editorial direction of *Free Russia* should not be overstated, though, and Robert Spence-Watson continued to work amicably with Volkhovskii despite his staunch Quaker beliefs and role as President of the National Liberal Association.[74] The paper still published numerous accounts detailing the harsh treatment suffered by critics of the tsarist regime, which had been its staple fare since it was first established, providing continuing impetus for much of the support attracted by the 'cause' in Britain.

Volkhovskii was at first determined that the plans for *Zemskii sobor* should go ahead despite Stepniak's death. Other fundists agreed that the loss of their friend should inspire them to continue his work.[75] Yet the plans for the new journal stalled over the following months, even though funding had been promised from Russia, almost certainly with the help of Vladimir Korolenko. The reasons are not altogether clear, but

73 F. Volkhovsky, 'The Maximum Working Day', *Free Russia* (1 August 1897).
74 The correspondence between the two men gives no hint of any fundamental difference of opinion at this time. See, for example, Volkhovskii Papers (Houghton Library), MS Russ 51, Folder 362 (Various letters from Spence Watson to Volkhovskii).
75 See for example 'Ot komiteta V. R. Pressy v Londone' and the obituaries by Lazarev and Volkhovskii in *Letuchie listki*, 28 (18 January 1896).

Volkhovskii doubtless came to recognise that his work for *Free Russia* and the Free Press Fund would take up much of his time, making it difficult for him to edit a new journal. Nor was planning made any easier by the personal and ideological differences that emerged in the months that followed Stepniak's death.

By the spring of 1896, P. A. Dement'ev had become the unlikely central figure in plans for the new journal. Dement'ev had known Lazarev for some years in America, and discussed the new journal in correspondence with him, although he only seems to have considered the possibility of becoming editor following Stepniak's death.[76] While liberals in Russia looked favourably on Dement'ev, most fundists, including Volkhovskii, were less positive given his lack of experience in running such a venture. Nor were they sympathetic to his decidedly moderate programme. Dement'ev was in any case something of a maverick ('completely Americanised' and 'an extreme individualist' in his own words).[77] The idea of transforming *Letuchie listki* into a new journal was tacitly dropped, and Volkhovskii continued as editor, although with increasing input from Chaikovskii, who published numerous pseudonymous articles over the initials N. Ch. Dement'ev nevertheless continued with his plans, and in the spring of 1897 a new journal appeared in London under the title *Sovremennik: Ezhemesiachnoe politicheskoe izdanie* (*The Contemporary: A Monthly Political Publication*). The quality of the journal was poor and the political programme obscure. It ceased publication after three issues. Volkhovskii refused to support efforts to save the journal, partly because he did not trust Dement'ev, but perhaps too because he was starting to doubt the wisdom of promoting the kind of accommodation between Russian liberals and revolutionaries that he had once favoured so strongly.

The death of Stepniak also increased tensions between the fundists and other émigré groups in Western Europe. When Dement'ev was planning his new journal in the spring of 1896, he wrote to Petr Lavrov in Paris asking for his cooperation. The reply was scathing. Lavrov attacked the Russian liberals as too poorly organised and hesitant to bring about change. He also dismissed any strategy that focused on

---

76   See, for example, Volkhovskii Papers (HIA), Box 3, Folder 21, Dement'ev to Lazarev, 9 January 1896; 14 January 1896.
77   Hamburg, 'London Emigration', 334.

the need for political reform that was not combined with a struggle to build socialism, which he argued was 'the only way to eradicate the economic, political, and other evils that currently plague humanity in general, and our homeland in particular'. Lavrov made little secret that the real target of his attack was the London emigration grouped around *Free Russia* (he may not have realised that Dement'ev's links with the group were quite perfunctory).[78] He was particularly incensed that many Russians both in Russia and abroad seemed to think he endorsed the 'National Front' strategy that Stepniak and Volkhovskii had pursued over the previous few years. The death of Stepniak encouraged Lavrov to express himself more boldly about what he saw as the weaknesses of a purely political strategy.

Stepniak's death also complicated relations between the London emigration and the Emancipation of Labour Group centred in Geneva. Vera Zasulich had moved to London in 1894, in part to continue a long-planned biography of Rousseau, although she may also have wanted to see more of the country that had shaped Marx's understanding of capitalism. The experience was a dispiriting one, leading her to doubt the revolutionary instincts of the British proletariat, who seemed to view the world through the narrow prism of material self-interest. Zasulich had known Stepniak well for many years. In *Underground Russia* he had painted a vivid picture of her as an almost painfully shy introvert, unprepossessing in appearance, yet with 'a mind full of the highest poetry, profound and powerful, full of indignation and love'.[79] She, for her part, admired Stepniak for his energy and dynamism, even if she did not share his lingering nostalgia for terrorism, which Zasulich had long come to believe was nothing more than an impotent cry of rage.

Zasulich's relationship with members of the London emigration grouped around *Free Russia* and the Free Press Fund declined rapidly after Stepniak's death, for reasons that seem to have been as much personal as ideological, perhaps tinged with concern on the part of the fundists that Zasulich's lingering status as an icon of terrorism might

---

78 G. M. Hamburg and P. L. Lavrov, 'P. L. Lavrov in Emigration. An Unpublished Letter', *Russian Review*, 37, 4 (1978), 449–52.

79 Sergei Stepniak, *Underground Russia* (London: Smith Elder, 1883), 108.

complicate their position in Britain.[80] She certainly believed that the fundists discouraged members of the SFRF from inviting her to speak at their meetings. The situation was made more complicated by tension about managing Stepniak's literary and political legacy. Volkhovskii and Kropotkin corresponded extensively about publishing a biography of Stepniak, which never appeared,[81] while Stepniak's wife Fanni complained bitterly to Zasulich that the fundists were trying to prevent her benefitting financially from her late husband's work.[82] Zasulich for her part complained repeatedly to Plekhanov in Geneva about the pettiness and opportunism of the London emigration (reserving her strongest venom for Volkhovskii).[83] Plekhanov himself doubted whether the fundists were capable of any serious analysis of the political and economic situation in Russia. When David Soskice approached him in the summer of 1896 about possible cooperation with the fundists, he replied firmly that while he had been ready to work with Stepniak, the situation had changed: 'I certainly have no personal animus against the honourable Feliks Volkhovskii, but I am equally certain that I do not agree with his views. Both he and I are naturally opposed to Russian absolutism but that is hardly sufficient to allow us to pull amicably together under the same literary harness'.[84] The tensions became still more stark at the 1896 Fourth Congress of the Second International discussed later in the chapter.

Zasulich's criticism of the 'petty feuds' within the London emigration presumably referred to the debates that took place about the publication of a new journal in the months following Stepniak's death. Vladimir

---

80 For a useful summary of the tensions, see Jay Bergman, *Vera Zasulich: A Biography* (Stanford, CA: Stanford University Press, 1983), 135–36.

81 See, for example, Volkhovskii Papers (HIA), Box 3, Folder 17, Kropotkin to Volkhovskii, 27 January 1896; Volkhovskii to Kropotkin, 28 January 1896.

82 On the financial aspect of Stepniak's legacy, and the lack of any remaining payments from his publisher, see Volkhovskii Papers (Houghton Library), MS Russ 51, Folder 362, Spence Watson to Volkhovskii, 31 December 1895.

83 L. G. Deich (ed.), *Gruppa Osvobozhdenie truda (Iz arkhivov Plekhanova, Zasulich i Deicha)*, 6 vols (Moscow: Gosudarstvennoe izdatel'stvo, 1923-28), V, 152, (Zasulich to Plekhanov, mistakenly dated 1895 but in fact 1896). Zasulich found Volkhovskii particularly hostile which may have reflected the fact that he was also strongly disliked by Stepniak's widow.

84 Letter from Plekhanov to Soskice, 1 November 1896, in P. F. Iudin et al. (eds), *Literaturnoe nasledie G. V. Plekhanova*, 8 vols (Moscow: Gosudarstvennoe sotsial'no-eknomicheskoe izd-vo, 1934-40), IV, 305.

Burtsev regularly discussed such problems with Volkhovskii, recalling that his friend was often 'severely attacked' for his views on 'revolutionary issues', and 'found it hard to endure' the hostile attitude he sometimes encountered.[85] It is not entirely clear whether Burtsev was describing tensions between the fundists or relations between Volkhovskii and other members of the Russian revolutionary movement like Zasulich. Nor is it clear if the divisions were personal or ideological in character. Volkhovskii had a reputation among many of his British friends for charm and good nature, but his Russian colleagues often found him sarcastic and rude, traits that were made worse by his deafness and bouts of ill-health. There were also more substantial disagreements about the character of *Letuchie listki* in the wake of Stepniak's death. Chaikovskii wanted the paper to focus less on reprinting material smuggled out of Russia and more on showing how the growth of labour unrest in Russia signalled the need for changes to revolutionary strategy.[86] Volkhovskii agreed about the importance of rising industrial militancy, but he was at least initially sceptical about changing the character of the *listki* to one that focused less on reportage and more on polemic, believing that the tone of crafted neutrality actually increased its impact on readers and attracted a wide readership.[87]

This growing tension among the fundists may explain a letter sent to Chaikovskii by Egor Lazarev, in the spring of 1897, in which he noted that differences over the editorial character of the *listki* had become an issue of

> ideology and principle. We have had differences with Felix from the very first. We must clarify them for our own sake and explain them to him ... His own life and prejudices were formed under the influence of the monied elite, which may be progressive and liberal in the general cultural sense, but which has little ideological sympathy for the 'working class'. This aloofness from the crowd, from the gray masses, is strongly

---

85 Burtsev, *Bor'ba za svobodnuiu Rossiiu*, 97–98.

86 Many of the articles Chaikovskii contributed to *Letuchie listki* dealt with issues of strikes and labour militancy both in Russia and abroad. See, for example, N. Ch. (Chaikovskii), 'Mezhdunarodnaia federatsiia rabochikh soiuzov korabel'nykh, portovykh i rechnykh rabochikh', *Letuchie listki*, 36 (23 December 1896).

87 The *listki* undoubtedly moved in a more 'Socialist Revolutionary' direction from 1897 onwards, not least because of Chaikovskii's growing influence, but there is little evidence that Volkhovskii seriously opposed the development. For a nuanced discussion of the change, see Senese, *Stepniak-Kravchinskii*, 113–14.

reflected in his attitudes, emotions, and writing ... He has seen in the
workers' strikes, in the labor movement, in the social confrontation only
superficial facts, incidental news that might conveniently be exploited by
the *Listki*; he has not seen here the epic and unbroken growth of a new
and powerful world force which must in the end either conquer and rule
or perish.[88]

Lazarev also suggested that Volkhovskii was most comfortable in 'a
bourgeois Anglo-American milieu'. His words were not altogether fair,
given Volkhovskii's comparatively impoverished background, while
his articles in both *Free Russia* and *Letuchie listki* showed that he was
well-aware of the significance of growing labour unrest in Russia. And,
while Lazarev's letter may have reflected growing scepticism among
some fundists about building a 'National Front' against autocracy, at
a time when burgeoning worker radicalism heralded the rise of a new
revolutionary force in Russia, Volkhovskii's own refusal to help save
Dement'ev's short-lived journal suggests that he too was rethinking his
ideas about cooperation with Russian liberals. A sceptic might indeed
point out that Lazarev himself, although the son of a peasant, was by
now spending most of his time in Switzerland where he was married
to a wealthy woman and lived as a gentleman farmer.[89] A decision was
nevertheless taken in the spring of 1897 to drop Volkhovskii as the
named editor of *Letuchie listki* in favour of a general statement that the
journal was edited by members of the Free Press Fund in London.[90]

Lazarev's comments about Volkhovskii probably captured a sense
among some fundists that their friend was not only remote from the 'grey
masses' of Russia, but also too inclined to immerse himself in English
society in a way that distanced him from the struggle for revolution.
While Stepniak had used his social contacts to build support for the
'cause' in Britain, Volkhovskii never commanded the same level of
respect as his old friend, making him more vulnerable to the charge that

---

88 The translation is that found in Hamburg, 'London Emigration', 337. The letter
    has been re-catalogued since Hamburg consulted it and can now be found in
    Volkhovskii Papers (Houghton Library), MS Russ 51, Folder 188, Lazarev to
    Chaikovskii, 19 March 1897.

89 N. A. Ekhina, 'Emigranty, revoliutsionery i koronovannye osoby: "russkaia
    volost'" E. E. i Iu. A. Lazarevykh v Bozhi nad Klaranom', *Ezhegodnik Doma russkogo
    zarubezh'ia im. Aleksandra Solzhenitsyna* (2014–15), 20–30.

90 The first edition of *Letuchie listki* to appear without Volkhovskii's name as editor
    was published in May 1897.

his personal ties in Britain made him (in Lazarev's words) 'aloof' from the revolutionary struggle. Too much should not perhaps be made of these tensions. Lazarev and Chaikovskii were both by the late 1890s less interested in pursuing a strategy that focused on shaping international opinion against the tsarist government, and more concerned with identifying other ways to advance the cause of revolution in Russia itself. The same was increasingly true of Volkhovskii. The differences certainly appear to have dissipated by the early years of the twentieth century, as the fundists gradually coalesced into the Agrarian-Socialist League, which itself in turn subsequently merged with the Socialist Revolutionary Party.

Volkhovskii kept up his interest in literary matters during the second half of the 1890s, using the pages of *Free Russia* to print translations of new stories unfamiliar to British readers, while negotiating with Constables to write a biography of Turgenev (which never appeared).[91] He still instinctively viewed literature in Russia through a political lens, suggesting that for all Tolstoy's genius his emphasis on 'striving after personal self-perfection', which so appealed to his British readers, was almost a 'vice' to Russians since it obscured understanding of the causes of 'oppression in the present'.[92] He admired Vladimir Korolenko, but the two men were never on particularly close terms, even though Volkhovskii organised the translation of some of Korolenko's stories and met him in person when the author came to London in 1893 (the two men had also corresponded at some length when they were both exiled in Siberia).[93] Nor was Volkhovskii particularly interested in following

---

91 Volkhovskii Papers (Houghton Library), MS Russ 51, Folder 246, Archibald Constable and Co. to Volkhovskii, 27 June 1898.

92 Felix Volkhovsky, 'Preface', in G. H. Perris, *Leo Tolstoy: the Grand Muzhik A Study in Personal Evolution* (London: T. Fisher Unwin, 1898), viii. Volkhovskii's correspondence shows that he had many connections with the various Tolstoian communities in Britain but few of these were particularly close. For further details of Tolstoian communities in England, see W. H. G. Armytage, 'J. C. Kenworthy and the Tolstoyan Communities in England', *The American Journal of Economics and Sociology*, 16, 4 (1957), 391–405; Charlotte Alston, *Tolstoy and His Disciples. The History of a Radical International Movement* (London: I. B. Tauris, 2013).

93 See N. V. Zhiliakova, 'Obsuzhdenie professional'nykh tsennostei zhurnalista v perepiske F. V. Volkhovskogo i V. G. Korolenko', *Zhurnalistskii ezhegodnik*, 3 (2014), 38–42. On Korolenko's later journalism in the Russian legal press, most notably *Russkoe bogatstvo*, see L. G. Berezhnaia, 'Zhurnal "Russkoe Bogatstvo" v 1905–1913 gg.', in B. I. Esin (ed.), *Iz istorii russkoi zhurnalistiki nachala XX veka* (Moscow: Izd-vo Moskovskogo universiteta, 1984), 59–93.

literary developments in Britain during this time. He seldom visited
Edward and Constance Garnett after they moved in 1895 to a new
'Arts and Crafts' house ('The Cearne') near the village of Limpsfield in
Surrey, which became the focus of a small colony of Fabians, as well as
a disparate group of Russian émigrés (Edward Garnett later flippantly
named the area Dostoievskii Corner).[94] Stepniak was among those
who moved to Limpsfield for a time, in the months before his death,
to be close both to the Garnetts and his old friend Edward Pease. Many
prominent literary figures visited the Garnetts, including Stephen
Crane and Joseph Conrad, whose distinctive mixture of insecurity and
Russophobia proved rather trying to Constance.[95] Ford Maddox Ford
also lived in the area for a while, playing at being a farmer, although
his commitment seemed to be limited to sinking an old bath into the
ground so that the local ducks could 'queue, waiting their turn to swim
in it'.[96] Not only did Volkhovskii seldom visit The Cearne, but he also
showed little interest in the development of what one scholar has called
'Limpsfield Modernism' (associated above all with Edward Garnett and
Ford Maddox Ford).[97] Nor did he ever really become a central figure
in facilitating the Russian craze in Britain, despite his translations of
Russian stories and his early success in encouraging Constance Garnett
to learn Russian, admittedly a service to literature that was of lasting
importance.

Volkhovskii's growing distance from the Garnetts was not just
a consequence of his focus on *Free Russia* and *Letuchi listki*. Olive
Garnett noted in her diary early in 1894 that Constance had told her

---

94   For descriptions of life at The Cearne, see Garnett, *Constance Garnett*, 145–59; Helen
     Smith, *The Uncommon Reader: A Life of Edward Garnett* (London: Jonathan Cape,
     2017), passim.
95   Garnett, *Constance Garnett*, 165–69. On Conrad see, for example, Jeffrey Meyers,
     Joseph Conrad. A Biography (New York: Cooper Square Press, 2001); John Stape, *The
     Several Lives of Joseph Conrad* (London: William Heinemann, 2007).
96   Garnett, *Constance Garnett*, 169. For Ford's less than effusive memories of
     Limpsfield, see Maddox Ford, *Return to Yesterday*, 33 ff. For Ford's critical view of
     the Limpsfield aesthetic and political 'ecosystem', see Nathan Waddel, *Modernist
     Nowheres: Politics and Utopia in Early Modernist Writing, 1900–1920* (Basingstoke:
     Palgrave Macmillan, 2012), 88 ff.
97   Rebecca Beasley, *Russomania. Russian Culture and the Creation of British Modernism,
     1881–1922* (Oxford: Oxford University Press, 2020), 61–80.

that Volkhovskii and Edward Garnett 'mutually enrage one another'.[98] Several Britons who knew Volkhovksii noted that he could be moody and detached. The more astute recognised he was lonely.[99] Constance Garnett's observation that Volkhovskii was a 'tremendous ladies' man' was not an idle observation. Fanni Stepniak, who never liked him, wrote sarcastically to Olive Garnett in the spring of 1897 that 'poor uncle Felix [is] in decline altogether. No more flirtations, no expectations, even old maids are not available. C'est fini'.[100] Olive herself noted that her sister-in-law believed that 'F. V. has demanded devotion from women all his life, & is always offended if he doesn't get it to the uttermost. He was a spoiled child, adored by his mother, one of seven children of whom the other six died young, & till he was 18, he never lifted a finger to do a thing for himself. He always fascinated women but was not in love with his first wife who adored him'.[101]

Olive also recorded in her diary that Volkhovskii's attitude towards women, at least as it was seen by her brother and sister-in-law, was sometimes a cause for concern. Constance told Olive that 'When he [Volkhovskii] comes into a family he can't help making one member of it jealous'. Sometimes he demanded too much by way of support for the 'cause'. He was impatient with one female friend ('Gracie') who would not agree to give help to Russian exiles without her husband's agreement, berating her for 'not saving a fellow creature's life', and petulantly refusing to shake hands when he left her house. Constance Garnett also hinted to her sister-in-law that such behaviour reflected a deeper pattern of emotional manipulation or at least unbridled self-centredness:

---

98 Johnson, *Olive and Stepniak*, 20. Olive's episodic dating of her diary entries makes it difficult to identify precisely when some entries were written, although Constance's comments seem to have been made in January around the time when Ivanoff's diatribe against the members of the London emigration appeared in the *New Review*.

99 G. H. Perris later recalled that Volkhovskii had been on the point of marriage soon after arriving in London, although for some reason the ceremony never took place, in part because the whole plan was in Perris' view 'slightly absurd'. G. H. Perris, *Russia in Revolution* (London: Chapman and Hall, 1905), 66.

100 Garnett Papers (Northwestern University), Box 23, Folder 3, Fanni Stepniak to Olive Garnett, 9 March 1897.

101 Johnson, *Olive and Stepniak*, 20.

F. V.'s morals are quite different; he would do nothing clandestinely but he would think it quite fair to come openly & steal—say Gracie away from her husband—and then in a year's time if he got tired of her, he would say 'Go back'.

This is not English. We agreed that it was pathetic that now on account of F. V.'s age, ill-health, etc, he is no longer attractive to women, & yet he needs them more than ever, & we agree that of all the Russians we know, he is most devoted to the cause, most single-minded, the greatest idealist & in spite of many childish faults in some respects the most lovable.[102]

* * * * *

Volkhovskii's private correspondence certainly shows that he craved the emotional intensity that had been such a marked feature of the *kruzhki* that shaped his early adult life in Russia. Female acquaintances were sometimes forced to rebuff what appeared to them as inappropriate if rather clumsy advances. One engaged Unitarian woman gently told him ('old chap') that however much she wished convention could be thrown to 'the four winds', in a world of 'old fogies' she had to be cautious: 'I am bound, there are restrictions on me ... I have to bow and submit'.[103] Another female correspondent who wrote to Volkhovskii, asking for advice about how she could contribute to the cause of Russian liberation, was startled to receive by return a request for a photograph. She gently declined on the grounds—probably untrue—that she had not had one taken since she was six.[104] Volkhovskii's behaviour sometimes caused more serious problems. His flirtatious relationship with one married correspondent—she called him her 'grumpatious old bear "Bruin"' and he called her 'Puck'—exploded when an outraged husband found the correspondence (he condemned Volkhovskii as 'dishonourable' and demanded that he 'drop the friendship').[105]

The most intense emotional relationship that Volkhovskii had during these years was with Margaret Heath, the sister of the painter Nellie

---

102 Johnson, *Olive and Stepniak*, 20.
103 Volkhovskii Papers (Houghton Library), MS Russ 51, Folder 249, Daisie to Volkhovskii, 25 May 1896; Daisie to Volkhovskii, 11 June 1896.
104 Volkhovskii Papers (Houghton Library), MS Russ 51, Folder 244, Laura Coates to Volkhovskii, 3 April 1897.
105 Volkhovskii Papers (Houghton Library), MS Russ 51, Folder 283, Janet Hooton to Volkhovskii, 13 July 1898; Folder 282, Henry Hooton to Volkhovskii, 30 August 1898.

Heath (Nellie was a close intimate of the Garnett family and had a long-term relationship with Edward Garnett that seems to have been tolerated by Constance).[106] Margaret was a member of the Independent Labour Party and later married the son of Edward Pease. The precise nature of her relationship with Volkhovskii remains unclear, but it seems to have been rooted in a desire for a deep emotional and intellectual intimacy, as well as shared political interests. Margaret's correspondence was punctuated with laments about 'how lonely life gets', and rueful acknowledgements of Volkhovskii's claim that he could never really know her since she guarded her inner life so closely (not, it must be said, something that comes over in her correspondence). She in turn told Volkhovskii that it was hard to know him since 'you have so many different selves ... There is one self of yours wh[ich] helps me so much more than most people do—but that is not always there'.[107] Such words were interspersed with more prosaic discussion both about the future of Russia ('you can dream what Russia will be one day') and political developments in Britain (Heath toured Britain speaking at numerous ILP and trade union meetings).[108]

In one of her letters sent to Volkhovskii, Heath anxiously asked about his attitude towards the recent fourth Congress of the Second International held in London in July 1896, seeking his views on everything from the treatment of the anarchists through to the quality of the leaders of the British socialist movement.[109] Volkhovskii's reply to Heath has not survived, but he was clearly incensed by much that had taken place. His anger stemmed from the behaviour of Plekhanov and other representatives of the Marxist wing of the Russian revolutionary movement. The composition of the Russian delegation at the Congress caused confusion from the start. Volkhovskii himself spoke at the opening rally in Hyde Park,[110] and when the Congress proper began

---

106 Garnett, *Constance Garnett*, 175; Smith, *Edward Garnett*, 99 ff.

107 Volkhovskii Papers (Houghton Library), MS Russ 51, Folder 272, Margaret Heath to Volkhovskii, 20 August 1896.

108 Volkhovskii Papers (Houghton Library), MS Russ 51, Folder 272, Margaret Heath to Volkhovskii, 29 November 1896.

109 Volkhovskii Papers (Houghton Library), MS Russ 51, Folder 272, Margaret Heath to Volkhovskii, 16 August 1896. For a dated but still lucid discussion of the history of the Second International, see James Joll, *The Second International, 1889–1914* (London: Routledge and Kegan Paul, 1955).

110 *Justice* (25 July 1896).

there was a general mood of celebration at the growth of the labour movement in Russia, given the recent strikes in St Petersburg. Things became much tenser as proceedings got underway. Plekhanov insisted that his country should be formally represented by Marxist delegates from both the emigration and Russia itself. He dismissed the *narodniki* as ineffective and rejected the idea that a socialist revolution would come from the field rather than the factory.[111] Russian representatives from the *narodnik* wing of the revolutionary movement were, following Plekhanov's verbal report, refused any formal status as delegates. It appears that Volkhovskii was one of their number.[112]

The conflict at the Congress was part of the broader tension between members of the London emigration and the Emancipation of Labour Group discussed earlier. Volkhovskii quickly took to the pages of the *Labour Leader* to express his frustration to British readers:

> We Russians who have the cause of Russian liberty and justice at heart, and have worked for it, know perfectly well that all fractions of Russian Socialism, and even some people who, though advanced, do not call themselves socialists, have equally wanted to bring about that awakening of the Russian workers which resulted in the St Petersburg strike.

He went on to attack the 'intolerance and partisanship' shown by Plekhanov and other delegates from the Emancipation of Labour Group.[113] His charges were predictably rebuffed a few weeks later in the same paper by Vera Zasulich and, even more vehemently, in *Justice* (where she wrote that Volkhovskii had 'no relations whatsoever ... with the international movement of the socialist workers').[114] Volkhovskii's defence of the need for a broad opposition—of all 'fractions of Russian Socialism'—was of

---

111 For a description of how the Congress struggled with the question of credentials, see *Full Report of the Proceedings of the International Workers' Congress, London, July and August 1896* (London: The Labour Leader, 1896). The *Full Report* also noted that the Congress met amid rumours that 'the Marxists had made up their mind ... to expel by main force all who disagreed with them' (16).

112 G. D. H. Cole, *A History of Socialist Thought. The Second International 1889–1914*, Part 1 (London: Macmillan, 1956), 23. For a different perspective, which suggests that the exclusion was of the veteran *narodnik* Esper Serebiakov, along with a delegate from Berne, see A. Hamon, *Le socialisme et le Congrès de Londres: étude historique* (Paris: Ancienne Librairie Tresse and Stock, 1897), 128, 247–49.

113 *Labour Leader* (8 August 1896). See, too, the long article (by Chaikovskii), 'Mezhdunarodnyi kongress', *Letuchie listki*, 35 (15 September 1896).

114 *Labour Leader* (5 September 1896); *Justice* (29 August 1896).

course precisely what Plekhanov condemned as 'opportunism'. Yet Volkhovskii was correct in arguing that revolutionaries in Russia who looked to Marx for inspiration had been greatly helped by those who articulated more *narodnik* views when fostering labour unrest. And he was also right in suggesting that the fundists in London had from the start welcomed the strike movement as evidence of the growth of labour militancy in Russian factories. Volkhovskii was nevertheless naïve in not recognising that Plekhanov was likely to succeed in presenting the Social Democrats as the authentic voice of the Russian revolutionary movement. Marxist sympathies were strong in most of the delegations at the London Congress, while revolutionary 'nihilists' were often conflated in the mind of many Western socialists with anarchists, who were from the start effectively excluded from the Congress.

While Volkhovskii knew leading figures in the Independent Labour Party and the Trade Union movement, including Ramsay MacDonald and Tom Mann, he never made such a strong impression on the British labour movement as Stepniak. Nor was he as well-connected with leading Fabians like Edward Pease. Volkhovskii was, as seen earlier, finding it increasingly difficult by the second half of the 1890s to keep together the distinctive coalition of socialists and liberals grouped around the SFRF and *Free Russia* (an echo, of course, of the tensions that undermined the strategy of building the fragmented Russian opposition into a united front against autocracy). In October 1897, one correspondent wrote to Volkhovskii, apparently in response to a letter from him about possible changes to trade union legislation, arguing that 'Progress indeed would become impossible' if trade unions were allowed to become more powerful. He went on to note that 'it is the capitalist who is the slave of the trade unionist', adding that unionism was bringing about the 'decay' of British industry.[115] Yet Henry Simon— the author of these words—was an active member of the SFRF. He was by his own lights 'a sincere well-wisher of the working-classes'. Simon represented an element in the Liberal tradition—stretching back as far as the campaign by Richard Cobden and John Bright against the corn laws—which identified political freedom at home and peace abroad as intimately bound up with *laissez-faire* economics and free trade. Such an

---

115 Volkhovskii Papers (Houghton Library), MS Russ 51, Folder 346, Henry Simon to Volkhovskii, 19 October 1897.

outlook was by the end of the century fading among those most active in Britain in the campaign to support Russian freedom, as they were increasingly eclipsed by others drawn from a more radical tradition, sympathetic not only to the cause of political reform in Russia but to more far-reaching radical economic and social revolution as well.

Henry Simon was, despite his concerns, still happy to contribute to a fund set up by the SFRF at the end of 1887 to pay for the legal defence of Vladimir Burtsev, after he was prosecuted for publishing an article justifying the cause of regicide in Russia.[116] The Burtsev case provided a test for many supporters of the SFRF, raising the question of whether they should support free expression by political émigrés when it was used to encourage violence (albeit not in Britain). It also casts light on the suspicion with which both the *Okhrana* and Special Branch still viewed members of the Russian exile community in London two years after the death of Stepniak. One of the most striking features of Burtsev's arrest and imprisonment was, indeed, the extent to which his 'crimes' were in many ways no different from those committed by Stepniak in the ten years or so prior to his death (or indeed Mazzini several decades before that). While Stepniak had openly defended Narodnaia volia's use of terrorism in Russia, he never faced arrest or prosecution, instead becoming a well-known public figure and journalist. The public mood had changed by the second half of the 1890, though, and Burtsev was found guilty and sentenced to hard labour for offences that might have gone unpunished just a few years before.

The death of Stepniak had done little to weaken Inspector Melville's antipathy towards the remaining members of the London emigration. While one of his assistants later acknowledged that Russian nihilists only 'plotted against their own country', unlike many anarchists who believed in 'no system of government',[117] his chief made no such fine distinctions. When Nicholas II visited Britain in 1896—a visit that

---

116 For a detailed discussion of the Burtsev case, see Henderson, *Vladimir Burtsev*, 83–99. Also see Alan Kimball, 'The Harassment of Russian Revolutionaries Abroad: The London Trial of Vladmir Burtsev in 1898', *Oxford Slavonic Papers*, New Series, 6 (1973), 48–65; Saunders, 'Burtsev and the Russian Revolutionary Emigration'; Donald Senese, '"Le vil Melville": Evidence from the *Okhrana* File on the Trial of Vladimir Burtsev', *Oxford Slavonic Papers*, New Series, 14 (1981), 47–53.

117 John Sweeney, *At Scotland Yard: Being the Experiences during Twenty-Seven Years' Service of John Sweeney* (London: Grant Richards, 1904), 71.

was met with predictable anger by Volkhovskii on the pages of *Free Russia*[118]—the Inspector worked closely with Rachkovskii to ensure the royal visitor's safety (there had been reports that an attempt might be made on the Tsar's life by Fenian terrorists, perhaps in an unlikely alliance with Russian nihilists).[119] While there is no record of the British Prime Minister Lord Salisbury discussing the issue of terrorism with the Tsar, when the two men met at Balmoral,[120] the visit helped to deepen relations between the Paris *agentura* and Special Branch. Rachkovskii himself was closely involved in the events leading up to Burtsev's arrest the following year.

The fundists had reacted with concern to Burtsev's decision in early 1897 to establish a new journal, *Narodovolets* (*The People's Supporter*), recognising that its endorsement of the use of terror could make the position of Russian political exiles in London more vulnerable. Volkhovskii and Chaikovskii knew that the German anarchist Johann Most had been imprisoned in Britain in 1881 for praising the murder of Aleksandr II.[121] When the first number of *Narodovolets* eventually appeared, it contained an article by Burtsev arguing that 'the name of our journal clearly reflects its programme', before going on to endorse the principle of regicide and 'systematic terror' (though he carefully noted that this only applied to actions carried out by Russians on Russian soil).[122] Rachkovskii in Paris contacted Melville demanding action. The inspector advised the head of the Paris *agentura* to ask the Russian ambassador in London, Baron Staal, to make a formal complaint to the British government (he made his own position clear when telling Rachkovskii that 'I will be glad to do you a service and grab these scoundrels').[123] The ambassador duly made a protest to the

---

118 F. Volkhovsky, 'The Tzar's Visit', *Free Russia* (1 October 1896).

119 See, for example, the reports from various European papers in *The Standard* (18 September 1896).

120 On the meeting, see Margaret M. Jefferson, 'Lord Salisbury's Conversations with the Tsar at Balmoral, 27 and 29 September 1896', *Slavonic and East European Review*, 39, 92 (1960), 216–22.

121 On Most, see Frederic Trautmann, *The Voice of Terror. A Biography of Johann Most* (Westport, CN: Greenwood Press, 1980). For the prosecution of Most, see Bernard Porter, 'The *Freiheit* Prosecutions, 1881–1882', *Historical Journal*, 23, 4 (1980), 833–56.

122 *Narodovlets. Sotsialnoe-politicheskoe obozrenie*, 1 (April 1897).

123 Henderson, *Vladimir Burtsev*, 88.

Foreign Office, although Lord Salisbury warned him that a prosecution might not be successful, given that the jury could choose not to convict. Melville meanwhile pushed things along by sending one of his men to purchase copies of *Narodovolets* from a shop in Tottenham Court Road.[124] The journal was translated into English, and Melville obtained a warrant to arrest Burtsev, finding his quarry in the British Museum Library. Burtsev handed the keys to his flat over to the inspector, who duly organised a thorough search, seizing numerous documents used in the compilation of *Za sto let* (Burtsev's history of the Russian revolutionary movement). Burtsev was sent for trial. The material seized by the police was never seen again.

Burtsev was not particularly close to most members of the Russian Free Press Fund, although when researching *Za sto let* he lived at its headquarters and received fifteen shillings a week for his efforts, but he was on good terms with Volkhovskii.[125] He had shown his friend the final proofs of the first edition of *Narodovolets* before it appeared, who cautioned that it would be 'mad' to publish it, since it would do great damage to 'the common cause'.[126] Burtsev was nevertheless determined to press ahead with further issues despite more warnings from Volkhovskii about the potential consequences.[127] Following his arrest, though, the fundists had no option but to support Burtsev, not least to fight back against what they saw as the *de facto* extension of the Russian government's claims to authority over its subjects wherever they were in the world.

Volkhovskii took a leading role in the campaign to persuade British supporters of the 'cause' to offer financial and rhetorical support to Burtsev. He worked closely with Robert Spence Watson to identify a

---

124 For the depositions of Melville and the police constable see Volkhovskii Papers (HIA), Box 1, Folder 14.

125 On the support offered to Burtsev when writing *Za sto let*, see Tuckton House Archive (Leeds Brotherton Library), MS 1381/26 (typescript of later parts of L. Goldenberg, 'Reminiscences'), 64–65. The warm tone of correspondence between Burtsev and Volkhovskii can be seen clearly in the various letters found in Volkhovskii Papers (HIA), Box 1, Folder 12. The trial was extensively covered in articles in *Letuchie listki* which expressed deep concern about the process. See, for example, 'Delo Burtseva', *Letuchie listki*, 42 (23 March 1898).

126 Burtsev, *Bor'ba za svobodnuiu Rossiiu*, 106.

127 See, for example, Volkhovskii Papers (Houghton Library), 66M-197 (miscellaneous material relating to the Volkhovskii family), Volkhovskii to Burtsev, 1 November 1897.

defence counsel who would take on the case *pro bono* or at least at a reduced rate. Spence Watson advised Volkhovskii to avoid publishing anything that could prejudice the trial and give rise to contempt of court proceedings. He also cautioned that it would be difficult for Burtsev to get a fair trial since it was so 'difficult to fight the police. They all stick together like wax and swear through thick and thin'.[128] Spence Watson, like Volkhovskii, believed that the case was a political one, and that the British government had instigated the prosecution at the behest of St Petersburg, and he was doubtful about success in Court.[129] He was also shrewd enough to realise that whatever the rights and wrongs of the case, the public mood had changed over the previous few years, making it difficult to mount a defence of a foreigner in Burtsev's position. Volkhovskii himself contemplated a libel action against Inspector Melville, who had during the course of the investigation said that he had purloined funds sent from abroad for his personal use, but Volkhovskii's solicitors persuaded him not to proceed at such a febrile time (Melville predictably said he know nothing about the supposed statement).[130] A few weeks after the Court returned a guilty verdict, Spence Watson told an English correspondent that 'The whole subject is one of much sadness and great difficulty. I cannot possibly express to you what I should like to do in a letter. I believe the action of our Government to have been entirely wrong ... In the meantime I feel more than ever the importance of keeping our Society alive. It is very difficult, and I scarcely, at times, see how it can be done'.[131]

Many contributors to the Burtsev defence fund made it clear that they did not approve of terrorism but were concerned about the principles raised by the case. Such a view was expressed most eloquently by Rosalind Howard (Lady Carlisle), when she sent a cheque for £10 towards Burtsev's defence costs, noting in her letter that she wanted to

---

128 Volkhovskii Papers (Houghton Library), MS Russ 51, Folder 362, Spence Watson to Volkhovskii, 9 January 1898.

129 Volkhovskii Papers (Houghton Library), MS Russ 51, Folder 362, Spence Watson to Volkhovskii, 13 January 1898.

130 Volkhovskii Papers (HIA), Box 18, Folder 4, Radford to Volkhovskii, 11 January 1898; 20 January 1898; 22 January 1898. Letter by Melville, 25 January 1898.

131 Volkhovskii Papers (Houghton Library), MS Russ 51, Folder 388, Spence Watson to Cecily Sidgwick, 7 March 1898.

see 'a perfectly fair trial for a Russian patriot', but hoped that if he had indeed advocated the murder of the Tsar he should

> suffer penalty, as I have never swerved from the conviction that no good can come from such a method ... I glory in the execution of Charles the First, but regicide is one thing, & assassination is another. You need not recapitulate to me the deeds of shame committed by the Russian government. I hate that Government & all its works with my whole soul; but we shall not exterminate the Tzar & his dynasty by murderous acts ... I fully agree with you that the search for Russian papers in an English domicile, & the possible publication of those papers for some dastardly Government object is most deplorable.[132]

Volkhovskii was shrewd enough to play on such sentiments when raising money for Burtsev's defence. Yet it was difficult for him to know how to present the case in public. His passionate condemnation of the Burtsev trial in *Free Russia* started even when the case was still *sub judice*. He argued—although in slightly oblique terms—in defence of the use of terror by Narodnaia volia nearly two decades earlier as a justified response to the oppression of the tsarist regime. He also suggested that when Burtsev invoked the names of those involved in the murder of Aleksandr II—such as Sof'ia Perovskaia and Andrei Zheliabov—he was simply behaving like a British republican inspired by the example of Oliver Cromwell. Volkhovskii told his readers that, since *Narodovolets* 'was published in the Russian language, [and] the argument was carried on, so to say, on the soil of Russian thought, of Russian political circumstances', the British government had no reason to become involved in something that was of little consequence to it.[133]

His words had little effect. Volkhovskii attended Burtsev's trial when it took place in February 1898, although he was at one stage asked along with other Russians to leave the courtroom, and he was astute enough to recognise that the judge presiding over the case was determined to secure a guilty verdict. When the jury duly reached its decision— Burtsev was sentenced to imprisonment with hard labour for eighteen months—the British press overwhelmingly endorsed the outcome,

---

132 Volkhovskii Papers (Houghton Library), MS Russ 51, Folder 236, Letter by Lady Carlisle, 8 January 1898.
133 F. Volkhovsky, 'The Case of V. Bourtzev', *Free Russia* (1 February 1898).

though perhaps in more muted terms than might have been expected.[134] Volkhovskii was left to fret that 'The whole affair from beginning to end was not one of justice, nor was it even one of a necessity to enforce law, but merely a matter of political convenience of the moment. It was thought imperatively necessary to pay a visible compliment to one of "our neighbours" at the lowest possible cost'.[135]

The Burtsev trial marked a distinct stage both in the campaign to mobilise British public opinion against tsarist Russia as well as the fundists' relations with other revolutionary groups in emigration and in Russia itself. There was by the end of the 1890s a growing tension among members of the SFRF between those who were concerned above all at the harsh way the tsarist government treated its opponents and others who were convinced that lasting change could only come about in Russia through building a new socialist society. In the years before 1900, the 'liberal-pacifist' wing had generally prevailed. In the years after 1900, the voices of more radical supporters became stronger. And, following the creation of the Agrarian-Socialist League in 1900, and its merger two years later with the Socialist Revolutionary Party, the fundists themselves effectively became a more integral part of a larger if fissiparous 'neo-populist' movement committed to fomenting violent revolution in Russia. The next two chapters explore Volkhovskii's role in these developments during the last fifteen years of his life.

---

134 For the somewhat muted reactions, see, for example, *Daily Telegraph* (12 February 1898); *Morning Post* (12 February 1898); *Times* (12 February 1898). For a more dramatic account of the trial and Burtsev's conviction, see *Irish Independent* (12 February 1898).
135 F. Volkhovsky, 'A Russian's View of the Bourtzev Case', *Free Russia* (1 March 1898).

6. Returning to the Revolutionary Fray

The trial and conviction of Vladimir Burtsev highlighted the declining sympathy in Britain for revolutionary opponents of the Russian government. The appeal of the 'cause' had for some years been damaged by growing concern about anarchism, along with the Salisbury Government's determination to reduce the threat to public order supposedly posed by aliens living in Britain.[1] Volkhovskii's anger at the outcome of the Burtsev case was clear on the pages of *Free Russia*, where he was unusually trenchant in criticising not only the legal process, but other aspects of life in modern Britain as well. In May 1898, he wrote a piece condemning the poor quality of food and medical care in British prisons, arguing that 'English prison life might be greatly improved by borrowing from Russia that humanitarian disposition and attitude of mind towards the fallen which characterises the Russian people'.[2] Eighteen months later, at the Annual Meeting of the SFRF, he spoke dismissively of the 'Podsnappian' complacency that permeated public life in Britain (a reference to the character in Charles Dickens' *Our Mutual Friend* who embodied smug insularity and reluctance to face unpleasant truths). He described how, at one of his lectures, the local

---

1   For an examination of the development of anti-alien discourses before 1905, see David Glover, *Literature, Immigration and Diaspora in Fin-de-Siècle England. A Cultural History of the 1905 Aliens Act* (Cambridge: Cambridge University Press, 2012). For a more dated but still useful discussion, see Bernard Gainer, *The Alien Invasion. The Origins of the 1905 Aliens Act* (London: Heinemann, 1972). Much of the focus in these debates was on the Jewish population in London's East End. For an imaginative spatial analysis of shifting attitudes towards British Jews in this period, and the way the associated discourses paved the way for the 1905 Aliens Act, see Hannah Ewence, *The Alien Jew in the British Imagination, 1881–1905. Space, Mobility and Territoriality* (Cham: Palgrave Macmillan, 2019).

2   F. Volkhovsky, 'English & Russian Prisons', *Free Russia* (1 May 1898).

          https://doi.org/10.11647/OBP.0385.06

mayor 'patted him on the shoulder, and urged him never to go back to Russia since "there was no country above England"'. Volkhovskii told his audience that while he had:

> nothing against "Mr Podsnap's" pride in his country, he had everything against that gentleman imagining that any man of any nationality must be happy in being turned—forcibly, if necessary—into a Britisher. "Mr Podsnap" forgets, or does not understand that to every man *his own* country and *his own* personality is dear—whatever be the glory and advantages of England and the English.[3]

* * * * *

Volkhovskii's words partly reflected his disdain for the outburst of jingoism that erupted in Britain at the end of 1899, following the outbreak of the South African War,[4] but they also hinted at wider changes in his outlook that shaped his activities during the last fifteen years of his life. While he never abandoned the campaign to influence perceptions of the Russian revolutionary movement abroad, Volkhovskii devoted less time to it in the years after 1900, focusing more attention on producing propaganda designed to foment revolutionary sentiment in Russia itself. He also became less concerned about reassuring his British audience about the essential moderation of the Russian opposition movement, acknowledging even on the pages of *Free Russia* that many revolutionaries like himself wanted to bring about not just political reform in Russia, but more far-reaching social and economic change as well.

Both the SFRF and *Free Russia* faced a major financial crisis by the end of the 1890s. Sales of the paper were poor and donations proved elusive in the wake of the Burtsev trial. Members of the Society sought to take advantage of the Russia 'craze' by organising exhibitions of Russian peasant crafts, including one in London's New Bond Street,

---

3   'Our Annual Gathering', *Free Russia* (1 January 1900). Volkhovskii had used the Podsnap image as a criticism of English insularity as early as 1898 in his preface to G. H. Perris, *Leo Tolstoy. The Grand Mujik* (London: T. Fisher Unwin, 1898).

4   For Volkhovskii's comparatively restrained views on developments in South Africa, see F. Volkhovsky, 'The South African Affair', *Free Russia* (November 1899). His words nevertheless caused controversy among readers, not least because some of them believed that *Free Russia* was *too* cautious in not opposing the war. See, for example, Spence Watson / Weiss Papers (Newcastle University), SW 1/19/3, Volkhovskii to Spence Watson, 4 January 1900. See, too, the article by Robert Spence Watson, 'South Africa and the Russians', *Free Russia*, 1 February 1900.

hoping that such initiatives could provide a useful source of income.[5] *Free Russia* ran illustrated articles explaining how the Russian peasantry had for centuries supplemented their income by making a wide range of high-quality decorative goods.[6] Volkhovskii approached Herbert Thompson, who chaired the SFRF branch in Cardiff, to see if he would provide the capital to fund the expansion of the venture. His answer was unpromising. Thompson noted that 'Such an undertaking ... would require ... an able manager (or manageress) at its head devoting his whole time and energies to it and well-acquainted with the conditions of peasant industry in Russia and of the market for the goods in England. A manager with such qualities would be hard to find'.[7] It was a shrewd assessment of the situation.

The situation in North America was no brighter, but Volkhovskii still hoped to increase sales of *Free Russia* there, as well as attract donations from wealthy sympathisers.[8] In 1899, he corresponded at length with Edmund Noble, a leading figure in the American SFRF, discussing how to increase the appeal of *Free Russia* to an American audience. Noble replied noting pointedly that he could not himself provide financial support, adding that he lacked the right 'social connections' to seek philanthropic funding. He did however agree to write a regular letter 'From Across the Atlantic' reporting on developments in North America. Volkhovskii also discussed potential new publishing ventures with Noble, including a lavishly illustrated magazine depicting scenes of Russian life, as well as a series of 'nihilist' novels about the revolutionary struggle in Russia (a proposal that was less far-fetched than it sounds, given the success that authors including Stepniak and Le Queux had found in writing about Russian revolutionaries). Noble remained sceptical about the prospects for 'making Russian material pay'.[9] There was indeed something rather desperate about Volkhovskii's efforts to

---

5   'An Exhibition and Sale of Russian Peasants' Work', *Free Russia* (1 December 1899).
6   'What Are They Capable of?', *Free Russia* (1 April 1899).
7   Volkhovskii Papers (Houghton Library), MS Russ 51, Folder 354, Thompson to Volkhovskii, 29 January 1900.
8   For a discussion of the decline of interest in Russian affairs in the USA in the late 1890s, see D. M. Nechiporuk, *Vo imia nigilizma. Amerikanskoe obshchestvo druzei russkoi svobody i russkaia revoliutsionnaia emigratsiia, 1890–1930 gg.* (St Petersburg: Nestor-Istoriia, 2018), 168–85.
9   Volkhovskii Papers (Houghton Library), MS Russ 51, Folder 318, Letters from Noble to Volkhovskii, 16 October 1899; 22 December 1899; 13 February 1899.

put *Free Russia* on a stable footing. The paper appeared less regularly after 1900—typically between four and six editions a year—reflecting both the financial constraints and Volkhovskii's involvement in other activities.

Many of the pieces Volkhovskii wrote for *Free Russia* following the Burtsev trial continued to attack the tsarist regime's 'militant and cannibalistic attitude towards its own people'.[10] He condemned the 'Philosophy of Reaction' espoused by the Procurator of the Holy Synod, Konstantin Pobedonostsev, who was widely considered by critics of the regime to exert great influence on the Tsar,[11] dismissing Pobedonostsev himself as 'a kind of wooden ruling machine in human shape, to whom the living units of mankind are nothing'.[12] It was a striking image which characterised the tsarist government less as a relic of traditionalism and more as a modern manifestation of arbitrary power.[13] Volkhovskii also continued to criticise the British press for providing too positive a coverage of Nicholas II. When the Tsar put forward proposals in the summer of 1898 for an international conference on disarmament, which attracted positive reactions around the world, he dismissed the idea as a publicity stunt, writing that, while Nicholas called for 'peace on earth', millions of his subjects had 'no bread, no fuel, no fodder and no money; they do not know how to exist until the next crop'.[14]

Volkhovskii devoted much of *Free Russia* to developments in Finland, following the Tsar's proclamation of a manifesto in February 1899 that weakened the authority of the Finnish Diet and promoted further

---

10   F. Volkhovsky, 'The Latest Horrors', *Free Russia* (1 November 1898).
11   On Pobedonostsev, see Robert Byrnes, *Pobedonostsev: His Life and Thought* (Bloomington, IN: Indiana University Press, 1968); A. Iu. Polunov, *K. P. Pobedonostsev v obshchestvenno-politicheskoi i dukhovnoi zhizni Rossii* (Moscow: Rosspen, 2010). For a treatment of Pobedonostsev as a reactionary rather than a conservative, see Richard Pipes, *Russian Conservatism and Its Critics* (New Haven, CT: Yale University Press, 2005), 139–44.
12   F. Volkhovsky, 'The Philosophy of Reaction', *Free Russia* (1 January 1900).
13   For a fascinating discussion of the changing pattern of efforts to establish the legitimacy of the tsarist government, including extensive references to Pobedonostev, who played a critical role in fostering ideas and ceremonies designed to show how the Russian government was rooted in tradition, see Richard Wortman, *Scenarios of Power. Myth and Ceremony in Russian Monarchy from Peter the Great to the Abdication of Nicholas II* (Princeton, NJ: Princeton University Press, 2006).
14   F. Volkhovsky, 'Peace on Earth, Goodwill Towards Men', *Free Russia* (March 1899).

Russification of the country.[15] He had for some years been anxious
about Russian ambitions to dominate Scandinavia, and hoped that
unrest in Finland could resist such a move and foster opposition capable
of destabilising the tsarist regime itself.[16] Volkhovskii's knowledge of
developments was helped by his long-standing links with many Swedish
and Danish socialists, who had for some years played a role in the
dispatch of illegal literature into the Tsarist Empire,[17] and shortly after
the February Manifesto was issued he urged the leader of the Swedish
Social Democrats, Hjalmar Branting, to adopt a stronger anti-Russian
position.[18] Volkhovskii described the assault on Finnish autonomy
to readers of *Free Russia* as an example of 'Russian Imperialism', and
criticised those in Britain, like William Stead and Charles Dilke, who
tried to justify the new policy on the grounds that it would help the
Russian state to manage ethnic tensions in the western borderlands.[19]

> There are other elements in my country. There are Constitutionalists,
> Socialists, and Trade Unionists exercising now influence over thousands
> of factory workers. There are adherents of Local Self-Government. There
> are the Polish, Georgian, Oukrainien nationalists and other sections of

15 For a useful series of essays on the Russification of Finland from the late
    nineteenth century onwards, see Edward C. Thaden (ed.), *Russification in the
    Baltic Provinces and Finland, 1855–1914* (Princeton, NJ: Princeton University
    Press, 1981). A more recent account can be found in Tuomo Polvinen, *Imperial
    Borderland: Bobrikov and the Attempted Russification of Finland, 1898–1904* (London:
    Hurst and Co., 1995). A brief but helpful discussion of the Russification process
    in the north-west of the Empire can be found in Kari Alenius, 'Russification in
    Estonia and Finland Before 1917', *Faravid*, 28 (2004), 181–94. A useful discussion
    of the Russification process on the western periphery of the Empire other than
    Finland can be found in Theodore R. Weeks, *Nation and State in Late Imperial
    Russia: Nationalism and Russification on the Western Frontier, 1863–1914* (DeKalb, IL:
    Northern Illinois University Press, 1996).
16 The situation in Finland was discussed extensively by Volkhovskii with British
    members of the SFRF. See, for example, Volkhovskii Papers (Houghton Library),
    MS Russ 51, Folder 354, Thompson to Volkhovskii, 2 April 1899; MS Russ 51,
    Folder 362, Spence-Watson to Volkhovskii, 14 March 1899.
17 Michael Futrell, *Northern Underground. Episodes of Russian Revolutionary Transport
    and Communications through Scandinavia and Finland, 1863–1917* (London: Faber,
    1963), 37.
18 William Copeland, *The Uneasy Alliance: Collaboration between the Finnish Opposition
    and the Russian Underground, 1899–1904* (Helsinki: Suomalainen Tiedeakatemia,
    1973), 97.
19 For a useful review of British policy on the Finnish question in these years, see
    George Maude, 'Finland in Anglo-Russian Diplomatic Relations, 1899–1910',
    Slavonic and East European Review, 48, 113 (1970), 557–81.

the educated and semi-educated class, whose ideas about systems of government are decidedly different from those of Mr Pobyedonostsev and Company. And all these very large sections of the population have certainly more right to claim the representation of the National view than a handful of Reactionaries and Imperialists, who profit by their strong position at Court and in ruling circles to put a new blot on the honour of the Russian people.[20]

While the harsh treatment of Finland made for excellent anti-tsarist propaganda, Volkhovskii was still more struck by the changing character of the opposition movement in Russia itself. The student unrest that broke out in Moscow and St Petersburg early in 1899 signalled the beginning of a long period of disruption in Russian universities. Student protests were hardly unprecedented in pre-revolutionary Russia—Volkhovskii himself had helped to foment student unrest when a young man—but the protests of 1899-1901 were notable for the sympathy they attracted from sections of the urban workforce.[21] The disturbances also took place at a time of growing unrest in the Russian countryside. For Volkhovskii, as for many others, the start of the twentieth century seemed to mark the start of a new phase in the revolutionary struggle which brought together student and worker and peasant in a common front against the government. He was keen to explain the significance of developments to his Western readers.

In the spring of 1901, Volkhovskii published an article in *Free Russia* on 'The Meaning of Recent Events', telling his readers that

the Russian people are making their first attempt at no less a thing than the turning of a new leaf in their history. The Russian people long ago became sick of the lack of any personal security and of any official regard for the law, but they have been divided in their estimate of the causes of this state of things, and consequently in the recognition of their friends and enemies.

The change now was that 'thousands of artizans, factory workers, cabmen and journeymen' in cities across Russia responded to 'the cry of

---

20 F. Volkhovsky, 'Russian Imperialism and the Finns', *Free Russia* (1 April 1899).
21 On the student unrest in this period, see Samuel D. Kassow, *Students, Professors and the State in Tsarist Russia* (Berkeley, CA: University of California Press, 1989), 88–140. For a rather different discussion of the student movement in the years before Revolution, see Susan K. Morrissey, *Heralds of Revolution: Russian Students and the Mythologies of Radicalism* (New York: Oxford University Press, 1998).

the students for justice'. Volkhovskii also suggested that faith in the Tsar as the 'little father' of his people was fading rapidly in the countryside, as the peasantry began to understand how their poverty was rooted in the very structure of the existing social and economic order.[22] Volkhovskii expanded on these ideas in an article on the 'Russian Awakening' that appeared in the *Contemporary Review*, in which he once again argued that students and workers were joined in close bonds of sympathy ('a hearty compact') against 'horrible' assaults by Cossack troops armed with whips and guns. He also described how the authorities were using force to suppress peasant unrest in provinces like Poltava and Kharkov, where many peasants had been shot or birched, suggesting that such repressive measures were bound to fail given the level of discontent.[23] His views seemed to be confirmed in the spring of 1902, when further outbreaks of peasant unrest took place across the Empire, which Volkhovskii told readers of *Free Russia* was 'a thing expected and only a matter of time'.[24] He was confident that more extensive disorder would soon erupt in both the countryside and the city.

Many *narodniki* of the 1870s had believed that revolution could halt the development of capitalism in Russia and preserve intact the egalitarian instincts of the Russian peasantry.[25] Such hopes were by 1900 clearly untenable. Population growth in the countryside had created pervasive land hunger and poverty, as well as considerable economic differentiation, while the rapid growth of major urban centres created complex patterns of rural migration that disrupted traditional patterns of behaviour and belief.[26] It was for this reason that, by the closing years of the nineteenth century, several groups had emerged within the Tsarist Empire which—while more or less consciously identifying themselves

22 F. Volkhovsky, 'The Meaning of Recent Events', *Free Russia* (1 May 1901).

23 Felix Volkhovsky, 'The Russian Awakening', *Contemporary Review*, 81 (January 1902), 823–35.

24 F. Volkhovsky, 'The Rebellious Peasantry', *Free Russia* (1 June 1902).

25 For competing interpretations of this aspect of Populism, see Richard Pipes, '*Narodnichestvo*: A Semantic Inquiry', *Slavic Review*, 23, 3 (1964), 441–58; Andrzej Walicki, *The Controversy over Capitalism: Studies in the Social Philosophy of the Russian Populists* (Oxford: Clarendon Press, 1969).

26 On the question of 'stratification', see Daniel Field, 'Stratification and the Russian Peasant Commune: A Statistical Inquiry', in Roger Bartlett (ed.), *Land Commune and Peasant Community in Russia. Communal Forms in Imperial and Early Soviet Society* (London: Macmillan in Association with School of Slavonic and East European Studies, 1990), 143–64.

as heirs to the *narodnik* tradition of a previous generation—recognised that the social and economic changes of the previous twenty years or so demanded new ideas and tactics.[27]

The Union of Socialist Revolutionaries, led by A. A. Argunov, was sceptical about the revolutionary potential of the peasantry given its poverty and lack of education (the Union's programme instead emphasised, in the tradition of Narodnaia volia, the importance of terror in the struggle against the tsarist state).[28] The so-called Southern Party by contrast believed that the peasantry itself had a key role to play in the struggle for political freedom and economic transformation, not least because class divisions in the countryside had created a rural strata eager to bring about the destruction of the existing order.[29] Other smaller groups like the Worker's Party for the Liberation of Russia, established by G. A. Gershuni, focused more on fomenting revolution among urban workers. Although these groups came together in 1901-2 to form the Socialist Revolutionary Party, many ideological and tactical divisions remained, reflecting different perspectives on such questions as the revolutionary potential of the Russian peasantry and the use of terror to bring about political and economic change. One distinguished historian of the Party has suggested that the membership of the Socialist Revolutionary Party was defined by a common 'state of mind' rather than any more tangible agreement.[30] It was a verdict that could be applied to the SRs right down to 1917 and beyond.

---

27 For a useful discussion of the various groups that coalesced to form the SR Party, see Manfred Hildermeier, *The Russian Socialist Revolutionary Party Before the First World War* (New York: St Martin's Press, 2000), 27–42; M. I. Leonov, *Partiia sotsialistov-revoliutsionerov v 1905–1907 gg.* (Moscow: Rosspen, 1997), 26–38; A. I. Spiridovich, *Partiia sotsialistov-revoliutsionerov i eia predshestvenniki, 1886–1916* (Petrograd: Voennaia tipografiia, 1918), 47–91. For an examination of the development of the SR Party focusing on its relations with the urban workers, see Christopher Rice, *Russian Workers and the Socialist-Revolutionary Party through the Revolution of 1905–07* (Basingstoke: Macmillan, 1988).
28 For Argunov's memoirs of the developments culminating in the creation of the Socialist-Revolutionary Party, see A. Argunov, 'Iz proshlago partii sotsialistov-revoliutsionerov', *Byloe* (October 1907), 94–112.
29 On the Southern Party, see Maureen Perrie, *The Agrarian Policy of the Russian Socialist-Revolutionary Party* (Cambridge: Cambridge University Press, 1976), 44–46.
30 Oliver H. Radkey, *The Agrarian Foes of Bolshevism: Promise and Default of the Russian Socialist Revolutionaries from February to October 1917* (New York: Columbia University Press, 1958), 47.

The relationship between the nascent socialist revolutionary groups in Russia and the former *narodniki* in exile abroad was uncertain in the years before 1900, reflecting fragmentation on both sides, as well as the practical constraints imposed by police surveillance in Russia and Western Europe. The most important initiative to develop closer ties during the early years of the twentieth century came through the creation of the Agrarian-Socialist League, which was established following the death of Petr Lavrov in Paris at the start of 1900. While Volkhovskii had often disagreed with Lavrov during the previous decade, he recognised his central place in the Russian revolutionary pantheon, writing several poems in his honour including one that was recited at his funeral in Paris. A number of those who attended the funeral, including Volkhovskii, agreed to continue an initiative that Lavrov had set in motion before his death to create a new émigré organisation to support those seeking to foster revolutionary sentiment among the Russian peasantry.[31] The founding members of the Agrarian-Socialist League included a number of former fundists—among them Shishko, Chaikovskii and Lazarev— as well as Volkhovskii himself.[32] Viktor Chernov, who had arrived in Western Europe from Tambov province the previous year, and subsequently became the most important figure in shaping the ideology of the Socialist Revolutionary Party, was also a founding member.[33]

The principal focus of the Agrarian-Socialist League, at least in its early days, was on developing propaganda for circulation in Russia. Its publications were often distributed through the networks built up by the Russian Free Press Fund over the previous decade (although the

---

31   Viktor Chernov, *Pered burei* (Moscow: Direct Media, 2016), 200.

32   On the Agrarian League, see Perrie, *Agrarian Policy*, 24–33; Hildermeier, *Russian Socialist Revolutionary Party*, 38–41; Spiridovich, *Partiia sotsialistov-revoliutsionerov*, 85–87.

33   For Chernov's account of his life before leaving Russia, see Viktor Chernov, *Zapiski sotsialista-revoliutsionera* (Berlin: Izd-vo Z. I. Grzhebina, 1922). For a useful biography of Chernov, see A. I. Avrus, A. A. Goloseeva and A. P. Novikov, *Viktor Chernov: zhizn' russkogo sotsialista* (Moscow: Kliuch-S, 2015). For a valuable discussion of Chernov's career and development, see Hannu Immonen, *Mechty o novoi Rossii. Viktor Chernov (1877–1952)* (St Petersburg: Izd-vo Evropeiskogo universiteta v Sankt-Peterburge, 2015). Immonen's earlier work *The Agrarian Programme of the Russian Socialist Revolutionary Party, 1900–1914* (Helsinki: Suomen Historiallinen Seura, 1988) argued that Chernov's role as the main architect of SR policy, especially in the countryside, may have been somewhat overstated given the role played by other key figures like N. I. Rakitnikov.

Northern Underground was used less than the route through Ukraine). The first publication to appear was headed an appeal 'To Comrades in Thought and Deed', which was printed together with an essay on 'The Immediate Question of the Revolutionary Cause' (written by Chernov). Volkhovskii was among the five signatories to the appeal, which began by noting that the Agrarian-Socialist League had been created to broaden 'the revolutionary movement in general and the workers's movement in particular by attracting 'the working masses of the countryside'. It went on to list the key tasks of the League as:

1. The publication and distribution of popular revolutionary literature, suitable for the peasants as well as the urban factory and craft workers, especially those who have links to the countryside.

2. Familiarising Russian comrades with methods of socialist propaganda employed in the West among the working peasant masses (*truodvye krest'ianskie massy*), and with the forms of their organisation for the agrarian class struggle; assessing the historical experience of the 'movement to the people' by the Russian revolutionaries; studying all manifestations of social-political unrest among the contemporary peasantry; the theoretical development of general problems of agrarian socialism.

3. Practical and immediate aid of all kinds to Russian comrades whose activity corresponds to the programme of the Agrarian-Socialist League.

Members of the League were expected to acknowledge 'the ability of the working mass of the Russian peasantry to participate in active movement and struggle that will contribute to the evolution of Russian life in the direction indicated by ... the principles of international socialism'. They also had to accept the legitimacy of a revolutionary strategy focused on 'carrying out appropriate social-revolutionary propaganda and agitation' among the peasantry. The two principles taken together in effect recognised that successful revolutionary activity required careful guidance and planning while also needing to build on the energy of the *narod* itself.[34] Chernov's accompanying essay reinforced the idea that the countryside was an important site of revolution, arguing that propaganda and agitation should take place among the peasantry as well as the urban workers, a position that rejected the traditional Marxist view of the rural population as backward-looking and insular, while still acknowledging the critical role of the proletariat in forging revolution.[35] The League's subsequent publications marked a break with the populism of an earlier generation, acknowledging that economic relations in the countryside were already permeated by capitalism, with the result that the peasant commune was no longer necessarily a place where social relations were characterised by a spirit of egalitarian harmony.[36]

Volkhovskii was determined that the League should attract a broad spectrum of members, reflecting his long-standing impatience with ideological and tactical disputes of the kind that were soon to lead to the division of the Social Democrats into Bolsheviks and Mensheviks in 1903 (his daughter Vera noted many years later that her father always sought to maintain good relations with Russian revolutionaries from all parties, regularly meeting them for dinner, and attending the same meetings in London and Switzerland).[37] Volkhovskii was responsible for inviting David Soskice to join the League, even though his views at the time were closer to the Social Democrats, a move opposed by some other members.[38] The League's membership was nevertheless very small. Only fifteen people attended its first Congress at Geneva in 1902, including Lazarev and Shishko, while the total membership was just twenty-one. Volkhovskii was, for some reason, not present. The report of the Congress noted that the League had produced five pamphlets and organised the dispatch of a significant amount of material to Russia,

---

34 Spiridovich, *Partiia sotsialistov-revoliutsionerov*, 85–86. The translation here is taken from Perrie, *Agrarian Policy*, 30. For the composition of the League and a fuller statement of its aims sometime later, see SR Party Archive (Amsterdam), 131 ('Proekt Ustava Agrano-Sotsialisticheskoi Ligi').

35 [V.M. Chernov], *Ocherednoi vopros revoliutsionnago dela* (London: Agrarian League, 1900).

36 For a somewhat different view, arguing that this change only came later after the 1905 Revolution, see Radkey, *Agrarian Foes of Bolshevism*, 83–84.

37 Bertrand Russell Papers (McMaster University), 710.057280, Vera Volkhovskii to Bertrand Russell, 1 November 1920.

38 SR Party Archive (Amsterdam), 131, Volkhovskii to comrades, 21 April 1902.

although much of it had been seized by the tsarist authorities, following receipt of information from an agent who had established friendly relations with one of the League's own members.[39]

The Congress also approved the production of material to train a cadre of 'future leaders', who were to come from the areas where they carried out agitation, ensuring they had an understanding of local (*mestnoe*) conditions that would allow them to take the lead in 'revolutionising all the mass of the peasantry, cultivating in it a warlike spirit and preparation for struggle'.[40] The aim of this struggle was the removal (*ustranenie*) of the tsarist government as the principal obstacle to 'the freedom of the *narod* and the handing over of the land to the working people'. The programme said little about the situation in the towns and cities. Although Volkhovskii was not present at the Congress, he approved of the programme, which was in some ways more conventionally *narodnik* than the informal principles adopted by the Socialist Revolutionary Party the same year.[41]

The Congress also gave a good deal of attention to relations with the Socialist Revolutionary (SR) Party in Russia as well as more general questions of ideology and tactics. The *Okhrana* double agent Evno Azef told his superiors in St Petersburg at the end of 1901 that most of the League's members wanted to merge with the SRs, reporting that there was already an agreement for the League to focus on producing agitational literature, while SR publications like *Revoliutsionnaia Rossiia* [*Revolutionary Russia*] and *Vestnik russkoi revoliutsii* [*Herald of the Russian Revolution*] would be aimed at the *intelligentsia*.[42] Azef's views were not

SR Party Archive (Amsterdam), 131 ('Pervyi s"ezd Agrarno-Sotsialisticheskoi Ligi', 20 July 1902).

40 'Programma revoliutsionnoi deiatel'nosti v derevne', in Erofeev (ed.), *Partiia sotsialistov-revoliutsionerov. Dokumenty i materialy*, I, 48–51.

41 For the SR Programme, see 'Nasha programa', in Erofeev (ed.), *Partiia sotsialistov-revoliutsionerov. Dokumenty i materialy*, I, 51–58. The programme originally appeared in *Vestnik russkoi revoliutsii*, 1 (1902), edited by N. S. Rusanov, the journal which along with *Revoliutsionnaia Rossiia* provided the most authoritative locus of policy statements at a time when the SR Party lacked a coherent organisational structure. For a useful discussion of the evolution of the SR programme before and after the 1905 Revolution, see Leonov, *Partiia sotsialistov-revoliutsionerov*, 103–25. For another statement of key SR principles before the 1905 Revolution, see 'Osnovnye voprosy russkoi revoliutsionnoi programmy', *Revoliutsionnaia Rossiia*, 33 (1 October 1903).

42 D. B. Pavlov and Z. I. Peregudova (eds), *Pis'ma Azefa, 1893–1917* (Moscow: Terra, 1994), 64–67 (Azef to Rataev, 26 December 1901). On Azef see Anna Geifman,

altogether accurate. Volkhovskii had doubts about too hasty a union, believing the League should maintain its non-party character, although he also seems to have entertained hopes that it might at some point serve as the kernel of a new peasant socialist party in Russia.[43] Some other *stariki* (party elders) including Shishko shared his views.[44] Chernov was, by contrast, keen on union. His views eventually won out. The League and the SR Party were already cooperating closely in the spring of 1902 while a more formal federation took place a few months later.[45]

Some of the older émigrés may have struggled to accept that a new revolutionary generation had come to the fore in Russia, fearing their own influence was likely to be limited once the Agrarian-Socialist League merged with the SRs. Volkhovskii certainly disagreed with Chernov on various issues during this period. He was adamant that carrying out effective revolutionary work in the Russian countryside required strong direction, which he believed could only come from abroad, in effect asserting the leadership of the émigrés while casting doubt on the ability of those in Russia to conduct an effective campaign of agitation without firm guidance. Chernov was wary of such centralism. He had been in Russia far more recently than Volkhovskii, and his experience in areas like Tambov led him to take a more positive view of the capacity of local groups to develop a well-crafted programme of agitation. He also believed that it was impractical for 'generals' living abroad to run a revolutionary campaign from outside the country. The relationship between the two men at one point became very tense (Chernov accused Volkhovskii of using 'bitter and unpleasant' words about him). It is difficult to read the correspondence between them without sensing that Volkhovskii was out of touch with the way that things had changed in

---

   Entangled in Terror: The Azef Affair and the Russian Revolution (Wilmington, DE: Scholarly Resources, 2000).

43   SR Party Archive (Amsterdam), 131, Volkhovskii to comrades, 21 April 1902. Perrie, *Agrarian Policy*, 43.

44   See, for example, 'Iz pokazanii S. N. Sletova (Zemliakova) sudebno-sledstvennoi komissii pri Ts. K. PSR po delu Azefa', in Erofeev (ed.), *Partiia sotsialistov-revoliutsionerov. Dokumenty i materialy*, I, 139.

45   SR Party Archive (Amsterdam), 131 ('Federativnyi dogovor mezhdu Partii Sotsialistov-Revoliutsionerov i Agrarno-Sotsialisticheskoi Ligoi'). A briefer version of the document can be found in Erofeev (ed.), *Partiia sotsialistov-revoliutsionerov. Dokumenty i materialy*, I, 68–69.

Russia since his flight from Vladivostok a decade earlier.[46] Nor was he
alone. The tension between locals and émigrés became a major theme in
the development of the SR Party down to 1917.

While the League's members recognised that peasant uprisings
might involve violence, if only in response to official repression, the
question of using terror as a revolutionary tactic was seldom addressed
directly in its publications. The League was particularly cautious about
'agrarian terrorism'—the use of violence against landlords, whether in
the form of murder or destruction of property—instead stressing the
pivotal role of strikes and boycotts in creating the kind of mass movement
needed to bring about change. Nor did its programme say much about
questions of political terror. One leading scholar has rightly noted that
Chernov's original essay outlining the League's programme owed
more to the second Zemlia i volia than to Narodnaia volia,[47] although
Chernov himself later contributed an article to *Revoliutsionnaia Rossiia* in
1903 endorsing 'the implementation of terror' as one of 'many kinds of
weapons' to be used in the 'assault on the government',[48] subsequently
becoming the leading SR theorist defending the use of terror to bring
about political reform.[49] The question of political terror does not,

46   Volkhovskii Papers (Houghton Library), MS Russ 51, Folder 87, Chernov (pseud.
     B. Olenin) to Volkhovskii [no date but probably 1902]. I am indebted to the work
     of Dr Lara Green for alerting me to the significance of this correspondence which
     I had previously overlooked. See Lara Green, 'Russian Revolutionary Terrorism in
     Transnational Perspective: Representations and Networks, 1881–1926' (PhD thesis,
     Northumbria University, 2019), 144.
47   Hildermeier, *Russian Socialist Revolutionary Party*, 39.
48   Anna Geifman, *Thou Shalt Kill. Revolutionary Terrorism in Russia 1894-1917*
     (Princeton, NJ: Princeton University Press, 1993), 46. A useful series of essays on
     terrorism in Russia during the years before 1917 can be found in S. V. Deviatov
     et al. (eds), *Terrorizm v Rossii v nachale XX v.*, Istoricheskii vestnik, 149 (Moscow:
     Runivers, 2012). On attitudes towards terrorism within the SR Party generally,
     see O. V. Budnitskii, *Terrorizm v rossiiskom osvoboditel'nom dvizhenii: ideologiia,
     etika, psikhologiia (vtoriaia polovina XIX–nachalo XX v)* (Moscow: Rosspen, 2000),
     134–217; Maureen Perrie, 'Political and Economic Terror in the Tactics of the
     Russian Socialist-Revolutionary Party before 1914', in Wolfgang J. Mommsen
     and Gerhard Hirschfeld (eds), *Social Protest, Violence and Terror in Nineteenth- &
     Twentieth-Century Europe* (London: Macmillan, 1982), 63–79; Manfred Hildermeier,
     'The Terrorist Strategies of the Socialist-Revolutionary Party in Russia, 1900–1914',
     in Mommsen and Hirschfeld (eds), *Social Protest*, 80–87.
49   For the clearest programmatic statement of the role of terror for the SRs, see
     Chernov's 'Terroristicheskii element v nashei programme', which originally
     appeared in *Revoliutsionnaia Rossiia*, 7 (June 1902), reproduced in *Po voprosom
     programmy i taktiki. Sbornik statei iz Revoliutsionnoi Rossii* (n.p.: Tip-ia Partii

though, seem to have been a stumbling block in the discussions that led to federation between the League and the SR Party. Any differences were probably ones of degree. Volkhovskii was certainly not opposed to the use of terror against leading figures in the tsarist regime, believing that such attacks could weaken the state apparatus, although he was convinced that real change could only come about in Russia through popular revolution in both the city and the countryside.

The SRs use of terror did create something of a challenge for Volkhovskii when writing for a British audience. Although he had previously joined Stepniak in defending Narodnaia volia, both men repeatedly stressed on the pages of *Free Russia* that the Russian revolutionary movement had largely abandoned terrorism by the early 1890s, a claim that could no longer be made ten years later. The problem was made somewhat easier by the response of many leading British newspapers to the assassinations carried out by the Combat Organisation of the SR Party, which was headed first by Grigorii Gershuni and then, following his arrest, by Evno Azef. When the Minister of the Interior Dmitrii Sipiagin was assassinated in April 1902, the *Times* noted that although such an action was 'regrettable and reprehensible ... the odious system of government which continues in force cannot by any means be exonerated from its share of the blame'.[50] It responded in a similar vein two years later to the murder of Viacheslav Pleve (who had replaced Sipiagin). An editorial in the paper noted that while 'Murder as a political weapon is universally condemned by civilized man and the assassination of M. de Pleve cannot escape reprobation from the point of view of public and private morality', his role in promoting harsh measures to preserve the autocratic system of government represented an 'extreme provocation' and 'an explanation of what can never be ethically justified'.[51] Many other papers took a similar line, suggesting that such actions were understandable, even if they were morally

---

sotsialistov-revoliutsionerov, 1903), 71–84. For a discussion of attitudes towards terror within the SRs during this period, see Leonov, *Partiia sotsialistov-revoliutsionerov*, 125–36. Leonov suggests (126) that Volkhovskii was 'indifferent' on questions of terror which, as will be seen in both this and the following chapter, does not capture his views accurately.

50   *Times* (17 April 1902).
51   *Times* (29 July 1904).

dubious.[52] Anti-tsarist feeling in Britain still remained strong enough in
the early 1900s to ensure there was at least some level of sympathy for
the regime's revolutionary opponents.

The murder of Pleve in July 1904 came just a few weeks after the
assassination of the Governor-General of Finland Nikolai Bobrikov by
a Finnish nationalist, a killing that also attracted sympathy (or at least
understanding) in much of the British press, given his role in suppressing
Finnish autonomy within the Tsarist Empire.[53] *Free Russia* was only
appearing quarterly by 1904—testimony to the perennial character of the
financial challenges it faced—with the result that the shock of the Pleve
assassination had faded by the time the July-October edition appeared.
An unsigned editorial noted that the killing had been 'as inevitable and
natural as the explosion of gunpowder in an overheated oven ... the
great masses of the people have everything to lose and nothing to gain
by further submission to the tyranny of their oppressors'. It added that
autocracy was 'at its last gasp' and that the whole world would become
more peaceful once the tsarist government was overthrown.[54] The same
edition carried, without any negative comment, a translation of the
manifesto released by the SRs explaining that the assassination of Pleve
was designed to remove 'the omnipotent tyrant of Russia' who had
played a critical role in preserving 'the barbarous mould of despotism'.[55]

The Combat Organisation that carried out the murder of Pleve
operated with a high degree of autonomy within the SR Party. Émigrés
like Volkhovskii knew little about its activities.[56] He was however closely

---

52   See, for example, *The Referee*, 31 July 1904.
53   The liberal *Daily News* without praising the killing noted on 18 June 1904 that
     Bobrikov had for some years sought 'to destroy all semblance of liberty in
     Finland'. The conservative *Morning Post* by contrast on the same day referred to
     the killing as 'The Helsingfors Outrage'. On the killing, see Richard Bach Jensen,
     'The 1904 Assassination of Governor-General Bobrikov: Tyrannicide, Anarchism
     and the Expanding Scope of "Terrorism"', *Terrorism and Political Violence*, 30, 5
     (2018), 828–43. For a discussion of the worldwide press coverage of the killing,
     see Mila Oiva et al., 'Spreading News in 1904. The Media Coverage of Nikolay
     Bobrikov's Killing', *Media History*, 26, 4 (2020), 391–407.
54   'The Events of the Last Three Months', *Free Russia* (1 October 1904). Volkhovskii
     was out of Britain a good deal in the late summer of 1904, and it is possible that
     the editorial was penned by David Soskice.
55   'Why M. de Plehve was Assassinated: A Manifesto', *Free Russia* (1 October 1904).
56   A comprehensive history of the Combat Organisation can be found in R. A.
     Gorodnitskii, *Boevaia organizatsiia partii sotsialistov-revoliutsionerov v 1901–1911
     gg.* (Moscow: Rosspen, 1998). See, too, Geifman, *Thou Shalt Kill*, passim. For

involved with the Foreign Committee of the SR Foreign Organisation (Zagranichnaia organisatsiia), which effectively absorbed many of the operations of the Agrarian-Socialist League following its merger with the SRs.[57] The Foreign Organisation was tasked, among other things, with providing support for revolutionary activities in Russia, including the production and transport of revolutionary literature, although since it was made up of a number of national groups it was too unwieldy to operate effectively. As a result, the Foreign Committee was in practice responsible for carrying out much of the work. Volkhovskii himself continued to play a significant role in producing propaganda. He was not a regular contributor to the main SR publications *Revoliutsionnaia Rossiia* and *Vestnik russkoi revoliutsii*, although he contributed a long piece to the former in 1903, attacking Pleve's policy towards Finland and criticising those in Britain, like William Stead, who were too ready to accept the principle of Russification.[58] He also occasionally published verse in the two journals.[59] He was, though, still active in the years before 1905 in producing other revolutionary literature for illegal circulation in Russia.

Volkhovskii helped to edit the miscellany *Narodnoe delo*, which appeared irregularly in 1902–04 as a publication of the Socialist Revolutionary Party, contributing several pieces under his own name.[60]

---

a statement of its organisation and aims dating from 1904, see 'Ustav boevoi organizatsii partii SR, priniatyi ee chlenami v Avguste 1904 g.', in Erofeev (ed.), *Partiia sotsialistov-revoliutsionerov. Dokumenty i materialy*, I, 149–51. For the justification of the murder by the SR leadership, see 'Dve voiny', *Revoliutsionnaia Rossiia*, 50 (1 August 1904).

57   Among the limited literature on the Foreign Organisation, see M. I. Leonov, 'Zagranichnaia organizatsiia i Zagranichnyi komitet partii eserov v nachale XX veka (Na putiakh partiinoi institutsionalizatsii)', *Vestnik Samarskogo universiteta: istoriia, pedagogika, filologiia*, 27, 2 (2021), 27–36. For a brief useful discussion in English, see Hildermeier, *Russian Socialist Revolutionary Party*, 111–14. The discussion in K. N. Morozov, *Partiia sotsialistov-revoliutsionerov v 1907–1914 gg.* (Moscow: Rosspen, 1998), 249–65, focuses on the Foreign Organisation after 1907 when its role and organization were very different.

58   F. Volkhovskii, 'Inostrannaia kritika teorii Fon-Pleve', *Revoliutsionnaia Rossiia*, 36 (15 November 1903).

59   *Vestnik russkoi revoliutsii*, 3 (March 1903) printed one of Volkhovskii's poems dedicated to the memory of Petr Lavrov.

60   Lara Green rightly points out that there is little surviving archival material relating to *Narodnoe delo* (see Green, 'Russian Revolutionary Terrorism', 119). It is possible that Volkhovskii was only one of the editors, particularly since he did not formally join the SRs till 1904, although the limited material in the SR Party archive shows

Narodnoe delo was aimed at an audience of what the second issue called 'urban and rural workers', although the content was quite demanding, and more likely to appeal to a readership of students and *intelligenty*. The opening number contained an article describing how the private ownership of property was the principal cause of poverty among both workers and peasants.[61] The third issue included long articles on urban unemployment and the development of new forms of economic 'serfdom' in the countryside.[62] The fourth issue explored the historical and contemporary significance of 1 May for the workers' movement in Russia and beyond, while the fifth included a long piece on the differences between the attitudes of the Social Democrats and Socialist Revolutionaries towards the peasantry.[63] Most numbers contained short stories and poems, reflecting Volkhovskii's long-standing policy of including literary content in the journals he edited, while his main editorial role appears to have been the practical one of organising and reviewing submissions rather than setting down a firm ideological line for the journal.

Among the pieces Volkhovskii himself published in *Narodnoe delo* was 'Pochemu armiane "buntuiut"' ('Why the Armenians Are Rebelling'),[64] which was written shortly after violent protests broke out in Russian Armenia against the confiscation of the property of the Armenian Church. He accused the tsarist authorities of deliberately stoking up ethnic tension in the Caucasus, to keep the Armenians in a state of 'slavish submission', without 'their own schools, libraries, newspapers … clergy and national property'. The Armenians were, Volkhovskii suggested, simply defending 'their rights not to climb into the wolf's mouth of the tsarist government', and far from being the enemies of the

---

that he was certainly involved in reviewing and amending articles submitted to the journal.
61　Opening editorial, *Narodnoe delo*, 1 (1902), 1–2.
62　'Krizis i bezrabotitsa', *Narodnoe delo*, 3 (1903), 3–20; 'Novoe krepostnoe pravo', *Narodnoe delo*, 3 (1903), 46–71.
63　'Sotsialism i 1-oe Maia', *Narodnoe delo*, 4 (1904), 3-30; 'Kak smotriat' sotsialisty-revoliutsionery i sotsial-demokraty na krest'ianstvo i na zemel'nyi vopros', *Narodnoe delo*, 5 (1904), 1–27 (the title of the piece is curiously listed slightly differently in the contents page).
64　F. Volkhovskii, *Pochemu armiane "buntuiut"* (Geneva: Partiia sotsialistov-revoliutsionerov, 1904). The article first appeared in the fifth number of *Narodnoe delo*.

Russian people, 'are helping us ... to free ourselves from the kulak, the landlord and the bureaucratic yoke. If all the peoples inhabiting Russia strike unanimously at these bloodsuckers, then it will be much easier for them to break the strength of the present ... government'. Volkhovskii's argument echoed his long-standing commitment to fostering greater cultural self-awareness among Ukrainians and Siberians, as well as the SR Party's somewhat hazy commitment to a post-revolutionary federal order that recognised the autonomy of national minorities within a new socialist union.[65] It also reflected his view that the development of nationalist sentiment on the fringes of the Empire could strengthen opposition against the tsarist government.

Volkhovskii also sought to engage with a rather different audience during these years through writing fables and short stories. The ones he wrote for English children, including 'The Story of the Clever Fox' and 'In the Sun',[66] were little more than entertaining pieces leavened with gentle warnings about the importance of cooperation and the pitfalls of deceiving the unwary. He also, though, wrote other stories aimed at a peasant readership in Russia that were far more radical in character. Volkhovskii's experience in producing poems for children and satirical fantasies for adults had long convinced him that skilfully-written tales of magic and mystery could shape popular attitudes towards real social and political questions. In 1902, he published *Skazanie o nespravedlivom tsare* (*The Tale of the Unjust Tsar*), subsequently reprinted as 'The Tale of Tsar Simeon', which began in time-honoured fashion with the words 'Once upon a time there lived an unjust tsar [who] was arrogant and merciless towards his people'.[67] The story tells how a delegation of villagers sought the help of an old magician to ease their plight, who responds by transforming the appearance of the kindest man in the village, one Ivan Krasnoperov, to look exactly like the Tsar himself. The real Tsar, meanwhile, falls from his horse while out hunting, destroying both his finery and his memory, transforming him into a poverty-stricken tramp

65   See, for example, the sentiments expressed by the anonymous author of 'Natsional'nyi vopros i revoliutsiia', *Revoliutsionnaia Rossiia*, 35 (1 November 1903).

66   Felix Volkhovsky, 'In the Sun', *Little Folks* (1 June 1900); Felix Volkhovsky, 'The Story of the Clever Fox', *Little Folks* (1 July 1900).

67   Feliks Volkhovskii, *Skazanie o nespravedlivom tsare i kak on v razum voshel i kakoi sovet liudiam dal* (London: Izd-vo. Partii sotsialistov-revoliutsionerov i Agrarno-sotsialisticheskoi ligi, 1902).

forced to beg for food and shelter. Five years pass, during which time
Krasnoperov starts to behave like a ruthless and suspicious autocrat,
flattered and deceived by his courtiers, while the true Tsar is chastened
by witnessing the injustice and poverty that scar his kingdom. When
the two men are changed back into their former selves, the Tsar refuses
to return to his old role, while Krasnoperov slips away into the crowd
and vanishes. The villagers are at first unsure what to do in the absence
of a ruler, until they hear the wind whispering in the trees, telling them
that 'You are people not cattle. Help yourselves for nobody else will'.
The moral of the *skazka* was clear. The failings of an autocratic system of
government were not simply rooted in the character of the Tsar but were
instead an inevitable consequence of giving unlimited power to any
single person. A 'good' tsar would not, as many peasants still hoped,
take action to end their poverty and improve their place in society.

Volkhovskii published a second story in *Narodnoe delo*, in 1904, that
was reprinted a year later at the height of the 1905 Revolution. 'Kak
muzhik u vsekh v dolgu ostalsia' ('How the Peasant Owes Everyone')
tells how the devil created a kulak, a nobleman and a priest to trick
an honest peasant out of his possessions.[68] When the peasant refuses
to hand over his land, the devil and his accomplices seek the advice of
the mythical Baba Yaga, who tells them to find a magic egg in the forest
and sit on it until it hatches out a tsar. The tsar then carves an army
of soldiers and police from the nearby trees, who arrest the luckless
peasant and seize his possessions, forcing him to survive by labouring in
the kulak's factory and working in the fields of the nobleman. The priest
blesses the arrangement, in return for payment, with the result that 'the
muzhik from that time has been in debt with everyone: the kulak, the
priest, the nobleman, and the tsar'. The fable offered no happy ending. It
was instead designed to show how the existing social and political order
was not 'natural' or divinely ordered. The figures of authority—tsar,
nobleman, priest, kulak—were all rapacious exploiters rather than the
protectors of the *muzhik*.

Volkhovskii's stories were crafted to echo the motifs of a Russian
folk-tale tradition that itself often challenged social and political

---

68   F. Volkhovskii, 'Kak muzhik u vsekh v dolgu ostalsia. Skazka', *Narodnoe delo*, 5
     (1904), 28–48.

hierarchies.[69] His approach was apparently successful. Both stories were reprinted many times, including in the wake of the 1917 February Revolution, when the SRs published 100,000 copies of the 'The Tale of Tsar Simeon' and 30,000 copies of 'How the Peasant Owes Everyone'.[70] A significant number were also smuggled into Russia during the unrest of 1905 as part of the SR Foreign Organisation's efforts to foment peasant uprisings. 'The Tale of the Unjust Tsar' was translated into Ukrainian in 1903, by the poet Lesia Ukrainka, and circulated widely in the south-western provinces of the Tsarist Empire. Ukrainka was the niece of the Ukrainian nationalist writer and historian Mykhailo Drahomanov, who had himself known Volkhovskii for many years, and been an important source of information for the fundists during the 1890s. While Ukrainka's political sympathies lay with the Marxist Social Democrats rather than the Socialist Revolutionaries, she was astute enough to realise that the SRs were more positive about the cause of national self-determination, corresponding regularly with Volkhovskii in 1902–03 about how to promote political change that would allow Ukrainian culture to flourish.[71]

Volkhovskii also continued to write poetry throughout the years leading up to the 1905 Revolution, although the lyrical-pastoral turn that characterised his work in the 1880s was largely abandoned in favour of a return to the more overtly political verse he penned in the 1870s. He wrote several poems in homage to leading figures in the revolutionary movement, including a new 1902 poem praising the memory of Petr Lavrov, whose 'grave is not silent' but rather 'a living source of inspiration' for all those struggling for freedom.[72] Two years

---

69 For a lucid analysis of the Russian folktale tradition, see Jack V. Haney, *An Introduction to the Russian Folktale* (Armonk, NY: M. E. Sharpe, 1999).

70 Elizabeth Jones Hemenway, 'Telling Stories: Russian Political Culture and Narratives of Revolution, 1917–1921' (PhD thesis, University of North Carolina at Chapel Hill, 1998), 51. See, too, the same author's article 'Nicholas in Hell: Rewriting the Tsarist Narrative in the Revolutionary *Skazki* of 1917', *Russian Review*, 60, 2 (2001), 185–204.

71 On Ukrainka (born Larysa Petrivna Kosach), including material on her relations with Volkhovskii, see George S. N. Luckyj, *Seven Lives: Vignettes of Ukrainian Writers in the Nineteenth Century*, *The Annals of the Ukrainian Academy of Arts and Sciences in the US*, 20, 47–48 (1998–99), 161–87. The correspondence between Ukrainka and Volkhovskii can be found in Volkhovskii Papers (HIA), Box 3, Folder 39.

72 F. Volkhovskoi (*sic*), 'Dorogaia mogila (Pamiati P. L. Lavrova)', in F. Volkhovskoi, *Sluchainyia pesni* (Moscow: Knigoizdatel'stvo L. I. Kolevatova, 1907), 65. The poem first appeared in *Revoliutsionnaia Rossiia*, 9 (July 1902).

earlier, in 1900, he had published a poem, 'Maiak' ('The Lighthouse'), in honour of the *narodnik* theorist Nikolai Mikhailovskii, complete with laden metaphors of how words could be used to illuminate the world as light cut through fog.[73] Volkhovskii also reworked some of his old poems, including 'Duda', originally published in the 1870s, in order to attract a wider audience, adding some scathing lines about money-grubbing priests ('long-haired Satans') who exploited the peasantry under the guise of holiness.[74] The new version was intended to be sung to the well-known tune 'Zdrastvui, milaia, khoroshaia moia' ('Greetings My Sweet Girl'). 'Voina' ('War')—which described the plight of soldiers sent thousands of miles from home—was set to music traditionally used to train soldiers to march in time (the poem was clearly designed to strike a chord with troops during the Russo-Japanese War of 1904–05).[75] Whether such 'song-poems' circulated widely is difficult to say. Nor is it clear, as with the *skazki*, what lasting impact they had. Yet the time Volkhovskii spent on instilling radical motifs into poems and short stories designed to ape familiar forms of popular culture reflected a thoroughly *narodnik* desire to shape the political consciousness of peasants and workers by engaging with them in their own vernacular.

****

Volkhovskii's contribution to the neo-*narodnik* revival before 1905 was not limited to journalism and propaganda. In the early years of the twentieth century, he also became involved in procuring false passports for individuals wanting to travel to and from Russia illegally (he had indeed sought advice about how to get passports under a false name as early as 1895).[76] The Fabian Socialist and Quaker Samuel Hobson recalled many years later that 'It was the mild and persuasive Volkhovsky who lured me into evil ways' by asking him to obtain English passports to help Russian exiles flee Siberia. It was a practice that continued 'off and on for years ... Then a personal friend in the Foreign Office sent for me.

---

73 F. Volkhovskoi, 'Maiak', in *Sluchainyia pesni*, 61.
74 For this variant, see N. A. Alikina and L. S. Kashikhin (eds), *Pesni revoliutsionnogo podpol'ia* (Perm: Permskoe Knizhnoe Izd-vo, 1977), http://a-pesni.org/starrev/duda.htm.
75 F. Volkhovskoi, 'Voina', in *Sluchainyia pesni*, 81–82.
76 Volkhovskii Papers (HIA), Box 17, Folder 11, Letter to Volkhovskii dated 31 May 1895.

"Sorry old chap, but we know about it. It must stop"'.[77] Hobson believed the passports were destined for those fleeing Russia, but there was a more sinister side to the trade as well. Volkhovskii was almost certainly involved in 1904 in helping the journalist H. N. Brailsford procure passports for three Russians seeking to return to their country. One of the passports was later found on the body of a terrorist who died while planting a bomb in a St Petersburg hotel, leading the Russian government to make a formal protest to London, which in turn prompted an inquiry that resulted in Brailsford being tried and convicted for obtaining a passport under false pretences. Brailsford claimed that he obtained the passports at the request of someone 'on the continent' with close ties to the Russian revolutionary movement, who told him that they would be used to facilitate smuggling illegal literature into Russia,[78] but declined to name his interlocutor. Despite the best efforts of his defence counsel—the future Liberal MP and Minister Sir John Simon—he was found guilty and fined £100. Volkhovskii for his part seems to have been unrepentant and continued his efforts to obtain passports for use by revolutionaries seeking to enter and leave Russia.[79]

Volkhovskii was also involved in several other attempts to support the opposition movement in Russia. He was by the early 1900s confident that fomenting revolution in areas on the periphery of the Empire could help to weaken the tsarist government (a conviction that had shaped his response to the unrest in Armenia and prompted his collaboration with Lesia Ukrainka to translate radical material into Ukrainian). Volkhovskii's sympathy for Ukrainian nationalist aspirations also

---

77   S. G. Hobson, *Pilgrim to the Left: Memoirs of a Modern Revolutionist* (London: Edward Arnold, 1938), 126.

78   F. M. Leventhal, *The Last Dissenter: H. N. Brailsford and his World* (Oxford: Clarendon Press, 1985), 52–54. Leventhal speculates that Soskice rather than Volkhovskii may have been instrumental in helping Brailsford, but Volkhovskii had returned to Britain from the continent for some weeks at this time, and the whole affair bears his hallmark. The two men were certainly regular correspondents, as can be seen in Volkhovskii Papers (Houghton Library), MS Russ 51, Folder 266 (letters from Brailsford to Volkhovskii). For a report of the trial, which took place in 1905, see the *Times* (24 May 1905).

79   For example, Volkhovskii Papers (HIA), Box 17, Folder 11 contains a passport for an American woman Ida Rauh dated 1906 to be used for any purpose 'so long as it is not terrorism'. The same folder contains a letter by Volkhovskii asking for advice about how to organise quick marriages, presumably designed to allow foreign nationals to obtain British passports.

reflected something more than simple revolutionary pragmatism, given his long-standing interest in Ukrainian history and culture (during his later years he collected numerous photographs of Ukrainian villages and noted in one unpublished piece that 'my thoughts ... are Ukrainian').[80] Yet despite his Ukrainophilism, Volkhovskii believed that it was in Finland that nationalism was most likely to fuel revolutionary sentiment, given popular resentment against the Russification programme set in motion by Governor-General Bobrikov. Not all his contacts agreed. The Swedish journalist N. C. Frederickson, who in August 1903 interviewed Pleve about the government's policies, warned Volkhovskii a few weeks later 'that revolutionary movements as in Russia are and always will be impossible in Finland'. In another letter, Frederickson noted that moderate nationalists in Finland, like the jurist and academic Leo Mechelin, looked at the Russian revolutionary movement with considerable wariness.[81] A rather different view of the Finnish opposition movement was taken by Konrad (Konni) Zilliacus, a charismatic Swedish-speaking Finnish nationalist and journalist, who had since the late 1890s been involved in smuggling literature into the Russian Empire through Scandinavia.[82]

Volkhovskii and Zilliacus probably first came into contact in the spring of 1899 at a time when they were both seeking to rally opinion in Sweden against the tsarist government.[83] They certainly began to correspond regularly from the summer of 1902, initially discussing ways of preventing Swedish customs from seizing revolutionary literature sent from London for onward dispatch to Russia.[84] Volkhovskii became

---

80   Volkhovskii Papers (HIA), Box 22, Folder 4 (Selection of photographs of Ukrainian villages). The unpublished article quoted from here is unsigned but appears to be in Volkhovskii's handwriting. See Volkhovskii Papers (HIA), Box 11, Folder 7 (Untitled and undated fragment).

81   Volkhovskii Papers (HIA), Box 3, Folder 24, Frederickson to Volkhovskii, 18 September 1903; 26 October 1903.

82   For a useful brief discussion of Zilliacus' career, see Ira Jänis-Isokongas, 'Konrad (Konni) Zilliacus and Revolutionary Russia', *Nordic and Baltic Studies Review*, 3 (2018), 366–79. Also of value is Zilliacus' own admittedly unreliable autobiography *Sortovuosilta. Poliittisia muistelmia* (Porvoo: WSOY, 1920) which has not yet been translated into English. I would like to thank staff at the Slavonic Library at Helsinki who helped me read the relevant pages of the book.

83   Copeland, *Uneasy Alliance*, 96–98.

84   Volkhovskii Papers (HIA), Box 3, Folder 36, Zilliacus to Volkhovskii, 13 November 1902.

a regular contributor to publications edited by Zilliacus in Stockholm, including *Fria Ord* (*Free Word*), submitting pieces on subjects ranging from his revolutionary experiences through to the challenges facing Russian women.[85] The two men quickly came to trust one another. There were also some striking similarities in their views, even though Zilliacus was first and foremost a nationalist and Volkhovskii a socialist. In 1902, Zilliacus published in Swedish a book describing the development of the Russian revolutionary movement,[86] subsequently telling Volkhovskii that it was designed to do what *Free Russia* had done over the previous decade,[87] presenting revolutionary opponents of the tsarist regime as reasonable people who only turned to violence in the face of oppression and cruelty. Volkhovskii was impressed enough to work with Zilliacus on producing an English version.[88] He also shared Zilliacus' view that opponents of the tsarist regime needed to set aside their ideological differences and cooperate more effectively. Zilliacus struggled, though, to persuade moderate figures in the Finnish opposition, like Mechelen, that their best hope for securing greater independence rested on cooperating with revolutionary groups across the Russian Empire.[89] Despite his frustrations, he nevertheless told Volkhovskii in the spring of 1903 that he planned to launch an ambitious personal initiative 'to come to an understanding about a concerted plan of action ... with all the various elements of the Russian opposition', including the Finns.[90]

85 Volkhovskii Papers (Houghton Library), MS Russ 51, Folder 372, Zilliacus to Volkhovskii, 6 January 1903. Volkhovskii's contributions to the journal appeared under a pseudonym.

86 Konni Zilliacus, *Det revolutionära Ryssland: en skildring af den revolutionära rörelsens i Ryssland uppkomst och utveckling* (Stockholm: K. P. Boströms Forlag 1902). The book was updated and translated into English three years later including further material provided by Volkhovskii. See Konni Zilliacus, *The Russian Revolutionary Movement* (London: E. P. Dutton, 1905).

87 Volkhovskii Papers (Houghton Library), MS Russ 51, Folder 372, Zilliacus to Volkhovskii, 6 January 1903.

88 See the positive draft review of Zilliacus, *Det revoliutionära Ryssland*, which appears to be in Volkhovskii's handwriting, in Volkhovskii Papers (HIA), Box 8, Folder 12.

89 On relations between the Finnish constitutionalists and revolutionaries both in Finland and Russia, see Antti Kujala, 'Finnish Radicals and the Russian Revolutionary Movement, 1899–1907', *Revolutionary Russia*, 5, 2 (1992), 172–192. See, too, Steven Duncan Huxley, *Constitutionalist Insurgency in Finland. Finnish "Passive Resistance" against Russification as a Case of Nonmilitary Struggle in the European Resistance Tradition* (Helsinki: Suomen Historiallinen Seura, 1990).

90 Volkhovskii Papers (Houghton Library), MS Russ 51, Folder 372, Zilliacus to Volkhovskii, 21 April 1903.

Zilliacus had, by the autumn of 1903, convinced at least some
representatives of the Finnish constitutionalist movement to support the
establishment of a news agency that would coordinate the propaganda
activities of all groups that were critical of the tsarist autocracy
(although he carefully downplayed the role of Russian revolutionary
organisations). At the start of December, he told Volkhovskii that he was
about to depart on 'a pilgrimage through Europe to personally meet and
become acquainted with representatives of all the [various] groups of
the opposition against the present government in Russia', in the hope
of getting them to pull together 'to overthrow the ruling order'.[91] Two
weeks later, Zilliacus was in Paris, meeting with the SRs Evno Azef and
Ilia Rubanovich (a former member of Narodnaia volia who had worked
closely with Lavrov during his final years). He followed this up with a
trip to London where he met Volkhovskii, Chaikovskii and Kropotkin.
The outbreak of the Russo-Japanese War a few weeks later made his task
more timely than ever,[92] since the conflict promised to exacerbate the
social and political tensions that had been building up for many years,
providing fresh hope to opponents of the tsarist government.[93] In the
early March of 1904, Zilliacus told Volkhovskii that the time was ripe for
revolutionary groups to submit a joint manifesto to the Tsar demanding
concessions including freedom of speech and constitutional reform.[94]
Volkhovskii was sceptical about the wisdom of such a proposal, fearing
that Zilliacus was too sensitive to the concerns of Russian and Finnish
liberals, and wrote a detailed response arguing that Nicholas would
never agree to such reforms. Zilliacus, in turn, replied that he had
not meant to suggest that the course of action he proposed would be
effective without holding out the possibility of more direct forms of

---

91 Volkhovskii Papers (HIA), Box 3, Folder 36, Zilliacus to Volkhovskii, 7 December
1903. For a discussion of Zilliacus' activities over the next few months, with a
particular focus on his efforts to reassure Finnish constitutionalists about his
discussions with Russian revolutionaries, see Copeland, *Uneasy Alliance*, 147–60.

92 For the diplomatic and military history of the Russo-Japanese War, see John W.
Steinberg et al. (eds), *Russo-Japanese War in Global Perspective: World War Zero*,
2 vols (Leiden: Brill, 2005–07); Ian Nish, *The Origins of the Russo-Japanese War*
(London: Longman, 1985).

93 The war with Japan and its potential to increase the prospects of revolution was
the subject of a special column, 'Voina', in almost all editions of *Revoliutsionnaia
Rossiia* during 1904 and into 1905.

94 Volkhovskii Papers (HIA), Box 3, Folder 36, Zilliacus to Volkhovskii, 1 March
1904.

action.[95] The two men had previously discussed how best to provoke armed uprisings in the countryside, as a way of putting pressure on the Government, and Volkhovskii was convinced that only such radical action would bring about change.

Although he had been ill for some weeks, Zilliacus once again met with Volkhovskii and Chaikovskii in London, in April 1904, to discuss plans for a possible conference that would bring together revolutionaries, nationalists and liberals to discuss ways of overthrowing the tsarist regime.[96] Volkhovskii was ready to consider any strategy that could weaken the government, although past experience made him fearful that divisions among Russian liberals made them unreliable collaborators.[97] The two most prominent figures among the liberals—Petr Struve and Pavel Miliukov—were both ready to cooperate with more radical groups, but as Zilliacus quickly discovered, others were uncertain about how far they should go in cooperating with the revolutionary parties. Zilliacus' correspondence with Volkhovskii over the following months was full of

---

95   The gist of Volkhovskii's letter can be determined from the reply by Zilliacus found in Volkhovskii Papers (HIA), Box 3, Folder 36, Zilliacus to Volkhovskii, 31 March 1904.

96   While there was, by the early summer of 1904, a growing recognition within the SR Party of the potential significance of growing unrest in Finland, the main Party publications still tended to see it more as an expression of growing radicalism rather than nationalism, at least until later in the year. See, for example, 'Revoliutsionnoe dvizhenie v Finliandii', *Revoliutsionnaia Rossiia*, 48 (15 June 1904).

97   For the multi-faceted character of Russian liberalism in this period see, for example, the relevant sections of Anton A. Fedyashin, *Liberals under Autocracy. Modernization and Civil Society in Russia, 1866–1904* (Madison, WI: University of Wisconsin Press, 2012); Klaus Frolich, *The Emergence of Russian Constitutionalism 1900–1904: The Relationship between Social Mobilization and Political Group Formation in Pre-Revolutionary Russia* (The Hague: Martinus Nijhoff, 1981); Shmuel Galai, *The Liberation Movement in Russia, 1900–1905* (Cambridge: Cambridge University Press, 1973); Randall Poole, 'Nineteenth-Century Russian Liberalism: Ideals and Realities', *Kritika: Explorations in Russian and Eurasian History* 16, 1 (2015), 157–81; Susanna Rabow-Edling, *Liberalism in Pre-Revolutionary Russia. State, Nation, Empire* (Abingdon: Routledge, 2019); Vanessa Rampton, *Liberal Ideas in Tsarist Russia. From Catherine the Great to the Russian Revolution* (Cambridge: Cambridge University Press, 2020); Konstantin I. Shneider, *Mezhdu svobodoi i samoderzhaviem: istoriia rannego russkogo liberalizma* (Perm: Permskii gos. natsional'nyi issledovatel'skii universitet, 2012); Andrzej Walicki, *Legal Philosophies of Russian Liberalism* (Oxford: Clarendon Press, 1987). Useful biographies of key figures in this period include Richard Pipes, *Struve: Liberal on the Left* (Cambridge, MA: Harvard University Press, 1970); Melissa Kirschke Stockdale, *Paul Miliukov and the Quest for a Liberal Russia, 1880–1918* (Ithaca, NY: Cornell University Press, 1996).

irritation that he could not 'bring them [the liberals] into line'.[98] Among
the points at issue was whether decisions by the planned conference
would be binding on all the parties represented there (particularly any
proposal to support an armed uprising). Miliukov was in principle
happy to cooperate with revolutionary groups as part of his emerging
'no enemies on the left' strategy, while Struve acknowledged that the
terror attacks mounted by the SRs were not 'melodramatic whims', but
rather 'the logical development of a dying autocracy'.[99] Many other
liberals were by contrast reluctant to support an armed uprising, a
sentiment rooted both in ethical unease about the use of violence, as well
as recognition that it would make them vulnerable to harsh repression
by the authorities.

Zilliacus also struggled to win support among the Social Democrats
for a conference (although Plekhanov in Geneva was unusually amenable
to the proposal).[100] The recent split of the Party into Mensheviks and
Bolsheviks complicated discussions, while many Social Democrats were
suspicious of claims for national autonomy made by the Finns and other
minorities. Volkhovskii and Zilliacus corresponded over the summer of
1904 about the challenges involved in organizing a conference. The two
men probably met in Geneva in the early summer of 1904. They certainly
met in August at the sixth Congress of the Second International, in
Amsterdam, where delegates from several European countries put
pressure on their Russian colleagues to overcome their divisions.[101]
Zilliacus recalled that questions of political violence and terrorism
loomed large in discussion with the various Socialist Revolutionaries
present in Amsterdam.[102] The subsequent report in *Revoliutsionnaia
Rossiia* suggests that although many SR delegates were concerned about

98   Volkhovskii Papers (HIA), Box 3, Folder 36, Zilliacus to Volkhovskii, 1 July 1904.
99   Pipes, *Struve, Liberal on the Left*, 357.
100 Volkhovskii Papers (HIA), Box 3, Folder 36, Zilliacus to Volkhovskii, 5 April 1904.
101 For the SR's articulation and defence of their programme at Amsterdam, see *Report
     of the Russian Socialist Revolutionary Party to the International Socialist Congress,
     Amsterdam, 1904* (London: Twentieth Century Press, 1904). For a discussion
     of Russian questions at the Amsterdam Congress, including the build-up, see
     Bruno Naarden, *Socialist Europe and Revolutionary Russia: Perception and Prejudice,
     1848–1923* (Cambridge: Cambridge University Press, 1992), 145–56.
102 For Zilliacus' memories of the Conference, see Zilliacus, *Sortovuosilta*, 42–47. Both
     Shishko and Lazarev were also members of the SR delegation and presumably
     took part in the discussions (Shishko in particular corresponded in some detail
     with Zilliacus in the summer of 1904).

the principle of working with non-revolutionary opposition groups, most were ready to endorse such a strategy if it could advance the revolutionary cause.[103]

The 'Conference of Oppositional and Revolutionary Organisations' finally took place in the autumn of 1904 at the Hotel d'Orleans in Paris. Eight organizations sent delegations.[104] The Social Democrats did not attend. Miliukov and Struve were among the representatives of the Union of Liberation (whose members sought various reforms including the establishment of a constitutional monarchy). Azef, Chernov and Natanson represented the SRs. The remaining six delegations were made up of representatives from the various nationalist parties. The Conference agreed a common program that committed participants to work for the overthrow of autocracy, the adoption of a new form of government based on full adult suffrage, and the principle of national self-determination.[105] Articles in *Revoliutsionnaia Rossiia* noted that any agreement between revolutionaries and liberals could never be more than a temporary accommodation of convenience.[106] Volkhovskii was not a delegate for reasons that are not entirely clear. He had already effectively handed over the editorship of *Free Russia* to David Soskice, in part so he could move to Switzerland for medical treatment, although

103 'Mezhdunarodnyi sotsialisticheskii kongress v Amsterdame', *Revoliutsionnaia Rossiia*, 51 (25 August 1904). The report in the paper noted that the SR delegation generally took an 'extreme' left position on the range of issues discussed at the Congress.

104 The fullest discussion of the conference, including the negotiations leading up to it, can be found in Antti Kujala, 'March Separately – Strike Together', in Olavi K. Fält and Antii Kujala (eds), *Rakka ryūsui: Colonel Akashi's Report on his Secret Cooperation with the Russian Revolutionary Parties during the Russo-Japanese War* (Helsinki, Suomen Historiallinen Seura, 1998), 85-168.

105 Galai, *Liberation Movement in Russia*, 214–19; Pipes, *Struve: Liberal on the Left*, 365–66; P. N. Miliukov, *Vospominaniia* (Moscow: Izd-vo Politicheskoi literatury, 1991), 168–71. Useful material can also be found in D. B. Pavlov, *Khroniki tainoi voiny. Iaponskie den'gi dlia pervoi russkoi revoliutsii* (Moscow: Veche, 2011), 67–97, discussing how agreement at the Conference was made conditional by the Japanese government in return for providing funding to the opposition in an effort to undermine the Russian war effort in the Far East. The resolutions agreed at the Conference can be found in Erofeev (ed.), *Partiia sotsialistov-revoliutsionerov. Dokumenty i materialy*, I, 158–61.

106 See, for example, 'Na dva fronta', *Revoliutsionnaia Rossiia*, 53 (30 September 1904). The paper returned regularly to the subject in the following months. See 'Sotsialisty-revoliutsionery i nesotsialisticheskaia demokratiia', *Revoliutsionnaia Rossiia*, 56 (5 December 1904).

he continued to travel quite extensively in the final months of 1904.[107] While he was one of the main confidantes of Zilliacus, Volkhovskii had been hesitant in supporting the merger of the Agrarian-Socialist League with the Socialist Revolutionaries, which may have ruled him out as a Party delegate at the Paris Conference.[108]

There was a further dimension to Volkhovskii's relationship with Zilliacus. Soon after the outbreak of the Russo-Japanese war at the start of 1904, Zilliacus established close links with the former Japanese Military Attaché in St Petersburg, Col. Akashi Motojiro, who had moved to Stockholm after the start of hostilities (Zilliacus himself had lived in Japan for two years in the 1890s which helped him to win Akashi's trust). Over the next eighteen months or so, Akashi became a key figure in channelling funds from the Japanese government to the Russian opposition through Zilliacus, designed to foster popular unrest that could weaken the Russian war effort.[109] The money that was eventually provided by the government in Tokyo was used to buy weapons for use in uprisings in St Petersburg and other major cities. Zilliacus for his part went to great lengths to conceal his links with Akashi, recognising that they would alienate some of the opposition parties he was trying to bring together, particularly members of the Union of Liberation. He was however ready to discuss the issue openly with Volkhovskii as early as March 1904, when he told his friend that although he could not say anything definite about procuring weapons for use by the SRs and other revolutionary parties in Russia, he would shortly meet 'a man' in Stockholm, presumably Akashi, after which he would be able to say

---

107 Useful material relating to Soskice's time editing *Free Russia*, and more particularly his role in shaping the response of the SFRF to the 1905 Revolution, can be found in the Stow Hill Papers. Soskice devoted considerable effort to promoting greater cooperation between the myriad groups and individuals committed to supporting change in Russia.

108 Some sources suggest that Volkhovskii—along with Chaikovskii—only formally joined the SRs in 1904, although the incomplete records of the Party make it difficult to determine the precise date.

109 For a detailed discussion of relations between Akashi and Zilliacus, including some material relating to Volkhovskii, see Fält and Kujala (eds), *Rakka ryūsui*, passim. A great deal of useful material looking at Akashi's activities through the prism of Russian police files, rounding out the story, can be found in Pavlov, *Khroniki tainoi voiny*.

more when he met Volkhovskii in April in London.[110] There is no record of this latter meeting—where they were joined by Chaikovskii—but over the following weeks Zilliacus continued to liaise with Akashi to obtain money for purchasing weapons.

Zilliacus' role was not an easy one, not least because the Japanese government was reluctant to make any money available until it was confident there was some degree of unity among the opposition (one of the reasons that Zilliacus was so anxious to secure agreement among potential participants at the planned Paris Conference). The Russian government was in any case well-aware of Akashi's activities through the reports of Azef (Zilliacus himself was under almost constant observation by the *Okhrana*).[111] Still more complex was the actual procurement and distribution of weapons. A letter that appears to be from Volkhovskii, written in Geneva in July 1904, gives an insight both into his own views and those of other SR comrades. He told Zilliacus that the situation in Russia was particularly febrile since the Government was calling out the reserves 'at a time when agriculture work is most urgent', adding that 'This creates such a tension among the peasantry that there would be no difficulty in starting a successful agitation in terms of refusing to pay taxes as well as supplying recruits'. He went on to note that the situation in the towns was equally tense and that 'Our party acknowledges the necessity of at once starting and pushing forward such an agitation in both towns & the country'. Volkhovskii told Zilliacus that the SRs were ready to

> organise a number of armed attacks on single representatives of the *regime*, as well as—where possible—on certain governmental institutions (police stations, etc) ... The carrying out of this programme and its success will among other things depend on our possessing the necessary means, among which are adequate amounts of proper arms ...

He went on to suggest that importing weapons would 'cost us far more' than obtaining them within the Russian Empire, adding that foreign weapons such as Browning revolvers were of limited value given the

---

110 Volkhovskii Papers (HIA), Box 3, Folder 36, Zilliacus to Volkhovskii, 1 March 1904.

111 Pavlov, *Khroniki tainoi voiny*, 53–54.

shortage of ammunition. Volkhovskii believed it would be more helpful to send money which could be used to buy weapons in Russia itself.[112]

Akashi was in the summer of 1904 still struggling to get Tokyo to commit major financial support to the Russian opposition movement, which meant that he was unable to provide Zilliacus with the money needed to buy arms in Russia. The talks between Zilliacus and Akashi did however lay the foundation for a separate scheme, launched several months later, to transport weapons to Russia from Britain in barrels of lard. The architect of the scheme was Chaikovskii, along with J. F. Green of the SFRF, who persuaded Samuel Hobson to set up a 'dummy' company exporting goods to Russia.[113] Volkhovskii does not seem to have been directly involved. He left Geneva in August 1904 to go to Amsterdam, and from there returned for a time to London, but was back in Switzerland by the end of the year. Nor does he seem to have been involved in Zilliacus' most ambitious effort to smuggle weapons into Russia, which took place the following year, when the Finn used a series of intermediaries to hire the steamship *John Grafton* to transport thousands of rifles and millions of cartridges from London to the Baltic (Chaikovskii was once again the main conspirator among the London emigration). The Russian authorities were well-aware of the plot through information supplied by Azef, and the crew were forced to scuttle the ship off the coast of Finland, with the loss of most of its cargo, after failing to *rendez-vous* with the individuals who were meant to collect the weapons.[114] Whether Volkhovskii was aware of the scheme is uncertain,

---

112 SR Party Archive (Amsterdam), 161, Volkhovskii to Zilliacus, 3 July 1904. The precise provenance and transmission of this letter is not altogether clear, but Volkhovskii seems to have written it having discussed the issue at length with Chaikovskii, suggesting both men were by now heavily involved in the plans to support armed uprising in Russia.

113 Hobson, *Pilgrim*, 127–29.

114 Antti Kujala, 'The Russian Revolutionary Movement and the Finnish Opposition, 1905. The John Grafton Affair and the Plans for an Uprising in St Petersburg', *Scandinavian Journal of History*, 5, 1–4 (1980), 257–75; Pavlov, *Khroniki tainoi voiny*, 135–70. Miliukov noted in his memoirs that plans to smuggle weapons into Russia were discussed at the Paris Conference of opposition parties that opened in October 1904. See Miliukov, *Vospominaniia*, 169. In the wake of the John Grafton affair, Special Branch provided the Russian authorities with information to help them unravel who was behind the plot. See, for example, Okhrana Archive (HIA), Index Vc, Folder 1, Letter by George Edwards, 6 November 1905 (microfilm 69). For further information about subsequent efforts to smuggle arms to Russia, in some cases using British firms and boats, see Okhrana Archive (HIA), Index

but it seems likely that he was, given that it was known to a number of revolutionaries in Switzerland where he was himself living at the time.[115]

Free Russia noted slightly cryptically early in 1905 that its principal editor had 'for a time' stood down 'to devote himself to the work of the Russian liberation movement at another centre'.[116] Volkhovskii had in fact gone to Switzerland for medical treatment, which he had been planning for some months,[117] but the move allowed him to play a bigger role in the SR Foreign Committee.[118] The decision-making structure of the SRs was extraordinarily fluid and ill-defined right down to 1917, resulting in almost constant skirmishing between various committees and editorial boards, with a consequent lack of any clear hierarchy. The Foreign Committee was as noted earlier elected by local groups of the SR Foreign Organization, whose 'statutes' set out its role as the provision of financial and human support for the revolutionary struggle in Russia, but the Committee served in practice as a more general decision-making body of the Party in emigration from 1903 down until the middle of 1905 (it included most senior SRs in exile including Volkhovskii, Chaikovskii, Shishko and Chernov). There were often tensions between the Foreign Committee based in Geneva and SR groups in Russia. Volkhovskii himself was part of a small commission set up in 1904 to examine complaints

XIIc(2), Folder 1 and Folders 2 a–e (microfilm 169); Okhrana Archive (HIA), Index VIk, Folder 23, Reports by Farce, 18 October 1905; 9 January 1906; 12 January 1906; 9 February 1906 (all microfilm 108).

115 Among those who seem to have known of the plans was Lenin. See Pavlov, *Khroniki tainoi voiny*, 160

116 'Report for the Year 1904', *Free Russia* (1 March 1905). David Soskice as acting editor of *Free Russia* was instrumental in encouraging the SFRF to raise money to help striking workers in Russia, although the issue raised familiar tensions, as Robert Spence Watson continue to point out that he could not as President of the Peace Society be associated with efforts 'to buy ammunition and the like'. Stow Hill Papers (Parliamentary Archives), STH/DS/1/WAT/7, Spence Watson to David Soskice, 24 January 1905.

117 Volkhovskii Papers (HIA), Box 12, Folder 4, Vera Volkhovskii to father, 29 April 1904. Some insight into Volkhovskii's daily life in Switzerland can be gleaned from the letters sent to him by his daughters. Vera's letters focused heavily on personal matters but provided her father with some details about events in Britain. The letters from Sof'ia in Russia, found in Volkhovskii Papers (HIA), Box 14, Folder 1, were also largely personal in character and contained limited information about the turbulent political developments taking place around her.

118 For a valuable analysis of the history and amorphous organizational identify of the Foreign Organisation, see Leonov, *Zagranichnaia organizatsiia*.

that representatives sent by the Committee to Russia regularly behaved in an arrogant manner that alienated their 'hosts'. While its report acknowledged the problem, the authors could not identify any positive ways to improve matters, and the gulf between exiles in Western Europe and party members in Russia festered for many years to come.[119]

Perhaps the most vexing question facing the Foreign Committee in 1904 was the issue of 'agrarian terrorism' (a term loosely applied to acts of violence and expropriation aimed against landowners and other symbols of rural authority). Chaikovskii noted at the second Conference of the Foreign Organisation, held in July 1904, that there were sharp differences within the Party about how best to foment unrest in the countryside.[120] Three months later, in October, Chaikovskii and Volkhovskii both attended a meeting of the Geneva Group of the Foreign Organisation, at which they contributed to a draft resolution warning against

> The local uncoordinated character of acts of 'agrarian terror', which makes their regulation and control by the party difficult, and, consequently, cannot prevent unwarranted excesses which may be harmful to the moral prestige of the movement; and the danger of the degeneration in the movement if the spread of an 'agrarian-terrorist' mood should outstrip the development of the social-revolutionary consciousness and organisation of the masses and turn the movement from a collective struggle for the socialisation of the land into a guerrilla struggle by individual groups for the immediate improvement of their own economic position.[121]

The fear that encouraging agrarian terror might undermine the long-term cause of revolution echoed the position adopted by the Agrarian-Socialist League at its 1902 Congress, but it was not shared by many of the younger SRs in Western Europe, and a majority of those attending the meeting in Geneva voted for an alternative resolution that endorsed the spontaneous seizure of property as an effective means of radicalising the peasantry. Volkhovskii was well respected by the new generation of

119 Hildermeier, *Russian Socialist Revolutionary Party*, 113–14.
120 The full minutes of the Conference, along with other material about the proceedings, can be found in the SR Party Archive (Amsterdam), 199.
121 Quoted in Perrie, *Agrarian Policy*, 95. Perrie's analysis of events in October, which relied heavily on printed sources, is largely borne out by archival material relating to the meeting that can be found in SR Party Archive (Amsterdam), 199.

revolutionaries like Vladimir Zenzinov, who later remembered him in Switzerland as 'an old man' with 'a beard that was almost completely white', but there was by 1905 significant resistance among many younger SRs to letting the *stariki* make all the critical decisions about how to conduct the struggle against tsarism.[122] Volkhovskii was frustrated by what he saw as a lack of discipline. In early January 1905, he wrote to Ekaterina Breshko-Breshkovskaia, who unlike him supported the young maximalists, lamenting that the supporters of agrarian terrorism wanted to create 'a Party within a Party'.[123] By the time she received the letters, though, the situation in Russia had been transformed by the events of Bloody Sunday, which sparked the 1905 Revolution and threatened for a time to sweep away the tsarist government.

The slaughter of unarmed demonstrators by imperial troops in front of the Winter Palace, in January 1905, shocked opinion both in Russia and abroad. The 'Bloody Sunday' protest was largely peaceful, although it had been infiltrated by revolutionaries, and the demands put forward by its leaders were distinctly radical, even if they were expressed in the conventional language of respect for the Tsar as the father of his people. In the weeks that followed, the government's authority rapidly disintegrated, as waves of strikes brought thousands of workers on to the streets, and a new 'Soviet' was set up that served for a time as a kind of shadow government in the Russian capital. *Zemstvo* liberals demanded a national assembly with real powers, while strikes by middle-class professionals including lawyers and doctors symbolised the growing importance of the 'third element', frustrated by both the banality and brutality of the autocratic government.[124] Tsar Nicholas responded

---

122 V. Zenzinov, *Perezhitoe* (New York: Izd-vo im. Chekhova, 1953), 103–04. Zenzinov's memoirs are inaccurate in identifying the time he met Volkhovskii (Zenzinov spent two periods of time in Geneva).

123 Volkhovskii's views during this time can be seen in the numerous letters and postcards he sent to Breshkovskaia, in SR Party Archive (Amsterdam), 691. Although Volkhovskii and Breshkovskaia disagreed on a range of issues, the relationship between them was still warm. See, for example, the correspondence between them dating from this period in Volkhovskii Papers (HIA), Box 1, Folder 9.

124 Among the large literature on the 1905 Revolution, for a still unrivalled general account see Abraham Ascher, *The Revolution of 1905. Russia in Disarray* (Stanford, CA: Stanford University Press, 1988). The same author examines developments in the immediate wake of 1905 in his book *The Revolution of 1905. Authority Restored* (Stanford, CA: Stanford University Press, 1992). A lively account in English of

with a characteristic mixture of stubbornness and inconsistency. By the autumn of 1905, he was forced to turn to his former Finance Minister, Sergei Witte, who advised the Tsar to issue a manifesto promising civil liberties and a new assembly elected on a wide franchise. The October Manifesto helped to win over a section of moderate opinion, although working-class unrest continued in the major cities until the end of the year, when an uprising in Moscow was brutally supressed, while the countryside remained in turmoil throughout 1906. Although order was gradually restored, the political reforms set in motion by the Manifesto, complete with the rhetoric and institutions of a quasi-liberal democratic system, ultimately failed to set the Russian political system on the path to a Western-style government.[125]

Volkhovskii's activities during the 1905 Revolution and its immediate aftermath are hard to trace, in part because of a paucity of personal letters, while the SR archives themselves throw surprisingly little light on the subject.[126] Although his health was poor, he continued to correspond regularly with Zilliacus, seeing him early in 1905 to discuss arrangements for a second conference to coordinate the work of liberal and revolutionary groups, but when it eventually took place in Paris in early spring the meeting did nothing to create a more united

---

the 1905 revolution can be found in Orlando Figes, *A People's Tragedy. The Russian Revolution, 1891–1924* (London: Pimlico, 1996), 157–212.

125 On this subject, see Geoffrey Hosking, *The Russian Constitutional Experiment: Government and Duma, 1907–1914* (Cambridge: Cambridge University Press, 1973). A more sanguine attitude towards democratisation and modernisation in Russia can be found in some other works published during the late 1960s and 1970s, such as Theofanis George Stavrou (ed.), *Russia Under the Last Tsar* (Minneapolis, MI: University of Minnesota Press, 1969). See, too, Edith W. Clowes, Samuel D. Kassow and James L. West (eds), *Between Tsar and People. Educated Society and the Quest for Public Identity in Late Imperial Russia* (Princeton, NJ: Princeton University Press, 1991). For a useful if now somewhat dated summary of some of the literature, and more especially on how to think quizzically about the difference between 'optimists' and 'pessimists' when considering the prospects of effective democratisation and modernisation in Russia before 1917, see Christopher Read, 'In Search of Liberal Tsarism: The Historiography of Autocratic Decline', *Historical Journal*, 45, 1 (2002), 195–210.

126 For helpful discussions of the SR Party in the 1905 Revolution, see Leonov, *Partiia sotsialistov-revoliutsionerov*; Michael Melancon, 'The Socialist Revolutionaries from 1902 to 1907. Peasant and Workers' Party', *Russian History*, 12, 1 (1985), 2–47; Rice, *Russian Workers*, esp. 57–70. See, too, Hildermeier, *Russian Socialist Revolutionary Party*, esp. 129–76. The best source for tracing Volkhovskii's views on developments in Russia can be found in the letters he sent back to Vera in England.

opposition.[127] The pace of events heightened still further the schism between SRs abroad and those living in Russia. Volkhovskii helped to oversee the dispatch of SR representatives to Russia on behalf of the Foreign Committee,[128] but many of them failed to report back, with the result that party members in Western Europe found it increasingly difficult to keep up with developments. Members of SR organisations in Russia for their part often complained about lack of central direction, even as they rebelled against the idea of outside control, preferring to act according to their own volition. The Combat Organisation continued to be active, assassinating Grand Duke Sergei in February 1905, but SR terrorism increasingly assumed a spontaneous and chaotic character, sometimes taking the form of semi-criminal enterprises in which the 'expropriators' held on to the money they had liberated.[129] Such activities owed little to the earlier *narodnik* tradition of 'ethical terrorism' and its emphasis on the selfless moral character of those who used violence to promote the welfare of the people.

The anxieties expressed by Volkhovskii and some other SR leaders in exile about agrarian terrorism were not rooted in any rejection of armed revolt *per se*. Nikolai Chaikovskii, whose views were usually close to his old friend, complained in the summer of 1905 that many SR leaders in Western Europe were if anything not *sufficiently* committed to supporting armed uprisings.[130] Volkhovskii himself welcomed attacks on senior bureaucrats, including the murder of the Governor of Ufa in May 1905, along with the killing of tsarist officials in Baku. He also warmly praised Ivan Kaliaev's killing of the Grand Duke Sergei. Volkhovskii had met Kaliaev in Switzerland, subsequently telling Vera back in England that the murder of the Grand Duke had been a work of 'popular justice', and that 'an aura of eternal glory' would forever

---

127 For details of the second Paris Conference, see Kujala, 'March Separately – Strike Together'. Also see 'Nekotorye itogi Parizhskoi konferentsii', *Revoliutsionnaia Rossiia*, 61 (15 March 1905); 'Dokumenty mezhdupartiinoi konferentsii', *Revoliutsionnaia Rossiia*, 65 (25 April 1905).

128 See, for example, SR Party Archive (Amsterdam), 211 (Minutes of the Foreign Committee, 5 July 1905; 6 August 1905).

129 For a discussion of this seamy 'terrorism of a new type', see Geifman, *Thou Shalt Kill*, 123–80. For a rather different view, focusing on the activities of the SR Combat Organisation in the 1905 Revolution and its aftermath, see Gorodnitskii, *Boevaia organizatsiia*, esp. 87–132.

130 Hildermeier, *Russian Socialist Revolutionary Party*, 132.

'surround his [Kaliaev's] blond head'.[131] Yet while the SR newspaper *Revoliutsionnaia Rossiia* welcomed the first outbreaks of disorder in 1905, as evidence that workers and peasants were interested in something more than economic reform, both Chaikovskii and Volkhovskii feared that spontaneous local uprisings would have little impact unless they were carefully coordinated. The subsequent loss of the *John Grafton* and its cargo symbolised how difficult it was for SR leaders in emigration to provide any real support for the struggle in Russia itself. The debacle also made it harder for leaders abroad to assert their authority. The disorder that shook Russia to its core in 1905 created tensions and divisions within the SR Party, as its leaders attempted to apply existing ideological shibboleths and organisational practices to a rapidly changing landscape.

Volkhovskii continued to contribute to the SR Party's propaganda work during 1905, although his activities were constrained both by his work for the Foreign Committee and his poor health. He nevertheless periodically made 'fiery' speeches at various Party meetings in Geneva,[132] and took a leading role in organising the translation and dispatch of material to the Ukraine.[133] He also contributed two poems to *Krasnoe znamia: sbornik na 1-e Maia 1905* (*Red Banner: A Miscellany for 1 May 1905*) published by the SR Party in Geneva.[134] The first of Volkhovskii's poems, 'Pervoee Maia' ('The First of May'), was written in the rhythm of a march and proclaimed the day as 'a festival of work and spring', when the rays of the sun brought warmth and light like the struggle for 'holy freedom'. It ended with a rousing declaration that 'brothers we are many ... / and before us is the whole world! / Justice is with us! Our strength lies in hope! / To battle as to a festive banquet'. His second

---

131 Volkhovskii Papers (Houghton Library), 66M-197 (miscellaneous material relating to the Volkhovskii family), Feliks Volkhovskii to Vera, 22 May 1905.

132 Leonov, *Partiia sotsialistov-revoliutsionerov*, 151. Volkhovskii does not seem to have been closely involved in plans to send agitators to work among the Russian peasantry, and among his old colleagues he seems to have sided with Chaikovskii against Shishko in emphasising the importance of establishing links among the urban workers as well as the peasants, something of a change from his position a few years before.

133 For an appeal by Volkhovskii for funds to support such work, printed in Ukrainian, see *Revoliutsionnaia Rossiia*, 74 (15 September 1905).

134 *Krasnoe znamia: sbornik na 1-e Maia 1905 goda* (Geneva: Partiia sotsialistov-revoliutsionerov, 1905).

poem, 'Videnie' ('The Vision'), which had probably been written rather earlier, began with a description of the grim fortress of Shlissel'burg, before continuing with a hopeful description of how the political system it represented could soon be swept away ('I hear the sound of the tocsin'). As well as contributing to *Krasnoe znamia*, Volkhovskii probably edited it as well, including in its pages warm tributes to several terrorists who had been executed for their actions, along with other material designed to persuade readers that the chaos that had erupted in Russia would soon mark the end of the tsarist government. The *sbornik* appeared at a time when it seemed that the hopes of those who had for years opposed the tsarist autocracy were about to come to fruition.

The 1905 Revolution transformed the environment in which all the Russian revolutionary groups operated. The reforms set in motion by the October Manifesto, including the creation of a new representative assembly (*Duma*), promised to expand the scope of legitimate political activity. So, too, did the end of censorship. Yet the scale of unrest in both city and countryside indicated that there was potential for more far-reaching social and economic change. In the event, developments in the years after 1905 proved unpredictable and uncertain, as the regime sought to maintain at least some of the traditional pattern of autocratic rule, pushing back on the changes set in motion by the launch of the constitutional experiment. Members of the SR Party in Russia and abroad had to respond to a new world in which familiar questions were raised in new forms. Divisions inevitably emerged in the Party as it sought to respond to the challenges and opportunities posed by a political environment that combined constitutional and autocratic elements in new and unfamiliar ways. The following chapter examines how Volkhovskii responded to these changes, at a time when he developed his role as a leading figure in producing SR propaganda, while continuing his efforts to shape attitudes in Britain towards the Russian government and the Russian revolutionary movement.

7. Final Years

Many Russian revolutionaries in exile abroad began to return home in the second half of 1905, a stream that became a flood following the proclamation of the October Manifesto, which at least rhetorically guaranteed freedom of the press and open political debate. Volkhovskii was—eventually—among those who made their way back to Russia. One of the leading historians of the Socialist Revolutionary Party, Manfred Hildermeier, has suggested that Volkhovskii was already in St Petersburg by the end of December, in time to take part in the first Congress of the SR Party using the pseudonym Glazov, although he acknowledges that the real identity of Glazov 'is not completely secure'. If the suggestion were correct then it would cast some interesting light on Volkhovskii's views, since his putative *alter ego* argued—*contra* Volkhovskii's long-standing position—that the revolutionary parties should call for an immediate mass revolution. Hildermeier goes so far as to suggest that Volkhovskii / Glazov pushed their position to one of 'suicidal heroism' in supporting such a revolt, even though most of the peasantry lacked a developed political consciousness.[1]

Volkhovskii was not in fact Glazov, and not only because Glazov's views were so different from the ones he had expressed over the

---

[1] Manfred Hildermeier, *The Russian Socialist Revolutionary Party Before the First World War* (New York: St Martin's Press, 2000), 138–39. For a discussion of the Conference, see M. I. Leonov, *Partiia sotsialistov-revoliutsionerov v 1905–1907 gg.* (Moscow: Rosspen, 1997), 226–48. Glazov's views were in many ways a curious mixture of Blanquism—with a strong focus on the role of the Party in creating revolution—and faith in the spontaneous revolutionary instincts of the *narod*. A trenchant discussion of the Conference and the Programme approved there can be found in Oliver H. Radkey, *The Agrarian Foes of Bolshevism: Promise and Default of the Russian Socialist Revolutionaries from February to October 1917* (New York: Columbia University Press, 1958), 24–46. The Congress was held in Imatra in Finland.

      https://doi.org/10.11647/OBP.0385.07

previous few years.[2] Volkhovskii's health was too poor to allow him
to travel to Russia for the Congress. He was still sending letters *from*
a hospital in Switzerland at the start of January 1906, including one to
his daughter Vera in England,[3] and a second to Robert Spence Watson
listing his various ailments (the wound of an operation had failed to heal
properly creating an abscess on the skin).[4] While one delegate recalled
that Volkhovskii was present throughout the proceedings, the accuracy
of his memories are negated by the minutes, which include a note
that Congress sent greetings to Volkhovskii 'detained abroad through
illness'.[5] Although some questions remain about the real identity of
Glazov, it seems likely that it was the pseudonym of Mark Natanson,
another *narodnik* veteran and former Chaikovets.[6]

Volkhovskii was convinced by reports filtering through to him in
Switzerland that the revolution taking place in Russia was 'not only
political but also social'. He believed that both workers and peasants had
'shown splendid capacities, in solidarity, in organising, in self-sacrifice
for an ideal'. He was confident that what he called 'autobureaucracy'
was dead, and that while the regime might seek to fight to regain its lost
power, 'it will be unable to establish its rule with any steadiness again'.
He was also confident that the old peasant demands for 'Land and
freedom through a good Tzar' had been replaced by a desire for 'Land
and freedom through democratic self-government and nationalisation
of land'. Volkhovskii glumly told Spence Watson from his hospital bed
in Lausanne that despite the massive upheavals in Russia his own plans
were 'very unsettled'. He had a few months earlier hoped to return to
Russia to work for the Socialist Revolutionary press in St Petersburg,
since 'the centre of gravity of all ... political activity has been fully and
entirely transferred to Russia', but he was subsequently warned by

2   It is, though, worth noting that Volkhovskii was seen by some of his comrades as
     being on the left of the SR Party during his final years. See, for example, Ritina [I.
     I. Rakitnikova], Obituary of Volkhovskii, *Mysl'*, 40 (January 1915).
3   Volkhovskii Papers (Houghton Library), 66M-197 (miscellaneous material relating
     to the Volkhovskii family), Feliks Volkhovskii to Vera, 3 January 1906.
4   Spence Watson / Weiss Papers (Newcastle University), SW 1/19/4, Volkhovskii to
     Spence Watson, 2 January 1906.
5   Maureen Perrie (ed.), *Protokoly pervogo s"ezda Partii Sotsialistov-Revolyutisonerov*
     (Millwood, NY: Kraus International Publications, 1983), 354.
6   Glazov was however listed as a member of the London delegation in the *Protokoly*,
     which is curious given that Natanson had few links with Britain.

friends in the Russian capital that he could face arrest if he did so. Nor was his health likely to be up to the journey. Volkhovskii nevertheless found it excruciatingly hard to remain abroad at a time when his country was going through such an upheaval, telling his old friend that 'to an active man inactivity is one of the worse trials'.[7]

Volkhovskii's absence from the first Congress meant that he missed a critical moment in the evolution of the SR Party. The Congress approved a Minimum and a Maximum Programme (which had been under discussion within the Party for nearly two years).[8] The Minimum Programme specified among other things the need for a democratic republic and full civil rights, the socialisation of the land, and the creation of a federal state structure that would provide national minorities with a high degree of autonomy including the right to secede. The Maximum Programme outlined the more fundamental socialist transformation that the Party was committed to pursuing over the longer term. The discussions at the Congress highlighted the wide range of views within the SRs. There were particularly sharp divisions over the land question. Chernov defended the inclusion in the Minimum Programme of the principle of 'socialization' of the land, rejecting 'nationalization', which he feared might increase the power of a bourgeois state apparatus over the countryside. The 'Maximalists', by contrast, emphasised the right of poor peasants to take land without interference from outside. Beneath the abstruse language was the perennial question of the peasantry's capacity to create a rural revolution through its own efforts. The Congress eventually supported Chernov's position, which sought to maintain a balance between *étatist* and *syndicalist* views, supporting the 'right to land' within a framework that maintained it was the 'general property' of the people.[9] While the Minimum Programme was still ready to accept

---

7   Spence Watson / Weiss Papers (Newcastle University), SW 1/19/4, Volkhovskii to Spence Watson, 2 January 1906.

8   For a discussion of the SR programme, see Radkey, *Agrarian Foes*, 24–46; Maureen Perrie, *The Agrarian Policy of the Russian Socialist-Revolutionary Party* (Cambridge: Cambridge University Press, 1976), 143–52. For a lucid discussion of attitudes within the Socialist Revolutionaries towards revolution, see Manfred Hildermeier, 'The Socialist Revolutionary Party of Russia and the Workers, 1900-1914', in Reginald E. Zelnik (ed.), *Workers and Intelligentsia in Late Imperial Russia: Realities, Representations, Reflections* (Berkeley, CA: University of California Press, 1998), 206-27.

9   Hildermeier, *Russian Socialist Revolutionary Party*, 83.

the temporary continuation of private property in the industrial sphere, its commitment to an immediate end of the private ownership of land reflected the *narodnik* roots of the SRs.

Vera Figner wrote in her memoirs that when Volkhovskii did eventually return to Russia, he played an important role producing propaganda targeted at the military rank-and-file. She also noted that he was active in the SR Military-Organisation Bureau, created in the summer of 1906, which sought to coordinate the Party's efforts to promote revolutionary sentiment in the army and navy.[10] Viktor Chernov similarly recalled that Volkhovskii was 'closely connected' with the Military-Organisation Bureau during the months he spent in Finland and St Petersburg in 1906–07.[11] Another SR activist, Inna Rakitnikova, described in her obituary of Volkhovskii how he had 'rushed' back to Russia like a 'youth' in 1906, despite his age and poor health, editing publications aimed at soldiers and sailors before fleeing the country to avoid arrest.[12] Other references to Volkhovskii's time in Russia are scattered through memoirs and SR documents, although once again without much detail, with the result that his activities can only be sketched out from the fragments of information available.[13]

Konni Zilliacus suggested to Volkhovskii that he should consider moving to Finland at the end of 1905, when he was still living in Switzerland, telling his old friend that it was comparatively easy to enter the country without a passport. Zilliacus also noted that 'mutual friends' would provide him with assistance once he was there. He added that it would be easy to move on from Finland to St Petersburg.[14] Volkhovskii's health meant that he could not put such a plan into effect until the summer of 1906, when he travelled from Britain to Finland via Denmark and Sweden, staying for a time in the countryside outside Helsingfors (Helsinki), where he 'contrived to enter into communication with our Finnish friends'. When he moved to the Finnish capital, he

10 Vera Figner, *Posle Shlissel'burga* (Moscow: Direct Media, 2016), 347–48. Figner wrongly recalled that Volkhovskii returned to Russia at the end of 1905.
11 Viktor Chernov, *Pered burei* (Moscow: Direct Media, 2016), 495.
12 Ritina [I. I. Rakitnikova], Obituary of Volkhovskii, *Mysl'*, 40 (January 1915).
13 For one of Volkhovskii's few public comments on his whereabouts during this period, including his time in Finland, see SR Party Archive (Amsterdam), 148 (Minutes of the fifth Party Council, Session 11, 6 May 1909).
14 Volkhovskii Papers (HIA), Box 3, Folder 36, Zilliacus to Volkhovskii, 23 December 1905.

found things easier than he expected, despite the large number of troops on the streets, in part because the local police were reluctant to arrest political agitators. Although the local revolutionary parties were not well organised, Volkhovskii was confident that the SRs and their allies commanded considerable popular support, noting approvingly that preparations were underway to launch two new publications.[15] He was also surprised at how easy it was to travel from Helsingfors to St Petersburg (Vera travelled to Finland with him, and regularly moved between the two cities, while Volkhovskii's elder daughter Sof'ia came to Finland on several occasions to see her father and sister). Volkhovskii went to St Petersburg on short visits, almost certainly for meetings of the Military-Organisation Bureau, but spent most of his time in Finland, finding the country safer than Russia even though some of the towns were 'full of spies'. He remained there until April or May 1907, living for most of the time in the house of a local SR sympathiser, before returning to London. He spent some time trying to develop a new commercial venture, which would if successful have provided funds to support revolutionary activities, but it does not appear to have come to anything.[16] Volkhovskii devoted most of his energy to producing propaganda aimed at soldiers and sailors, including the SR newspaper *Soldatskaia gazeta* (*The Soldier's Gazette*), which contained articles on issues of interest to a military readership.[17]

The first SR Party Congress recognised that the government would try to use the army and navy to put down any mass uprising,[18] and the Party leadership subsequently allocated a good deal of money to

---

15   The SR leadership was, though, worried about both the loyalty and behaviour of some of its putative supporters in Finland. See 'Bulletin du Parti Socialiste Révolutionnaire', *La Tribune Russe* (31 January 1907). *La Tribune Russe* was produced in Paris, where it was edited by Ilia Rubanovich, who regularly reproduced information from other SR publications.

16   For Volkhovskii's trip to Helsingfors and his early impressions, see GARF, f. P5805, op. 2, del. 156 (Letters between Volkhovskii and Chaikovskii), in particular Volkhovskii to Chaikovskii, 14 September 1906; Volkhovskii to Chaikovskii, 19 October 1906. The commercial enterprise was presumably meant to make money to support SR Party activities.

17   On the establishment of *Soldatskaia gazeta*, see 'Bulletin du Parti Socialiste Révolutionnaire de Russie', *La Tribune Russe* (15 June 1906).

18   For consideration of the SR's views about the Government's likely response to an armed uprising, and the need for agitation among the troops, see Perrie (ed.), *Protokoly pervogo s"ezda Partii Sotsialistov-Revolyutisonerov*, 307–09, 313.

supporting agitation in the military, while allowing both local SR military
organisations and the Military-Organisation Bureau extensive freedom
to determine their *modus operandi*. It also agreed that agitation among
soldiers and sailors should have a revolutionary non-party character
that focused on broad issues rather than demanding full commitment to
the SR program. It is not entirely clear how Volkhovskii's activities fitted
into this broader picture, although he almost certainly acted as editor of
Soldatskaia gazeta,[19] while playing a significant if uncertain role in the SR
Military-Organisation Bureau.[20] He had throughout the 1905 Revolution
believed that promoting local armed uprisings would undermine the
regime, since soldiers and sailors would be reluctant to use force against
civilians whose revolutionary sentiments they shared.[21] Volkhovskii
appears to have already been in Finland when a significant mutiny took
place at the military fortress of Sveaborg, close to his place of residence
in Helsingfors, and it seems likely that it helped to reinforce his interest
in identifying ways of building on unrest in the military as a way of
fomenting a wider revolution. On returning to London in spring 1907,
he became the principal editor of a new newspaper targeted at readers
in the army and navy, *Za narod* (*For the People*), which was smuggled
back into Russia using many of the routes used by the Free Press Fund
in the 1890s.

Soldatskaia gazeta first appeared in August 1906, shortly after
Volkhovskii moved to Finland, and it is possible that he had been asked
to set up the new publication while still living in Western Europe. He
had certainly decided as early as February 1906 that 'the most vivid

19   Chernov recalled in his memoirs that Volkhovskii became editor of the journal
     Narodnaia armiia, although the publication did not appear until 1907, while
     Volkhovskii certainly later edited *Za narod* which had a format that was closely
     modelled on *Soldatskaia gazeta*. See Chernov, *Pered burei*, 495.
20   For a useful brief discussion of the Military-Organisation Bureau, see A. A.
     Okseniuk, 'Voennye organizatsii eserov v 1905–1907 gg', *Vestnik Moskovkogo
     Universiteta*, Ser. 8 (Istoriia), 6 (2012), 74–82. For an excellent discussion of the
     impact of the 1905 Revolution on the tsarist military, see John Starkes Bushnell,
     'Mutineers and Revolutionaries: Military Revolution in Russia, 1905–1907' (PhD
     thesis, University of Indiana, 1977). See, too, the book based on the thesis, *Mutiny
     Amid Repression. Russian Soldiers in the Revolution of 1905–1906* (Bloomington,
     IN: Indiana University Press, 1985). Bushnell's PhD contains useful material,
     particularly on events in 1907, not included in the book.
21   See, for example, Volkhovskii Papers (Houghton Library), 66M-197, Feliks
     Volkhovskii to Vera, 13 January 1906.

propaganda is now needed [for] the soldiers and the working people ... I can do whatever is necessary. I have some weapons—the power to instill my beliefs and the ability to express them'.[22] *Soldatskaia gazeta* was written in a lively and engaging manner, and included articles and reports about developments across Russia, as well as short stories and poems. The second issue contained an article arguing that recent events showed how the patience of the Russian people with arbitrary bureaucratic rule had finally run out after centuries of oppression. It also included first-hand accounts of the Sveaborg uprising and a description of the recent mutiny on board the warship *Pamiat' Azova* off Reval (modern-day Tallin).[23] The following edition continued in a similar vein, reporting on outbreaks of disorder across Russia, and listing assassinations of senior officials and military leaders that had taken place over the previous year.[24] The fifth number opened with a piece celebrating the importance of freedom, [25] while the sixth included a long discussion of recent developments in the Duma, arguing that political rights were only a means to achieving more fundamental social and economic goals.[26] Poems that appeared in *Soldatskaia gazeta* were typically rousing pieces with titles such as 'Pesnia o pravde i krivde' ('Songs of Truth and Falsehood'),[27] while short stories were usually about soldiers and sailors fighting for justice in the face of oppression. *Soldatskaia gazeta* was more than crude *agitprop*, instead combining emotional appeals and logical argument with reportage, and was designed to encourage soldiers and sailors to feel that they were part of a process of dramatic change. The paper was apparently produced in Finland, and transported back into Russia, although it did not list either the editor or the place of publication. While the contents were printed anonymously, or with obvious pseudonyms, Volkhovskii probably wrote many of the articles and *belles-lettres* himself. When *Za narod* began to appear in the spring of 1907, in London, it was closely modelled on *Soldatskaia gazeta*.

22 Volkhovskii Papers (Houghton Library), 66M-197, Feliks Volkhovskii to Vera, 14 February 1906.
23 'Otkuda poshla Russkaia Revoliutsiia?'; Razskaz uchastnika Sveaborgskago vozstaniia'; 'Vozstanie na kreisere Pamiat Azova'; all in *Soldatskaia gazeta*, 2 (22 September 1906).
24 *Soldatskaia gazeta*, 3 (8 October 1906).
25 'O svobode', *Soldatskaia gazeta*, 5 (1 January 1907).
26 'O Gosudarstvennoi Dume', *Soldatskaia gazeta*, 6 (10 February 1907).
27 'Pesnia o pravde i krivde', *Soldatskaia gazeta*, 3 (8 October 1906).

While still living in Finland, Volkhovskii also wrote a lengthy pamphlet, *Pro voinskoe ustroistvo* (*On the Organisation of the Military*),[28] which examined the economic cost to Russia of maintaining a large standing army. He was still more exercised by the government's use of the army as an instrument for suppressing dissent (the SR Party had at its first Congress committed itself to eliminating the army in favour of a popular militia). Volkhovskii argued that military service by its nature broke the psychological ties that bound young soldiers to the *narod*, turning them into servants of the autocratic state, while blinding them to the suffering of ordinary workers and peasants. He praised the system of military service found in Switzerland, where every young man went through a short period of initial training, after which they were required to report annually for special instruction to keep their skills up to date. Volkhovskii believed that such a system allowed a country to defend itself while ensuring that soldiers remained rooted in society rather than forming a separate estate. While there was no prospect of adopting such a system in Russia, so long as the tsarist state remained intact, he was convinced that revolutionary parties needed to foment military unrest to weaken the government's ability to crush a popular uprising.

Volkhovskii's growing interest in military matters was in many ways surprising. Unlike some other SR veterans, like Leonid Shishko, he had never served in the army. Nor had he shown much interest in the subject earlier in his career. Yet Volkhovskii's previous cooperation with Zilliacus and Chaikovskii in putting together plans to smuggle weapons into Russia reflected his conviction that armed uprisings would be central to a successful revolutionary struggle. He also recognised that such uprisings could only be effective if they had the means to avoid being crushed by force. His private papers suggest that he read a good deal of history to improve his knowledge of military affairs, particularly at times of political unrest, focusing in particular on how 'the citizen soldier' could be more effective than his professional counterpart since 'he willingly gives his life in defence of [his] country'.[29] Volkhovskii continued to believe in the importance of propaganda, but in the years after 1905 he focused his attention less on peasants and workers, and

---

28   F. Volkhovskii, *Pro voinskoe ustroistvo* (Moscow: Knigoizdatel'stvo E. D. Miakova 'Narodnaia mysl', 1906).

29   Volkhovskii Papers (HIA), Box 11, Folder 1 (various notes by Volkhovskii).

more on producing material to persuade soldiers and sailors of the
pivotal role they could play in forging a successful revolution.[30] He also
established a wider reputation within the SR Party as an expert on the
growing challenge posed to the European left by the rise of militarism,
attending conferences of the Second International, and contributing to
debates about how best to counter the growing influence of nationalism
across the continent.

Following Volkhovskii's return to London in the spring of 1907,
he immediately devoted much of his energy to producing *Za narod*,
working out of an office in Hammersmith almost next door to the old
premises of the Russian Free Press Fund.[31] The paper was also printed in
London (including some copies on thin paper designed for smuggling
back into Russia).[32] Volkhovskii was assisted by Vasilii Iarotskii, who
was at this stage of his career close to the SRs, although he subsequently
joined the Bolsheviks. In later years, an important editorial role was
played by Vladimir Lebedev, who had been active in the SR Party's
Military Organisation in the aftermath of the 1905 Revolution, before
fleeing to Paris in 1907. Volkhovskii also consulted regularly with other
leading figures in Paris, including Andrei Argunov, who kept him
informed about the Central Committee's views on important issues
(Argunov headed the transport commission responsible for dispatching
SR literature to Russia and his Paris address was often listed in *Za
narod* for correspondence).[33] Volkhovskii's own role was not formally

---

30 In 1906 Volkhovskii published a story, *Vylechennyi prints* (*The Cured Prince*) which
    featured the antics of an imaginary royal family. The story was more ironic in tone
    than his previous *skazki* and seems to have been aimed at a broader readership
    than the peasantry alone.

31 For details of Volkhovskii's addresses during his final years in London, see
    Lara Green, 'Russian Revolutionary Terrorism in Transnational Perspective:
    Representations and Networks, 1881–1926' (PhD thesis, Northumbria University,
    2019), 124.

32 For useful details on the production of *Za narod*, see Green, 'Russian Revolutionary
    Terrorism', 123 ff. K. N. Morozov among others suggests that the paper was based
    in Paris, but in practice production and much of the editorial work took place in
    London, although as Volkhovskii got older more of the business was transferred
    to the French capital. Volkhovskii himself travelled regularly to Paris, both to
    coordinate editorial work and to discuss developments with senior figures in the
    SR leadership, including Argunov (whose office address was listed in *Za narod* for
    readers wishing to contact the editors).

33 For Volkhovskii's letters to Argunov, including a good deal on the finances of
    Za narod, as well as discussions about its content and distribution, see SR Party

identified on the masthead of the paper, while the editorials typically reflected the (sometimes uncertain) views of the Party leadership, but he was still able to put his own stamp on *Za narod*. The paper was, like *Soldatskaia gazeta*, no crude propaganda publication, but while it in some respects resembled the *Letuchie listki* of the 1890s, printing information about what was taking place across Russia, and downplaying divisions between the Socialist Revolutionaries and the Social Democrats, the tone was far more radical in calling for revolution.[34] Volkhovskii once again included a significant amount of literary material, including poems and short stories, believing that it would engage the sympathies of readers in ways that more polemical articles could not always achieve.

The first number of *Za narod* appeared in April 1907, shortly after a meeting of the St Petersburg SR Military Organisation proposed setting up a new non-party All Russian Union of Soldiers and Sailors, tasked with creating closer links between revolutionaries in military units across the country.[35] The SR leadership was ready to allow its own local organisations significant autonomy in determining relations with other parties,[36] believing that such a strategy would prove more effective than trying to control events from above. It was an approach defended on the pages of *Za narod*, although building ties with other parties in the event proved difficult, both because of local tensions and disagreement about tactics and strategy. While the Mensheviks and (especially) Bolsheviks had come to believe by 1907 that revolutionary fervour was subsiding in the army and navy, the SRs still hoped that a well-planned programme of agitation could weaken the loyalty of the armed forces, making it harder for the government to restore order in cases of further civilian unrest.

Archive (Amsterdam), 645; Volkhovskii Papers (HIA), Box 1, Folder 4. Argunov had, when still in Russia, been less than complimentary about SR members in emigration, believing they had little sense of what was taking place 'on the ground', but following his arrival in Western Europe he seems to have established good personal relations with Volkhovskii.

34	For a useful discussion of the relationship between the SR Party organisation and SR agitators in the military, see Bushnell, 'Mutineers and Revolutionaries', 379–91. *Za narod's* non-party status was emphasised by its claim to be the paper of the All-Russian Union of Soldiers and Sailors, although in practice that organisation was itself dominated by the SRs.

35	The decision to launch *Za narod* was part of a bigger reorganisation of the SR press which saw the journal *Znamia truda* launched just a few weeks later.

36	Bushnell, 'Mutineers and Revolutionaries', 384-86.

The opening editorial in *Za narod* argued magisterially that the outcome of 'the great struggle of the working people with the tsarist government for freedom and land depends on ... what position in the struggle will be taken by the army and navy'.[37] Volkhovskii was probably the author of an article on 'Socialism' in the same issue, which avoided any detailed discussion of the kind of complex economic questions that preoccupied the SR *intelligentsia*, preferring to ask the simple question of 'Why is it today that the rich can live without working?', concluding that 'Things will only change when the worker can look at the factory as their property and the peasant at the land as theirs'.[38] The same edition of *Za narod* contained a lengthy article on the second Duma, which included a number of SR representatives, urging radical deputies to build closer links with the wider revolutionary movement in order to strengthen the opposition to tsarism.[39] The paper supported SR participation in the Duma—a subject of controversy within the Party—and defended the record of socialist deputies in the face of official hostility.[40] It bitterly attacked the Government's attempt to arrest a number of left-wing deputies, in the days leading up to the dissolution of the second Duma in June 1907,[41] and condemned the new electoral law subsequently announced by the Prime Minister Petr Stolypin, which was designed to reduce the electorate in order to minimise radical voices among those serving in a future Duma.[42]

The early numbers of *Za narod* also had to deal with the vexed question of terrorism. During the upheavals of 1905-6, a huge increase took place in the number of attacks on officials throughout the Empire. More than two hundred killings were the work of individuals claiming affiliation to

---

37 'V edinenii voiska s narodom – sila neodolimaia', *Za narod*, 1 (2 April 1907).

38 'O sotsialisme', *Za narod*, 1 (2 April 1907).

39 'Vtoraia Duma i voiska', *Za narod*, 1 (2 April 1907). For a description of the attitude of the SR Party towards the Duma, including decisions taken at an Extraordinary Congress held in February 1907, see *Rapport du Parti Socialiste Révolutionnaire de Russie au Congrès Socialiste International de Stuttgart* (Gand: Volksdrukkerij, 1907), 193–99. For a broader discussion of SR views towards the Duma, see Leonov, *Partiia sotsialistov-revoliutsionerov v 1905–1907 gg.*, 260–95 and 353–80.

40 'Bezsilie Dumy', *Za narod*, 2 (20 April 1907).

41 'Khlopnulo, grianulo: komar s duba svalilsia', *Za narod*, 4 (6 June 1907). For a review of the dissolution in another leading SR paper, see 'Le Coup d' État', *La Tribune Russe* (30 June 1907).

42 'Tret'ia Duma', *Za narod*, 5 (8 July 1907).

the SRs (although many had no official sanction).[43] Many other attacks simply formed part of a campaign of 'expropriations' of somewhat dubious character.[44] The whole question of terrorism had prompted renewed debate within the SR Party, following the decision to take part in elections to the second Duma, given that it seemed inconsistent to pursue a programme of assassinations while deputies took their place in the state legislature. The rather tortured formula used by the Party early in 1907—in effect that acts of terror could still be directed against tsarist officials and officers guilty of particularly egregious behaviour[45]—was echoed on the pages of *Za narod*. Volkhovskii himself still had no ethical qualms about the use of terror, although he continued to believe like most of the *stariki* (party elders) in emigration that it should form part of a broader strategy, reflecting his concern that uncoordinated and isolated acts of violence could not alone weaken the power of the tsarist state.

Volkhovskii's activities were not confined to journalism in the years following his return to London from Finland. While much of his attention focused on promoting revolutionary sentiment within the tsarist army and navy, he was also increasingly concerned about the rise of 'militarism' across Europe. Many of those active in the Second International feared that international tension could create divisions among the European working class, allowing governments to use nationalism to justify using force against those who challenged the existing order. Volkhovskii was not, for some reason, among the seventeen SR delegates who attended the 1907 seventh Congress of the Second International,[46] held at Stuttgart in August, which passed a resolution on militarism condemning war as a product of capitalist competition that allowed the bourgeoisie to

---

43 More than 200 individuals were killed in some 250 attacks by individuals at least notionally associated with the SRs. See see O. V. Budnitskii, *Terrorizm v Rossiiskom osvoboditel'nom dvizhenii: ideologiia, etika, psikhologiia (vtoriaia polovina XIX–nachalo XX v)* (Moscow: Rosspen, 2000), 177.

44 The 'degradation' of terror during 1905–07 is discussed at length in Budnitskii, *Terrorizm*, 177–217; Anna Geifman, *Thou Shalt Kill. Revolutionary Terrorism in Russia 1894-1917* (Princeton, NJ: Princeton University Press, 1993), 123–53.

45 See, for example, *Rapport du Parti Socialiste Révolutionnaire de Russie*, 199; 'Bulletin du Parti Socialist Révolutionnaire', *La Tribune Russe* (28 February–31 March 1907).

46 While Michael Melancon suggests that Volkhovskii led the SR delegation at Stuttgart, his name does not seem to appear in the records. See Michael Melancon, *The Socialist Revolutionaries and the Russian Anti-War Movement 1914–1917* (Columbus, OH: Ohio State University Press, 1990), 21.

maintain its power and advance its economic interests.[47] Nor, despite the significance of the Stuttgart Congress, was much attention given to its proceedings in *Za narod*. The first edition of the paper to appear after the Congress instead contained a piece celebrating the life of the SR veteran Mikhail Gots on the first anniversary of his death,[48] along with the usual articles on 'Voices from the Army and Navy' and 'The Revolutionary Struggle in the City and Countryside'. Since Volkhovskii attended both the previous Congress in Amsterdam in 1904, and the following Congress in Copenhagen in 1910, it seems likely that his non-attendance at Stuttgart was due either to his indifferent health or the need to devote his energy to overseeing *Za narod*. The lack of coverage of the Stuttgart Congress in a paper aimed at a readership of soldiers and sailors was nevertheless both striking and curious.

The years following the Stuttgart Congress were difficult ones for the Socialist Revolutionary Party. Deputies from the Centre and Right dominated the third Duma, which Volkhovskii denounced as a mere 'semblance' of parliamentary government, which could not conceal the fact that 'the country is being more arbitrarily governed than ever by an irresponsible bureaucracy with a despot at its head'.[49] Stolypin's repressive policies, which included mass executions of thousands of peasants, brought a degree of order back to the countryside while making it harder for revolutionary parties to organise effectively in the cities.[50] The

---

47 *Internationaler Sozialisten-Kongress zu Stuttgart 1907* (Berlin: Buchhandlung Vorwäts, 1907), 64-66. Detailed coverage of the Conference and its resolutions, written from a distinctly SR perspective, can be found in *La Tribune Russe*, 31 July 1907.

48 For a brief discussion of Gots' career, see L. E. Shishko, 'M. I. Gots', *Byloe* (November 1906), 283–92. Chaikovskii and Lazarev were among those who had provided fulsome tributes on Gots' death. See the supplement to *La Tribune Russe* (30 September 1906).

49 Volkhovskii Papers (HIA), Box 11, Folder 1 (Untitled and apparently unpublished article by Volkhovskii).

50 While the use of force to end revolution in the Russian countryside led to the familiar description of Stolypin as a 'hangman', his views on political questions, in particular the challenge of creating orderly change, were more complex than sometimes supposed. For a good discussion of Stolypin's time in government, see Abraham Ascher, *P. A. Stolypin. The Search for Stability in Late Imperial* Russia (Stanford, CA: Stanford University Press, 2001). For a valuable discussion of attitudes within the SR leadership concerning the potential of armed uprisings to achieve any significant results at this time, see Konstantin Morozov, *Partiia sotsialistov-revoliutsionerov v 1907–1914 gg.* (Moscow: Rosspen, 1998), 278–304.

failure of SR agitators in the military to build momentum, culminating
in the collapse of a planned mutiny at Sevastopol' in September 1907,
meant that it was increasingly difficult for the revolutionary parties to
challenge the state directly.[51] So too did the collapse of an uprising in
Vladivostok.[52] A meeting held in November 1907 between members of
the SR Central Committee and local representatives agreed to continue
work among rank-and-file soldiers and sailors,[53] but the resources
devoted to such activities were cut drastically, as the Party struggled to
raise funds both in Russia and abroad.[54] The publication of *Za narod* was
also suspended due to lack of funds and the paper only began to appear
once more at the start of 1909.

Although many left-wing 'Maximalists' and right-wing 'Legalists'
had broken away from the SRs in 1906, in principle allowing for greater
unity among those who remained, the Party was still disorganised and
demoralised at the time of the first All-Party Conference that convened
in the summer of 1908.[55] Most leading SRs in emigration believed, like
Volkhovskii, that the tsarist state's resilience in the face of the challenges
of 1905-6 showed that it was naïve to think that uncoordinated unrest
could bring about lasting change. A significant number of SRs based
in Russia by contrast believed that local organisations should be free
to determine their own course of action. The disagreement was about
more than tactics. It also reflected competing views about the locus

---

51 On the events at Sevastopol, see 'Sevastopol'skiia sobytiia', *Za narod*, 9 (5 October
    1907).
52 Volkhovskii Papers (HIA), Box 4, Folder 19, ('Izvlechenie iz doklada Ts. Kom. PSR
    o Vladivostokom vozstanii v oktiabre 1907 goda'). The Central Committee report
    concluded among other things that the uprising, which was supported by SR
    Maximalists, had taken place without sufficient preparation.
53 SR Party Archive (Amsterdam), 153 ('Soveshchanie Ts. K. s gruppoi voenn.
    rabotnikov, November 1907').
54 On the financial crisis, see Morozov, *Partiia sotsialistov-revoliutsionerov*, 265–78.
55 The collection edited by N. D. Erofeev, *Partiia sotsialistov-revoliutsionerov.
    Dokumenty i materialy. 1900–1907 gg.* 3 vols., II (Moscow: Rosspen, 2001), suggests
    that the first All-Party Conference took place in Paris, although other sources
    suggest that it met in London (see, for example, Hildermeier, *Russian Socialist
    Revolutionary Party*, 12). For a useful discussion of the Conference, see Morozov,
    Partiia sotsialistov-revoliutsionerov, 305 ff. Morozov's work, which is based on an
    extensive use of the archives, contains a wealth of detail about the organisation
    and membership of the SR Party, along with the debates about tactics, and has
    been used extensively in the pages that follow.

of decision-making in the Party. The tension between 'centralists' and 'democrats' loomed large in the debates that took place at the Conference.[56]

Volkhovskii opened the Conference thanks to his status as the oldest delegate present (Breshko-Breshkovskaia, who was two years older, had recently been arrested in Russia). He planned his speech to give heart to the delegates, drawing on examples from his own long revolutionary career to argue that the SRs could achieve their goals even with little money, as long as they remained enthusiastic and determined. He reminded delegates of the revolutionary pantheon to which they were heirs, recalling the contribution of Grigorii Gershuni, who had died a few weeks earlier, and Lev Sinegub, son of his old friend Sergei, who had been hanged in 1906 for the attempted murder of a tsarist minister. It was striking that these names, both so closely associated with terrorism, were the first that Volkhovskii chose to mention. The SR leadership had reasserted its commitment to the use of terror in its report to the 1907 Stuttgart Congress of the Second International, noting that it did so not out of any 'sanguinary fetish', but rather as a tactic to secure a popular insurrection against the tsarist government.[57] The tactic was nevertheless increasingly questioned by some on the right of the Party, who believed that recent setbacks showed that it should focus its energy on working with legal organisations such as trade unions. Despite such tensions, Volkhovskii's opening speech remained positive about the prospects for revolution, suggesting that each wave was like an incoming tide, pulling back before returning higher than before.[58] His words were those of a revolutionist rather than an evolutionist.

Volkhovskii joined other leading SRs at the Party's first All-Party Conference in seeking compromise between the various factions. He echoed Chernov in supporting the view that using terror was still

---

56   Hildermeier, *Russian Socialist Revolutionary Party*, 305.

57   The report noted firmly that the SR Party 'will not cease using the tactic of terror in the political struggle'. *Rapport du Parti Socialiste Révolutionnaire de Russie*, 21. On shifting attitudes towards terror among the SRs, and the determination of the Party leadership to bring the use of terror by the Combat Organisation more firmly under central control, see Morozov, *Partiia sotsialistov-revoliutsionerov*, 375–442; 484–95.

58   Volkhovskii's speech along with the corrected minutes of the first All-Party Conference and other related material can be found in SR Party Archive (Amsterdam), 138.

an acceptable tactic in the struggle against the government, but only
when combined with a policy of building up the cadres of workers and
peasants necessary to lay the foundations for a popular revolution. It
was a position that reflected Volkhovskii's own long-standing view that
successful insurrection depended on effective agitation and propaganda.
Yet it did not really address the Party's past failures nor consider how
such principles might be put into practice in the future. Nor did it allay
the fears of delegates who fretted that the principle of hierarchical
centralization was supplanting intra-party democracy. The proceedings
of the Conference showed how difficult it was to achieve much at a time
when the tsarist regime was looking more secure and the SRs, like the
rest of the revolutionary movement, were increasingly divided.[59]

Divisions within the Party were even more visible at the fifth Party
Council that met at Paris in the spring of 1909, shortly after Vladimir
Burtsev's unveiling of Evno Azef as an *Okhrana* agent, which created
an enormous crisis of confidence across the SR Party both in Russia
and abroad (it also led to a fall in sales of SR publications including
Za narod).[60] The Party's Central Committee was already facing sharp
criticism for not acting more quickly once concerns about Azef's
loyalties had been raised, and the rancor quickly spread to debates about
tactics and strategy, including the value of the continuing use of terror.[61]
Volkhovskii was like many SRs shattered by the revelations about Azef,
which he described as 'an enormous blow to our Party', that could
only be overcome by a wholesale process of 'moral disinfection' and

---

59   For the *Okhrana's* view of the Conference, which emphasised that the SR Party was
     still committed to regicide, see GARF, fond 102, op. 260, delo 281 (Secret Circular,
     7 October,1908).
60   See, for example, Volkhovskii Papers (HIA), Box 17, Folder 1 (Bulletin 9 of the
     Foreign Committee of the SR Foreign Organisation). See, too, the financial appeal
     to comrades by the editors of *Za narod* in the same folder. The rapid decline in
     circulation for all SR publications can be found by comparing the figures in *La
     Tribune Russe*, 11 November 1907 with those given just three years later in *Znamia
     truda*, 32 (November 1910).
61   See, for example, the numerous criticisms of the Central Committee made
     by delegates to the third Conference of the Foreign Organisation in SR Party
     Archive (Amsterdam), 207–08 (Minutes of the third Conference of the Foreign
     Organisation, 27 March–1 April 1909). For a useful example of discussion over the
     issue of terror, see G. Borisov, 'Nuzhen li eshche terror?', *Znamia truda*, 19 (July
     1909).

transformation of its 'facilities and arrangements'.[62] His contribution to the discussions in Paris was however limited almost entirely to military questions. In a long intervention on 5–6 May,[63] he argued that while it was critical to continue distributing propaganda among the soldiers and sailors, the Party also needed to support a more ambitious programme of agitation that would actively prepare the ground for insurrection. He also maintained that both propaganda and agitational work should retain a 'non-party' character to ensure the greatest impact. Volkhovskii's words were, like his interventions in London the previous year, designed to support a 'middle course' between Party members who still believed in the spontaneous revolutionary instincts of the Russian people and others who doubted whether a successful revolution could take place in Russia for many years to come.

While Volkhovskii played a significant role at the 1908 SR All-Party Conference and the fifth Party Council, he does not seem to have attended many other Party meetings, although the cumbersome nature of the SR records makes it difficult to trace his activities in much detail. He was not present at the third and fourth conferences of the Foreign Organisation,[64] held in March 1909 and April 1911 respectively, although it was admittedly by now a more marginal body in the Party's decision-making. His correspondence shows that he remained in close contact with many leading figures in the SR Party, like Argunov in Paris, but developed fewer close relations with the new generation of Party members. Nor was Volkhovskii particularly active among SRs resident in London (his name seldom appears in the London group's accounts and reports).[65] He was nevertheless selected as a member and *de facto* leader of the SR delegation to the eighth Congress of the Second International,

---

62   Spence Watson / Weiss Papers (Newcastle University), SW 1/19/5, Volkhovskii to Spence Watson, 4 June 1909.

63   SR Party Archive (Amsterdam), 148 (Minutes of the fifth Party Council, Session 9, 5 May 1909; Session 11, 6 May 1909).

64   For the records of the third Conference of the Foreign Organisation, see SR Party Archive (Amsterdam), 207–08; for the records of the fourth Conference, see SR Party Archive (Amsterdam), 209. For the role of the revamped Foreign Organisation in the wake of the 1905 Revolution, see M. I. Leonov, 'Zagranichnaia organizatsiia i Zagranichnyi komitet partii eserov v nachale XX veka (Na putiakh partinoi institutsionalizatsii)', *Vestnik Samarskogo universiteta: istoriia, pedagogika, filologiia*, 27, 2 (2021), 27–36; Morozov, *Partiia sotsialistov-revoliutsionerov*, 249–65.

65   For various records relating to the London group of SRs see, for example, SR Party Archive (Amsterdam), 239.

which met in Copenhagen in 1910, where he played a significant if ultimately ineffective role in discussions about military matters.

The Copenhagen Congress established a series of commissions, including one on antimilitarism, which set up a sub-commission to produce a resolution building on the one agreed at Stuttgart three years earlier. The group did not at first include any Russian representatives, a decision met with fury by Volkhovskii, who pointed out that such a proposal made no sense given that Russia was one of the most militarised countries on earth. He was himself eventually selected to take part in this sub-commission, where discussions were often fractious, given the different views about how best to mobilise workers to prevent war. Volkhovskii argued that the proposed resolution should include a demand that the civil rights of soldiers and sailors be enshrined in national legal systems. More controversially, he also called for the resolution to emphasise the need to conduct socialist propaganda in the armed forces, making it harder for governments to use soldiers to snuff out any incidences of revolution. He criticised a draft proposal tabled by the British Labour politician Keir Hardie and the French socialist Édouard Vaillant for being too timid. The chair of the sub-commission rejected Volkhovskii's proposal for being outside the remit of the Commission on Antimilitarism, much to the indignation of its architect, and it was set aside in favour of the one put forward by Hardie and Vaillant. Volkhovskii's defeat was in part due to his failure to master the bureaucratic machinations and compromises that were an inevitable consequence of the deep fissures within the Second International.[66] He also failed to understand that some socialist parties in Western Europe were more or less eager participants in mainstream politics and wary of agreeing to anything that could compromise their increasingly 'established' status. The SR press by contrast predictably endorsed Volkhovskii's views and attacked the timidity of the resolution endorsed by the Commission on Antimilitarism.[67]

---

66 For details of Volkhovskii's protests and the eventual rejection of his draft resolution, see *Huitième Congrès Socialiste International tenu à Copenhague du 28 août au 3 septembre 1910: compte rendu analytique* (Gand: Volksdrukkerij, 1911), 187–90.

67 See the articles 'VIII Mezhdunarodnyi Sotsialisticheskii Kongress' and 'Vopros o militarizme na Kopengagenskom kongresse' in *Znamia truda*, 31 (October 1910).

Volkhovskii continued to devote much of his energy to *Za narod* after it resumed publication in 1909, although with a much lower print run, given a sharp fall in demand.[68] The paper continued to take a 'non-party' revolutionary line, carrying reports of disturbances across Russia, and printing letters from revolutionaries of all political colours including Social Democrats. It dismissed the third Duma and the constitutional experiment more generally without setting down any clear views about the political direction that the SRs should follow (a subject that continued to cause division within the Party). Despite the generally bleak revolutionary climate, Volkhovskii argued that there were still a number of positive developments, including the growing radicalism of the peasantry.[69] He also wrote further pieces showing his interest in the Swiss political system, arguing that it gave electors real power, not least through the use of referenda on important issues of policy.[70] Although he did not spell it out, Volkhovskii was clearly pondering how new forms of 'direct democracy' could avoid the compromises of parliamentary politics while dovetailing with the political culture of the Russian countryside, in effect keeping alive at least a remnant of the traditional *narodnik* idealization of the peasant *mir*.

Volkhovskii was determined that *Za narod* should continue to publish poetry and short stories. The literary content of the paper remained unashamedly propagandistic and the titles of many of the poems provided a vivid clue to their character. 'Pesnia o tirane' ('The Song of Tyranny') condemned a government 'drunk on the people's blood' that ruled over a land where 'there is no law or love'.[71] 'Pamiati pavshikh' ('To the Memory of the Fallen') celebrated 'the torch' lit by revolutionaries who had been executed for their actions.[72] Each verse

---

68 See, for example, Volkhovskii Papers (HIA), Box 7, Folder 4, Bowman to Chevin, 31 July 1907 (indicating that 2,000 copies of the paper had been sent to Paris); Woodruffe to 'Comrade', 2 February 1910 (noting that the radical East End publishing house which printed *Za narod* made almost no money from the business); Woodruffe to Volkhovskii, 23 April 1910 (discussing arrangements for the Cyrillic type face used to print *Za narod*, which may have been the type face previously used for publications of the Russian Free Press Fund).

69 'Chto narod dumaet o tsare', *Za narod*, 28 (April 1910).

70 See, for example, 'Kak shveitsartsy vybiraiut svoikh deputatov', *Za narod*, 14 (February 1909).

71 'Pesnia o tirane', *Za narod*, 5 (8 July 1907).

72 'Pamiati pavshikh', *Za narod*, 6 (25 July 1907). The poem was described as a 'hymn'.

of 'Druzheskaia beseda Rossii s tsarem' ('A Friendly Conversation of
Russia with the Tsar') began with the ironic claim that Nicholas was the
little father (*batiushka*) of his people.[73] Most of the poems had a strong
beat, in some cases with a suggested tune, indicating that they were
intended to be recited or sung out loud. The stories published in *Za narod*
were also typically short—often no more than fifteen hundred words—
and written in an easily-readable style.[74] Many stories had a soldier
as the central character, who was typically portrayed sympathetically,
while officers were depicted as incompetents who had no interest in
the welfare of the men who served under them. Only a few stories
were attributed to a named author. Some were written by the novelist
Aleksandr Amfiteatrov.[75] Volkhovskii probably contributed many of the
poems and stories himself.

Volkhovskii's editorial activities were not limited to *Za narod*. He
was also involved in the production of several numbers of *Narodnoe
delo: sbornik* that was published irregularly by the SR press between
1909 and 1912.[76] The *sbornik* included less literary material than the
issues of *Narodnoe delo* that Volkhovskii edited a few years earlier, in
favour of articles on such questions as 'Autocracy and Revolution' and
'What Kind of Agricultural Order Should There Be in Russia?'[77] It is
not easy to identify Volkhovskii's role in editing the *sbornik*, although
some of the work of production and distribution appears to have been
done in Paris by Argunov,[78] suggesting it may have been quite limited.
There is nevertheless evidence that the *sbornik* and *Za narod* were
closely connected, not least through occasional transfers of money
between them, although some of this once again seems to have been the

---

73 'Druzheskaia beseda Rossii s tsarem', *Za narod*, 14 (February 1909).
74 Some stories were however significantly longer. See, for example, 'Nashel', *Za
    narod*, 8 (12 September 1907).
75 See I. S. Zilbershtein and N. I. Dikushina (eds), *Gorkii i russkaia zhurnalistika XX
    veka: Neizdannaia perepiska, Literaturnoe nasledstvo*, 95 (Moscow: Nauka, 1985), 133
    (Amfiteatrov to Gorkii, 10 December 1908).
76 For a useful discussion of *Narodnoe delo: sbornik*, including its relation to other SR
    publications, see Green, 'Russian Revolutionary Terrorism', 118–22.
77 A. Bakh, 'Samoderzhavie i revoliutsiia', *Narodnoe delo: sbornik*, 1 (1909), 4–38;
    Dikii, 'Kakovy dolzhny byt' zemel'nye poriadki na Rusi?', *Narodnoe delo: sbornik*, 5
    (1910), 27–54.
78 Argunov was regularly in St Petersburg until 1909 but subsequently seems to have
    based himself in Paris.

work of Argunov.[79] The regular use of pseudonyms makes it difficult
to identify how much of the content Volkhovskii contributed to the
sbornik. He certainly wrote 'Skazka o soldatskoi dushe' ('The Tale of a
Soldier's Soul') that appeared in the fourth issue,[80] in which the devil
discusses with some of his minions how to corrupt ordinary soldiers,
who seem to be far less responsive to Satan's blandishments than their
officers. The story was simpler in tone than many of the more serious
pieces published in the same number, none of which were written by
Volkhovskii, and it was probably intended as light relief in an issue that
also included articles on 'The Glory Days of the Turkish Army' and 'The
Army and the Great French Revolution of 1789'.

Although Volkhovskii did not publish much new poetry under his
own name in the final years of his life, when he lived in Finland in 1907
he arranged for publication of some of his earlier verses (although most
copies were confiscated and destroyed soon after he fled the country).[81]
A new collection of his children's stories appeared in Moscow the
following year, dedicated to his daughters, under the title *Diuzhina skazok*
(*A Dozen Tales*).[82] He also appears to have cooperated on the translation of
a number of Ukrainian stories about peasant life in the south-west of the
Empire into Russian,[83] as well as publishing in *Sovremennik* a translation
of Clementina Black's novel 'The Agitator', described by Eleanor Marx
as one of the most realistic fictional portrayals of the British socialist
movement (Black was a long-time Fabian and sister of Volkhovskii's old
friend Constance Garnett).[84] There is, too, an intriguing question as to
whether Volkhovskii turned his hand to writing novels during his final

---

79   Green, 'Russian Revolutionary Terrorism', 122. At least some of the practical
     work of editing *Za narod* was done in Paris in the years before 1914, by Vladimir
     Lebedev, making it still more difficult to establish the relationship between the two
     publications.
80   F. Volkhovskii, 'Skazka o soldatskoi dushe', *Narodnoe delo: sbornik*, 4 (1909), 5–12.
81   This was the collection, *Sluchainyia pesni* (Moscow: Knigoizdatel'stvo L. I.
     Kolovatova, 1907), which appeared under Volkhovskii's own name.
82   Ivan Brut (Feliks Volkhovskii), *Diuzhina skazok* (Moscow: V. M. Sablin, 1908). A
     further collection appeared five years later. See Ivan Brut, *Rakety. Skazki dlia detei
     sovershennago vozrasta* (Paris: L. Rodstein, 1913).
83   M. Kotsiubinskii, *Razskazy*, trans. F. Volkhovskii and Mikh. Mogilianskii (Moscow:
     Knigoizdatel'stvo pisatelei v Moskve, 1914). Volkhovskii and Mogilanskii also
     translated an edition of children's stories from Ukrainian into Russian.
84   *Sovremennik* 10 (1911), 120–60; *Sovremennik*, 11 (1911), 135–72; *Sovremennik*, 12
     (1911), 28–58.

few years. In 1913, the German publisher Heinrich Caspari issued a book entitled *Admiral Chagin*, under the pseudonym Brut, which was loosely based on the real-life suicide of its eponymous hero (Volkhovskii had of course often used the pseudonym Ivan Brut in his earlier work and started to make considerable use of it once again in the years after 1905).[85] Chagin had enjoyed a distinguished naval career before his appointment as captain of the Royal Yacht *Shtandart*, which he was commanding when it hit a rock off the Finnish coast in August 1907 (the boat remained afloat and the Royal Family was unharmed). An investigation largely cleared Chagin of responsibility for the accident, and he continued to command the *Shtandart*, but it seriously damaged his reputation, and according to some accounts led to a cycle of depression that led five years later to his suicide. The inquiry following his death concluded by contrast that he took his life in despair following his rejection by a young woman. The rumour mill quickly provided a more dramatic account. Stories circulated that the Admiral's lover had been a member of the SRs who used her relationship with Chagin to help Party members infiltrate the ship's crew. Reports even circulated that the Tsarevich had been shot on board the *Shtandart* through Chagin's negligence (claims repeated in a garbled form in several newspapers abroad).[86] The whole affair clearly appealed to Volkhovskii's sense of the dramatic. He may also have hoped that penning a novel could bring him some much-needed income.

The plot of *Admiral Chagin* revolves around the relationship between the Admiral and 'Annochka', a young provincial woman, who attracts the romantic interest of a group of radical students whose conversation is replete with stilted discussion of such ideological questions as the nature of economic development in Russia and the need to build closer relations between the revolutionary *intelligentsia* and the *narod*. She also, however, attracts the love of Admiral Chagin who has known her since she was a child. Annochka is in this telling of the story genuinely torn between her respect for the Admiral and her love for a student (Bronnikov), who becomes an agitator among

85   [Ivan] Brut, *Admiral Chagin* (Berlin: Heinrich Caspari, 1913). The published version in fact only gives the author as 'Brut', raising the question of authorship discussed below.

86   See, for example, the *Daily Mail* (25 October 1912). The rumours probably gained extra credence because Aleksei was very ill at the time and widely believed to be close to death.

the sailors at the Krondstadt naval base, after narrowly escaping arrest in a student demonstration. The story lacks clear heroes and villains. The Admiral is portrayed as a sympathetic character ready to turn his back on a possible marriage to a prominent aristocrat to win the hand of Annochka. Bronnikov by contrast shows a streak of ruthlessness, threatening to denounce Annochka as an *agent provocateur* if she does not use her relationship with the Admiral to further the revolutionary cause. The book is at its heart a melodramatic love story set against a revolutionary background rather than a revolutionary novel *per se*. One Russian academic has suggested that *Admiral Chagin*—and a second novel *Peterburg* published by 'Brut' the following year—were written by the journalist and translator M. A. Sukennikov.[87] The evidence he provides is quite thin. But neither, it must be said, can a draft of either novel be found in Volkhovskii's papers (nor indeed any other material relating to its publication). Both the pseudonym of the author and the subject matter—not least Bronnikov's role in agitation among the military—suggest that Volkhovskii was the more likely author. Material in his papers certainly shows that he had previously tried his hand at writing novels.[88] It nevertheless seems unlikely that the authorship of *Admiral Chagin* can ever be conclusively determined.

While Volkhovskii focused much of his energy on supporting the revolutionary cause in Russia, he still spent most of his last ten years in Britain, although his social and literary connections there were never as extensive as they had been during his first few years in London. There was also a change in his political networks. Although many members of the SFRF continued to be drawn from the Liberal milieu personified by Robert Spence Watson, who continued to be active in support of the 'cause' down to his death in 1911, criticism of the Russian government increasingly found its strongest expression in trade unions and the newly formed Labour Party. In 1907, Volkhovskii penned 'An Open Letter to the Socialists and Workers of Great Britain', noting that the 'self-sacrifice' and 'heroic energy' of the Russian labour movement had always appealed to British workers. He went on to argue that while in the 1860s

---

87   K. M. Azadovskii, 'Iz slovaria "Russkie pisateli. 1800–1917" (M. A. Sukennikov. S. N. Shil')', *Literaturnyi fakt*, 7 (2018), 358–84.

88   Volkhovskii Papers (HIA), Box 11, Folder 6, for example, contains the title page of Ivan Brut, 'Novel Without a Hero'.

and 1870s 'the fight in the interests of the working man was carried on almost exclusively by the advanced, idealistic elements of the educated, privileged, governing classes', today 'the numerical strength of the army of progress is supplied by these masses themselves'. Volkhovskii added that the events of 1905–06 had given 'working people' practical experience in 'municipal affairs ... the land question and parliamentary elections'.[89] The letter was presumably written to help raise funds. It also reflected Volkhovskii's recognition that the political complexion of support for the cause of Russian freedom had changed.

In an astute article published in June 1906 in the short-lived SR paper *Mysl'*—a few weeks before he set off for Finland—Volkhovskii had been sharply critical of the Liberal Government in London. He told his readers that many ministers, above all the Foreign Secretary Sir Edward Grey, were fervent imperialists who always put the interests of empire ahead of such principles as freedom of conscience. By contrast prominent members of the Labour Party, including Keir Hardy and Will Thorne, were active in calling for a tougher policy towards Russia (both men had recently spoken out strongly in Parliament against a planned visit to Kronstadt by a flotilla from the Royal Navy). While Volkhovskii expressed hope that the British government would be forced to listen to public opinion in such matters, he acknowledged that interests of *Realpolitik* usually prevailed in foreign policy, and that it was naïve to expect ministers to take a hard line against Russia at a time of growing fear about the threat posed by Germany.[90] It was a shrewd assessment of the challenge involved in bringing public opinion to bear on British foreign policy.

The whole question of Britain's relationship with Russia was thrust to the centre of the political stage by the signing of the Anglo-Russian Convention in August 1907, a few weeks after Volkhovskii returned to London from Finland. The Convention was designed to reduce imperial tensions between the two countries in central Asia, establishing clear spheres of influence, while freeing them up to focus on the threat posed

89	Volkhovskii Papers (HIA), Box 11, Folder 2, ('An Open Letter to the Socialists and Workers of Great Britain'). The letter appears to be in Volkhovskii's handwriting although it is not clear if it was ever published.
90	F. Volkhovskii, 'Chto delaetsia za granitsei—Angliskii liberalizm i Rossiia', *Mysl'* (24 June 1906).

by the erratic policy of Wilhelmine Germany.[91] Although it did not bring
a complete halt to the tension between Russia and Britain, particularly
in Persia,[92] the agreement was an important step in shaping the two
international blocs that went to war in 1914. The decision to seek an
entente with Russia was driven by the views of senior figures in the
Foreign Office, including Sir Edward Grey, and took place despite
significant misgivings among some Cabinet ministers and a wider
strand of public opinion. Volkhovskii acknowledged in his article in
Mysl' the previous year that some ministers including James Bryce and
John Morley were opposed to any policy of building better relations with
St Petersburg. The Liberal Prime Minister Henry Campbell-Bannerman
had also reacted to news of the suspension of the first Duma with a
rallying cry of 'La Douma est morte, Vive la Douma'.[93] Grey and his
Permanent Secretary, Sir Charles Hardinge, were however adepts in the
culture and practice of the Old Diplomacy. They were able to shepherd
the agreement onto the books in part through using a veil of secrecy to
limit public debate.[94]

There was significant public opposition in Britain to any attempts to
improve relations with the Russian government. Six weeks before the
Convention was announced, the SFRF organised a meeting in Trafalgar
Square to protest at the recent suspension of the second Duma. A
number of those present subsequently headed to the Foreign Office,

---

91 Among the large literature on Anglo-Russian relations in this period, including
the 1907 Convention, see Michael Hughes, *Diplomacy before the Russian Revolution:
Britain, Russia and the Old Diplomacy, 1894–1917* (Basingstoke: Palgrave Macmillan,
2000); Keith Neilson, *Britain and the Last Tsar: British Policy and Russia, 1894–1917*
(Oxford: Oxford University Press, 1995); Jennifer Siegel, *Endgame: Britain,
Russia and the Final Struggle for Central Asia* (London: I. B. Tauris, 2002); Fiona K.
Tomaszewski, *A Great Russia: Russia and the Triple Entente, 1905–1914* (London:
Praeger, 2002). For an account emphasising how fear of Germany shaped British
policy towards Russia, see John Charmley, *Splendid Isolation? Britain and the Balance
of Power, 1874–1914* (London: Hodder and Stoughton, 1999).

92 See, in particular, Siegel, *Endgame*, 50–116.

93 For details of the Prime Minister's outburst and the subsequent 'Memorial' signed
by many prominent Britons, see Barry Hollingsworth, 'The British Memorial to the
Russian Duma, 1906', *Slavonic and East European Review*, 53, 133 (1975), 539–57.

94 On the idea of the Old Diplomacy, see Hughes, *Diplomacy before the Russian
Revolution*, 3–18. For a useful brief discussion of changing patterns of diplomacy,
see Kenneth Weisbrode, *Old Diplomacy Revisited. A Study in the Modern History of
Diplomatic Transformations* (Basingstoke: Palgrave Macmillan, 2014). Also see Keith
Hamilton and Richard Langhorne, *The Practice of Diplomacy: Its Evolution, Theory
and Administration* (Abingdon: Routledge, 2011), 93–140.

where they were forcibly dispersed by the police after a demonstrator attempted to enter the building, a form of direct action that would have been anathema to many original members of the Society.[95] Emotions were running particularly high given that rumours of talks between London and St Petersburg had been circulating for months. Once the Anglo-Russian Convention was signed, the Society's Executive Committee sent a memorial to the British government condemning the treaty 'as calculated to improve the credit of the Russian Government and to discourage those who were fighting for liberty in Russia'.[96] It also argued that the agreement should be submitted to Parliament for approval, a move that was not constitutionally required, but echoed a growing sense among some on the left of the need to open up the secret world of diplomacy to public gaze.

While the cause of improved Anglo-Russian relations attracted opposition, it also found considerable support in some quarters, not least from the *Times*, which in later years published a Russian supplement that combined articles about the country's buoyant commercial prospects with other pieces praising the unique character of its culture. The development of the 'Russia craze' in Britain since the 1890s—which manifested itself in everything from interest in Russian literature through to the Ballets Russes—undoubtedly helped to reshape attitudes towards Russia by challenging old notions of the Russian 'bear'. Writers like Maurice Baring produced books and articles presenting Russia as a place of mystery and intrigue.[97] Bernard Pares of the University of Liverpool worked to develop Russian Studies in Britain, in order to build up a cadre of young men with the expertise required to strengthen the country's commercial presence in Russia.[98] Many yearbooks and gazetteers were published containing detailed commercial information for those interested in doing business with Russia. Volkhovskii was quick to recognise the challenges posed by this

---

95   *Daily Telegraph* (15 July 1907).

96   'Our Activity', *Free Russia* (January–March 1908).

97   Among Baring's numerous writings on Russia, see, for example, Maurice Baring, *With the Russians in Manchuria* (London: Methuen, 1905); Maurice Baring, *The Russian People* (London: Methuen, 1911).

98   Michael Hughes, 'Bernard Pares, Russian Studies and the Promotion of Anglo-Russian Friendship, 1907–14', *Slavonic and East European Review*, 78, 3 (2000), 510–35.

new wave of cultural and commercial Russophilia. Following his return to Britain in 1907, he used the columns of *Free Russia* to persuade readers that the 1905 Revolution had in reality changed very little, and that the tsarist government remained a threat both to its own people and the wider world.

Free Russia continued to print numerous articles reporting abuses committed by the tsarist government, as well as condemning its neglect of the welfare of the people, including its failure to respond to such crises as the cholera outbreaks that swept across parts of the country in the summer of 1908.[99] The paper also regularly criticised West European governments that extradited members of the Russian opposition back to Russia.[100] Particularly striking was the harsh criticism of the Tsar himself, who was the subject of a number of unflattering cartoons, as well as several pieces by Volkhovskii challenging the claim that Nicholas knew little of the abuses carried out in his name. In the first edition of *Free Russia* to appear in 1908, he savagely condemned the Tsar for being the effective head of the Black Hundreds—the bands of thugs who carried out anti-Jewish pogroms across European Russia—adding confidently that in the face of such evils 'the British people acknowledges in the last resort for improvement the sacred right of revolution'.[101] Volkhovskii repeated his claims in the next number, insisting that the Tsar welcomed the pogroms and was personally responsible for the 'heartless tyranny' of his government.[102] In an unpublished article, apparently intended for *Free Russia*, Volkhovskii argued that the Russian people were ready to fight for their freedom, and attacked the complacency of many Britons who believed that 'terrorist methods ... are wrong as well as mistaken'. He argued that Britons too would be ready to turn to violence, if faced with similar circumstances, adding that if 'the atrocities ... of the official world never met with revolutionary punishments the masses would by now have lost all faith in the eventual triumph of equity over injustice'.[103] The fact that the article remained unpublished suggests that Volkhovskii

99 'Cholera', *Free Russia* (July–September 1908).
100 'The Extradition of Vassilev', *Free Russia* (April–June 1908).
101 F. Volkhovsky, 'The Present Situation', *Free Russia* (January–March 1908).
102 F. Volkhovsky, 'The Tzar's Responsibility', *Free Russia* (April–June 1908).
103 Volkhovskii Papers (HIA), Box 11, Folder 1 (Untitled and unpublished article by Volkhovskii, c. January 1908).

recognised that such sentiments were still likely to alienate many of his British readers.

Both the SFRF and *Free Russia* attacked attempts to build closer relations between Britain and Russia in the wake of the signing of the Anglo-Russian Convention. In the early summer of 1908, in response to news that Edward VII was going to meet with the Tsar on board ship in the Bay of Reval, the Liberal MP Charles Trevelyan established a Russian Committee in the House of Commons. Volkhovskii took a leading role in editing the Committee's Bulletin, circulated to MPs and the press, which was predicated on the view that Russia was an unsuitable diplomatic partner for Britain given the despotic character of its government. Copies included numerous articles on such subjects as 'The Tsar and the Organisers of the Pogroms', as well as detailed evidence about the use of torture, along with extensive statistical information on the number of exiles condemned by the regime without trial.[104] The question of royal visits became still more pressing the following year, when it was announced that Nicholas was to come to Britain, although in the event he only set foot on the Isle of Wight (home of the royal residence Osborne House).[105] Volkhovskii inveighed against the visit on the pages of *Free Russia*, condemning the British government for welcoming 'the head of the Black Hundred', pointing out with some justice that the unpopularity of the Tsar in Britain meant that he could only be received in 'a remote corner' where he would not have to face protesters.[106]

Volkhovskii was encouraged by the opposition to the Tsar's visit from the Labour Party and the Independent Labour Party, as well as various trade unions and the Church Socialist League, along with newspapers like *Justice* which carried a column referring to Nicholas as 'the prince of butchers'.[107] The *Daily News* was more restrained, but it too condemned the visit, suggesting that the Tsar had given tacit support to the Black Hundreds.[108] Thousands attended a mass meeting in Trafalgar

---

104 'Bulletin Issued by the Russian Committee in the House of Commons: No. 4' (16 September 1908).

105 For a useful analysis of the symbolic importance of the visit, see Fiona Tomaszewski, 'Pomp, Circumstance, and Realpolitik: The Evolution of the Triple Entente of Russia, Great Britain, and France', *Jahrbücher für Geschichte Osteuropas*, 47, 3 (1999), 362–80.

106 F. Volkhovsky, 'The Tzar's Visit to England', *Free Russia* (July 1909).

107 *Justice* (14 August 1909).

108 *Daily News* (16 June 1909).

Square to demonstrate against the visit.[109] Many more attended protest meetings up and down the country.[110] Such demonstrations did little to influence British policy towards Russia. The Foreign Office was remarkably successful at insulating policymaking from the influence of the *hoi polloi*—whether in the form of Labour MPs, Church of England bishops or émigré journalists—while most of the British press in any case defended both the visit and the broader principle of the 1907 agreement. The *Times* argued that Russian foreign policy was peaceful and condemned politicians who attacked the visit for 'mischief-making'.[111] Many local papers reported with approval the Tsar's gift of £1000 to support those in need on the Isle of Wight.

Free Russia also regularly carried pieces criticising the 1905 Aliens Act, which was passed by Parliament to limit immigration, although it also represented the culmination of more than a decade of concern that political violence and 'anarchism' were imports contrary to British political traditions and values.[112] The nature and composition of the Russian revolutionary emigration in London changed significantly during the first decade of the twentieth century. Jewish émigrés from the western borderlands of the Tsarist Empire continued to find a home in the self-contained diaspora in the East End,[113] where it was possible

---

109 *Justice* (24 July 1909).
110 See, for example, a description of various protests by trade unions at the prospect of the Tsar's visit in the *Daily News* (22 June 1909).
111 *Times* (2 August 1909).
112 The paper had opposed the legislation long before it was passed. See, for example, 'The Aliens Bill', *Free Russia* (1 May 1904). Prominent members of the SFRF had for some time taken a leading role in opposing the Bill. See Stow Hill Papers, (Parliamentary Archives), STH/DS/1/GRE 12 (Flyer headed 'The Aliens Bill'). For a useful overview of the Aliens Act, see Helena Wray, 'The Aliens Act and the Immigration Dilemma', *Journal of Law and Society*, 33, 2 (2006), 302–23. See, too, Jill Pellew, 'The Home Office and the Aliens Act, 1905', *Historical Journal*, 32, 2 (1989), 369–85. For an examination of the Act in its historical context, see Bernard Gainer, *The Alien Invasion. The Origins of the 1905 Aliens Act* (London: Heinemann, 1972). For a very different approach to the history and significance of the Aliens Act, see David Glover, *Literature, Immigration and Diaspora in Fin-de-Siècle England. A Cultural History of the 1905 Aliens Act* (Cambridge: Cambridge University Press, 2012).
113 On the development of the Jewish community in Britain see, for example, David Feldman, *Englishmen and Jews: Social Relations and Political Culture, 1840–1914* (New Haven, CT: Yale University Press, 1994); Lloyd P. Gartner, *The Jewish Immigrant in England, 1870–1914* (Detroit, MI: Wayne State University Press, 1960). For a valuable examination of radicalism among the Jewish population in London's East

for new arrivals to live a life that seldom brought them into contact with the host communities surrounding them.[114] Some of the most prominent figures in the revolutionary movement also made London their home, including Vladimir Lenin, although few of these new arrivals developed many friendships with Britons beyond a small coterie of radical socialists.[115] While the names of Stepniak and Kropotkin resonated widely among a section of British society in the 1880s and 1890s, made familiar through their writings in newspapers and journals, the 'new' revolutionaries who flitted in and out of Britain in the years following the 1905 Revolution were altogether more shadowy figures.

A short piece in the first number of *Free Russia* that appeared in 1908 noted that several members of the SFRF had the previous year attended the fifth Congress of the Russian Social Democratic Party that took place in London (which included Lenin and Stalin among its delegates). The paper did not, though, provide many details about the proceedings.[116] A reporter from the conservative *Morning Post* noted at the time that there was no secrecy about the event, describing his interviews with delegates milling round the Socialist Club in Whitechapel, including one who told him that the Marxist Social Democrats had no sympathy for 'anarchism'.[117] Other papers took a bleaker view, detailing rumours that the delegates hoped to buy arms in London,[118] and that some of those who had previously been expelled from Denmark planted a bomb there in revenge.[119] The press was nevertheless still fairly relaxed about the presence of Russian revolutionaries in London. The *Daily News* went so far as to complain about police harassment of delegates to the

---

End, see William J. Fishman, *East End Jewish Radicals, 1875–1914* (London: Five Leaves Publications, 2004).

114 For a wealth of useful material on the pattern of ethnic settlement in the East End, see the relevant sections of James Perry, 'Foreigners, Aliens and Strangers: Foreign-Born Migration and Settlement in England and Wales, 1851–1911' (PhD thesis, Lancaster University, 2019).

115 On Lenin in London, see Robert Henderson, *The Spark that Lit the Revolution. Lenin in London and the Politics that Changed the World* (London: I. B. Tauris, 2020). Also see the relevant sections of Helen Rappoport, *Conspirator: Lenin in Exile. The Making of a Revolutionary* (New York: Basic Books, 2010).

116 'Our Activity', *Free Russia* (January–March 1908).

117 *Morning Post* (11 May 1907).

118 *Evening Mail* (13 May 1907).

119 *Leeds Mercury* (11 May 1907).

Congress, given there was no evidence that they sought to create any unrest in Britain.[120]

Things changed sharply over the next few years. At the start of 1909, two Jewish immigrants from Latvia, Paul Helfeld and Jacob Lepidus, killed two passers-by when fleeing from a factory in north-east London where they had carried out an armed robbery. They may—or may not—have intended to use the money to support revolutionary activities both in Russia and abroad.[121] The *Morning Post* reported that many émigrés from Russia refused to denounce Helfeld and Lepidus.[122] The *Daily Telegraph* attacked the Metropolitan Police for allowing foreign revolutionaries to remain at liberty, despite knowing that many plots were hatched in the British capital to carry out killings abroad.[123] The Siege of Sidney Street that took place two years later, after several members of a gang of Latvian refugees killed three policemen who interrupted a raid on a jewellery shop in Hounsditch, re-enforced growing concern about the threat posed by foreign 'anarchists'.[124] The *Times* printed a long editorial arguing that the British police were now confronting the same kinds of challenges that had faced the Russian authorities for many years, as 'the old blaze ... leapt out into the country to which so many of the refugees have escaped—that is, East London'.[125] The image of the ethical Russia revolutionary, so carefully cultivated in the pages of *Free Russia* over the previous fifteen years or so, was undermined not by the insinuations of tsarist agents but rather by real sanguinary events in London's East End.

The *Okhrana* continued to use retired Scotland Yard detectives to monitor the activities of Russian revolutionaries in London (as well as

---

120 *Daily News* (23 May 1907).

121 For a lively account of the events in Tottenham see, for example, Geoffrey Barton, *The Tottenham Outrage and Walthamstow Tram Chase: The Most Spectacular Hot Pursuit in History* (Hook: Waterside Press, 2017).

122 *Morning Post* (26 January 1909).

123 *Daily Telegraph* (26 January 1909).

124 On the siege and the events leading up to it, see Colin Rogers, *The Battle of Stepney. The Sidney Street Siege: Its Causes and Consequences* (London: Robert Hale, 1981); Donald Rumbelow, *The Houndsditch Murders and the Siege of Sidney Street* (London: W. H. Allen, 1988).

125 *Times* (25 January 1911). The *Okhrana* provided London with information likely to help them identify the culprits in the Houndsditch murders. See Okhrana Archive (HIA), Index Vc, Folder 1, Letter of thanks for information to A. Krassilnikoff, 31 December 1910; Letter of thanks for information by John Ottoway, 6 February 1911 (microfilm 69).

maintaining good working relations with some serving officers). The Paris *agentura* became increasingly frustrated by the poor character of the reports submitted by their principal agent in London, Edgar Farce, who seems to have been curiously silent about the activities of Jewish radicals in the East End despite claiming to know Yiddish.[126] Volkhovskii himself made regular trips to East London, to meet with couriers who carried material to and from the continent, presumably including both confidential letters and material relating to the publication of *Za narod*. He also had close links with the Free Russian Library in Whitechapel, which served as an important cultural hub for the Russian community in the area, but was in the opinion of the Russian and French secret police 'the rallying centre of the Russian revolutionary movement in London'.[127] Volkhovskii did not, though, ever develop close links with the more prominent members of the Bolshevik Party who regularly made London their home (he does not appear to have ever met Lenin).[128] Nor did he develop close links with the Jewish radical émigré communities of Whitechapel, and he had no connections with the networks to which the perpetrators of the Tottenham and Houndsditch murders belonged. *Free Russia* itself was oddly silent on the Tottenham Outrage, perhaps reflecting the challenge posed by such events to the paper's long-standing mission to present a positive picture of the revolutionary movement, but Volkhovskii did write a long letter to the *Manchester Guardian* intended to counter the potential damage to the 'cause' resulting from the dramatic events that had been played out on the streets of London.

Volkhovskii described the events in Tottenham as 'a particularly sore spot' for Russians who had found 'friendly asylum' in Britain after being

---

126 Developments in the East End became more prominent in some of Farce's later reports, though the Paris *agentura* continued to be frustrated about the lack of definite information. Farce for his part feared (wrongly) that Melville wished to replace him. See Okhrana Archive, Index VIk, Folder 23, Report by Edgar Farce, 9 May 1904 (microfilm 107).

127 Henderson, *Spark That Lit the Revolution*, 26. On the Whitechapel Library see Robert Henderson, 'A. L. Teplov and the Russian Free Library in Whitechapel', *Solanus*, New Series, 22 (2011), 5–26.

128 While it is possible to exaggerate the fragmentation of Russian émigré communities in London and other west European cities, at least in the ten years or so before the First World War, the divisions certainly complicated the pattern of life in Russian émigré communities set out in such magisterial terms in Faith Hillis, *Utopia's Discontents: Russian Émigrés and the Quest for Freedom, 1830s–1930s* (New York: Oxford University Press, 2021).

driven from their own country by 'tyranny and official lawlessness'. He also acknowledged that the killing of a policeman and a young boy seemed a poor 'repayment for political hospitality'. Volkhovskii went on to argue that the brutality of the Russian government had effectively 'trained' men like Helfield and Lapidus to turn to violence since, like thousands of young men, they saw no other way of bringing about change. He also claimed that the Socialist Revolutionaries and the Social Democrats 'most emphatically' condemned 'expropriations of private persons and institutions' and could not therefore be held accountable for the actions of Helfield and Lapidus.[129] Such words were disingenuous. All the main revolutionary parties raised money in Russia through robbery and expropriations. The boundary between political and criminal activity was in any case often porous. Helfield and Lapidus had criminal records, but they were also active in smuggling revolutionary literature into Russia, and they had both been living in Paris when Helfield's brother was killed by the premature explosion of a bomb designed to assassinate the French President. The two men belonged to the Latvian Socialist Party, which was formally distinct from both the Socialist Revolutionaries and the Social Democrats, but in the confused maelstrom of revolutionary organisations such categories were seldom precise ones. Volkhovskii must have realised that his skilfully chosen words did not fully capture the complex reality of the East End revolutionary diaspora.

Volkhovskii was more comfortable when welcoming Vera Figner to Britain in the summer of 1910, introducing her to a meeting in north London as 'the embodiment of all the sorrow, all the martyrdom but also of all the best hopes and sublime aspirations of our beloved country'. Similar sentiments were expressed by other members of the London emigration, including Petr Kropotkin, who suggested that her ideals were not simply Russian but 'universal'.[130] Such language was designed to create a rhetoric of integrity that not only celebrated a revolutionary icon but also wrapped the contemporary revolutionary movement in her mantle.[131] The same was true of other revolutionary

---

129 *Manchester Guardian* (27 January 1909).
130 'To Welcome Vera N. Figner', *Free Russia* (July 1909).
131 Figner's presence in Britain was also welcomed by much of the Liberal press. See, for example, *Daily News* (22 June 1909).

veterans. After Ekaterina Breshko-Breshkovskaia was sentenced to a further bout of exile in Siberia, at the start of 1910, Volkhovskii described her on the pages of *Free Russia* as an icon of 'the whole revolutionary cause'.[132] In the same number, he wrote an obituary of his old friend Leonid Shishko, warmly recalling his revolutionary career from his time in the Chaikovskii circle ('His memory ... will shine with a permanent, unflagging soft starlight').[133] Volkhovskii may well have been genuine in believing there was a vital connection between the revolutionaries of the 1870s and their successors of the 1900s. He was indeed himself a living expression of the lineage. Yet there was also something calculated in his attempt to persuade British readers to see the contemporary revolutionary movement through the prism of the past. The perpetrators of the killings in Tottenham and Hounsditch were very different in both background and ideological outlook from the young men and women who flocked to the Russian countryside in the 1870s and later joined the ranks of Narodnaia volia.

Volkhovskii's health declined still further in the last few years before his death in 1914. Constance Garnett heard that he had developed kidney problems to add to his other woes. Several correspondents urged him not to allow his physical ailments to undermine his good spirits ('It is only your illness that makes you downcast. You must not allow yourself to think sadly of the past').[134] He nevertheless kept up a regular correspondence with old friends including Korolenko and Vera Figner. And, despite the challenges, he remained as hard working as ever, even though he periodically made clear that he wanted to 'retire' (he told Robert Spence Watson as early as 1909 that 'I can no longer do the same amount of work I did in times gone').[135] One of his obituarists subsequently noted that Volkhovskii edited the main SR newspaper *Znamia truda* (*Banner of Labour*) from 1912–14,[136] while

---

132 F. Volkhovsky,'The Grandmother of the Russian Revolution', *Free Russia* (April 1910).

133 F. Volkhovsky, 'A Great Loss', *Free Russia* (April 1910).

134 Volkhovskii Papers (HIA), Box 6, Folder 11, 'Teddie' to Volkhovskii, 5 January 1911.

135 Spence Watson / Weiss Papers (Newcastle University), SW 1/19/4, Volkhovskii to Spence Watson, 4 June 1909.

136 Ritina [I. I. Rakitnikova], Obituary of Volkhovskii. The author—I. I. Rakitnikova—was a regular contributor to *Znamia truda* and there is no reason to doubt her claim.

continuing to edit *Za narod*, although the surviving material suggests that his contribution to the former may have been quite limited.[137] His work for *Za narod* by contrast continued unabated, although Vladimir Lebedev in Paris took on an increasingly active role, editing many of the submissions and contributing a good deal of material (including short stories and poems as well as articles on military questions). Lebedev was however careful to keep Volkhovskii informed of his decisions, addressing numerous letters to 'grandfather', a correspondence that continued until shortly before Volkhovskii's death.[138] Andrei Argunov also continued to be involved in overseeing the production and distribution of *Za narod* in his role as head of the SR Transport Commission. The Russian authorities still considered Volkhovskii to pose a threat. When the former Scotland Yard detective Francis Powell, who had for many years worked closely with William Melville monitoring Russian revolutionaries in London, began working for the *Okhrana* in 1912, he devoted significant time reporting to the Paris *agentura* on the ageing Volkhovskii's activities.[139]

Za narod continued to appear every two or three months, following the familiar format, with regular columns on 'Voices from the Army and Navy' and 'What is Happening in Russia'. Lebedev appears to have taken a growing role in collecting material, typically provided by informants in Russia, although, like Volkhovskii, he regularly scoured the European press for information. The paper also published numerous obituaries of SRs, including a lengthy one of 'Jan' (Stanislav Mikhailevich), who had played a central role directing the work of the Party's Military-Organisation Bureau in fomenting agitation among the

---

137 Victor Chernov also suggested that Volkhovskii was closely involved with *Znamia truda* although without spelling out his precise role. See Chernov, *Pered burei*, 495.

138 See, for example, the correspondence between Volkhovskii and Lebedev contained in Volkhovskii Papers (HIA), Box 2, Folder 17. The description of Volkhovskii as 'grandfather'—a clear counterpart to the description of Breshko-Breshkovskaia as 'grandmother'—had been increasingly common among some SRs since at least 1908.

139 Okhrana Archive (HIA), Index Vlk, Folder 39, Reports by Powell, 30 June 1912; 21 September 1912; 8 November 1912; 3 January 1913; 4 July 1913; 21 July 1913 (all microfilm 119). Okhrana Archive (HIA), Index Xe, Folder 38, Report by Powell, 17 August 1913 (microfilm 152). See, too, the surveillance reports on Volkhovskii during one of his regular visits to Paris, in 1912, almost certainly to discuss publishing issues with Lebedev and Argunov, in Okhrana Archive (HIA), Xe, Folder 45 (microfilm 154).

troops.[140] *Za narod* continued to print articles on more general themes likely to be of interest to its readers, ranging from elections to the fourth Duma to the rumours and scandals surrounding Rasputin and his arch-opponent Iliodor.[141] Another piece discussed the growing labour unrest in Britain.[142] The paper still avoided the shrill tone characteristic of some other publications, instead combining restrained anger with detailed descriptions of abuses to create the greatest impact. A typical piece on 'Russia's Disgrace' described how Russian troops occupying territory in northern Persia had hanged many locals suspected of opposition, complete with a graphic photograph, even though the country was not at war and Persia was a 'foreign land'.[143]

In December 1912, *Za narod* published a lengthy account of the ninth Congress of the Second International held at Basel, presumably written by Volkhovskii, who, despite his indifferent health, served as one of the SR representatives.[144] The war that had recently erupted in the Balkans, threatening to suck in the great powers, seemed to many delegates both a threat and an opportunity. The Congress passed a resolution that, in the event of a major war, '[the workers] shall be bound to intervene for it being brought to a speedy end', while taking advantage of the situation 'to rouse the masses of the people and to hasten the downfall of the predominance of the capitalist class'.[145] Volkhovskii welcomed the rhetoric of proletarian internationalism, telling readers of *Za narod* that there were no differences on the subject between the Socialist Revolutionaries and the Social Democrats, a claim that was not entirely accurate and reflected his habitual impatience with ideological squabbling. He enthusiastically endorsed the principle that the workers of all countries had a shared interest in mobilising to prevent their

---

140 'Ian', *Za narod*, 54 (March 1913).
141 'Vybory', *Za narod*, 49 (August 1912); 'Skandal v tsarskoi sem'e', *Za narod*, 48 (June 1912).
142 'Stachka transportnykh rabochikh v Londone', *Za narod*, 49 (August 1912).
143 'Opozorenie Rossii', *Za narod*, 50 (September 1912).
144 On the Basel Congress, see Egbert Jahn, *World Political Challenges. Political Issues Under Debate* (Berlin: Springer, 2015), 55–72. See, too, the piece probably penned by Volkhovskii on the 'Chrezvychainyi mezhdunarodnyi sotsialisticheskii kongress v Bazele', *Znamia truda*, 47 (December 1912).
145 *Justice* (25 December 1912).

governments from going to war.[146] Despite the air of international crisis surrounding the Congress, Volkhovskii like many other delegates was hopeful that international working-class solidarity would prove stronger than the call of patriotism.

Volkhovskii's reputation as one of the SR's leading experts on military matters meant that he often received requests for practical advice and assistance. He had back in 1905 been asked to support efforts to help the sailors who had found refuge in Romania following the mutiny on the Battleship Potemkin.[147] Six years later, he met representatives of the men to offer advice about how they could move to Canada, at a time when they were increasingly anxious that the Romanian government was about to expel them, writing to the British authorities asking them to facilitate their emigration.[148] Volkhovskii was also approached in 1912 by a leading figure in the newly established Union of Black Sea Sailors, Mikhail Adamovich, asking him to use *Za narod* to support efforts to organise sailors at a time when the leading figures in the movement had been forced to flee abroad to avoid arrest.[149] The Union had established a newspaper, *Moriak (The Sailor)*, which shared the commitment of *Za narod* to avoid party factionalism, in order to coordinate efforts to promote revolutionary sentiment in the military (most of those involved in the Union of Black Sea Sailors were in fact Mensheviks). Although Volkhovskii was not able to offer much more than rhetorical support in such cases, he was despite his age and growing infirmity still seen as an influential figure in the revolutionary movement, as well as someone who had extensive insight into the challenges involved in fostering revolution in the military.

Volkhovskii also cooperated with Vladimir Lebedev during his final years on a new series titled 'On Military Matters'. Three numbers

---

146 'Mezhdunarodnyi sotsialisticheskii kongress (S"ezd') v g. Bazele', *Za narod*, 52 (December 1912).

147 Volkhovskii was also involved in plans to publish an account in English of the mutiny by one of its leading figures, Afanasii Matiushenko, although this appears to have come to nothing at the time. See Volkhovskii Papers (HIA), Box 5, Folder 5, Perris to Volkhovskii, 31 October 1905.

148 Volkhovskii Papers (HIA), Box 5, Folder 5, Undated draft of letter from Volkhovskii to Smith (Asst. Superintendent of Emigration).

149 Volkhovskii Papers (HIA), Box 5, Folder 6, Adamovich to Volkhovskii, 17 January 1912. For Adamovich's memoirs of this time, see M. Adamovich, *Na Chernom more: ocherki proshloi bor'by* (Moscow: Politkatorzhan, 1928).

appeared before the outbreak of war in the summer of 1914. The essays covered issues ranging from the role of officers in promoting revolution through to the readiness of the Russian army to conduct wartime military operations. Volkhovskii contributed to each of the publications. The collection *O nashei sovremennoi armii* (*About Our Army Today*) included his article on the scandal surrounding the dismissal of General E. I. Martynov, who had raised questions about corruption and embezzlement in the tsarist military from the time of the Russo-Japanese War onwards.[150] Volkhovskii described Martynov as 'an exemplary officer' who was disliked by many senior figures in the tsarist regime as much for his left-wing (*vlevo*) views as his efforts to expose wrong-doing.[151] In a second piece, in *Oborona strany* (*The Defence of the Country*), Volkhovskii pointed out that Russian army officers had in the past often been on the side of the 'nation', noting that some prominent figures in the revolutionary movement including Stepniak and Shishko had served in the military. He concluded that officers should inform themselves about social and political questions, while 'revolutionary workers' needed to make every effort to understand the more technical aspects of warfare, breaking down the sharp distinction between soldier and worker in ways that would make it harder for the government to use force to crush future disorders.[152]

In a third collection, *Koe-Chto o nashikh zadachakh* (*Something About Our Tasks*),[153] Volkhovskii contributed a piece designed to spell out the most effective ways to approach 'military-revolutionary work', noting that the editors of 'On Military Matters' had received numerous letters from soldiers and sailors asking for practical advice about how best to promote the cause of revolution. He added that the letters had come from Socialist Revolutionaries and Social Democrats alike, which he believed

---

150 F. Volkhovskii, 'Delo generala E. I. Martynova', in Aleksandrov and F. Volkhovskii (eds), *O nashei sovremennoi armii* (Paris: n.p., 1914), 37-54. Lebedev used the name Aleksandrov for much of his published work including numerous pieces in *Za narod*.

151 Martynov did later hold senior military positions in the Red Army after 1917, suggesting that his political views were indeed left-wing, though he later fell foul of Stalin's purge of the officer corps in 1937.

152 See the introduction by Volkhovskii in Aleksandrov and F. Volkhovskii (eds), *Oborona strany* (Paris: n.p., 1913), 3-6.

153 F. Volkhovskii, 'Konkretizatsiia voenno-revoliutsionnoi zadachi', in Aleksandrov and F. Volkhovskii (eds), *Koe-Chto o nashikh zadachakh* (Paris: n.p., 1914), 17-43.

showed that ideological and organisational divisions on the ground were often of little importance, going on to praise those like Adamovich who had pursued a non-party line when setting up the Union of Black Sea Sailors. Volkhovskii argued that sympathetic members of the officer corps had a critical role to play in preparing for revolution—a view he had held for many years—and believed that every effort should be made to coordinate future military uprisings with popular unrest to increase the chance of overthrowing the government. Volkhovskii had read extensively about the career of Giuseppe Garibaldi to help him understand how volunteers could be mobilised into an effective military force, and although he did not spell out his ideas in detail, he clearly once again believed that in a revolutionary situation the boundary between soldier and civilian would fade, and that militants and radically-minded officers could work together to create a new force that would fight on the side of the people.

Although Volkhovskii's attention was focused during his final years on fostering revolutionary sentiment in the army and navy, he could not ignore other issues altogether. The assassination of the Prime Minister Petr Stolypin in Kyiv, in September 1911, once again raised the issue of the efficacy and ethics of terrorism as a tool in the struggle against autocracy. The question was made still more stark by the fact that the assassin, Dmitrii Bogrov, was a sometime *Okhrana* informant who may have carried out the killing in part to assert his revolutionary credentials and persuade his fellow revolutionaries to spare his life.[154] Volkhovskii appears to have been the author of pieces defending the murder on the pages of *Za narod* and *Znamia truda*, noting that foreigners often struggled to understand how such violent actions could be justified,[155] since they had no personal experience of the ways in which the Russian Government regularly acted in ways that were totally unconstrained by law. He went on to argue that Stolypin's repressive policies had

---

154 On the Bogrov affair see, for example, Geifman, *Thou Shalt Kill*, 237–40.

155 Although unsigned, making it impossible to identify authorial provenance with certainty, both internal and external evidence suggests that Volkhovskii was the author of 'Terror i delo Bogrova', *Znamia truda*, 38 (October 1911) and 'Kievskie vystrely', *Za narod*, 43 (October 1911). The argument of both articles closely resembles pieces signed by Volkhovskii that appeared in the English press, while as the principal editor of *Za narod* it seems certain that he must at least have approved the inclusion of the piece.

led to thousands of executions, usually without anything like a fair trial, leaving behind grieving families bereft of any means of support. Volkhovskii's defence of Stolypin's assassination also made much of the fact that the Prime Minister had acted in ways that challenged the collective values and material interests of the Russian *narod*. The SRs had always been intensely suspicious of the Prime Minister's agrarian reforms, 'a wager on the strong', which sought to transform the social and economic character of the Russian countryside by allowing peasants to secede from the commune and farm the land as individual proprietors.[156] Although he did not spell out the comparison, Volkhovskii seemed to hope that the assassination of Stolypin would ease the tide of change that threatened the communal foundations of peasant life, just as an earlier generation of Russian revolutionaries believed they were in a race to protect the peasant commune from the development of capitalist relations in the countryside.

There was nevertheless something rather muted about Volkhovskii's articles about Stolypin's assassination in both *Za narod* and *Znamia truda*. He knew that growing numbers of SRs believed that the Party should focus on legal forms of opposition at a time when the Azef *débacle* continued to cast a long shadow. In an exchange of letters with Boris Savinkov, that took place early in 1912, Volkhovskii responded cautiously to the idea of expressing himself more forcefully in support of using terror. Savinkov had replaced Azef as head of the SR Fighting Organisation, and was frustrated by the Central Committee's growing ambivalence over terrorism, which he believed was both a tactical mistake and a betrayal of those who had given their lives for the cause.[157]

---

156 On the long-term background of the Stolypin agrarian reforms, see David A. J. Macey, *Government and Peasant in Russia, 1861–1906: The Prehistory of the Stolypin Reforms* (DeKalb, IL: Northern Illinois University Press, 1987). See, too, the same author's useful revisionist essay '"A Wager on History": The Stolypin Agrarian Reforms as Process', in Judith Pallot (ed.), *Transforming Peasants. Society, State and the Peasantry, 1861–1930* (Basingstoke: Palgrave Macmillan, 1998), 149–73. On the reforms themselves and their consequences, see Judith Pallot, *Land Reform in Russia, 1906–1917: Peasant Responses to Stolypin's Project of Rural Transformation* (Oxford: Clarendon Press, 1999).

157 On Savinkov, see Richard B. Spence, *Boris Savinkov: Renegade on the Left* (Boulder, CO: East European Monographs, distributed by Columbia University Press, 1991). See, too, Morozov, *Partiia sotsialistov-revoliutsionerov*, 396–442. Some insight into Savinkov's views and activities can be drawn from his less than reliable memoirs, *Vospominaniia terrorista* (Kharkov: Izd-vo 'Proletarii', 1926).

He was therefore anxious to encourage Volkhovskii to speak out on this issue.[158] Volkhovskii, for his part, drafted a reply urging caution on a subject that could so easily cause division among the SRs.[159]

Volkhovskii also faced substantial constraints when writing about Stolypin's assassination in the British press, since he was well aware that the use of terror appalled many of his readers. His articles were crafted in response to the coverage in newspapers like the *Times*, which condemned the 'dastardly attempt' on the Prime Minister's life, praising him as 'the stoutest and most formidable' opponent of the 'anarchical designs' of those who wanted to kill him.[160] Volkhovskii told the *Manchester Guardian* that, while 'we all regard the taking of human life as deplorable', the killing was a natural response to the Prime Minister's brutal repression of dissent, and was welcomed by many Russians as proof there was 'justice in the world'.[161] He nevertheless recognised that the assassination of the Prime Minister could damage still further the image of the Russian revolutionary movement in Britain, telling the paper in rather convoluted terms that the Central Committee of the SRs had opposed the killing. He wrote a further piece in *Free Russia* on 'Spy Rule', suggesting that the killing of Stolypin had been authorised at the highest levels of the *Okhrana* (a charge that may have contained some truth although the full picture remains unclear). It was a shrewd move. By suggesting that Stolypin's murder had been actioned by 'the secret police, that pet child of the Tzar's rule', Volkhovskii was not only able to echo his earlier justification of terror as a legitimate response to brutal despotism, but also locate the crime within the corrupt world of the tsarist government itself.[162]

During his final years, Volkhovskii also continued to use *Free Russia* to campaign against efforts to treat tsarist Russia as a 'normal' European country and a suitable diplomatic and trade partner for Britain. The paper railed against the visit of a delegation of 'representative Englishmen' to

158 Volkhovskii Papers (HIA), Box 3, Folder 9, Savinkov to Volkhovskii, 9 April 1912. I am indebted to Dr Lara Green for this reference, which escaped my attention during my first visit to the Hoover archives.
159 Volkhovskii Papers (HIA), Box 3, Folder 9 (incomplete draft of reply by Volkhovskii).
160 *Times* (16 September 1911).
161 *Manchester Guardian* (22 September 1911). See, too, the sentiments Volkhovskii expressed in F. Volkhovsky, 'The End of Stolypin', *Free Russia* (October 1911).
162 F. Volkhovsky, 'Spy-Rule and the Douma', *Free Russia* (January 1912).

Russia in 1912, organised by Bernard Pares, as part of his campaign to improve Anglo-Russian relations.[163] Following its return to Britain, the writer Maurice Baring, who had been part of the delegation, took part in an angry dialogue with J. F. Green and Thomas Unwin, suggesting that the 'so-called' friends of Russia should really be regarded as enemies for perpetuating outdated ideas about the Tsarist Empire at a time when it was undergoing a process of rapid change.[164] The intensity of the polemic revealed that both sides understood how the image of Russia in Britain had become a significant factor in framing the economic and diplomatic relationship between the two countries. Writers like Baring sought to mobilise the Russia 'craze' as part of a broader Anglo-Russian rapprochement in which cultural affinities and understandings bolstered diplomatic and economic relations. Unwin and Green by contrast followed Volkhovskii's lead in arguing that everything that was valuable about Russian culture, and indeed Russian life, was an authentic expression of a society fighting to emancipate itself from the harsh rule of autocracy.

Volkhovskii still contributed occasional pieces on Russian culture to *Free Russia*, including one following Tolstoi's death in 1910, in which he emphasised Tolstoi's role as a moralist rather than a novelist.[165] Volkhovskii was, though, more focused on the campaign against closer Anglo-Russian political and economic relations. *Free Russia* gave enormous coverage to the Lena goldfield massacres that took place in the spring of 1912, when troops fired on striking workers, with the loss of hundreds of lives. Volkhovskii railed against 'British Responsibility' for the killings, suggesting (wrongly) that most of the capital invested in the mine works was British. He told readers that since 'gentlemen of the type of Professor Pares and Mr Maurice Baring are nowadays very assiduous in their invitations to British capital to back up Russian enterprises [surely] the British investor ought to give a little thought as to the kind of dealings he is going to support'. While an individual investor might be ignorant of the situation on the ground, it was wrong of them as 'a Christian and an Englishman' to close their eyes to 'the

---

163 On Pares's role in organising the trip, see Hughes, 'Russian Studies'.
164 The debates which took place in the journal *Eyewitness* were reproduced almost
      verbatim in 'The British Visit', *Free Russia* (April 1912).
165 F. Volkhovsky, 'Leo Tolstoy', *Free Russia* (January 1911).

blood and sweat out of which his profits are squeezed'.[166] Although he may not have been aware of it, Volkhovskii's words pointed to a profound tension in early twentieth-century British liberalism. Its *laissez-faire* strand held that free trade and freedom of investment flows would improve material conditions around the world and make war less likely. Its nonconformist-humanitarian strand believed that decisions about foreign policy, and by extension foreign investment, should be based on ethical judgements about the rights and wrongs of the issues involved.

****

Europe seemed to be at peace during the last few months before Volkhovskii's death. The two Balkan wars had ended without leading to conflict between the great powers, and the rhythms of international life continued as normal in the fine summer of 1914, as diplomats and ministers headed for the fashionable spas and resorts dotted across the continent. The assassination of Archduke Franz Ferdinand at the end of June was at first met with a shrug in many quarters, even if the following weeks were to shatter such complacency, as the great powers stumbled into war. Volkhovskii lived alone at this time, for Vera had long since left Somerville College in Oxford and was teaching at a girl's boarding school. When David Soskice saw him a few weeks before his death, 'there could be no mistaking the fact he was terribly ill ... His limbs were swollen with dropsy, his waxen bloodless face bore traces of intolerable suffering, and he was stone deaf'.[167] Vladimir Burtsev, who visited his old friend around the same time, later recalled that 'He was already old and very sick. He talked a lot about death'. But even though in suffering and pain, he found that Volkhovskii continued to 'be the same [person] I knew ... He knew how to live and knew how to die—calmly, with faith in the future'.[168] Volkhovskii ruefully told his old friend that he believed he would after death get the recognition that had often eluded him in life. He also told Burtsev that he had left instructions that he wanted to be cremated. He got his wish. A few days after his death, on 2

166 F. Volkhovsky, 'British Responsibility', *Free Russia* (July 1912).
167 David Soskice, 'Feliks Volkhovsky', *Free Russia* (October 1914–January 1915). This was the last number of *Free Russia* to appear.
168 V. L. Burtsev, *Bor'ba za svobodnuiu Rossiiu. Moi vospominaniia* (Moscow: Direct Media, 2014), 100.

August 1914, Volkhovskii's funeral service took place at Golders Green Crematorium in north London. His ashes were scattered on the crocus lawn there.

It was perhaps inevitable that Volkhovskii's death was rather lost among the tumultuous events of the July Crisis and its aftermath. His cremation service was held the day after Britain declared war on Germany. The *Manchester Guardian* carried a short obituary two days after his death celebrating a man whose health had been ravaged by his fight against the tsarist government.[169] The *Daily Telegraph* carried a shorter piece that confined itself to a brief account of Volkhovskii' life.[170] The *Times* did not even refer to his death. Those who had worked closely with Volkhovskii in Britain were more generous in their memories. J. F. Green praised 'the loveableness of his disposition', his acute literary sense and his devotion 'to animals and children'. Herbert Thompson recalled Volkhovskii's 'sweetness of character'. Henry Hyndman praised him as 'a martyr type whose self-service and sacrifice lasted as long as his life'.[171] Obituaries in the Russian radical press also praised Volkhovskii's personal qualities and literary talent, while focusing more on showing how his life fitted into the broader history of the Russian revolutionary movement,[172] evidence perhaps of the fact that there had always been something of a distinction between Volkhovskii's 'English' and 'Russian' identities. Even David Soskice, who like Volkhovskii lived a life defined in large part by its division between the two countries, acknowledged that it was only when he began to write his friend's obituary that he really understood the scale and drama of his 'trials'. Obituaries are by their nature a place for eulogy rather than critical analysis, but Soskice was neither a sentimentalist nor a hypocrite, and there was something genuine in the warmth with which he finished his account:

> He is dead, but his memory will live long not only in the hearts of his own people, but also in those of his foreign friends for whom he was a glorious example of a man whose spirit throughout his long career of

169 *Manchester Guardian* (4 August 1914).
170 *Daily Telegraph* (4 August 1914).
171 See the memoir notes by J. F. Green, H. M. Thompson and H. Hyndman, 'Death of Volkhovsky', *Free Russia* (October 1914–January 1915).
172 N. V. Chaikovskii, Obituary of Volkhovskii, *Golos minuvshago*, 10 (1914), 231–35; N. E. Kudrin, Obituary of Volkhovskii, *Russkoe bogatstvo*; Ritina [I. I. Rakitnikova], Obituary of Volkhovskii.
173 Soskice, 'Feliks Volkhovsky'.

8. Conclusion

There was something ironic about the date of Volkhovskii's death, given that he had devoted so much of his time and energy over the previous few years to the struggle against 'militarism', for he died the day after Berlin declared war on Russia and two days before Britain declared war on Germany.[1] The armed forces of the main European states remained loyal to their governments. So, for the most part, did the people. Although there were protests in Britain and France in the days following the declaration of war, they were insignificant compared with the patriotic demonstrations that took place on the streets of London and Paris, while thousands of young men flocked to join the fight against their country's enemies.[2] Middle-class support for the war was strong in Germany, and although working-class opinion was more divided, protests soon faded as recognition grew that the conflict had become inevitable.[3] Even Russia was not immune to the wave of patriotic sentiment, despite recent outbreaks of disorder in several cities, which had raised hopes among some revolutionary groups that a new phase in the fight against tsarism was about to begin.[4] The fervent hope repeatedly expressed at conferences of the Second International—that

---

1   Volkhovskii died on 2 August, although a few sources give the following day as the date of death.

2   Among the large literature on this subject, see Catriona Pennell, *A Kingdom United. Popular Responses to the Outbreak of the First World War in Britain and Ireland* (Oxford: Oxford University Press, 2012); Jean-Jacques Becker, *L'année 1914* (Paris: Armand Colin, 2004).

3   Wolfgang J. Mommsen, 'The Topos of Inevitable War in Germany in the Decade Before 1914', in Volker R. Berghahn and Martin Kitchen (eds), *Germany in the Age of Total War. Essays in Honour of Francis Carsten* (London: Croom Helm, 1981), 23–45.

4   For a useful discussion of the reaction to war in Russia, see Joshua Sanborn, 'The Mobilization of 1914 and the Question of the Russian Nation. A Reexamination', *Slavic Review*, 59, 2 (2000), 267–89.

   https://doi.org/10.11647/OBP.0385.08

the spirit of proletarian internationalism would outweigh the siren call of nationalism—appeared at least for a time to be nothing more than the quixotic fantasy of radicals loathe to acknowledge the stubborn realities of the world they hoped to transform.

It is impossible to know how Volkhovskii would have reacted to a war that eventually cost millions of lives and transformed the continent forever. The SR Party quickly split over the conflict. Most of the populist veterans Volkhovskii had known for many years—including Lazarev, Chaikovskii and Breshko-Breshkovskaia—supported Russia's war effort on the grounds that a German victory would set back the cause of revolution. Other prominent SRs like Chernov and Natanson took a different view, arguing for a revolutionary internationalism designed to mobilise popular opposition to war in all the combatant nations, even if they never endorsed the outright 'defeatism' of Lenin and the Bolsheviks.[5] It seems likely that if Volkhovskii had lived then he would have remained committed to the cause of revolutionary internationalism, even at the cost of a break with old friends, although such a judgement must remain tentative given the sheer number of imponderables. It is by contrast almost certain that if he had survived to witness the events that followed the October Revolution of 1917, then he would have joined other SRs, including Chernov and Chaikovskii, as an active participant in the fight against the Bolshevik government.[6] The brutal suppression of dissent that became a hallmark of the new regime would have appalled Volkhovskii as a betrayal of the principles he had espoused for half a century. He was perhaps fortunate in being spared the disillusion and danger that became the lot of so many of his old comrades.

The suppression of the Socialist Revolutionaries in the months following the October Revolution has been seen by some scholars as a key moment in the disintegration of the revolutionary promise of 1917,

---

5   Michael Melancon, *The Socialist Revolutionaries and the Russian Anti-War Movement 1914–1917* (Columbus, OH: Ohio State University Press, 1990), 20–56.

6   Among the large literature on the SRs in the wake of the October Revolution, see Oliver Radkey, *The Sickle under the Hammer: The Russian Socialist Revolutionaries in the Early Months of Soviet Rule* (New York: Columbia University Press, 1963); Scott B. Smith, *Captives of Revolution: The Socialist Revolutionaries and the Bolshevik Dictatorship, 1918–1923* (Pittsburgh, PA: University of Pittsburgh Press, 2011). For a lively discussion of the SRs in emigration between the world wars, see Elizabeth White, *The Socialist Alternative to Bolshevik Russia: The Socialist Revolutionary Party, 1921–1939* (Abingdon: Routledge, 2011).

signifying the Bolsheviks' determination to defend their position, even at the cost of eliminating other radical voices and movements.[7] There was, though, even before 1917, a recognition in some quarters that the seeds of authoritarianism were deep-rooted in the culture of the Russian revolutionary *intelligentsia*. The contributors to the celebrated *Vekhi (Landmarks)* Symposium of 1909, including Petr Struve and Nikolai Berdiaev, argued that a quasi-millenarian instinct had fostered a deep-seated intolerance and opposition to compromise among many Russian radicals.[8] It was an insight that subsequently found an echo in much of the scholarly literature produced in Western Europe and North America, both on the pre-revolutionary Russian *intelligentsia* and the post-revolutionary Soviet state,[9] as well as the vast literature on totalitarianism as a form of political religion that came to prominence after the Second World War.[10] Although seldom spelt out in detail, much of this work assumed that Bolshevik authoritarianism was simply one expression of a broader revolutionary tradition, characterised by an oppositional mentality that focused above all on the need to destroy the

---

7   See, for example, Geoffrey Swain, *The Origins of the Russian Civil War* (London: Longman, 1995). For a superbly detailed examination of the establishment of Bolshevik power, and the marginalisation of other left-wing groups, see Alexander Rabinowitch, *The Bolsheviks in Power. The First Year of Soviet Rule in Petrograd* (Bloomington, IN: Indiana University Press, 2007).

8   Marshall S. Shatz and Judith E. Zimmerman (eds), *Vekhi / Landmarks* (London: M. E. Sharpe, 1994).

9   Among the numerous examples of such works see, for example, Alain Besançon, *The Intellectual Origins of Leninism*, trans. Sarah Matthews (Oxford: Blackwell, 1981); Tibor Szamuely, *The Russian Tradition* (London: Secker and Warburg, 1974); Adam Ulam, *Prophets and Conspirators in Prerevolutionary Russia* (New Brunswick, NJ: Transaction Publishers, 1998).

10   The classic early text on this theme, which exerted enormous influence on later writers, was Eric Voeglin's 1938 book *Die politischen Religionen* available in translation by T. J. DiNapoli and E. S. Easterly III, *Political Religions* (Lewiston, NY: Edward Mellen Press, 1986). See, too, the chapter by Arthur Versluis, 'Eric Voeglin, Anti-Gnostics, and the Totalitarian Emphasis on Order', in Arthur Versluis, *The New Inquisitions: Heretic-Hunting and the Intellectual Origins of Modern Totalitarianism* (Oxford: Oxford University Press, 2006), 69–84. The potential affinities between totalitarian political ideologies and religious belief systems became a standard motif in many works that sought to compare Nazi Germany and Soviet Russia as political systems with ruling ideologies and civic rituals informed by distinct religious memes. For a lively if rather simplistic article on this theme, see Marcin Kula, 'Communism as Religion', *Totalitarian Movements and Political Religion*, 6, 3 (2005), 371–81. For a more critical approach see Hans Maier, 'Political Religion. A Concept and its Limitations', *Totalitarian Movements and Political Religion*, 8, 1 (2007), 5–16.

tsarist regime, rather than confront the practical challenges of building a new socialist society. The obvious conclusion that flows from such a perspective is that other revolutionary parties might have followed the Bolshevik path if they had found themselves in power.

Such broad interpretations tend to fall apart when subjected to detailed historical investigation, even if they sometimes contain insights that remain of value, providing a broader context in which to view specific moments in the history of the Russian revolutionary movement. It was noted in the Introduction that Viktor Chernov characterised the life of Feliks Volkhovskii as 'a history of the Russian revolutionary movement'.[11] It is certainly true that his biography provides a way into the complex ideological and organisational mosaic that was the hallmark of the Russian opposition to tsarism over half a century. What the life of Volkhovskii shows above all, though, is precisely the danger of making neat generalisations about ideologies and organisations. This is partly because he was a revolutionary pragmatist, deeply committed to promoting popular welfare and destroying the autocratic state, while remaining open-minded in the face of the fervent debates about ideology and tactics that enthralled so many leading figures in the revolutionary movement. And, inevitably, his views about how best to promote revolution changed over fifty years as the world around him changed. Volkhovskii's life and thought was shaped as much by contingencies as by forethought and planning. It is, despite these caveats, possible to identify four broad periods in his revolutionary career, even if the chronological and thematic divisions between them were not always precise.

Whether or not the seeds of Volkhovskii's revolutionary instincts were sown in early childhood, when he witnessed the flogging of one of his grandfather's serfs, he was by his teenage years familiar with the radical ideas expressed in journals such as *Sovremennik*. He was just eighteen when in his first year at university he witnessed the civic execution of Nikolai Chernyshevskii. The youthful Volkhovskii was in all respects a typical *shestidesiatnik*—a person of the sixties—an *intelligent* whose outlook was shaped by a blend of opposition to the social and political *status quo* and a passionate if vague commitment to a utilitarian

---

11   V. M. Chernov, *Pered burei* (Moscow: Direct Media, 2016), 203.

scientism that rejected the idealism of the older generation of 'fathers'. He was part of a milieu that defined itself as much in terms of lifestyle and outlook as it did in more formal intellectual commitment. And, while he was not as a young man directly involved in any of the plots to assassinate the Tsar and foment violent revolution, whether the Ishutin-Karakazov conspiracy of 1865–66 or the Nechaevskoe delo of 1869–70, he was in contact with some who were. Volkhovskii was among the first of the young *intelligenty* of the 1860s to think seriously about how to build bridges to the Russian *narod*, whose welfare formed the focus of much radical talk, even as it remained, in German Lopatin's words, something of a 'sphinx' to those who spent their lives in the city. The short-lived Ruble Society, co-founded by Volkhovskii and Lopatin to foster closer ties between the peasantry and the *intelligentsia*, represented an early moment in the shift from the nihilism of the 1860s to the populism of the following decade. Even so, Volkhovskii himself never came to share the romanticised view of the *narod* held by many of those who subsequently flocked to the Russian countryside during the mad summer of 1874.

Volkhovskii's writings of the late 1860s—whether in the form of diary jottings or draft articles—suggest that he was for a short time open to a Jacobinism which held that the destruction of the tsarist state could only be brought about by a determined group ready to seize power in the name of the *narod*. By the time he was released from his second spell of imprisonment in 1871, though, he had once again come to believe that an effective revolution could only take place with the active involvement of the people. As leader of the Chaikovskii circle in Odessa, he was convinced that the cause of revolution was best advanced by developing a leadership cadre of young workers and members of the *intelligentsia*. It was a view shared by some (but not all) members of the wider Chaikovskii movement, although Volkhovskii's emphasis on organisation and discipline was unusually strong, as was the vigour and determination with which he built his organisation. Equally striking was his sense that urban workers rather than the peasantry represented the most natural focus for agitation and organisation (he seldom took much interest in the intense ideological debates that preoccupied many leading *narodniki* about the threat posed by the development of capitalism to the peasant commune). Volkhovskii was, by the 1870s, a pragmatist who was ready to work with liberals in Odessa if it could help to advance the cause of revolution. This did not necessarily make him a 'moderate', although he was throughout his life adept at reassuring those who were appalled by the brutality of the Russian state, even as they feared the chaos of revolution that was bound to result from its destruction. It was rather that Volkhovskii focused on practical questions of advancing the revolutionary cause rather than constantly interrogating its ideological foundations.

Volkhovskii was already established as a significant revolutionary leader by the time of his third arrest in 1874. His poetry was well known in radical circles. And, three years later, he was one of the most prominent defendants at the Trial of the 193, where his impassioned denunciation of the 'Court' became an important staging-post in reducing the process to a judicial farce. It is still not clear why Volkhovskii was not sentenced to hard labour, given his track record, but exile to Siberia in 1878 inevitably marked an important stage in his revolutionary career. The realities of exile, first in Tiukalinsk and then Tomsk, placed constraints on his freedom of action at a time when the reactionary government of Aleksandr III was hollowing out the heart of the revolutionary wave that had culminated in the assassination of his father in 1881. Whether Volkhovskii would have become a member of Narodnaia volia in the late 1870s, if he had still been at liberty, remains uncertain, but it is striking that many of those he worked with earlier in the decade subsequently committed themselves to a 'political' strategy of terrorism, in the hope that it would lead either to the destruction of the tsarist state or at least to reforms that could further the struggle for radical social and economic change.

Volkhovskii's outlook during his time in Siberia during the 1880s seems at first glance to have changed sharply, marking the development of a second phase in his revolutionary life, in which he became more convinced of the virtues of participating in legal forms of opposition, contributing extensively to *Sibirskaia gazeta* as well as publishing numerous short stories and poems. Distinctive radical and *narodnik* themes nevertheless still ran through many of Volkhovskii's writings. His theatre columns were informed by a literary aesthetic that emphasised the need for dramatic performances to engage with the outlook and needs of the people. Many of his short stories criticised the philistine values of the merchant class and the corruption that was commonplace among *chinovniki* in provincial towns. Such work was consistent with the broader development in the 1880s of a cultural populism that focused on accurately depicting the Russian *narod* in literature and art, in order to foster greater understanding of its character and needs, rather than articulating the more revolutionary social and political motifs of the previous decade. 'Legal populism'—to (mis)use a term that has its own uncertainties and ambiguities—was both a reaction to a political environment that limited the scope for truly revolutionary action as well as a search for new ways to promote a deeper understanding of the Russian *narod*.[12] Volkhovskii's emphasis on 'Siberianism', which was the hallmark of many of the articles published in *Sibirskaia gazeta*, was shaped by a desire to identify and defend patterns of popular identity in the face of a government bureaucracy that believed such 'regionalism' could threaten social and political order. The same was true of the 'Ukrainophilism' that had characterised his outlook since his time as a student in the 1860s. The constraints of censorship meant that such ideas and criticisms could only be expressed in veiled and elusive terms, but even the most cursory reading of Volkhovskii's writings of the 1880s often reveals a critical intent designed to shape the views of the audience, while remaining sufficiently Aesopian in character to pass the censor.

There was nevertheless another dimension to Volkhovskii's literary output during his time in Siberian exile. While much of his poetry of the 1870s had been thoroughly 'revolutionary' in character, designed to celebrate and inspire those who were committed to the fight against tsarism, some of his best work also captured the sadness and pathos that ran through his own life. The same was even more true of his poetry of the 1880s, which was less 'programmatic' than his earlier work, and more inclined to celebrate the beauty of the Siberian landscape and the heartache of his own tragic losses. Nor was there anything 'revolutionary' about many of the *feuilletons* he contributed to *Sibirskaia gazeta*, for while he sometimes used fantasy as a way of denouncing bureaucratic incompetence and corruption, much of his work was

---

12 For a discussion of legal populism, see G. N. Mokshin, *Evoliutsiia ideologii legal'nogo narodnichestva v poslednei trety XIX–nachale XX vv.* (Voronezh: Nauchnaia Kniga, 2010). See, too, B. P. Baluev, *Liberal'noe narodnichestvo na rubezhe XIX–XX vekov* (Moscow: Nauka, 1995).

simply whimsical and light-hearted. Volkhovskii was—throughout his life—not immune to the leaden demands of revolutionary aesthetic. He nevertheless possessed a real literary talent and imagination that meant his best work displayed a vivid quality that reflected his own suspicion of dogma in all its various forms.

Volkhovskii's literary talent was to become a significant factor in giving him an entrée to British society following his arrival in London in the summer of 1890. So too was his *persona*—part crafted and part genuine—that seemed to embody the suffering of those who dared to fight against the tsarist autocratic state. The seeds of Volkhovskii's future reputation (and reception) in Britain were planted by George Kennan, who was immensely impressed by Volkhovskii during their meetings in Tomsk in 1885-86, although the picture he painted for his Western audience in *Century Magazine* was distinctly one-sided. While not denying that many Siberian exiles like Volkhovskii were ready to support the use of violence to overthrow tsarism, Kennan presented such a strategy as the only one available to men and women confronted by a brutal autocratic state that snuffed out any demands for change. In doing so, he helped to shape Volkhovskii's image as a man whose moral and political *credo* placed him firmly within the boundaries of Anglo-American liberalism. Volkhovskii's meetings with Kennan in Siberia led him to recognise for his part that the cause of revolution could be advanced by winning over supporters in the West, and while his flight from Siberia in 1889 was partly the result of his desperate personal circumstances, he had already come to believe that he would be more effective at helping the revolutionary cause in exile abroad rather than by remaining in Russia.

The third phase in Volkhovskii's revolutionary career, roughly the years between 1890 and the early 1900s, was marked by a certain tension. Much of the support for the 'cause' of Russian freedom in Britain and North America came from liberals and nonconformists who viewed the country through a prism of moral universalism which encouraged a critical focus on the tsarist government's treatment of religious minorities and political opponents. Many members of this distinctive coalition were, though, firmly opposed to the use of terror and, more generally, quizzical about any ideology that challenged the supremacy of liberal constitutional values and the rights of private property. A large number of those active in the Society of Friends of Russian Freedom were curiously ready to believe that the Russian exiles in London were at heart political moderates rather than revolutionaries. Volkhovskii and Stepniak came to personify for many of their British sympathisers a beguiling mixture of strangeness and familiarity, representatives of an alien and intriguing culture, who were nevertheless inspired by the same values as fair-minded men and women in Western Europe and North America.

Nor was this simply the result of an elaborate self-fashioning on the part of political émigrés like Volkhovskii, designed to reassure Britons that in subscribing to *Free Russia*, or attending a lecture sponsored by the SFRF, they were not supporting violent revolution. The relations between the Russian émigrés and their English sympathisers were often genuinely warm and constructive. The vast appetite for all things Russian at the height of the 'Russia craze' helped open hearts and minds to Volkhovskii and other members of the London emigration. There was, though, always something unreal about the image of the Russian revolutionary movement presented in the pages of *Free Russia*. Individual revolutionaries were presented as heroic victims of the harsh rule of the tsarist state. Very little was said about their ideological views. While many readers of *Free Russia* thought of revolution in terms of individual freedom and rights, the same was seldom true of members of the more radical wing of the Russian opposition, whether *narodnik* or Marxist. Or, to put it more precisely, revolutionaries like Volkhovskii saw the struggle for freedom and constitutional reform as a struggle for changes that would in time make it easier to bring about a more far-reaching social and economic revolution. Some radical Fabians among the early supporters of *Free Russia* and the SFRF might have sympathised with such a position. Most by contrast believed that establishing constitutional government in Russia was something of supreme value in its own right. They thought that the revolutionaries were fighting for changes that would make Russia more like Britain.

The limits to the liberalism of Volkhovskii and Stepniak were, perhaps paradoxically, highlighted by their commitment in the first half of the 1890s to building a broad opposition movement of Russian revolutionaries and liberals alike. It was a strategy founded on a recognition that both 'parties' had a common interest in securing constitutional reform, whether as a fundamental political *desideratum*, or as a mechanism for facilitating the fight for revolutionary change. Neither Volkhovskii nor Stepniak ever saw themselves, though, as belonging to the ranks of the Russian liberals: quite the reverse. Nor did they believe that the existence of certain common ground eliminated the distance between the two groups (although Petr Lavrov in Paris was suspicious that they did). What is perhaps less clear is what kind of society Volkhovskii (and, indeed, Stepniak) hoped to see emerge in Russia beyond a vaguely articulated socialism. Nor were they alone in this. The social and economic changes that took place in Russia in the late nineteenth and early twentieth centuries rendered archaic the earlier *narodnik* focus on defending the peasant *mir* (commune). It was only in the first decade of the twentieth century that serious thought was given by members of the newly formed Socialist Revolutionary Party to such questions as what forms of land tenure would be most effective in advancing the welfare of the Russian peasantry. Volkhovskii, as has been seen throughout this book, preferred to focus his attention on identifying ways of undermining the tsarist state rather than pondering what kind of social and political order might emerge out of its destruction.

Volkhovskii's time in London helped to build further the journalistic and propagandistic skills he had developed when still living in Siberia. He was more or less from the moment he arrived in London the *de facto* editor of *Free Russia*, working closely with Stepniak to ensure that the tone of its coverage appealed to its British readers, through a sustained focus on the harshness of the Russian prison system and the iniquities of exile. He was also a leading figure in the Russian Free Press Fund, as well as the editor and main contributor to *Letuchie listki*, fostering a 'non-factional' approach designed to appeal to all strands of the opposition movement. Volkhovskii's role in these enterprises has often been eclipsed by his friendship with Stepniak, widely seen at the time and since as the main architect of both *Free Russia* and the Fund, as well as the principal author of the strategy of building a broad anti-tsarist opposition both in Russia and abroad. Yet while Stepniak possessed a charisma and authority that his old friend lacked, Volkhovskii played a more significant role in the practical side of propaganda work: obtaining Cyrillic typefaces, dealing with financial questions, building networks to smuggle material into Russia. Stepniak's death at the end of 1895 was without doubt a major blow to the fundists. It exposed tensions within the group and reduced their influence both with the *narodniki* grouped around Petr Lavrov in Paris and the Emancipation of Labour Group in Geneva. It also weakened links with revolutionaries from other European countries. The practical business of producing *Free Russia* and *Letuchie listki* nevertheless continued unabated. So, too, did the work of the Free Press Fund. Volkhovskii was the central figure in ensuring that Stepniak's death did not mark the end of such activities.

The campaign orchestrated by the *Okhrana* in the 1890s to discredit Stepniak and Volkhovskii, by equating them with the violent anarchists responsible for terrorist outrages across Europe, undoubtedly met with some success. It increased concern among more moderate British proponents of the 'cause' that their financial support might be used to promote violent revolution. Nor is there much doubt that some of the money collected by the Society of Friends of Russian Freedom was diverted to such ends. Volkhovskii was, though, throughout the 1890s concerned not to alienate potential supporters of the revolutionary movement in Britain. This began to change in the years after 1900, as he focused less on mobilising international support, and more on working with other Russian émigré groups across Europe to support the revolutionary cause, a development that marked the start of the fourth and final period of his revolutionary life. While Volkhovskii's work with Konni Zilliacus to build a broad-based opposition to tsarism was consistent with the strategy that he pursued with Stepniak in the 1890s, his support for smuggling weapons into Russia, to foment armed uprisings at a time when Russian forces were focused on war with Japan, represented a more direct entry (or perhaps return) to 'hands-on' revolutionary activity. So did his support for the assassination of senior tsarist officials in the years before the 1905 Revolution. It was not that Volkhovskii had ever opposed the use of force as a matter of principle. It was rather that he thought during the 1890s that Russian émigrés in Britain and elsewhere needed to be circumspect in expressing views that might make their position more difficult. He was by the opening years of the twentieth century increasingly ready to acknowledge that a successful revolution was unlikely to be bloodless.

The creation of the Agrarian-Socialist League, and its subsequent merger with the Socialist Revolutionary Party, shaped Volkhovskii's activities throughout the last fourteen years of his life. While he continued to edit *Free Russia*, support for the 'cause' in Britain increasingly came from radical socialists, who were sympathetic to demands for sweeping social and economic change as well as constitutional reform. It is striking that when Volkhovskii died, most of the Britons who attended his cremation service were drawn from left-wing socialist parties, rather than the distinctive liberal-nonconformist nexus that formed a large part of the audience for *Free Russia* in the 1890s. In the years following the 1905 Revolution, Volkhovskii also finally abandoned his earlier hopes of building a broad coalition of opposition between Russian revolutionaries and Russian liberals, in part because of his frustration at the latter's timidity, and even more because he believed that the situation on the ground had fundamentally changed. Like many SRs, Volkhovskii continued to believe that political reform could expedite far reaching social and economic change, but he was less inclined than before to think that it represented a critical stage on the road to revolution. Nor was he any clearer than before about what kind of society he hoped to see emerge in the wake of a successful revolution. While Volkhovskii remained committed to the development of socialism both in the city and the countryside, he was still remarkably silent on what he understood by such a term, and showed little interest in the agonised debates that took place in SR publications and at SR conferences about such things as the socialisation of the land and the nationalisation of the means of production in industry. He was by contrast intensely interested in identifying ways of weakening the tsarist state's capacity to prevent revolution and maintain the social and political *status quo*.

Volkhovskii's main contribution to the SRs was as ever in the sphere of propaganda. It is not entirely clear why he became involved in the production of material aimed at Russian soldiers and sailors during his months in Finland, at the end of 1906 and start of 1907, but it certainly became his main focus of activity down until his death in 1914. Volkhovskii's long experience in producing newspapers and flysheets meant that he was well-suited to take a leading role in the production of *Za narod* from its first publication in 1907, helping to develop a paper that blended analysis and reportage, while articulating an editorial position that assumed all the revolutionary parties were united in their desire to overthrow tsarism. He was also a significant figure within the

SR leadership in emigration, where his status as one of the veterans of the revolutionary movement gave him considerable prestige, although he never commanded such loyalty as figures like Ekaterina Breshko-Breshkovskaia, in part because he was seen by some younger Party members as increasingly out of touch with developments in Russia. While Volkhovskii played a significant role in the SR Foreign Committee during the 1905 Revolution, he never fully grasped that Party leaders abroad would always find it difficult to determine questions of strategy and tactics, not least given the chaotic character of the Party's administration and the instinctive suspicion of hierarchy that characterised many of its members. Nor was he ever really a dominant voice within the SR hierarchy. Although he participated in many of the key Party congresses and conferences in the years after the 1905 Revolution, his interventions were seldom decisive, even on such questions as the use of terror and the development of effective agitation within the military. And, while Volkhovskii could be adept at winning the respect and affection of some Party members, many more found him abrasive and out of touch. Yet his skills as a publicist were always in demand. When he sought to pull back from his commitments in the wake of the Azef affair, he was persuaded to continue his work, at a time when the SR Party was facing a deep-seated crisis of confidence and internal strife.

Volkhovskii's focus on producing propaganda to foment unrest in the military was a logical response to the widespread disorder that erupted in both the army and navy in 1905–07. So too was his involvement in meetings of the Second International that focused on how best to mobilise workers to counter the threat of war. It is hard, though, to see such activities as having any positive result. When war came in 1914, the Russian army for the most part remained loyal to the government, and it was only when massive failures of military supply resulted in defeat on the battlefield that spiralling levels of discontent and desertion led to the army and navy becoming important sites of revolutionary activity. The Bolsheviks were far more successful than the Socialist Revolutionaries after 1914 at building up support within the military rank and file, in part because of their uncompromising opposition to the war, which in turn ensured that the Party's leaders could rely on significant support in the army and navy during the chaos of 1917. The efforts made by Volkhovskii and other SRs before 1914 to foster revolutionary sentiment in the military seem to have had little long-term effect, at least in creating a deep well of support for the Party among soldiers and sailors, perhaps (ironically) because the insistence on a non-party approach masked the important role the SRs played in propaganda and agitation in the military in the years after 1905.

The success of the Bolsheviks in overthrowing the Provisional Government in October 1917, along with the subsequent repression of other revolutionary groups, has often prompted a teleological reading of history in which the triumph of Lenin is seen as the almost inevitable outcome of factors ranging from the superior organisation of the Bolsheviks through to the vacillation and division of other radical groups. More recent scholarship has questioned such a narrative, showing how Lenin's control of the Bolsheviks was far less complete than sometimes imagined, while the Bolshevik Party was itself often deeply fractious and impervious to the wishes of its leaders. The limited historiography on the Socialist Revolutionaries before 1914 has by contrast *always* tended to focus on its divisions and lack of clear leadership. There is a good deal of truth in this image of the Party, which reflected differences over important issues such as the use of terror and participation in the Duma, as well as the tension between SR leaders in emigration and those in Russia itself. While the Party periodically lost activists on both the left and the right, it was never ideologically cohesive nor united on questions of tactics. A moment's pause suggests that such divisions and disagreements should hardly be a cause for surprise, given that the SR Party contained tens of thousands of activists with a range of backgrounds and experiences, each with their own perspectives on how to bring about revolutionary change. Chaos and confusion are more often the stuff of human experience than order and certainty. The absence of so dominant a figure as Lenin was probably a factor in condemning the SRs to disagreement and division when the Party needed to coalesce more fully round a clear set of tactics and beliefs. But even Lenin followed events as much as he shaped them.

This is not to say there were no individuals who played a definite 'leading role' in the SRs. Viktor Chernov did more than anyone to shape the ideological character of the Party's programmes and statements. Mikhail Gots, Evno Azef and Boris Sazonov played an important role in shaping the Party's terrorist strategy. Ekaterina Breshko-Breshkovskaia established a kind of effortless influence that gave her voice real authority in the Party's counsels. Volkhovskii was never among these figures—but even influential figures like Chernov were seldom able to determine developments 'on the ground' in Russia, where local SR groups enjoyed considerable autonomy, rejecting instructions that did not fit with their own priorities and view of the immediate situation. It is once again unwise to assess individuals in the Russian revolutionary movement simply in terms of their agency or importance. The interest in studying any revolutionary life, perhaps any life, instead lies in seeing how it fitted into a wider pattern that was itself often uncertain and contradictory.

It has been seen throughout the previous chapters that the language traditionally used to discuss the development of the revolutionary movement in Russia before 1917 is as much a source of obfuscation as illumination. Terms such as 'populist', 'liberal', 'radical' and 'revolutionary' all have fluid meanings that reflect both historical and contemporary usage as well as a semantic tension between what might be termed their *a priori* and positional resonance. Or, to put it more simply, while such terms have their uses, they have their limitations too. Although it is possible to identify certain broad patterns of ideological development and disagreement in the Russian revolutionary movement in the half century before 1917, as well as shifting views about revolutionary tactics and organisation, the experience of being a revolutionary was more complex and fragmented than sometimes assumed. Many revolutionary careers were shaped not so much by well-defined ideological principles as by a powerful emotional commitment to bringing about the downfall of the economic and political *status quo*. This is not to argue that ideological conflicts within the revolutionary movement were not deep-seated and fierce. Nor is it to question whether 'ideology' helped to provide a framework for understanding the complex brew of social and political tensions that eventually destroyed the tsarist state. It clearly did. It is instead to suggest that a revolutionary 'instinct' was, for many members of the Russian revolutionary movement, more important than the nuances of ideological debate.

Feliks Volkhovskii was no exception to this pattern. His own published autobiographical writings (both Russian and English) were designed to convince his readers of the brutality of the tsarist state and by implication justify the actions of those who sought to overthrow it. They seldom touched on questions of ideology or revolutionary tactics narrowly understood. Opposition to the tsarist state and sympathy for the economic plight of the Russian people, whether in the countryside or the city, was the constant *leitmotif* of Volkhovskii's revolutionary life. He was instinctively flexible in addressing how change might be brought about. And, while his pragmatism appeared to some as lack of principle, it was informed above all by a deep fount of human sympathy that had little time for the kind of intolerance and factionalism that was so often a feature of the Russian revolutionary movement before 1917.

Bibliography

Archival Sources

While the two main collections of Volkhovskii's papers can be found at the Hoover Institution Library and Archives (Stanford University) and the Houghton Library (Harvard University), a great deal of other material relating to Volkhovskii's life and career can be found in numerous other archives around the world.

Bakhmeteff Archive of Russian and East European Culture (Columbia University)

- Sergei Stepniak-Kravchinskii Papers.
- Boris Sapir Papers.

British Library of Political and Economic Sciences (London School of Economics) Archives and Special Collections

- Peter Kropotkin Papers (COLL MISC 0530).
- Papers relating to *Free Russia* and the *Society of Friends of Russian Freedom* (COLL MISC 1028)
- Assorted Papers relating to *Letuchie listki* (COLL MISC 1156).

Leeds Russian Archive (Brotherton Library, Leeds University)

- Tuckton House Papers (LRA/MS 1381).

Gosudarstvennyi arkhiv Rossiiskoi Federatsii (GARF)

- Various papers relating to the commission for the investigation of cases of distribution of revolutionary appeals and propaganda, 1862-71 (fond 95).

- Various papers relating to the Department of Police of the Ministry of the Interior (fond 102).

- Various papers relating to the Third Section of his Imperial Majesty's own Chancellery (fond 109).

- Various papers relating to Nikolai Chaikovskii (fond P5085).

Gosudarstvennyi arkhiv Tomskoi oblasti (GATO)

- Papers relating to Volkhovskii's time as a political exile in Siberia (f. 3, op. 4, del. 820).

Hoover Institution Library and Archives, Stanford University (HIA)

- Egor Lazarev Papers (97002).

- Boris Nicolaevskii Papers (63013).

- Sergei Stepniak-Kravchinskii Papers (69068).

- Feliks Volkhovskii Papers (67046).

- Records of the Foreign Agency of the *Okhrana* (26001).

Houghton Library, Harvard University

- Feliks Volkhovskii Papers (MS Russ 51).

- Miscellaneous Papers relating to the Volkhovskii family (66M-197).

International Institute of Social History (Amsterdam)

- Papers of the Socialist Revolutionary Party.

Manuscript Division, Library of Congress, Washington DC

- George Kennan Papers, 1840-1937 (MSS 28456).

McMaster University Library

- Bertrand Russell Papers.

Newnham College (Cambridge) Library Special Collections

- Wallas Family Papers (GB 2911 PP WAL).

National Archives (Kew)

- Records of the Foreign Office (FO 371).

- The Security Service: First World War Historical Reports and Other Papers (KV 1).

New York Public Library (Manuscripts and Archives Division)
- George Kennan Papers, 1856-1987 (Mss Col 1630).

Parliamentary Archives (UK)
- Stow Hill Papers: David Soskice (STH/DS).

Philip Robinson Library (Newcastle University)
- Spence Watson / Weiss Papers (SW).

Rossiiskii gosudarstvennyi arkhiv literatury i iskusstva (RGALI)
- Correspondence between Sergei Stepniak-Kravchinskii and Volkhovskii, f. 1158, op. 1, ed. khr. 232.

Contemporary Newspapers and Journals

Anglo-Russian
Beverley and East Riding Recorder
Birmingham Daily Post
Blackburn Standard
Boston Globe
Buffalo Commercial
Byloe
Century Magazine
Chums
Contemporary Review
Daily Herald
Daily Mail
Daily News
Daily Telegraph
Delo
Derby Daily Telegraph
Evening Mail
Farringdon Advertiser

Fortnightly Review

Free Russia

Freeman's Advertiser

Frei Russland

Glasgow Evening Post

Glasgow Herald

Globe

Golos minuvshago

Golos minuvshego na chuzhnoi storone

Indianapolis News

Inverness Courier

Irish Independent

Istoricheskii vestnik

Justice

Katorga i ssylka

Lakes Herald

La Tribune Russe

Leeds Mercury

Leicester Chronicle

Letuchie listki

Little Folks

Liverpool Mercury

Manchester Guardian

Manitoba Free Press

Morning Post

Mysl'

Narodnoe delo (1868-70)

Narodnoe delo (1902-4)

Narodnoe delo: sbornik

Narodovlets. Sotsialnoe-politicheskoe obozrenie

New Review

New York Tribune

Norwich Mercury

Novoe vremia

Pedagogicheskii muzei

Pall Mall Gazette

Perthshire Advertiser
Pravitel'stvennyi vestnik
Review of Reviews
Revoliutsionnaia Rossiia
Russkii arkhiv
Sem'ia i shkola
Shields Daily Gazette
Sibirskaia gazeta
Sovremennik (1836-66)
Sovremennik (1911-15)
Sunderland Daily Echo
Times
[Toronto] Globe
Vestnik Evropy
Vospitanie i obuchenie
Vostochnoe obozrenie
Vestnik russkoi revoliutsii
Western Mail
Westmorland Gazette
Worcestershire Chronicle

Principal Writings of Feliks Volkhovskii

The vast majority of Volkhovskii's writings comprised short pieces published in newspapers and journals (which are cited accordingly in the notes). The items listed below are limited to Volkhovskii's longer pieces including those published as separate books or pamphlets.

Anon (compiled by F. Volkhovskii), *Iz-za reshetki* (Geneva: Tip-ia gazety 'Rabotnik', 1877).

Brut, I. [F. Volkhovskii], *Noch na novyi god* (Tomsk: Sibirskaia gazeta, 1885).

Brut, I. [F. Volkhovskii], *Shest' skazok* (Moscow: Tip-ia I. N. Kushnereva, 1888).

Brut, I. (ed.) [F. Volkhovskii], *Otgoloski Sibiri. Sbornik stikhotvorenii raznykh avtorov* (Tomsk: Tip-ia Mikhailova i Makushina, 1889).

Brut. I. (F. Volkhovskii), *Diuzhina skazok* (Moscow: V. M. Sablin, 1908).

Brut, I. (F. Volkhovskii), *Rakety. Skazki dlia detei sovershennago vozrasta* (Paris: L. Rodstein, 1913).

Brut [F. Volkhovskii], *Admiral Chagin. Roman* (Berlin: Heinrich Caspari, 1913).

Volkhovsky, F., 'The Suffering of Russian Exiles', *New Review*, 18, 3 (1890), 414–26.

Volkhovsky, F., 'My Life in Russian Prisons', *Fortnightly Review*, 48 (November 1890), 782-94.

Volkhovskii, F., *A China Cup and Other Stories for Children* (London: T. Fisher Unwin, 1892).

Volkhovsky, F. V. and V. G. Korolenko, *Russian Stories, Vol. I. Makar's Dream and Other Stories* (London: T. Fisher Unwin, 1892).

Volkhovskii, F., *Chemu uchit 'Konstitutsiia gr. Loris-Melikova?'* (London: Russian Free Press Fund, 1894).

Volkhovskii, F., *Russkii tkach. Petr Alekseevich Alekseev* (n.p.: Tip-ia 'Rabochago znamen', 1900).

Volkhovsky, F., 'The Russian Awakening', *Contemporary Review*, 81 (January 1902), 823-35.

Volkhovskii, F., *Pochemu armiane "buntuiut"* (Geneva: Partiia sotsialistov-revoliutsionerov, 1904).

Volkhovskii, F., *Skazanie o nespravedlivom tsare i kak on v razum voshel i kakoi sovet liudiam dal* (London: Izd-ie Partii sotsialistov-revoliutsionerov i Agrarno-sotsialisticheskoi ligi, 1902).

Volkhovskii, F, 'Kak muzhik u vsekh v dolgu ostalsia. Skazka', *Narodnoe delo*, 5 (1904), 28–48.

Volkhovskii, F., *Pro voinskoe ustroistvo* (Moscow: Knigoizdatel'sto E. D. Miakova 'Narodnaia Mysl', 1906).

Volkhovskii, F., Introduction to G. Kennan, *Sibir i ssylka v dvukh chastiakh* (St Petersburg: Izdanie Vl. Raspopova, 1906).

Volkhovskii, F., *Druz'ia sredi vragov. Iz vospominanii starago revoliutsionera* (St Petersburg: Knigozadel'stvo 'Narodnaia volia', 1906).

Volkhovskii, F., *Vylechennyi prints* (St Petersburg: Knigoizdatel'stvo 'Narodnaia volia', 1906).

Volkhovskoi, F. (*sic*), *Sluchainyia pesni* (Moscow: Knigoizdatel'stvo L. I. Kolovatova, 1907).

Volkhovskii, F., 'Pravdyve slovo Khliboroba', in M. Drahomanov (ed.), *Lysty do I. V. Franka i inshykh 1887–1895* (L'viv: Nakladom ukrainsko-ruskoi vydavnychoi spilky, 1908), 358–69.

Volkhovskii, F., 'Skazka o soldatskoi dushe', *Narodnoe delo: sbornik*, 4 (1909), 5-12.

Volkhovskii, F. (ed.), *Pamiati Leonida Emmanuilovicha Shishko* (n.p.: Partiia sotsialistov-revoliutsionerov, 1910).

Volkhovskoi, F. (*sic*), 'Otryvki odnoi chelovecheskoi zhizni', Parts 1-2, *Sovremennik* (April 1911), 254–67, *Sovremennik* (March 1912), 91–102.

Aleksandrov and F. Volkhovskii (eds), *Oborona strany* (Paris: n.p., 1913).

Aleksandrov and F. Volkhovskii (eds), *O nashei sovremennoi armii* (Paris: n.p., 1914).

Aleksandrov and F. Volkhovskii (eds), *Koe-chto o nashikh zadachakh* (Paris: n.p., 1914).

Collections of Documents

Full Report of the Proceedings of the International Workers' Congress, London, July and August 1896 (London: The Labour Leader, 1896).

Huitième Congrès socialiste international tenu à Copenhague du 28 août au 3 septembre 1910: compte rendu analytique (Gand: Volksdrukkerij, 1911).

Internationaler Sozialisten-Kongress zu Stuttgart 1907 (Berlin: Buchhandlung Vorwäts, 1907).

Partiia sotsialistov-revoliutsionerov. Dokumenty i materialy, ed. N. D. Erofeev, 3 vols (Moscow: Rosspen, 1996-2001).

Po voprosom programmy i taktiki. Sbornik statei iz 'Revoliutsionnoi Rossii' (Tip-ia Partii sotsialistov-revoliutsionerov, 1903).

Prilozheniia k trudam redaktsionnykh kommissii dlia sostavleniia polozhenii o krest'ianakh, 6 vols (St Petersburg: V tip-ii V. Bezobrazova i komp., 1860).

Protokoly pervogo s"ezda Partii Sotsialistov-Revolyutisonerov, ed. M. Perrie (Millwood NY: Kraus International Publications, 1983).

Rapport du Parti Socialiste Révolutionnaire de Russie au Congrès Socialiste International de Stuttgart (Gand: Volksdrukkerij, 1907).

Report of the Russian Socialist Revolutionary Party to the International Socialist Congress, Amsterdam, 1904 (London: Twentieth Century Press, 1904).

Stenograficheskii otchet po delu o revoliutisionnoi propagande v Imperii (St Petersburg, 1878).

Contemporary Writings and Memoirs

Adamovich, M., *Na Chernom more: ocherki proshloi bor'by* (Moscow: Politkatorzhan, 1928).

Agafonov, V. K., *Zagranichnaia okhranka* (St Petersburg: Kniga, 1918).

Argunov, A., 'Iz proshlago partii sotsialistov-revoliutsionerov', *Byloe* (October 1907), 94-112.

Asheshov, N. P. (ed.), *Andrei Ivanovich Zheliabov: Materialy dlia biografii i kharakteristiki* (Petersburg: Izdanie Petrogradskogo soveta rabochikh i krasnoarmeiskikh deputatov, 1919).

Aksel'rod, P. B., *Perezhitoe i peredumannoe* (Cambridge: Oriental Research Partners, 1975).

Baring, M., *With the Russians in Manchuria* (London: Methuen, 1905).

Baring, M., *The Russian People* (London: Methuen, 1911).

Bazilevskii, B., *Gosudarstvennyia prestupleniia v Rossii v XIX veke*, Vol. 3, *Protsess 193-kh* (St Petersburg: Sklad pri knigoizdatel'stve Donskaia Rech', 1906).

Bichter, A. (ed.), *Poety revoliutsionnogo narodnichestva* (Leningrad: Khudozhestvennogo literatura, 1967).

Blackwell, A. S. (ed.), *The Little Grandmother of the Revolution. Reminiscences and Letters of Catherine Breshkovsky* (London: T. Fisher Unwin, 1918).

Bland, F., *The Prophet's Mantle* (London: Drane, 1889).

Breshko-Breshkovskaia, E., *Skrytye korny russkoi revoliutsii. Otrechenie velikoi revoliutsionerki, 1873-1920* (Moscow: Tsentrpoligraf, 2007).

Burtsev, V. A., *Bor'ba za svobodnuiu Rossiiu. Moi vospominaniia* (Moscow: Direct Media, 2014).

Chaikovskii, N. V., 'F. V. Volkhovskii', *Golos Minuvshago*, 10 (October 1914), 231-35.

Chaikovskii, N. V., 'Cherez pol stoletiia', *Golos minuvshego na chuzhnoi storone*, 3 (1926), 179-96.

Chaleev-Kostromskoi, N. F., *Vospominaniia* (Kostroma: DiAr, 2006).

Charushin, N. A., *O dalekom proshlom. Kruzhok Chaikhovtsev. Iz vosmpominanii o revolitusionnom dvizhenii 1870-kh gg.* (Moscow: Vsesoiuznoe obshchestvo politicheskikh katorzhan i ssyl'no-poselentsev, 1926).

Chernov, V., *Zapiski sotsialista-revoliutsionera* (Berlin: Izd-vo Z. I. Grzhebina, 1922).

Chernov, V., *Pered burei* (Moscow: Direct Media, 2016).

Chernyshevsky, N. G., *Selected Philosophical Essays* (Moscow: Foreign Languages Publishing House, 1953).

Chicherin, B. N., *Vospominaniia*. 2 vols, I, Moskovskii universitet. Zemstvo i Moskovskaia duma (Moscow: Izd-vo im. Sabashnikovykh, 2010).

Chudnovskii, S. L., *Eniseiskaia guberniia: k trekhsotletnemu iubileiu Sibiri (statistiko-publitsisticheskie etiudy)* (Tomsk: n.p., 1885).

Chudnovskii, S. L., *Pereselenicheskoe delo na Altae* (Irkutsk: Vostochnoe obozrenie, 1889).

Chudnovskii, S. L., *Iz davnikh let. Vospominaniia* (Moscow: Izd-vo Vsesoiuznogo obshchestva politkatorzhan i ssyl'no-poselentsev, 1934).

Corder, P., *The Life of Robert Spence Watson* (London: Headley Bros., 1914).

Davitt, M., *Within the Pale. The True Story of Anti-Semitic Persecutions in Russia* (New York: A. S. Barnes and Co., 1903).

Deutsch, L., *Sixteen Years in Siberia. Some Experiences of a Russian Revolutionist*, trans. H. Chisholm (London: John Murray, 1903).

Dioneo [I. V. Shklovskii], 'Staraia londonskaia emigratsiia', *Golos minuvshego na chuzhoi storone*, 4 (1926), 41–62.

Durnovo, P. N., 'Aleksandr III i russkie emigranty', *Byloe*, No. 7 (1918), 198-203.

Edie, J. M., J. Scanlan and M. B. Zeldin (eds), *Russian Philosophy*, 2 vols (Chicago IL: Quadrangle Books, 1965).

Figner, V. *Memoirs of a Revolutionist*, trans. R. Stites (DeKalb, IL: Northern Illinois University Press, 1991).

Figner, V. N., *Posle Shlissel'burga* (Moscow: Direct Media, 2016).

Ford, F. M., *Return to Yesterday* (London: Victor Gollanz, 1931).

Gogol, N., 'Old World Landowners', *Evenings on a Farm near Dikanka and Mirgorod*, trans. R. English (Oxford: Oxford University Press, 1994).

Gruppa Osvobozhdenie truda (Iz arkhivov Plekhanova, Zasulich i Deicha), 6 vols (Moscow: Gosudarstvennoe izdatel'stvo, 1923-28).

Hambourg, M., *From Piano to Forte: A Thousand and One Notes* (London: Cassell, 1931).

Hamon, A., *Le socialisme et le Congrès de Londres: étude historique* (Paris: Ancienne Librairie Tresse and Stock, 1897).

Hobson, S. G., *Pilgrim to the Left: Memoirs of a Modern Revolutionist* (London: Edward Arnold, 1938).

Istoricheskaia zapiska 75-letiia S.-Peterburgskoi vtoroi gimnazii, 3 vols (St Petersburg: various publishers, 1880-1905).

Iudin, P. F. et al. (eds), *Literaturnoe nasledie G. V. Plekhanova*, 8 vols (Moscow: Gosudarstvennoe sotsial'no-eknomicheskoe izd-vo, 1934-40).

Ivanoff and Z, 'Anarchists. Their Methods and Organisation', *New Review*, 10, 56 (January 1894), 1-16.

Johnson, B. (ed.), *Tea and Anarchy! The Bloomsbury Diary of Olive Garnett, 1890-1893* (London: Bartlett's Press, 1989).

Johnson, B. C. (ed.), *Olive and Stepniak. The Bloomsbury Diary of Olive Garnett, 1893-95* (Birmingham: Bartletts Press, 1993).

Kapital sel'skikh bezplatnykh bibliotek v Sibiri (Tomsk: Tip-litografiia Sibirskago T-va Pechatnago dela, 1907).

Kennan, G., *Siberia and the Exile System*, 2 vols (New York: The Century Co. 1891).

Kennan, G., *Sibir i ssylka v dvukh chastiakh* (St Petersburg: Izdanie Vl. Raspopova, 1906).

Kennan, G., *A Russian Comedy of Errors with Other Stories and Sketches of Russian Life* (New York: The Century Co, 1915).

Klements, D. A. *Iz proshlogo. Vospominaniia* (Leningrad: Kolos, 1925).

Koni, A. F., *Vospominaniia o dele Very Zasulich* (Moscow: Direct Media, 2015).

Kornilova, O. I., *Byl' iz vremen krepostnichestva: vospominaniia o moei materi i eia okruzhaiushchem* (St Petersburg: Obshchestvennaia pol'za, 1894).

Kotsiubinskii, M., *Razskazy*, trans. F. Volkhovskii and M. Mogilianskii (Moscow: Knigoizdatel'stvo pisatelei v Moskve, 1914).

Kovalik, S. F., *Revoliutsionnoe dvizhenie semidesiatykh godov i protsess 193-kh* (Moscow: Izd-vo Vsesoiuznogo obshchestva politkatorzhan i ssyl'no-poselentsev, 1928).

Krasnoe znamia: sbornik na 1-e Maia 1905 goda (Geneva: Partiia sotsialistov-revoliutsionerov, 1905).

Krepkin, G. K., *Revnitel'sveta – P. I. Makushin: 50 let prosvetitel'noi deiatel'nosti* (Tomsk: n.p., 1916).

Kropotkin, P., *Memoirs of a Revolutionist* (London: Swann Sonneschein, 1908).

Lansdell, H., *Through Siberia* (Boston: Houghton Mifflin, 1882).

Lavrov, P. L., *Narodniki-propagandisty 1873-1878 godov* (St Petersburg: Tip-ia Andersona i Loitsianskago, 1907).

Lavrov, P. L., *Historical Letters*, trans. J. P. Scanlan (Berkeley, CA: University of California Press, 1967).

Lazarev, E. E., *Moia zhizn'. Vospominaniia, stati, pis'ma, materialy* (Prague: Pachetala Tip-ia Legiografiia, 1935).

Lemke, M. K., *Nikolaevskie zhandarmy i literatura, 1826-55 gg.* (St Petersburg: Tip-ia A. V. Orlova, 1909).

Le Queux, W., *Guilty Bonds* (London: Geo. Routledge and Sons, 1891).

Lopatin, V., 'Osvobozhdenie F. V. Volkhovskago', *Golos Minuvshago*, 4 (1914), 217-21.

Meredith, I., *A Girl Among the Anarchists* (London: Duckworth, 1903).

Miliukov, P. N., *Vospominaniia* (Moscow: Izd-vo Politicheskoi literatury, 1991).

Morozov, N. A., 'Andrei Franzholi', *Byloe* (March 1907), 283-89.

Morozov, N. A., *Povesti moei zhizni*, 3 vols (Moscow: Nauka, 1965).

Morozov, N. A., 'Vo imia bratstva', *Golos Minuvshago*, 11 (1913), 122–61; 12 (1913), 117–67.

Nihilism as It Is. Being Stepniak's Pamphlets Translated by E. L. Voynich, and Felix Volkhovsky's "Claims of the Russian Liberals" with an Introduction by Dr R. Spence Watson (London: T. Fisher Unwin, 1894).

Noble, E., *The Russian Revolt: Its Causes, Condition and Prospects* (Boston, MA: Houghton Mifflin, 1885).

Novikoff, O., 'A Cask of Honey with a Spoonful of Tears', *Contemporary Review*, 55 (February 1889), 207-15.

Novikoff, O., 'Russia and the Re-Discovery of Europe', *Fortnightly Review*, 61 (1897), 479-91.

Oksman, Iu. G. (ed.), *N. G. Chernyshevskii v vospominaniiakh sovremennikov*, 2 vols (Saratov: Saratovskoe knizhnoe izdatel'stvo, 1958).

Orlov, V. N. et al. (eds), *Poety-demokraty 1870-1880-kh godov* (Leningrad: Sovetskii Pisatel', 1968).

Perris, G. H., *Leo Tolstoy. The Grand Mujik* (London: T. Fisher Unwin, 1898).

Perris, G. H., *Russia in Revolution* (London: Chapman and Hall, 1905).

Peterson, A., 'Cherty starinnago dvorianskago byta', *Russkii arkhiv*, 8 (1877), 479-82.

Plekhanov, G. V., *Literaturnoe nasledie G. V. Plekhanova*, 6 vols (Moscow: Gosudarstvennoe sotsial'no-eknomicheskoe izd-vo, 1934-40).

Poluvekovoi iubilei P. I. Makushina 1866-1916 gg. (Tomsk: n.p., 1917).

Raevskii, I. A., 'Iz vospominanii', *Istoricheskii vestnik*, 101 (1905), 391-409.

Sapir, B. (ed.), *Lavrov. Gody emigratsii*, 2 vols (Dordrecht: D. Reidel, 1974).

Savinkov, B, *Vospominaniia terrorista* (Kharkov: Izd-vo 'Proletarii', 1926).

Shatz, M. S., and J. E. Zimmerman (eds), *Vekhi. Landmarks* (London: M. E. Sharpe, 1994).

Shilov, A. A. (ed.), *German Aleksandrovich Lopatin, 1845-1918. Avtobiografiя. Pokazaniia i pis'ma. Stat'i i stikhotvoreniia. Bibliografiia* (Petrograd: Gosudarstvennoe izdatel'stvo, 1922).

Shishko, L., *Sergei Mikhailovich Kravchinskii i kruzhok Chaikovtsev* (St Petersburg: Izd-ie Vl. Raspopova, 1906).

Shishko, L. E., 'M. I. Gots', *Byloe* (November 1906), 283-92.

Sinegub, Sergei, *Zapiski chaikovtsa* (Moscow: Molodaia gvardiia, 1929).

Soskice, J. M., *Chapters from Childhood: Reminiscences of an Artist's Granddaughter* (London: Selwyn and Blount, 1921).

Spence Watson, R., *The Proper Limits of Obedience to the Law* (Gateshead: Howe Brothers, 1887).

Spiridovich, A. I., *Partiia sotsialistov-revoliutsionerov i eia predshestvenniki, 1886-1916* (Petrograd: Voennaia tipografiia, 1918).

Stead, W. T., *The M.P. for Russia. Reminiscences and Correspondence of Madame Olga Novikoff*, 2 vols (London: Melrose, 1909).

Stepniak, *Underground Russia* (London: Smith Elder, 1883).

Stepniak, S., 'Terrorism in Russia and Terrorism in Europe', *Contemporary Review*, 45 (January 1884), 325-41.

Stepniak, S., *The Career of a Nihilist* (London: W. Scott, 1889).

Stepniak, S., *Chego nam nuzhno? i Nachalo kontsa* (London: Izd-ie Fonda Russkoi Vol'noi Pressy, 1892).

Stepniak, S., 'Nihilism as It Is (A Reply)', *New Review*, 10, 57 (February 1894), 215-22.

Stepniak-Kravchinskii, S. M., *V Londonskoi emigratsii*, ed. M. E. Ermasheva (Moscow: Nauka, 1968).

Sweeney, J., *At Scotland Yard: Being the Experiences during Twenty-Seven Years' Service of John Sweeney* (London: Grant Richards, 1904).

Von Samson-Himmelstern, H., *Russia under Alexander III. And in the Preceding Period* (London: T. Fisher Unwin, 1893).

Thompson, H. M., *Russian Politics* (London: T. Fisher Unwin, 1895).

Turgenev, I., *Fathers and Sons*, trans. Rosemary Edmonds (London: Penguin, 1979).

Turgenev, I., 'Apropos of Fathers and Sons', in D. Magarshack (ed.) *Turgenev's Literary Reminiscences* (London: Faber, 1984), 168–77.

Windt, H. de., *Siberia as It Is* (London: Chapman and Hall, 1892).

Zasulich, A., 'Vospominaniia shestidesiatnitsy', *Byloe*, 18 (1922), 19-45.

Zenzinov, V, *Perezhitoe* (New York: Izd-vo im. Chekhova, 1953).

Zilbershtein, I. S., and N. I. Dikushina (eds), *Gorkii i russkaia zhurnalistika XX veka: Neizdannaia perepiska, Literaturnoe nasledstvo*, 95 (Moscow: Nauka, 1985).

Zilliacus, K., *Det revolutionära Ryssland: en skildring af den revolutionära rörelsens i Ryssland uppkomst och utveckling* (Stockholm: K. P. Boströms Forlag, 1902).

Zilliacus, K., *The Russian Revolutionary Movement* (New York: E. P. Dutton, 1905).

Zilliacus, K., *Sortovuosilta. Poliittsia muistelmia* (Porvoo: WSOY, 1920).

Secondary Sources

The books and articles listed below are those cited in the footnotes along with a small number of others that have been of particular use in writing this book. The edition listed is the one that was used and not necessarily the first edition. In cases where there was more than one place of publication the first place alone is listed.

Abrosymova, S. V. and L. H. Hurai, 'A Chepa i nevidomi marhinalii z yoho biblioteky', *Sicheslavskyi almanakh: zb. nauk. prats z istorii ukr. kozatstva* (Dnipropetrovsk: NGU, 2006), 134–52, https://ir.nmu.org.ua/handle/123456789/1047.

Alenius, K., 'Russification in Estonia and Finland Before 1917', *Faravid*, 28 (2004), 181-94.

Alikina, N. A., and L. S. Kashikhin (eds), *Pesni revoliutsionnogo podpol'ia* (Perm: Permskoe Knizhnoe Izd-vo, 1977).

Alston, C., 'News of the Struggle: The Russian Political Press in London, 1853-1921', in C. Bantman and A. C. Suriani da Silva (eds), *The Foreign Political Press in Nineteenth Century London. Politics from a Distance* (London: Bloomsbury, 2017), 155-74.

Alston, C., *Tolstoy and His Disciples, The History of a Radical International Movement* (London: I. B. Tauris, 2013).

Armytage, W. H. G., 'J. C. Kenworthy and the Tolstoyan Communities in England', *The American Journal of Economics and Sociology*, 16, 4 (1957), 391-405.

Ascher, A., *Pavel Axelrod and the Development of Menshevism* (Cambridge, MA: Harvard University Press, 1972).

Ascher, A., *The Revolution of 1905: Russia in Disarray* (Stanford, CA: Stanford University Press, 1988).

Ascher, A., *The Revolution of 1905: Authority Restored* (Stanford, CA: Stanford University Press, 1992).

Ascher, A., *P. A. Stolypin. The Search for Stability in Late Imperial Russia* (Stanford, CA: Stanford University Press, 2001).

Avrich, P., *Bakunin and Nechaev* (London: Freedom Press, 1987).

Avrus, A. I., A. A. Goloseeva, and A. P. Novikov, *Viktor Chernov: zhizn' russkogo sotsialista* (Moscow: Kliuch-S, 2015).

Azadovskii, K. M., 'Iz slovaria "Russkie pisateli. 1800-1917" (M. A. Sukennikov. S. N. Shil')', *Literaturnyi fact*, 7 (2018), 358-84.

Balakhnina, M. V., 'Sotsial'no-ekonomicheskie i politicheskie aspekty sostoianiia Sibirskogo kraia v 1880-e gg. v publikatsiiakh D. A. Klementsa v "Sibirskoi gazete"', Interexpo GEO-Siberia (2022), 10-14, https://scholar.archive.org/work/bxh6lpr5uva5bfod3som4wl7ci.

Baluev, B. P., *Liberal'noe narodnichestvo na rubezhe XIX-XX vekov* (Moscow: Nauka, 1995).

Bantman, C., *The French Anarchists in London, 1890-1914: Exile and Transformation in the First Globalisation* (Liverpool: Liverpool University Press, 2013).

Baron, S. H., *Plekhanov. The Father of Russian Marxism* (London: Routledge and Kegan Paul, 1963).

Barton, G., *The Tottenham Outrage and Walthamstow Tram Chase: The Most Spectacular Hot Pursuit in History* (Hook: Waterside Press, 2017).

Beasley, R., *Russomania. Russian Culture and the Creation of British Modernism, 1881-1922* (Oxford: Oxford University Press, 2020).

Bebbington, D. W., *The Nonconformist Conscience: Chapel and Politics, 1870-1914* (London: George Allen and Unwin, 1982).

Becker, J.-J., *L'année 1914* (Paris: Armand Colin, 2004).

Beer, D., *The House of the Dead: Siberian Exile under the Tsars* (London: Penguin, 2016).

Bel'chikov, N. F., 'Rublevoe obshchestvo. Epizod iz istorii revoliutsionnogo dvizheniia 60-kh godov', *Izvestiia Akademii nauk SSSR. Seriia vii. Otdelenie obshchestvennykh nauk*, 10 (1935), 940-1001.

Berezhnaia, L. G., 'Zhurnal "Russkoe Bogatstvo" v 1905-1913 gg', in B. I. Esin (ed.), *Iz istorii russkoi zhurnalistiki nachala XX veka* (Moscow: Izd-vo Moskovskogo universiteta, 1984), 59-93.

Bergman, J., *Vera Zasulich: A Biography* (Stanford, CA: Stanford University Press, 1983).

Berlin, I., *Two Concepts of Liberty. An Inaugural Lecture Delivered before the University of Oxford on 31 October 1958* (Oxford: Clarendon Press, 1958).

Berlin, I., *Russian Thinkers* (London: Penguin, 1994).

Besançon, A., *The Intellectual Origins of Leninism*, trans. A. Matthews (Oxford: Blackwell, 1981).

Bilenky, S., *Romantic Nationalism in Eastern Europe: Russian, Polish, and Ukrainian Political Imaginations* (Stanford, CA: Stanford University Press, 2012).

Billington, J. H., *Mikhailovsky and Russian Populism* (New York: Oxford University Press, 1958).

Brachev, V. S., *Zagranichnaia agentura departmenta politsii (1883-1917)* (St Petersburg: Stomma, 2001).

Briggs, J., *A Woman of Passion. The Life of E. Nesbit, 1858-1924* (London: Hutchinson, 1987).

Broido, V., *Apostles into Terrorists. Women and the Revolutionary Movement in the Russia of Alexander II* (New York: The Viking Press, 1977).

Brower, D. R., *Training the Nihilists. Education and Radicalism in Tsarist Russia* (Ithaca, NY: Cornell University Press, 1975).

Brumfield, W. C., 'Bazarov and Rjazonov: The Romantic Archetype in Russian Nihilism', *Slavic and East European Journal*, 21, 4 (1977), 495–505.

Budd, L. J., 'Twain, Howells, and the Boston Nihilists', *New England Quarterly*, 32, 3 (1959), 351-71.

Budnitskii, O. V., *Terrorizm v rossiiskom osvoboditel'nom dvizhenii: ideologiia, etika, psikhologiia (vtoraia polovina XIX-nachalo XX v)* (Moscow: Rosspen, 2000).

Bujalski, N., '"Tuk, tuk, tuk!". A History of Russia's Prison Knocking Language', *Russian Review*, 81, 3 (2022), 491-510.

Burke, D., 'Theodore Rothstein, Russian Émigré and British Socialist', in J. Slatter (ed.), *From the Other Shore. Russian Political Emigrants in Britain, 1880-1917* (London: Frank Cass, 1984), 81-99.

Burke, D., *Russia and the British Left. From the 1848 Revolution to the General Strike* (London: I. B. Tauris, 2018).

Bushnell, J., *Mutiny Amid Repression. Russian Soldiers in the Revolution of 1905-1906* (Bloomington, IN: Indiana University Press, 1985).

Butterworth, A., *The World That Never Was. A True Story of Dreamers, Schemers, Anarchists and Secret Agents* (London: Bodley Head, 2010).

Byrnes, R., *Pobedonostsev: His Life and Thought* (Bloomington, IN: Indiana University Press, 1968).

Campbell, C., *Fenian Fire. The British Government Plot to Assassinate Queen Victoria* (London: Harper Collins, 2002).

Cavender, M. W., *Nests of the Gentry. Family, Estate and Local Loyalties in Provincial Russia* (Newark, DE: University of Delaware Press, 2007).

Charmley, J., *Splendid Isolation? Britain and the Balance of Power, 1874-1914* (London: Hodder and Stoughton, 1999).

Clowes, E. W., S. D. Kassow, and J. L. West (eds), *Between Tsar and People. Educated Society and the Quest for Public Identity in Late Imperial Russia* (Princeton, NJ: Princeton University Press, 1991).

Clutterbuck, L., 'The Progenitors of Terrorism: Russian Revolutionaries or Extreme Irish Republicans?', *Terrorism and Political Violence*, 16, 1 (2004), 154-81, https://doi.org/10.1080/09546550490457917.

Cohen, S. F., *Bukharin and the Bolshevik Revolution. A Political Biography, 1888-1938* (London: Wildwood House, 1974).

Cole, G. D. H., *A History of Socialist Thought. The Second International 1889-1914* (London: Macmillan, 1956).

Confino, M., *Violence dans le violence: Le débat Bakounine-Nečaev* (Paris: F. Maspero, 1973).

Cook, A., M. *MI5's First Spymaster* (London: Tempus, 2004).

Cooper, S. E., *Patriotic Pacifism. Waging War on War in Europe, 1815-1914* (New York: Oxford University Press, 1991).

Copeland, W., *The Uneasy Alliance: Collaboration between the Finnish Opposition and the Russian Underground, 1899-1904* (Helsinki: Suomalainen Tiedeakatemia, 1973).

Daly, J., *Autocracy under Siege. Security Police and Opposition in Russia, 1866-1905* (DeKalb, IL: Northern Illinois Press, 1998).

Dennison, T., *The Institutional Framework of Russian Serfdom* (Cambridge: Cambridge University Press, 2011).

Deviatov, S. V. et al. (eds), *Terrorizm v Rossii v nachale XX v.*, *Istoricheskii vestnik*, 149 (Moscow: Runivers, 2012).

Dianina, K., 'The Feuilleton: An Everyday Guide to Public Culture in the Age of the Great Reforms', *Slavic and East European Journal*, 47, 2 (2003), 187-210, https://doi.org/10.2307/3219943.

Dietze, C., *The Invention of Terrorism in Europe, Russia, and the United States* (London: Verso, 2021).

Di Paola, P., *The Knights Errant of Anarchy. London and the Italian Anarchist Diaspora (1880-1917)* (Liverpool: Liverpool University Press, 2013).

Dogliani, P., 'The Fate of Socialist Internationalism', in G. Sluga and P. Clavin (eds), *Internationalisms: A Twentieth Century History* (Cambridge: Cambridge University Press, 2016), 38-60.

Domanskii, V. A., 'F.V. Volkhovskii – neglasnyi redaktor "Sibirskoi gazety"', in E. A. Kol'chuzhkin et al. (eds), *Russkie pisately v Tomske* (Tomsk: Vodolei, 1996).

Doroshenko, D., 'First Efforts to Collect and Publish Ukrainian Historical Material', *The Annals of the Ukrainian Academy of Arts and Sciences in the US, Inc*, 5-6 (1957), 92-103.

Ekhina, N. A., 'Emigranty, revoliutsionery i kornovannye osoby: "russkaia volost'" E. E. i Iu. A. Lazarevykh v Bozhi nad Klaranom', *Ezhegodnik Doma russkogo zarubezh'ia im. Aleksandra Solzhenitsyna* (2014-15), 20-30.

Eklof, B., J. Bushnell and L. Zakharova (eds), *Russia's Great Reforms, 1855–1881* (Bloomington, IN: Indiana University Press, 1994).

Eklof, B. and T. Saburova, *A Generation of Revolutionaries. Nikolai Charushin and Russian Populism from the Great Reforms to Perestroika* (Bloomington, IN: Indiana University Press, 2017).

Eklof, B. and T. Saburova, ''Rembrances of a Distant Past': Generational Memory in the Collective Auto/Biography of Russian Populists in the Revolutionary Era', *Slavonic and East European Review*, 96, 1 (2018), 67-93.

Ely, C., *Underground Petersburg. Radical Populism, Urban Space and the Tactics of Subversion in Reform-Era Russia* (Dekalb, IL: Northern Illinois University Press, 2016).

Ely, C., *Russian Populism* (London: Bloomsbury, 2022).

Emmons, T., *Emancipation of the Russian Serfs* (New York: Holt, Rinehart and Winston, 1970).

Encyclopedia of Ukraine, ed. Danylo Husar Struk, 5 vols (Toronto: University of Toronto Press, 1993).

Ermolinskii, L. L., *Sibirskie gazety 70-80-kh godov XIX veka* (Irkutsk: Izd-vo Irkutskogo universiteta, 1985).

Esin, B. I. (ed.), *Iz istorii russkoi zhurnalistiki nachala XX veka* (Moscow: Izd-vo Moskovskogo gosudarstvennogo universiteta, 1984).

Ewence, H., *The Alien Jew in the British Imagination, 1881-1905. Space, Mobility and Territoriality* (Cham: Palgrave Macmillan, 2019).

Fält, O. K. and A. Kujala (eds), *Rakka ryūsui: Colonel Akashi's Report on His Secret Cooperation with the Russian Revolutionary Parties during the Russo-Japanese War* (Helsinki: Suomen Historiallinen Seura, 1998).

Fedyashin, A. A., *Liberals under Autocracy. Modernization and Civil Society in Russia, 1866-1904* (Madison, WI: University of Wisconsin Press, 2012).

Feldman, D., *Englishmen and Jews: Social Relations and Political Culture, 1840-1914* (New Haven, CT: Yale University Press, 1994).

Feuer, L. S., *The Conflict of Generations. The Character and Significance of Student Movements* (New York: Basic Books, 1969).

Field, D., 'Peasants and Propagandists in the Russian Movement to the People of 1874', *Journal of Modern History*, 59, 3 (1987), 415-38.

Field, D., 'Stratification and the Russian Peasant Commune: A Statistical Inquiry', in R. Bartlett (ed.), *Land Commune and Peasant Community in Russia. Communal Forms in Imperial and Early Soviet Society* (London: Macmillan in Association with School of Slavonic and East European Studies, 1990), 143-64.

Figes, O., *A People's Tragedy. The Russian Revolution, 1891-1924* (London: Pimlico, 1996).

Filippov, R. V., *Iz istorii narodnicheskogo dvizheniia na pervom etape "khozdeniia v narod" (1863-1874)* (Petrozavodsk: Karel'skoe knizhnoe izd-vo, 1967).

Fisher, B. B., (ed.), *Okhrana. The Paris Operations of the Russian Secret Police* (Washington DC: Central Intelligence Agency, 1997).

Fishman, W. J., *East End Jewish Radicals, 1875-1914* (London: Five Leaves Publications, 2004).

Foglesong, D. S., *The American Mission and the "Evil Empire". The Crusade for a "Free Russia" since 1881* (Cambridge: Cambridge University Press, 2007).

Footman, D., *Red Prelude. The Life of the Russian Terrorist Zhelyabov* (Westport, CT: Hyperion Press, 1979).

Frolich, K., *The Emergence of Russian Constitutionalism 1900-1904: The Relationship between Social Mobilization and Political Group Formation in Pre-Revolutionary Russia* (The Hague: Martinus Nijhoff, 1981).

Fuchs, J. A., 'Ein Yankee am Hofe des Zaren: Mark Twain und die *Friends of Russian Freedom', Forum für osteuropäische Ideen und Zeitgeschichte*, 15, 2 (2013), 69–86.

Futrell, M., *Northern Underground. Episodes of Russian Revolutionary Transport and Communications through Scandinavia and Finland, 1863-1917* (London: Faber, 1963).

Gainer, B., *The Alien Invasion. The Origins of the 1905 Aliens Act* (London: Heinemann, 1972).

Galai, S., *The Liberation Movement in Russia, 1900-1905* (Cambridge: Cambridge University Press, 1973).

Garnett, D., *The Golden Echo* (New York: Harcourt, Brace and Company, 1954).

Garnett, R., *Constance Garnett: A Heroic Life* (London: Sinclair-Stevenson, 1991).

Gartner, L. P., *The Jewish Immigrant in England, 1870-1914* (Detroit, MI: Wayne State University Press, 1960).

Geifman, A., *Thou Shalt Kill. Revolutionary Terrorism in Russia 1894-1917* (Princeton, NJ: Princeton University Press, 1993).

Geifman, A., *Entangled in Terror: The Azef Affair and the Russian Revolution* (Wilmington, DE: Scholarly Resources, 2000).

Gentes, A. A., *Exile to Siberia, 1590-1822* (Basingstoke: Palgrave Macmillan, 2008).

Gentes, A. A., *Exile, Murder and Madness in Siberia, 1823-1861* (Basingstoke: Palgrave Macmillan, 2010).

Gentes, A. A., *The Mass Deportation of Poles to Siberia, 1863-1881* (Cham: Palgrave Macmillan, 2017).

Getzler, I., *Martov: A Political Biography of a Russian Social Democrat* (Cambridge: Cambridge University Press, 1967).

Glover, D., *Literature, Immigration and Diaspora in Fin-de-Siècle England. A Cultural History of the 1905 Aliens Act* (Cambridge: Cambridge University Press, 2012).

Gol'dfarb, S. I., *D. A. Klements. Revoliutsioner, uchenyi, publitsist* (Irkutsk: Izd-vo Irkutskogo universiteta, 1986).

Gol'dfarb, S. I., *Gazeta "Vostochnoe Obozrenie" 1882-1906* (Irkutsk: Izd-vo Irkutskogo universiteta, 1997).

Gomme, R., *George Herbert Perris 1866-1920. The Life and Times of a Radical* (Oxford: Peter Lang, 2003).

Gorev, B. I., et al. (eds), *Istoriko-revoliutsionnaia khrestomatiia*, 3 vols (Moscow: Novaia Moskva, 1923).

Gorodnitskii, R. A., *Boevaia organizatsiia partii sotsialistov-revoliutsionerov v 1901-1911 gg.* (Moscow: Rosspen, 1998).

Grant, R., 'The Society of Friends of Russian Freedom (1890-1917): A Case-Study in Internationalism', *Scottish Labour History Society Journal*, 3 (1970), 3-24.

Green, L., 'Russian Revolutionary Terrorism, British Liberals, and the Problem of Empire (1884-1914)', *History of European Ideas*, 46, 5 (2020), 633-48, https://doi.org/10.1080/01916599.2020.1746083.

Greenblatt, S., *Renaissance Self-Fashioning: From More to Shakespeare* (Chicago, IL: Chicago University Press, 1980).

Haberer, E. E., *Jews and Revolution in Nineteenth-Century Russia* (Cambridge: Cambridge University Press, 1995).

Häfner, L., 'An Entangled World at the Beginning of the Twentieth Century: Socialist Revolutionary Terrorism, Transatlantic Public Sphere and American Capital', in F. Jacobs and M. Keßler (eds), *Transnational Radicalism. Socialist and Anarchist Exchanges in the 19th and 20th Centuries* (Liverpool: Liverpool University Press, 2021), 23-56.

Hamburg, G. M., 'The London Emigration and the Russian Liberation Movement: The Problem of Unity, 1889-1897', *Jahrbücher für Geschichte Osteuropas*, 25, 3 (1977), 321-39.

Hamburg, G. M., and P. L. Lavrov, 'P. L. Lavrov in Emigration. An Unpublished Letter', *Russian Review*, 37, 4 (1978), 449-52.

Hamilton, K. and R. Langhorne, *The Practice of Diplomacy: Its Evolution, Theory and Administration* (London: Routledge, 2011).

Haney, J. V., *An Introduction to the Russian Folktale* (Armonk, NY: M. E. Sharpe, 1999).

Harcave, S., *Count Sergei Witte and the Twilight of Imperial Russia. A Biography* (Abingdon: Routledge, 2015).

Hardy, D., *Petr Tkachev. The Critic as Jacobin* (Seattle, WA: University of Washington Press, 1977).

Hardy, D., *Land and Freedom. The Origins of Russian Terrorism, 1876–1879* (Westport, CT: Greenwood Press, 1987).

Hartley, J. M., *Siberia. A History of the People* (New Haven, CT: Yale University Press, 2014).

Hartnett, L., *The Defiant Life of Vera Figner. Surviving the Russian Revolution* (Bloomington, IN: Indiana University Press, 2014).

Hartnett, L., 'Relief and Revolution: Russian Émigrés' Political Remittances and the Building of Political Transnationalism', *Journal of Ethnic and Migration Studies*, 46, 6 (2020), 1040-56, https://doi.org/10.1080/13691 83X.2018.1554290.

Henderson, R., 'A. L. Teplov and the Russian Free Library in Whitechapel', *Solanus*, New Series, 22 (2011), 5-26.

Henderson, R., 'The Hyde Park Rally of 9 March 1890: A British Response to Russian Atrocities', *European Review of History / Revue européenne d'histoire*, 21, 4 (2014), 451-66, https://doi.org/10.1080/13507486.2014.933182.

Henderson, R., *Vladimir Burtsev and the Struggle for a Free Russia* (London: Bloomsbury, 2017).

Henderson, R., *The Spark That Lit the Revolution. Lenin in London and the Politics That Changed the World* (London: I. B. Tauris, 2020).

Herlihy, P., *Odessa. A History, 1794-1914* (Cambridge, MA: Harvard Ukrainian Research Institute, 1986).

Higgins, C., 'The Guttural Sorrow of the Refugees' – Constance Garnett and Felix Volkhovsky in the British Museum, *Materialy X Mezhdunarodnogo seminara perevodchikov*, https://www.repository.cam.ac.uk/items/ ee5b06e9-4ba2-43e4-a40f-4c1b4ed29f96.

Hildermeier, M., 'The Terrorist Strategies of the Socialist-Revolutionary Party in Russia, 1900-1914', in W. J. Mommsen and G. Hirschfeld (eds), *Social Protest, Violence and Terror in Nineteenth- & Twentieth Century Europe* (London: Macmillan, 1982), 80-87.

Hildermeier, M., 'The Socialist Revolutionary Party of Russia and the Workers, 1900-1914', in Reginald E. Zelnik (ed.), *Workers and Intelligentsia in Late*

Imperial Russia: Realities, Representations, Reflections (Berkeley, CA: University of California Press, 1998), 206-27.

Hildermeier, M., *The Russian Socialist Revolutionary Party Before the First World War* (New York: St Martin's Press, 2000).

Hillis, F., *Utopia's Discontents: Russian Émigrés and the Quest for Freedom, 1830s-1930s* (New York: Oxford University Press, 2021).

Hoch, S., *Serfdom and Social Control in Russia. Petrovskoe, a Village in Tambov* (Chicago, IL: Chicago University Press, 1986).

Hollingsworth, B., 'The Society of Friends of Russian Freedom: English Liberals and Russian Socialists, 1890-1917', *Oxford Slavonic Papers*, New Series, 3 (1970), 45-64.

Hollingsworth, B., 'The British Memorial to the Russian Duma, 1906', *Slavonic and East European Review*, 53, 133 (1975), 539-57.

Hosking, G., *The Russian Constitutional Experiment: Government and Duma, 1907-1914* (Cambridge: Cambridge University Press, 1973).

Hughes, M., 'Bernard Pares, Russian Studies and the Promotion of Anglo-Russian Friendship', *Slavonic and East European Review*, 78, 3 (2000), 510-35.

Hughes, M., *Diplomacy before the Russian Revolution: Britain, Russia and the Old Diplomacy, 1894-1917* (Basingstoke: Palgrave Macmillan, 2000).

Hughes, M., 'The English Slavophile: W. J. Birkbeck and Russia', *Slavonic and East European Review*, 82, 3 (2004), 680-706.

Hughes, M., 'Misunderstanding the Russian Peasantry: Anti-Capitalist Revolution or Third Rome?', in H. Schultz and A. Harre (eds), *Bauerngesellschaften auf dem Weg in die Moderne. Agrarismus in Ostmitteleuropa 1880 bis 1960* (Wiesbaden: Harrassowitz, 2010), 55-67.

Hughes, M., 'British Opinion and Russian Terrorism in the 1880s', *European History Quarterly*, 41, 2 (2011), 255-77.

Hughes, M., 'William Le Queux and Russia', *Critical Survey*, 31, 1-2 (2020), 119-38.

Huxley, S. D., *Constitutionalist Insurgency in Finland. Finnish "Passive Resistance" against Russification as a Case of Nonmilitary Struggle in the European Resistance Tradition* (Helsinki: Suomen Historiallinen Seura, 1990).

Iampol'skii, I. G., 'K bibliografii F. V. Volkhovskogo', *Uchenye zapiski Leningradskogo gosudarstvennogo universiteta*, 349, *Seriia filologicheskikh nauk*, 74 (1971), 184-90.

Immonen H., *The Agrarian Programme of the Russian Socialist Revolutionary Party, 1900-1914* (Helsinki: Suomen Historiallinen Seura, 1988).

Immonen, H., *Mechty o novoi Rossii. Viktor Chernov (1877-1952)* (St Petersburg: Izd-vo Evropeiskogo universiteta v Sankt-Peterburge, 2015).

Ingleby, M., 'Double Standards: Reading the Revolutionary Doppelgänger in *The Prophet's Mantle*', in D. Downes and T. Ferguson (eds), *Victorian Fiction beyond the Canon* (Basingstoke: Palgrave Macmillan, 2016), 181-199.

Ionescu, G. and E. Gellner, *Populism: Its Meaning and National Characteristics* (London: Weidenfeld and Nicolson, 1969).

Isakov, V. A., 'Sushchnost' rossiiskogo radikalizma vtoroi poloviny XIX veka v istoriograficheskom protsesse', in G. N. Mokshin et al. (eds), *Narodniki v istorii Rossii*, 2 vols (Voronezh: Istoki and Izdatel'skii dom VGU, 2013-16), I, 8-25.

Itenberg, B. S., *Dvizhenie revoliutsionnogo narodnichestva. Narodnicheskie kruzhkii i "khozdenie v narod" v 70-kh godakh XIX v.* (Moscow: Nauka, 1965).

Itenberg, B. S., *P. L. Lavrov v russkom revoliutsionnom dvizhenii* (Moscow: Nauka, 1988).

Izmozik, V. S., *"Chernye kabinety": Istoriia rossiiskoi perliustratsii, XVIII-nachalo XX veka* (Moscow: Novoe literaturnoe obozrenie, 2015).

Jahn, E., *World Political Challenges. Political Issues under Debate* (Berlin: Springer, 2015).

Jänis-Isokongas, I., 'Konrad (Konni) Zilliacus and Revolutionary Russia', *Nordic and Baltic Studies Review*, 3 (2018), 366-79.

Jefferson, M. M., 'Lord Salisbury's Conversations with the Tsar at Balmoral, 27 and 29 September 1896', *Slavonic and East European Review*, 39, 92 (1960), 216-22.

Jensen, R. B., 'The 1904 Assassination of Governor-General Bobrikov: Tyrannicide, Anarchism and the Expanding Scope of "Terrorism"', *Terrorism and Political Violence*, 30, 5 (2018), 828-43, https://doi.org/10.1080/09546553.2018.1445821.

Johnson, E. M., 'Revolutionary Romance: Love and Marriage for Russian Radicals in the 1870s', *Russian History*, 43, 3-4 (2016), 311-37, https://doi.org/10.1163/18763316-04304005.

Johnson, R. I., 'Zagranichnaia Agentura: the Tsarist Political Police in Europe', *Journal of Contemporary History*, 7, 1 (1972), 221-42.

Joll, J., *The Second International, 1889-1914* (London: Routledge and Kegan Paul, 1955).

Jones Hemenway, E., 'Nicholas in Hell: Rewriting the Tsarist Narrative in the Revolutionary *Skazki* of 1917', *Russian Review*, 60, 2 (2001), 185-204, https://doi.org/10.1111/0036-0341.00164.

Jones, W. G. (ed.), *Tolstoi and Britain* (Oxford: Berg, 1995).

Kafanova, O. B., 'Dialog kul'tur v teatral'nom khronotope Tomska na rubezhe XIX-XX vv.', *Knigoizdanie* 3 (2014), 45-64.

Kalinchuk, S. V., 'Revoliutsionnye narodniki i ukrainofily 1870-1880-kh gg.: sotrudnichestvo ili sopernichestvo?', in G. N. Mokshin et al. (eds), *Narodniki v istorii Rossii*, 2 vols (Voronezh: Istoki and Izdatel'skii dom VGU, 2013-16), II, 82-106.

Karpachev, M. D., 'O novykh i starykh podkhodakh k periodizatsii istorii russkogo narodnichestva', in G. N. Mokshin et al. (eds), *Narodniki v istorii Rossii*, 2 vols (Voronezh: Istoki and Izdatel'skii dom VGU, 2013-16), II, 7-19.

Kassow, S. D., *Students, Professors and the State in Tsarist Russia* (Berkeley, CA: University of California Press, 1989).

Keep, J., *The Rise of Social Democracy in Russia* (Oxford: Clarendon Press, 1963).

Kelly, A., *Mikhail Bakunin: A Study in the Psychology and Politics of Utopia* (Oxford: Clarendon Press, 1982).

Kelly, L., *British Humanitarian Activity in Russia, 1890-1923* (Cham: Palgrave Macmillan, 2017).

Kimball, A., 'The Harassment of Russian Revolutionaries Abroad: The London Trial of Vladmir Burtsev in 1898', *Oxford Slavonic Papers*, New Series, 6 (1973), 48-65.

Kindersley, R., *The First Russian Revisionists. A Study of 'Legal Marxism' in Russia* (Oxford: Clarendon Press, 1962).

Knowles, A. V., 'The "Book Affair" of the Chaykovsky Circle', *Slavonic and East European Review*, 51, 125 (1973), 554-66.

Kolesnikoff, N. and J., 'Leo Tolstoy and the Doukhobors', *Canadian Slavonic Papers / Revue Canadienne des Slavistes*, 20, suppl. 1 (1978), 37-44.

Kolakowski, L., *Main Currents of Marxism*, 3 vols (Oxford: Oxford University Press, 1978).

Kondratenko, A. I., 'Ot khozhdeniia v narod – k sozdaniiu fonda vol'noi russkoi pressy (S. M. Stepniak-Kravchinksii, ego politicheskie vzgliady i propagandistskaia deiatel'nost' v kontekste obshchestvennogo dvizheniia v Rossii 1870-1890-kh godov'), *Istoriia: Fakty i Simboly*, 3, 12 (2017), 62-72.

Koz'min, B. P., *P. N. Tkachev i revoliutsionnoe dvizhenie 1860-kh godov* (Moscow: Novyi Mir, 1922?)

Koz'min, B. P. (ed.), *Nechaev i Nechaevtsy. Sbornik materialov* (Leningrad: Gos. sotsialno-ekonomicheskoe izdatel'stvo, 1931).

Koz'min, B. P., 'S. G. Nechaev i ego protivniki v 1868-69 gg.', in B. I. Gorev and B. P. Koz'min (eds), *Revoliutsionnoe dvizhenie 1860-kh godov* (Moscow: Izd-vo vsesoiuznogo obshchestva politkatorzhan i ssyl'no-poselentsev, 1932), 168-226.

Kudriashev, V. N., 'M. P. Dragomanov i russkie sotsialisty: diskussiia o federalisme', *Vestnik Tomskogo gosudarstennogo universiteta*, 336 (July 2010), 82-5.

Kujala, A., 'The Russian Revolutionary Movement and the Finnish Opposition, 1905. The John Grafton Affair and the Plans for an Uprising in St Petersburg', *Scandinavian Journal of History*, 5, 1-4 (1980), 257-275.

Kujala, A., 'Finnish Radicals and the Russian Revolutionary Movement, 1899–1907', *Revolutionary Russia*, 5, 2 (1992), 172–192.

Kula, M., 'Communism as Religion', *Totalitarian Movements and Political Religion*, 6, 3 (2005), 371-81, https://doi.org/10.1080/14690760500317727.

Laity, P., *The British Peace Movement, 1870-1914* (Oxford: Oxford University Press, 2002).

Laverychev, V. Ia (ed.), *Gruppa "Osvobozhdenie Truda" i obshchevstvenno-politicheskaia bor'ba v Rossii* (Moscow: Nauka, 1984).

Leatherbarrow, W. J. (ed.), *Dostoievskii and Britain* (Oxford: Berg, 1995).

Lehning, A. (ed.), *Michel Bakounine et ses relations avec Sergej Nechaev, 1870-1872* (Leiden: Brill, 1971).

Leonov, M. I., *Partiia sotsialistov-revoliutsionerov v 1905-1907 gg.* (Moscow: Rosspen, 1997).

Leonov, M. I., 'Zagranichnaia organizatsiia i Zagranichnyi komitet partii eserov v nachale XX veka (Na putiakh partiinoi institutsionalizatsii)', *Vestnik Samarskogo universiteta: istoriia, pedagogika, filologiia*, 27, 2 (2021), 27-36.

Leventhal, F. M., *The Last Dissenter: H.N. Brailsford and His World* (Oxford: Clarendon Press, 1985).

Lincoln, W. B., 'The Problem of Glasnost' in Mid-Nineteenth Century Russian Politics', *European Studies Review*, 11, 2 (1981), 171-88.

Lincoln, W. B., *The Great Reforms. Autocracy, Bureaucracy, and the Politics of Change in Imperial Russia* (Dekalb, IL: Northern Illinois University Press, 1990).

Lindsay, V., *The Chinese Nightingale and Other Poems* (New York: The Macmillan Company, 1922).

Liubimov, L. S., *Istoriia Sibirskoi pechati* (Irkutsk: Izd-vo Irkutskogo universiteta, 1982).

Lovell, S., 'From Genealogy to Generation. The Birth of Cohort Thinking in Russia', *Kritika*, 9, 3 (2008), 567-94, https://doi.org/10.1353/kri.0.0016.

Luckyj, G. S. N., *Seven Lives: Vignettes of Ukrainian Writers in the Nineteenth Century. The Annals of the Ukrainian Academy of Arts and Sciences in the US*, 20, 47-48 (1998-99), 161-87.

Lyons, M. J., 'An Army Like That of Gideon. Communities of Transnational Reform on the Pages of *Free Russia*', *American Journalism*, 32, 1 (2015), 2-22, https://doi.org/10.1080/08821127.2015.999528.

Macey, D. A. J., *Government and Peasant in Russia, 1861-1906: The Prehistory of the Stolypin Reforms* (DeKalb, IL: Northern Illinois University Press, 1987).

Macey, D. A. J., '"A Wager on History": The Stolypin Agrarian Reforms as Process', in J. Pallot (ed.), *Transforming Peasants. Society, State and the Peasantry, 1861-1930* (Basingstoke: Palgrave Macmillan, 1998), 149-73.

Maier, H., 'Political Religion. A Concept and Its Limitations', *Totalitarian Movements and Political Religion*, 8, 1 (2007), 5-16, https://doi.org/10.1080/14690760601121614.

Malia, M., 'What Is the Intelligentsia?', *Daedalus*, 89, 3 (1960), 441-58.

Manchester, L., *Holy Fathers, Secular Sons: Clergy, Intelligentsia and the Modern Self in Revolutionary Russia* (DeKalb, IL: Northern Illinois University Press, 2008).

Matsuzato, K., 'Pol'skii faktor v pravoberezhnoi Ukraine s XIX po nachalo XX veka', *Ab Imperio*, 1 (2000), 123-44.

Maude, G., 'Finland in Anglo-Russian Diplomatic Relations, 1899-1910', *Slavonic and East European Review*, 48, 113 (1970), 557-81.

Mazurov, A. E. and N. V. Zhiliakova, '"Kartinka mestnogo nastroeniia": Obstoiatel'stva zapreshcheniia i soderzhanie pervogo fel'etona "Sibirskoi gazety" (1881)', *Vestnik Tomskogo gosudarstvennogo universiteta. Filologiia*, 66 (2020), 308-317.

McClellan, W., *Revolutionary Exiles. The Russians in the First International and the Paris Commune* (London: Frank Cass, 1979).

McKinsey, P. S., 'From City Workers to Peasantry. The Beginning of the Russian Movement "To the People"', *Slavic Review*, 38, 4 (1979), 629-49.

McKinsey, P. S., 'The Kazan Square Demonstration and the Conflict between Russian Workers and *Intelligenty*', *Slavic Review*, 44, 1 (1985), 83-103.

Melancon, M., 'The Socialist Revolutionaries from 1902 to 1907. Peasant and Workers' Party', *Russian History*, 12, 1 (1985), 2-47.

Melancon, M., *The Socialist Revolutionaries and the Russian Anti-War Movement 1914-1917* (Columbus, OH: Ohio State University Press, 1990).

Mendel, A. P., *Dilemmas of Progress in Tsarist Russia. Legal Marxism and Legal Populism* (Cambridge, MA: Harvard University Press, 1961).

Meyers, J., *Joseph Conrad. A Biography* (New York: Cooper Square Press, 2001).

Miller, A., *The Ukrainian Question: The Russian Empire and Nationalism in the Nineteenth Century* (Budapest: Central European Press, 2003).

Miller, M. A., 'Ideological Conflicts in Russian Populism: The Revolutionary Manifestoes of the Chaikovskii Circle, 1869-1874', *Slavic Review*, 29, 1 (1970), 1-21.

Miller, M. A., *The Russian Revolutionary Emigres, 1825-1870* (Baltimore, MD: Johns Hopkins University Press, 1986).

Miller, M. A., 'The Transformation of the Russian Revolutionary Émigré Press at the End of the Nineteenth Century', *Russian History*, 16, 2-4 (1989), 197-207.

Mokshin, G. N., *Evoliutsiia ideologii legal'nogo narodnichestva v poslednei trety XIX – nachale XX vv.* (Voronezh: Nauchnaia Kniga, 2010).

Mokshin G. N., et al. (eds), *Narodniki v istorii Rossii,* 2 vols (Voronezh: Istoki and Izdatel'skii dom VGU, 2013-16).

Mokshin, G. N. (ed.), *Kul'turnoe narodnichestvo 1870-1900-kh gg. Khrestomatiia* (Voronezh: Izdatel'skii Dom VGU, 2016).

Mokshin, G. N., 'Osnovnye etapy istorii "Kul'turnogo" narodnichestva', *Vestnik Rossiiskogo universiteta druzhby narodov. Ser. Istoriia Rossii,* 15, 2 (2016), 19-28.

Mommsen, W. J., 'The Topos of Inevitable War in Germany in the Decade before 1914', in V. R. Berghahn and M. Kitchen (eds), *Germany in the Age of Total War. Essays in Honour of Francis Carsten* (London: Croom Helm, 1981), 23-45.

Monas, S., *The Third Section. Police and Society in Russia under Nicholas I* (Cambridge, MA: Harvard University Press 1961).

Morozov, K. N., *Partiia sotsialistov-revoliutsionerov v 1907-1914 gg.* (Moscow: Rosspen, 1998).

Morrissey, S. K., *Heralds of Revolution: Russian Students and the Mythologies of Radicalism* (New York: Oxford University Press, 1998).

Moser, C. A., 'Korolenko and America', *Russian Review,* 28, 3 (1969), 303-14.

Naarden, B., *Socialist Europe and Revolutionary Russia: Perception and Prejudice, 1848-1923* (Cambridge: Cambridge University Press, 1992).

Nahirny, V. C., *The Russian Intelligentsia: From Torment to Silence* (New Brunswick, NJ: Transaction Books, 1983).

Naimark, N. N., *Terrorists and Social Democrats. The Russian Revolutionary Movement under Alexander III* (Cambridge, MA: Harvard University Press, 1983).

Nechiporuk, D. M., *Vo imia nigilizma. Amerikanskoe obshchestvo druzei russkoi svobody i russkaia revoliutsionnaia emigratsiia, 1890-1930 gg.* (St Petersburg: Nestor-Istoriia, 2018).

Nechkina, M. V., *Vstrecha dvukh pokolenii. Iz istorii russkogo revoliutsionnogo dvizheniia kontsa 50-kh – nachala 60-kh godov XIX veka. Sbornik statei* (Moscow: Nauka, 1980).

Neilson, K., *Britain and the Last Tsar: British Policy and Russia, 1894-1917* (Oxford: Oxford University Press, 1995).

Nish, I., *The Origins of the Russo-Japanese War* (London: Longman, 1985).

Offord, D., *Portraits of Early Russian Liberals. A Study of the Thought of T. N. Granovsky, V. P. Botkin, P. V. Annenkov, A. V. Druzhinin, and K. D. Kavelin* (Cambridge: Cambridge University Press, 1985).

Offord, D., *The Russian Revolutionary Movement in the 1880s* (Cambridge: Cambridge University Press, 1986).

Oiva, M. et al., 'Spreading News in 1904. The Media Coverage of Nikolay Bobrikov's Killing', *Media History*, 26, 4 (2020), 391-407.

Okseniuk, A. A., 'Voennye organizatsii eserov v 1905-1907 gg.', *Vestnik Moskovkogo Universiteta*. Ser. 8 (Istoriia), 6 (2012), 74-82.

Ol'khovskii, E. R., 'K istorii "Chernogo Peredela" (1879-1881 gg.)', in L. M. Ivanov et al. (eds), *Obshchestvenoe dvizhenie v poreformennoi Rossii'* (Moscow: Nauka, 1965), 124-78.

Pallot, J. *Land Reform in Russia, 1906-1917: Peasant Responses to Stolypin's Project of Rural Transformation* (Oxford: Clarendon Press, 1999).

Paperno, I., *Chernyshevsky and the Age of Realism. A Study in the Semiotics of Behaviour* (Stanford, CA: Stanford University Press, 1988).

Partridge, M., 'Alexander Herzen and the English Press', *Slavonic and East European Review*, 36, 87 (1958), 453-70.

Patrick, C. and S. Baister, *William Le Queux. Master of Mystery* (Purley: C. Patrick and S. Baister, 2007).

Patyk, L. E., 'Remembering "The Terrorism": Sergei Stepniak-Kravchinskii's *Underground Russia*', *Slavic Review*, 68, 4 (2009), 758-81, https://doi.org/10.1017/S0037677900024517.

Patyk, L. E., *Written in Blood. Revolutionary Terrorism and Russian Literary Culture, 1861-1881* (Madison, WI: University of Wisconsin Press, 2017).

Pavlov, D. B. and Z. I. Peregudova (eds), *Pis'ma Azefa, 1893-1917* (Moscow: Terra, 1994).

Pavlov, D. B., *Khroniki tainoi voiny. Iaponskie den'gi dlia pervoi russkoi revoliutsii* (Moscow: Veche, 2011).

Pellew, J., 'The Home Office and the Aliens Act', *Historical Journal*, 32, 2 (1989), 369-85.

Pennell, C., *A Kingdom United. Popular Responses to the Outbreak of the First World War in Britain and Ireland* (Oxford: Oxford University Press, 2012).

Pereira, N. G. O., 'The Idea of Siberian Regionalism in Late Imperial and Revolutionary Russia', *Russian History*, 20, 1-4 (1993), 163-78.

Perrie, M., *The Agrarian Policy of the Russian Socialist-Revolutionary Party* (Cambridge: Cambridge University Press, 1976).

Perrie, M., 'Political and Economic Terror in the Tactics of the Russian Socialist-Revolutionary Party before 1914', in W. J. Mommsen and G. Hirschfeld (eds), *Social Protest, Violence & Terror in Nineteenth- & Twentieth Century Europe* (London: Macmillan, 1982), 63-79.

Phillips, B., *Siberian Exile and the Invention of Revolutionary Russia, 1825-1917: Exiles, Émigrés and the International Reception of Russian Radicalism* (Abingdon: Routledge, 2022).

Pipes, R., '*Narodnichestvo*: A Semantic Inquiry', *Slavic Review*, 23, 3 (1964), 441-58.

Pipes, R., *Struve: Liberal on the Left* (Cambridge, MA: Harvard University Press, 1970).

Pipes, R., *Russian Conservatism and Its Critics* (New Haven, CT: Yale University Press, 2005).

Pipes, R., 'The Trial of Vera Z', *Russian History*, 37, 1 (2010), v-82.

Polunov, A. Iu., *K. P. Pobedonostsev v obshchestvenno-politicheskoi i dukhovnoi zhizni Rossii* (Moscow: Rosspen, 2010).

Polvinen, T., *Imperial Borderland: Bobrikov and the Attempted Russification of Finland, 1898-1904*, trans. S. Huxley (London: Hurst and Co., 1995).

Pomper, P., *Peter Lavrov and the Russian Revolutionary Movement* (Chicago, IL: Chicago University Press, 1972).

Pomper, P., 'Bakunin, Nechaev, and the "Catechism of a Revolutionary": The Case for Joint Authorship', *Canadian-American Slavic Studies*, 10, 4 (1976), 535-51.

Pomper, P., *Sergei Nechaev* (New Brunswick, NJ: Rutgers University Press, 1979).

Pomper, P., *The Russian Revolutionary Intelligentsia* (Wheeling, IL: H. Davidson, 1993).

Poole, R., 'Nineteenth-Century Russian Liberalism: Ideals and Realities', *Kritika: Explorations in Russian and Eurasian History*, 16, 1 (2015), 157–81.

Porter, B., 'The *Freiheit* Prosecutions, 1881-1882', *Historical Journal*, 23, 4 (1980), 833-56.

Porter, B., *The Origins of the Vigilant State: The London Metropolitan Police Special Branch before the First World War* (London: Weidenfeld and Nicolson, 1987).

Pozefsky, P. C., *The Nihilist Imagination: Dmitrii Pisarev and the Cultural Origins of Russian Radicalism (1860-1868)* (New York: Peter Lang, 2003).

Quail, J., *The Slow Burning Fuse. The Lost History of the British Anarchists* (London: Paladin, 1978).

Rabinowitch, A., *The Bolsheviks in Power. The First Year of Soviet Rule in Petrograd* (Bloomington, IN: Indiana University Press, 2007).

Rabow-Edling, S., *Liberalism in Pre-Revolutionary Russia. State, Nation, Empire* (Abingdon: Routledge, 2019).

Radkey, O. H., *The Agrarian Foes of Bolshevism: Promise and Default of the Russian Socialist Revolutionaries from February to October 1917* (New York: Columbia University Press, 1958).

Radkey, O. H., *The Sickle under the Hammer: The Russian Socialist Revolutionaries in the Early Months of Soviet Rule* (New York: Columbia University Press, 1963).

Raeff, M., *Origins of the Russian Intelligentsia. The Eighteenth-Century Nobility* (New York: Harcourt Brace and World, 1966).

Rahman, K. S., 'Russian Revolutionaries in London, 1853-70. A. I. Herzen and the Free Press Fund', in B. Taylor (ed.), *Foreign Language Publishing in London, 1500-1907* (London: British Library, 2002), 227-40.

Rampton, V., *Liberal Ideas in Tsarist Russia. From Catherine the Great to the Russian Revolution* (Cambridge: Cambridge University Press, 2020).

Rappoport, H., *Conspirator: Lenin in Exile. The Making of a Revolutionary* (New York: Basic Books, 2010).

Read, C., 'In Search of Liberal Tsarism: The Historiography of Autocratic Decline', *Historical Journal*, 45, 1 (2002), 195-210, https://doi.org/10.1017/S0018246X0100228X.

Remy, J., *Brothers or Enemies? The Ukrainian National Movement and Russia from the 1840s to the 1870s* (Toronto: Toronto University Press, 2016).

Riasanovsky, N., *Nicholas I and Official Nationality in Russia, 1825-1855* (Berkeley, CA: University of California Press, 1959).

Riasanovsky, N., *A Parting of Ways: Government and the Educated Public in Russia, 1801-1855* (Oxford: Clarendon Press, 1976).

Rice, C., *Russian Workers and the Socialist-Revolutionary Party through the Revolution of 1905-07* (Basingstoke: Macmillan, 1988).

Rindlisbacher, S., 'Living for a "Cause". Radical Autobiographical Writing at the Beginning of the 20th Century', *Avtobiografiя*, 6 (2017), 59-77, https://doi.org/10.7892/boris.130345.

Robbins, R. G., *Famine in Russia, 1891-1892: The Imperial Government Responds to a Crisis* (New York: Columbia University Press, 1975).

Robinson, P., *Russian Liberalism* (Ithaca, NY: Northern Illinois University Press, 2023).

Rodchenko, Iu. I., 'Istoriia pervogo Tomskogo teatra, 1850-1882 gg. (na materialy "Tomskikh gubernskikh vedomostei" i "Sibirskoi gazety")', *Vestnik Tomskogo gosudarstvennogo universiteta*, 366 (2013), 78-81.

Rogers, C., *The Battle of Stepney. The Sidney Street Siege. Its Causes and Consequences* (London: Robert Hale, 1981).

Rumbelow, D., *The Houndsditch Murders and the Siege of Sidney Street* (London: W. H. Allen, 1988).

Ruud, C. A. and S. A. Stepanov, *Fontanka 16: The Tsar's Secret Police* (Montreal: McGill-Queens's University Press, 1999).

Sablin I. and K. Kukushkin, '*Zemskii Sobor: Historiographies and Mythologies of a Russian "Parliament"*', in I. Sablin and E. M. Bandeira (eds), *Planting*

Parliaments in Eurasia, 1850-1950: Concepts, Practices and Mythologies (London: Taylor and Francis, 2021), 103-49, https://doi.org/10.31235/osf.io/bh8xg.

Sanborn, J., 'The Mobilization of 1914 and the Question of the Russian Nation. A Reexamination', *Slavic Review*, 59, 2 (2000), 267-89, https://doi.org/10.2307/2697051.

Saunders, D., 'Stepniak and the London Emigration: Letters to Robert Spence Watson, 1887-1890', *Oxford Slavonic Papers*, New Series, 13 (1980), 80-93.

Saunders, D., 'Vladimir Burtsev and the Russian Revolutionary Emigration (1888-1905)', *European History Quarterly*, 13, 1 (1983), 39-62.

Saunders, D., 'Russia and Ukraine under Alexander II: The Valuev Edict of 1863', *International History Review*, 17, 1 (1995), 23-50.

Scotto, P., 'The Terrorist as Novelist: Sergei Stepniak-Kravchinksii', in A. Anemone (ed.), *Just Assassins: The Culture of Terrorism in Russia* (Evanston, IL: Northwestern University Press, 2010), 97-126.

Senese, D., 'S. M. Kravchinskii and the National Front Against Autocracy', *Slavic Review*, 34, 3 (1975), 506-22.

Senese, D., '"Le vil Melville": Evidence from the Okhrana File on the Trial of Vladimir Burtsev', *Oxford Slavonic Papers*, New Series, 14 (1981), 47-53.

Senese, D., 'Felix Volkhovsky in London, 1890-1914', in John Slatter (ed.), *From the Other Shore: Russian Political Emigrants in Britain, 1870-1917* (London: Frank Cass, 1984), 67-78.

Senese, D., *S. M. Stepniak-Kravchinskii: The London Years* (Newtonville, MA: Oriental Research Partners, 1987).

Senese, D., 'Felix Volkhovskii in Ontario: Rallying Canada to the Revolution', *Canadian-American Slavic Studies*, 24, 3 (1990), 295-310.

Senese, D., 'Willie and Felix: Ill–Matched Acquaintances', *Ontario History* 84, 2 (1992), 141-8.

Serbyn, R., 'In Defence of an Independent Ukrainian Socialist Movement. Three Letters from Serhii Podolynsky to Valerian Smirnov', *Journal of Ukrainian Studies*, 7, 2 (1982), 3-32.

Service, R., *Lenin: A Political Life,* 2 vols, I, *The Strengths of Contradictions* (Basingstoke: Macmillan, 1985).

Service, R., *Lenin: A Biography* (London: Pan Macmillan, 2010).

Shevtsov, V. V., *Pravitel'stvennaia periodicheskaia pechat' Sibiri* (*vtoraia polovina XIX – nachalo XX veka*) (Izd-vo Tomskogo gosudarstvennogo universiteta, 2016).

Shilvoskii, M. V. et al. (eds), *Obshchestvenno-politicheskaia zhizn' Sibiri v kontse XIX – nachale XX veka* (Novosibirsk: Parallel, 2019).

Shirokova, V. V., *Partiia "Narodnogo prava". Iz istorii osvoboditelnogo dvizeniia 90-kh gg. XIX veka* (Saratov: Izd-vo Saratovskogo universiteta, 1972).

Shneider, K. I., *Mezhdu svobodoi i samoderzhaviem: istoriia rannego russkogo liberalizma* (Perm: Permskii gos. natsional'nyi issledovatel'skii universitet, 2012).

Shpayer-Makov, H., 'The Reception of Peter Kropotkin in Britain, 1886-1917', *Albion*, 19, 3 (1987), 373-390.

Shpayer-Makov, H., 'Anarchism in British Public Opinion, 1880-1914', *Victorian Studies*, 31, 4 (1988), 487-516.

Siegel, J., *Endgame: Britain, Russia and the Final Struggle for Central Asia* (London: I. B. Tauris, 2002).

Sifneos, E., *Imperial Odessa: People, Spaces, Identities* (Leiden: Brill, 2018).

Siljak, A., *Angel of Vengeance: The "Girl Assassin", the Governor of St. Petersburg, and Russia's Revolutionary World* (New York: St Martin's Press, 2008).

Simbirtsev, I., *Tret'e otdelnie. Pervyi opyt sozdaniia professional'noi spetssluzhbi v Rossiiskoi imperii, 1826-1880* (Moscow: Tsentrpoligraf, 2006).

Sizemskaya, I. N., 'Russian Nihilism in Ivan S. Turgenev's Literary and Philosophical Investigations', *Russian Studies in Philosophy*, 56, 5 (2018), 394-404.

Slatter, J., 'Jaakoff Prelooker and the Anglo-Russian', in J. Slatter (ed.), *From the Other Shore: Russian Political Emigrants in Britain, 1870-1917* (London: Frank Cass, 1984), 49-66.

Slatter, J., 'Stepniak and the Friends of Russia', *Immigrants and Minorities*, 2, 1 (1983), 33-49.

Smith, H., *The Uncommon Reader: A Life of Edward Garnett* (New York: Farrar, Straus and Giroux, 2017).

Smith, S. B., *Captives of Revolution: The Socialist Revolutionaries and the Bolshevik Dictatorship, 1918-1923* (Pittsburg, PA: University of Pittsburg Press, 2011).

Spence, R. B., *Boris Savinkov: Renegade on the Left* (Boulder, CO: East European Monographs, distributed by Columbia University Press, 1991).

Squire, P. S., *The Third Department: The Establishment and Practices of the Political Police in the Russia of Nicholas I* (Cambridge: Cambridge University Press, 1968).

Stape, J., *The Several Lives of Joseph Conrad* (London: William Heinemann, 2007).

Stavrou, T. G. (ed.), *Russia under the Last Tsar* (Minneapolis, MI: University of Minnesota Press, 1969).

Steinberg, J. W. et al. (eds), *Russo-Japanese War in Global Perspective: World War Zero*, 2 vols (Leiden: Brill, 2005).

Stites, R., *Serfdom, Society and the Arts in Imperial Russian Culture: The Pleasure and the Power* (New Haven, CT: Yale University Press, 2005).

Stockdale, M. K., *Paul Miliukov and the Quest for a Liberal Russia, 1880–1918*, (Ithaca, NY: Cornell University Press, 1996).

Swain, G., *The Origins of the Russian Civil War* (London: Longman, 1995).

Szamuely, T., *The Russian Tradition* (London: Secker and Warburg, 1974).

Talmon, J. L., *Myth of the Nation and Vision of Revolution: The Origins of Ideological Polarazation in the Twentieth Century* (Abingdon: Routledge, 2017).

Taratuta, E., *Nash drug Etel' Lilian Voinich* (Moscow: Pravda, 1957).

Taratuta, E., *S. M. Stepniak-Kravchinskii—revoliutsioner i pisatel'* (Moscow: Khudozhestvennaia literatura, 1973).

Thaden, E. C. (ed.), *Russification in the Baltic Provinces and Finland, 1855-1914* (Princeton, NJ: Princeton University Press, 1981).

Thorstensson, V., 'Nihilist Fashion in 1860s-1870s Russia: The Aesthetic Relations of Blue Spectacles to Reality', *Clothing Cultures*, 3, 3 (2016), 265-81.

Tikhomirov, M. N., et al. (eds), *Istoriia Moskovskogo universiteta*, 2 vols (Moscow: Izd-vo Moskovskogo universiteta, 1955).

Tiutiukin, S. V., *G. V. Plekhanov. Sud'ba russkogo marksista* (Moscow: Rosspen, 1997).

Tkachenko, P. S., *Uchashchaiasia molodezh' v revoliutsionnom dvizhenii 60-70-kh gg XIX v.* (Moscow: Mysl', 1978).

Tomaszewski, F., 'Pomp, Circumstance, and Realpolitik: The Evolution of the Triple Entente of Russia, Great Britain, and France', *Jahrbücher für Geschichte Osteuropa*, 47, 3 (1999), 362-80.

Tomaszewski, F. K., *A Great Russia: Russia and the Triple Entente, 1905-1914* (London: Praeger, 2002).

Trautmann, F., *The Voice of Terror. A Biography of Johann Most* (Westport, CN: Greenwood Press, 1980).

Travis, F. F., *George Kennan and the American-Russian Relationship, 1865-1924* (Athens, OH: Ohio University Press, 1990).

Troitskii, N. A., *Bol'shoe obshchestvo propagandy 1871-1874* (Saratov: Izd-vo Saratovskogo universiteta, 1963).

Troitskii, N. A., *Tsarskie sudy protiv revoliutsionnoi Rossii. Politicheskie protsessy v 1871-1880 rr.* (Saratov: Izd-vo Saratovskogo universiteta, 1976).

Troitskii, N. A., *Pervye iz blestiashchei pleiady. Bol'shoe obshchestvo propagandy 1871-1874 gody* (Saratov: Izd-vo Saratovskogo universitet, 1991).

Ulam, A., *Prophets and Conspirators in Pre-Revolutionary Russia* (New Brunswick, NJ: Transaction Publishers, 1998).

Vagina, T. V., 'Kniaz' Aleksandr Kropotkin: Pechalnyi udel nesostoiavshegosia talenta', *Vestnik arkhivista*, 1 (2017), 226-38.

Venturi, F., *Roots of Revolution. A History of the Populist and Socialist Movements in Nineteenth-Century Russia* (Chicago, IL: University of Chicago Press, 1983).

Verhoeven, C., *The Odd Man Karakazov. Imperial Russia, Modernity and the Birth of Terrorism* (Ithaca, NY: Cornell University Press, 2009).

Vernitski, A., 'Russian Revolutionaries and English Sympathizers in 1890s London. The Case of Olive Garnett and Sergei Stepniak', *Journal of European Studies*, 35, 3 (2005), 299-314, https://doi.org/10.1177/0047244105055105.

Versluis, A., *The New Inquisitions: Heretic-Hunting and the Intellectual Origins of Modern Totalitarianism* (Oxford: Oxford University Press, 2006).

Vishnyakova, O., 'Russian Nihilism: The Cultural Legacy of the Conflict between Fathers and Sons', *Comparative and Continental Philosophy*, 3, 1 (2011), 99-111, https://doi.org/10.1558/ccp.v3i1.99.

Voeglin, E., *Political Religions*, trans. T. J. DiNapoli and E. S. Easterly III (Lewiston, NY: Edward Mellen Press, 1986).

Volk, S. S., *Narodnaia volia, 1879-1882* (Moscow: Nauka, 1966).

Volk, S. S. et al. (eds), *"Narodnaia volia" i "Chernyi peredel": vospominaniia uchastnikov revoliutsionnogo dvizheniia v Peterburge v 1879-1882 gg.* (Leningrad: Lenizdat, 1989).

Von Laue, T., *Sergei Witte and the Industrialization of Russia* (New York: Columbia University Press, 1963).

Von Mohrenschildt, D., *Towards a United States of Russia: Plans and Projects of Federal Reconstruction of Russia in the Nineteenth Century* (London: Assoc. University Press, 1981).

Waddel, N., *Modernist Nowheres: Politics and Utopia in Early Modernist Writing, 1900-1920* (Basingstoke: Palgrave Macmillan, 2012).

Waddington, P. (ed.), *Ivan Turgenev and Britain* (Oxford: Berg, 1995).

Walicki, A., *The Controversy over Capitalism: Studies in the Social Philosophy of the Russian Populists* (Oxford: Clarendon Press, 1969).

Walicki, A., *Legal Philosophies of Russian Liberalism* (Oxford: Clarendon Press, 1987).

Weeks, T. R., *Nation and State in Late Imperial Russia: Nationalism and Russification on the Western Frontier, 1863-1914* (DeKalb, IL: Northern Illinois University Press, 1996).

Weisbrode, K., *Old Diplomacy Revisited. A Study in the Modern History of Diplomatic Transformations* (Basingstoke: Palgrave Macmillan, 2014).

Whelehan, N., *The Dynamiters: Irish Nationalism and Political Violence in the Wider World, 1867-1900* (Cambridge: Cambridge University Press, 2012).

White, E., *The Socialist Alternative to Bolshevik Russia: The Socialist Revolutionary Party, 1921-1939* (Abingdon: Routledge, 2011).

Whittaker, C., 'The Ideology of Sergei Uvarov: An Interpretive Essay', *Russian Review*, 37, 2 (1978), 158-76.

Williams, H., 'Vesti i slukhi: The Russian Émigré Press to 1905', *Revolutionary Russia*, 13, 2 (2000), 45-61, https://doi.org/10.1080/09546540008575726.

Wilson, R., *Special Branch: A History* (London: Biteback Publishing, 2015).

Woehrlin, W. F., *Chernyshevskii: The Man and the Journalist* (Cambridge, MA: Harvard University Press, 1971).

Wood, A., *Russia's Frozen Frontier: A History of Siberia and the Russian Far East, 1581-1991* (London: Bloomsbury, 2011).

Wortman, R., *Scenarios of Power. Myth and Ceremony in Russian Monarchy from Peter the Great to the Abdication of Nicholas II* (Princeton, NJ: Princeton University Press, 2006).

Wray, H., 'The Aliens Act and the Immigration Dilemma', *Journal of Law and Society*, 33, 2 (2006), 302-23.

Yekelchyk, S., *Ukraine: Birth of a Modern Nation* (New York: Oxford University Press, 2007).

Young, S. J., *Writing Resistance. Revolutionary Memoirs of Shlissel'burg Prison, 1884-1906* (London: UCL press, 2021).

Zaitsev, P., *Taras Shevchenko. A Life*, trans. George N. Luckyj (Toronto: University of Toronto Press, 1988).

Zhiliakova, N. V. (ed.), *"Sibirskaia gazeta" v vospominaniiakh sovremennikov* (Tomsk: NTL, 2004).

Zhiliakova, N. V., 'Mezhdu literaturoi i zhurnalistikoi: fel'etony F. V. Volkhovskogo v "Sibirskoi Gazete"', in *Amerikanskie issledovanie v Sibiri*, 9 (Tomsk: Izd-vo Tomskogo universiteta, 2008), 333-45.

Zhiliakova, N. V., *Zhurnalistika goroda Tomska (XIX – nachalo XX veka): stanovlenie i razvitie* (Tomsk: Izd-vo Tomskogo universiteta, 2011).

Zhiliakova, N. V., 'Knizhnye proekty redaktsii sibirskikh gazet (na primere Tomskoi "Sibirskoi gazety" 1880-e gg.', *Knigoizdanie*, 1 (2012), 89-97.

Zhiliakova, N. V., '"V zashchitu umstvennogo tsentra": polemika 'Sibirskogo vestnika' i 'Grazhdanina' po povodu otkrytiia Imperatorskogo Tomskogo Universiteta (1888 g.), *Vestnik Tomskogo gosudarstvennogo universiteta. Filologiia,* 17, 1 (2012), 129-39.

Zhiliakova, N. V., 'Obsuzhdenie professional'nykh tsennostei zhurnalista v perepiske F. V. Volkhovskogo i V. G. Korolenko', *Zhurnalistskii ezhegodnik*, 3 (2014), 38-42.

Zinov'ev, V. P., et al. (eds), *Obshchestvenno-politicheskaia zhizn' v Tomskoi gubernii v 1880-1919 gg.: khronika*. 3 vols (Tomsk: Izd-vo Tomskogo universiteta, 2013).

Zipperstein, S. J., *The Jews of Odessa. A Cultural History, 1794-1881* (Stanford, CA: Stanford University Press, 1985).

Zuckerman, F., *The Tsarist Secret Police Abroad: Policing Europe in a Modernising World* (Basingstoke: Palgrave Macmillan, 2003).

Zuckerman, F., 'Policing the Russian Emigration in Paris, 1880-1914: The Twentieth Century as the Century of Political Police', *French History and Civilisation*, 2 (2009), 218-27.

Theses

Bujalski, N. R., 'Russia's Peter and Paul Fortress: From Heart of Empire to Museum of the Revolution, 1825-1930' (PhD thesis, Cornell University, 2020).

Bushnell, J. S., 'Mutineers and Revolutionaries: Military Revolution in Russia, 1905-1907' (PhD thesis, University of Indiana, 1977).

Gamblin, G. J., 'Russian Populism and Its Relations with Anarchism, 1870-1881' (PhD thesis, University of Birmingham, 1999).

Grant, R., 'British Radicals and Socialists and Their Attitudes to Russia, c. 1890-1917' (PhD thesis, University of Glasgow, 1984).

Green, L., 'Russian Revolutionary Terrorism in Transnational Perspective' (PhD thesis, Northumbria University, 2020).

Hay, D. W., 'The Development of the Russian Revolutionary Movement in the South of the Russian Empire,1873-1883' (PhD thesis, University of Glasgow, 1983).

Henderson, R., 'Vladimir Burtsev and the Russian Revolutionary Emigration: Surveillance of Foreign Political Refugees in London, 1891-1905' (PhD thesis, Queen Mary College University of London, 2008).

Jones Hemenway, E., 'Telling Stories: Russian Political Culture and Narratives of Revolution, 1917-1921' (PhD thesis, University of North Carolina at Chapel Hill, 1998).

Nicoll, G. D., 'Russian Participation in the Second International, 1889-1914' (PhD thesis, University of Boston, 1961).

Peeker, C. L., 'Reading Revolution. Russian Emigres and the Reception of Russian Literature in Britain c. 1890-1905' (DPhil thesis, Oxford University, 2006).

Perry, J., 'Foreigners, Aliens and Strangers: Foreign-Born Migration and Settlement in England and Wales, 1851-1911' (PhD thesis, University of Lancaster, 2019).

Reading, F., 'Olive Garnett and Anglo-Russian Cultural Relations from the Crimean War to the Russian Revolutions, 1855-1917' (PhD thesis, University of Kent, 2022).

Tovrov, J., 'Action and Affect in the Russian Noble Family' (PhD thesis, University of Chicago, 1980).

Index

Cromwell, Oliver 188

Daily News 124, 160, 206, 258–261, 263
Daily Telegraph 130, 159, 188, 256, 261, 274
Davitt, Michael 121
'Dedushka Egor', Short story by Mariia Tsebrikova (translated into Ukrainian by Volkhovskii) 60
Deich, Lev 87
Dement'ev, P. A. 172–173, 176
De Windt, Harry 122
Dickens, Charles 69, 191
Dickstein, S. L. 141
Die Voraussetzungen des Sozialismus (The Prerequisites for Socialism), book by Eduard Bernstein 142
Dilke, Sir Charles 195
Diuzhina skazok (A Dozen Tales), 1908 collection of stories by Volkhovskii 251
Dostoievskii, Fedor 2, 6, 45, 133, 178
Doukhabors 123
Drahomanov, Mykhailo 61, 141, 145, 211
Drevnaia Rus' (Ancient Russia), book by Ivan Khudiakov 38
Druz'ia sredi vragov. Iz vospominanii starago revoliutsionera, 1906 pamphlet by Volkhovskii 40–41
'Duda', poem by Volkhovskii 212
Duma
  first 229, 237, 255
  fourth 266
  second 241–242, 255
  third 243, 249
Durnovo, Peter 152
Dvorianskoe gnezdo (Noble Nest), Novel by Ivan Turgenev 20

Fabian Society 112–114
Farce, Edgar 154–156, 262

Figner, Vera 5–7, 74, 82, 234, 263–264
Foma (pseudonym used by Feliks Volkhovskii) 94
Ford, Ford Maddox 134, 153–154, 178
Foreign Committee of the Socialist Revolutionary Party 5, 207, 223–224, 227–228, 246, 287
Foreign Organisation of the Socialist Revolutionary Party 207, 211, 223–224, 246–247
Franzholi, Andrei 56, 58
Frederickson, N. C. 214
Free Russia, newspaper produced by Society of Friends of Russian Freedom 2–3, 5, 71, 113, 115–118, 120–131, 134, 138–141, 144–145, 147, 152, 154–155, 157–159, 161–165, 167–173, 176–178, 183–184, 188, 191–197, 205–206, 215, 219–220, 223, 257–262, 264, 271–273, 283–286
Free Russian Library (Whitechapel) 262
Frei Russland (German edition of Free Russia) 139
Fritsche circle (Zurich) 82

Garibaldi, Giuseppe 113, 269
Garnett, Constance 52, 132, 146, 251, 264
Garnett, Edward 2, 131, 133–134
Garnett, Olive 133
Garrison, Francis 126
Gershuni, G. A. 198, 205, 245
Gladstone, William 122, 160
Globe 108, 159–160
Gogol, Nikolai 17, 21, 92–93
Goldenberg, Grigorii 80
Goldenberg, Lazar 31, 34, 106, 116, 126, 140–141
Goncharov, Ivan 132

About the Team

Alessandra Tosi was the managing editor for this book.

Maria Eydmans and Adèle Kreager proof-read this manuscript; Rosalyn Sword indexed it.

Jeevanjot Kaur Nagpal designed the cover. The cover was produced in InDesign using the Fontin font.

Cameron Craig typeset the book in InDesign and produced the paperback and hardback editions. The main text font is Tex Gyre Pagella. The heading font is Californian FB.

Cameron also produced the PDF and HTML editions. The conversion was performed with open-source software and other tools freely available on our GitHub page at https://github.com/OpenBookPublishers.

Jeremy Bowman created the EPUB.

This book was peer-reviewed by two anonymous referees. Experts in their field, these readers give their time freely to help ensure the academic rigour of our books. We are grateful for their generous and invaluable contributions.

This book need not end here...

Share

All our books — including the one you have just read — are free to access online so that students, researchers and members of the public who can't afford a printed edition will have access to the same ideas. This title will be accessed online by hundreds of readers each month across the globe: why not share the link so that someone you know is one of them?

This book and additional content is available at:
https://doi.org/10.11647/OBP.0385

Donate

Open Book Publishers is an award-winning, scholar-led, not-for-profit press making knowledge freely available one book at a time. We don't charge authors to publish with us: instead, our work is supported by our library members and by donations from people who believe that research shouldn't be locked behind paywalls.

Why not join them in freeing knowledge by supporting us:
https://www.openbookpublishers.com/support-us

Follow @OpenBookPublish

Read more at the Open Book Publishers BLOG

You may also be interested in:

Beyond Holy Russia
The Life and Times of Stephen Graham
Michael Hughes

https://doi.org/10.11647/obp.0040

In the Lands of the Romanovs
An Annotated Bibliography of First-hand English-
language Accounts of the Russian Empire (1613-1917)
Anthony Cross

https://doi.org/10.11647/obp.0042

Twentieth-Century Russian Poetry
Reinventing the Canon
Katharine Hodgson, Joanne Shelton, and Alexandra Smith (Eds)

https://doi.org/10.11647/obp.0076

Milton Keynes UK
Ingram Content Group UK Ltd.
UKHW020644110624
443938UK00012B/6